Editor: Martha V. Gottron
Associate Editor: Margaret C. Thompson
Major Contributers: Diane C. Hill, John L. Moore,
          Esther D. Wyss
Contributors: Sharon Clayton, Joseph A. Davis, Diane
          Granat, Bill Keller, Marc Leepson, William
          Sweet
Indexer: Beth Furbush
Cover Design: Richard A. Pottern
Graphics: George Rebh, Cheryl Rowe

Regulation
Process and Politics

Congressional Quarterly Inc.
1414 22nd Street, N.W.
Washington, D.C. 20037

Congressional Quarterly Inc.

Congressional Quarterly Inc., an editorial research service and publishing company, serves clients in the fields of news, education, business and government. It combines specific coverage of Congress, government and politics by Congressional Quarterly with the more general subject range of an affiliated service, Editorial Research Reports.

Congressional Quarterly was founded in 1945 by Henrietta and Nelson Poynter. Its basic periodical publication was and still is the CQ *Weekly Report,* mailed to clients every Saturday. A cumulative index is published quarterly.

CQ also publishes a variety of books. The CQ *Almanac,* a compendium of legislation for one session of Congress, is published every spring. *Congress and the Nation* is published every four years as a record of government for one presidential term. Other books include paperbacks on public affairs and textbooks for college political science classes.

The public affairs books are designed as timely reports to keep journalists, scholars and the public abreast of developing issues, events and trends.

They include such recent titles as *The Washington Lobby, Fourth Edition; The Soviet Union;* and *Dollar Politics, Third Edition.* College textbooks, prepared by outside scholars and published under the CQ Press imprint, include such recent titles as *American Politics and Public Policy: Seven Case Studies; Origins of Congress, Second Edition;* and *Congress and Its Members.*

In addition, CQ publishes *The Congressional Monitor,* a daily report on present and future activities of congressional committees. This service is supplemented by *The Congressional Record Scanner,* an abstract of each day's *Congressional Record,* and *Congress in Print,* a weekly listing of committee publications.

CQ Direct Research is a consulting service that performs contract research and maintains a reference library and query desk for clients.

Editorial Research Reports covers subjects beyond the specialized scope of Congressional Quarterly. It publishes reference material on foreign affairs, business, education, cultural affairs, national security, science and other topics of news interest. Service to clients includes a 6,000-word report four times a month, bound and indexed semi-annually. Editorial Research Reports publishes paperback books in its field of coverage. Founded in 1923, the service merged with Congressional Quarterly in 1956.

Library of Congress Cataloging in Publication Data

Main entry under title:

Regulation : process and politics

Bibliography: p.
Includes index.
1. Delegated legislation — United States. 2. Administrative law — United States. I. Congressional Quarterly, inc.
KF5407.R43 1982   342.73'066   82-14292
ISBN 0-87187-243-9   347.30266

Contents

Case Studies

Editor's Note. President Ronald Reagan entered office with a promise to end unnecessary, costly federal regulations. In his first months as president, Reagan froze dozens of regulations written during the Carter administration and set up a task force to weed out proposed rules carrying costs that would exceed the benefits. Congress, too, was unhappy with the regulatory bureaucracy. Many members believed that the rules issued by federal regulators overstepped congressional intent. They sought legislation that would give them more control over regulatory agency decisions. Although the number of regulations may decline, federal regulation itself will not disappear. Most experts agree that some regulation is necessary to preserve the country's economic well-being and to protect the public health and safety. The question is not whether regulation should exist but what form of regulation will be the most effective. *Regulation: Process and Politics* examines this question and more. How did the regulatory system develop and how does it operate? When is regulation justified? What are the alternatives? What headway have the president and Congress made toward eliminating costly, ineffective rules?

Regulation
Process and Politics

Introduction to Regulation

"Regulation." Webster's defines it as a "rule, ordinance or law by which conduct is regulated." Everyone regulates his or her life to some extent — if only to set the time of a meal or to meet the bus on schedule. Other regulations are imposed on individuals by their workplaces, their communities and their governments. Although at times it may seem obtrusive, regulation, like it or not, is necessary.

Of all the regulators that affect everyday life in the United States, the federal government is the largest. Virtually everything it does has a controlling impact on some part of society. Three-fourths of all federal revenues are devoted to aid programs, including Social Security; Medicare and Medicaid health plans for the elderly and indigent; and food stamp, education grants and welfare payments. These programs, demanded at various times by the American public in the name of social equity, entail not only huge dollar outlays but detailed regulations to determine who is eligible for how much aid and for how long. Such regulations require reams of paperwork heaped on government at all levels — federal, state and local — and frequently on the recipients of the benefits themselves. Few people advocate doing away with the programs, but many have proposed simplifying the procedures under which they operate.

Perhaps the most pervasive kind of government regulation is the federal income tax on both individuals and corporations. Americans are all too familiar with the onus of filling out federal income tax forms, which account for more than half of all government paperwork they must contend with.

But there is another form of regulation, one that to most Americans is less apparent than paying income taxes or Social Security. Although it consumes only a very small fraction of federal expenditures, it has a disproportionately far-reaching impact on the nation's economy, affecting both producers and consumers.

That kind of regulation is the subject of this book. It affects the quality of the air we breathe and the products we buy; the efficacy and safety of the medicine we take; the rates and routes of the airlines we fly and the trains and trucks that transport our goods; the operations of nuclear power plants, coal mines, oil wells and gas lines that supply our energy; the health and safety conditions in which we work; the purity of the water we drink; and the price tag,

crashworthiness and fuel efficiency of the automobiles we drive.

The printed volumes of federal regulations give some idea of the magnitude of the government's regulatory activity. The Senate Governmental Affairs Committee in 1977 pointed out that the Code of Federal Regulations, which contains the current general and permanent regulations of federal agencies, would fill a shelf 15 feet long with 60,000 pages of fine print.

Another survey found that federal departments and agencies send out more than 9,800 forms and receive 556,000,000 responses each year. At the Interstate Commerce Commission (ICC) alone, there are on file more than one trillion rates regulating the transportation of goods — more than 20,000 for each American family. In 1960 the number of pages in *The Federal Register*, the bureaucratic bible that contains all proposed and final rules, was 9,562 pages long. By 1981 its size had expanded to 63,553 pages.

But numbers alone do not provide the full picture of the scope of government regulation. "It sometimes seems that there is no area of human life left untouched by the multitude of regulations that have been issued to carry out the laws passed by Congress," said George E. Danielson, D-Calif., then chairman of the House Administrative Law and Governmental Relations Subcommittee, in March 1981. Regulations, which have the force of law, "probably have more impact on the average American" than actual statutes enacted by Congress, he said.

Compared with the vast size of the federal bureaucracy — more than two million civilian employees in 1982 — the number of people engaged solely in regulation is small. According to the Center for the Study of American Business at Washington University in St. Louis, there are approximately 76,500 permanent full-time employees working in 57 agencies that exist primarily to promulgate and enforce rules governing the state of the nation's economy and environment, the practices of its businesses and the health and safety of its citizens. The combined budgets of these agencies are only a fraction of total federal outlays, amounting to an estimated $6.3 billion in fiscal 1983 out of an anticipated budget of more than $800 billion. To most of the public, those people and the agencies they work for are unfamiliar. A study commissioned by the League of Women Voters found that less than a fifth of those surveyed knew who was responsible for writing federal rules.

Nonetheless the federal regulatory system was a major issue during the 1980 presidential campaign and continues to be the subject of intense debate both in the White House and on Capitol Hill. *(League of Women Voters poll, box, p. 5)*

The Rise of Regulation

Government control of various aspects of economic activity is an age-old phenomenon. But federal intervention in a major sector of the American economy began less than 100 years ago, with the establishment by Congress of the Interstate Commerce Commission in 1887 to oversee the nation's railroads. The rationale behind the move was rather surprising for a nation that had relied on the notion that the play of the free market would of itself bring about harmony in supply and demand and economic "justice."

But the railroads had grown too big. By the time the federal government intervened, it had become apparent that reliance on free market mechanisms was inadequate and that some kind of regulation was needed to control railroad rates, routes and operating licenses.

The mechanism chosen was the independent regulatory commission, a multi-member board created by congressional statute and endowed with authority to establish and enforce standards for certain economic activities. Appointed by the president, and subject to Senate confirmation, the ICC commissioners were independent from, yet responsible to, the legislative, executive and judicial branches of government.

As the nation's industrial life grew more complex, Congress set up more regulatory commissions to monitor other aspects of the business world. The ICC was followed by establishment of the Federal Reserve to regulate the nation's money supply network and the Federal Trade Commission to monitor unfair trade practices. By 1982 there were 17 independent commissions responsible for overseeing most of the nation's transportation, power and communications networks; fiscal and monetary matters; stock, bond and commodity transactions; labor relations; trade practices and product safety.

Independent Commissions

A number of features have led some observers to characterize the independent commissions as a "fourth branch" of government. Because independent commissioners may not be removed from office except for cause, they are insulated from political pressures emanating from the White House and Capitol Hill. One reason that Congress made the commissions independent was to remove political influences from the awarding of licenses or the determination of rates.

Setting fixed terms for independent commissioners contributed to continuity of policies and provided a buffer to changes resulting from congressional or presidential elections. And the relatively long terms of commission members were intended to help them develop expertise. Most commissions were set up so that no more than a simple majority of the commissioners could represent either major political party.

But the regulatory commissions are not wholly independent. They must be responsive to Congress, which sets their budgets and determines their mandates. Because the president chooses their members — and names their chairmen — the commissions tend to reflect his regulatory philosophy. The commissions also are responsive to the courts, which may hear appeals and overturn commission regulations.

There are drawbacks associated with the independent regulatory commission concept. Public responsibility and accountability is weakened by the fact that commissioners cannot be voted out of office if Congress and the White House are displeased with their actions. And the commissioners themselves lose some of the leverage over policy making that derives from political support.

Executive Agencies

Not all economic regulation is undertaken by independent regulatory commissions. Many important regulatory tasks have been given to agencies within the executive branch. Most, such as the Occupational Safety and Health Administration (OSHA) and the National Highway Traffic Safety Administration, are located within Cabinet departments. Others, such as the Environmental Protection Agency (EPA), are located within the executive branch but are separate entities within the bureaucratic structure.

The president appoints the administrators of most executive branch agencies. The nominees are subject to Senate confirmation. In a few cases such as the Food and Drug Administration, the director is appointed by the Cabinet secretary without Senate confirmation.

Although they have a great deal of independence and wide-ranging responsibilities, the administrators serve at the pleasure of the president. No executive branch agency head is likely to hold the job very long if he opposes the president's position. And most agency heads are changed when a new president takes office.

Regulatory Responsibilities

Just as the composition and degree of independence of regulatory agencies vary, so too does their purview. The agencies operate under laws that grant them specific rulemaking authority. These so-called "organic" statutes spell out the degree of discretion enjoyed by an agency or commission. The Federal Trade Commission, for example, has one of the broadest mandates: to regulate unfair trade practices. Nearly every business that participates in interstate commerce falls within its jurisdiction. At the other extreme, the Commerce Department's Patent and Trademark Office is authorized only to issue and register patents and trademarks.

Some independent commissions, often referred to as "old line," or "traditional," regulators — such as the ICC, the Civil Aeronautics Board (CAB), and the Federal Communications Commission — oversee the operations of specific economic sectors and are concerned primarily with ratemaking, licensing, market entry and so forth. That kind of regulation has also been referred to as "vertical" regulation because it controls many facets of a particular industry.

Other regulatory bodies, usually but not always located within the executive branch, make rules affecting a broad spectrum of industries and activities, engaging in what frequently is termed "horizontal" regulation. For example, one of the EPA's mandates is to administer the complex 1970 Clean Air Act, which affects virtually every sector of the economy, from requirements that auto manufacturers produce cars with pollution control devices to rules mandating industries to design plants whose emissions meet strict air quality standards. Because the act requires standards to be set to maintain areas where the air is relatively pure, regulations established by the EPA to implement the Clean Air Act also shape the decisions made by state and local governments concerning regional economic development policies.

Another agency that has a widespread impact on the economy is the Consumer Product Safety Commission (CPSC). Established as an independent commission in 1973, the CPSC has authority to set standards for and to recall, if necessary, more than 10,000 products on the market. The Occupational Safety and Health Administration in the Labor Department is authorized to promulgate and enforce health and safety regulations and standards extending to all employers in the 50 states, the District of Columbia, Puerto Rico, the Canal Zone and all other territories under federal jurisdiction.

Agencies such as EPA, CPSC and OSHA deal with what is commonly known as "social regulation," which involves consumer, environmental, health and safety issues. Many of the agencies involved in establishing and monitoring social, or "quality of life" standards — all of which have a broad impact on the functioning of the economy — were established in the early 1970s.

Whatever their form, Congress has endowed regulatory agencies and commissions with authority to pursue their activities in a number of ways — through ratemaking, licensing, standard setting and information disclosure. One approach to regulation is to set performance standards that require the achievement of certain goals (such as reducing workplace hazards) without detailing how they are to be reached. Another approach is to impose specification standards, which dictate the means of achieving a certain end.

A third alternative is to require industries to provide full disclosure of the dangers or possible problems of a product, rather than banning it entirely. Regulators also may use economic incentives, among them taxes and penalties for non-compliance, to regulate individual and corporate activities.

Justifications Questioned

Economic regulation in America arose as a set of specific answers to specific evils, without much attention to the overall philosophy behind it. It reflects a faith in experts, in rational administrative solutions to controversial problems.

Government regulation has been justified on economic, social and political grounds. However, just because regulation appears to be warranted in a particular situation does not mean that government-imposed controls will necessarily lead to better results than would occur in an unfettered market. There are many cases in which government intervention has resulted in less efficiency or equity than the original imperfect market.

By the same token, the failure of one type of regulation to meet desired objectives satisfactorily does not necessarily mean that deregulation is the answer. It may be that different tools or sets of rules would more efficiently achieve the desired result.

As the Senate Governmental Affairs Committee concluded in its 1978 report *A Framework for Regulation,* "Simply because a problem exists and, in theory, is remediable does not mean that regulation or other intervention is desirable, even on economic grounds. The potentially widespread indirect costs and consequences of regulation, subsidy, and other interventions are clear, and even direct costs are significant. In light of that burden, intervention should only be undertaken where there is a clearly identified problem, and where the potential achievements of government action are substantial."

A Haphazard System

By the late 1970s the federal regulatory system was under attack. Many agencies had been created in response to economic crises, but the economic problems of the 1970s and 1980s — unemployment, slow growth and inflation — focused attention on inefficiencies in the haphazardly developed regulatory apparatus. Increasingly the public, politicians and regulators themselves have been demanding that the benefits outweigh the costs of rules and that the most cost-effective method of regulation be chosen.

Much of the debate was directed toward the reform of regulatory activities rather than their total abolition. Most of the criticism did not involve the basic justifications for regulation so much as it centered on the way the system had worked in the past — the methods used, the rulemaking procedures followed, the way in which Congress wrote the regulatory statutes and the qualifications of the regulators themselves.

The overall performance of regulation was varied: sometimes it worked, sometimes not. The possible causes for regulatory failure in a particular situation were just as diverse. The fault could lie with the initial justification for imposing controls; with the congressional mandate given the agencies which, if contradictory or too broad or vague, could hinder effective performance; or with the regulatory process itself and the way a regulation was implemented or administered.

Many members of Congress believed that they had given too much leeway to federal regulators. "We in Congress have practically given *carte blanche* to the regulators to take the laws we passed and do with them what they choose," said William C. Wampler, R-Va., ranking minority member of the House Agriculture Committee. "To me this was a lot like placing Dracula in charge of the blood bank — and as a result a lot of the life of American business was drained by the bloodsuckers on the federal payroll."

Although that was a harsh assessment, it indicated the intensity of anti-regulatory sentiment on Capitol Hill. Congress has sought to regain some control through enactment of legislation that would allow it to veto agency rules and actions. The legislative veto issue was central to the bitter four-year fight to halt what critics called harassment by the activist FTC. The drive to clip the wings of the agency resulted in congressional imposition in 1980 of a two-house veto over future FTC rules. Congress also has expressed its displeasure with some agencies by amending their mandates to narrow their regulatory jurisdictions.

But efforts at overall regulatory reform during the late 1970s and early 1980s collapsed in controversy. While many, both within and outside the government, agreed on the need to take a close look at the federal regulatory system, there was no consensus on how the process should be changed and what should be regulated or deregulated.

Some critics of the existing scheme wanted major overhauls of the regulatory machinery. Others thought it needed just a tune-up. Some pressed the case for industry-by-industry deregulation (as was achieved during the Carter administration in the transportation and banking sectors), while others advocated changes in the way rules are promulgated or revisions in the basic statutes giving agencies their rulemaking authority.

Outside the government, many businessmen, unhappy with what they considered unnecessary and costly aspects of the bureaucratic maze, lobbied for more flexibility in health and safety standards and argued that the whole rulemaking process should be streamlined. Spokesmen for groups such as the Chamber of Commerce of the United States, the Business Roundtable and the National Federation of Independent Business said the labyrinth of federal rules and the time-consuming procedures for approving them dampened productivity, fueled inflation and blunted America's competitive strength abroad. They also argued that federal regulations penalized consumers in many cases because the extra costs of products and services resulting from complying with government rules were passed on to them.

In addition, business complained that agencies frequently chose the more expensive alternative when issuing a rule, thereby driving up production costs. OSHA "doesn't want to talk about ear plugs" for workers in noisy factories, said M. Kendall Fleeharty, former director of the Chamber of Commerce's Regulatory Action Center. "They only want to talk about noise abatement equipment, which costs millions of dollars."

In contrast to the general business view, consumer and environmental activists as well as labor groups warned that deregulatory "overkill" could negate the progress made in cleaning up the environment, providing safer and healthier working conditions and protecting consumers from hazardous products. Instead of relaxing those standards, the rules on the books should be enforced more vigorously, they suggested. Many of them also advocated reducing or abolishing federal controls that protected some economic sectors from marketplace competition.

In 1976 Sen. Charles H. Percy, R-Ill., a member of the Senate Governmental Affairs Committee, spelled out the difficulty of reaching a consensus on what is "good" and "bad" regulation and what should therefore be "reformed." "Often when I talk to business leaders, they tell me that too stringent environmental, health and safety regulations are ruining them. But they gloss over the widespread waste caused by much of today's economic regulation," he said. "When I talk to labor leaders, they complain about the anti-competitive regulation of certain industries, but overlook the costly effects of OSHA. And when I talk to consumer leaders, they decry the effects of a good deal of economic regulation but imply 'hands off' when it comes to health and safety. If we give all groups a prior veto on proposed reforms — if we exempt everyone's sacred cow from searching review — we will accomplish nothing."

Reagan and Regulation

President Ronald Reagan put regulatory reform high on his list of presidential priorities. "American society experienced a virtual explosion in government regulation during the past decade," Reagan said in an address to a joint session of Congress Feb. 5, 1981. "The result has been higher prices, higher unemployment and lower productivity growth.... We have no intention of dismantling the regulatory agencies — especially those necessary to protect [the] environment and to ensure the public health and safety. However, we must come to grips with inefficient and burdensome regulations — eliminate those we can and reform the others."

The new president asked Congress to join him in a concerted campaign to revise the federal regulatory structure and reduce the bewildering array of federal rules. Similar efforts had been undertaken by others before him, including Reagan's Democratic predecessor, Jimmy Carter, and Republican President Gerald R. Ford. But by the 1980s the time for an overhaul seemed riper than ever.

The Reagan administration, which estimated that it cost Americans $100 billion a year to comply with federal regulations (or $1,800 for every family), made regulatory reform a cornerstone of its economic program. During its first two years in office, the administration reduced the number of existing rules, revised some and postponed the promulgation of new ones. It supported efforts to curtail the statutory authority of some agencies, centralized White House oversight procedures by giving the Office of Management and Budget (OMB) additional power to review regulations and ordered agencies to weigh the costs of rules against their benefits.

"What the president is attempting to do in this area is find a balance between safety in the workplace and environmental protection and, at the same time, eliminate from our economy unneeded regulations so that we can grow and increase our nation's productive capacity," said Vice President George Bush in March 1981. Bush was chairman of a presidential task force established by Reagan to oversee review of major rules.

The regulatory agencies soon felt the impact of Reagan's "less-federal-government-is-better" approach. He proposed large cuts in regulatory agency budgets and staffs and named persons who shared his philosophy to head regulatory commissions and agencies.

During its first month in office the Reagan administration put a freeze on 172 rules that had been issued in the waning days of Carter's presidency.

In the following months the administration announced that scores of other rules would be withdrawn or postponed for further study. During 1981 OMB's Office of Information and Regulatory Affairs reviewed a total of 2,803 regulations. Thirteen percent were revised, returned or withdrawn during review. And in early 1982 Reagan put forward a "new federalism" policy that envisaged giving the states more authority to oversee and administer regulatory programs.

The administration claimed its actions had saved billions of dollars. But some observers noted that the calculation did not take into account the benefits that would have been gained if some rules had not been postponed or abandoned.

Doubts Expressed

Although the administration succeeded in delaying new regulations, by the end of 1982 it had offered no overall reform proposals. Nor had it sent to Capitol Hill many substantive plans to overhaul major regulatory statutes.

Among the most prominent of these laws was the 1970 Clean Air Act, amended and extended in 1977 and up for renewal in 1981. Business, labor, environmental and other groups generally agreed that although the act had helped to reduce pollution, it was inordinately complicated and needed to be revised. But the administration did not submit concrete legislative proposals to do so in 1981 or 1982. Many observers expressed the view that by its lack of initiative the administration had passed up an opportunity to effect substantial statutory changes in a far-reaching regulatory area. Having been given only a set of vague suggestions by the Reagan EPA, Congress simply kept the existing measure alive through continuing appropriations resolutions, while it worked sporadically and laboriously to extend and amend the bill.

Critics also found fault with Reagan's budget-cutting approach to deregulation. They pointed to the possibility that inadequate funds could result in less efficient implementation of regulatory revisions as well as enforcement of existing rules.

As far back as 1976, a Congressional Budget Office staff paper prepared for the House Commerce Subcommittee on Oversight and Investigations cautioned, "Enforcing regulations that affect the entire economy requires an enormous number of inspections. Agency heads often argue that they are operating with a skeleton staff, to the detriment of all concerned. In addition, many critics charge that regulation is ineffectual because the agencies cannot come close to matching [the] industries [they regulate] in technical expertise and information."

Many officials at regulatory agencies contended that real reform and overhaul of rules and procedures would require larger, not smaller, staffs and more expert personnel. For example, deregulation of the airline industry, a measure sought by Carter and passed by Congress in 1978, required the CAB to review, simplify or abolish hundreds of rules affected by the 1978 act. It also had to draw up new rules to put the law into effect. For example, to make certain no small community would lose air service for at least 10 years after the deregulation, as the law required, the CAB had to review service to more than 500 cities and set standards guaranteeing a certain number of daily flights and seats.

Little Awareness of Regulatory System

In March 1982, with government regulation the subject of heated debate in the nation's political arena, a Gallup poll measured public awareness of federal regulations on behalf of the League of Women Voters Education Fund. According to Dorothy S. Ridings, who headed the fund, the results were "appalling." A large segment of the American population was found to be in the dark about what federal regulations are, who makes them and the process by which they are made.

Among the most disturbing conclusions of the study, which consisted of 1,580 personal in-home interviews across the country, were:

• One-half of the Americans interviewed could not cite a single federal regulation most affecting them or their family;

• More than half of those surveyed could not name any differences between federal regulations and federal laws; some said there was little or no difference between them;

• Only 17 percent correctly believed that the executive branch had primary responsibility for writing federal regulations; nearly half (47 percent) said that regulation was in the hands of Congress; 10 percent believed the courts issued regulations. The remaining 26 percent said they did not know who made federal rules.

The study did show that 62 percent of those polled expressed interest in learning more about how federal regulations are made. "The results of this survey clearly indicate that more public education about all aspects of the regulatory process is needed," said Ridings.

While most observers agreed with the administration that greater consideration should be given to the costs and benefits of proposed rules and their alternatives, many acknowledged that it was difficult to quantify benefits such as cleaner air, healthier people, or safer automobiles. Often those benefits were underestimated. Moreover, critics warned that rigid and time-consuming cost-benefit analyses could hold up deregulatory as well as regulatory action and that OMB's review powers might shield regulatory decisions from oversight by Congress and the public.

The Reagan administration also was criticized for what some considered its piecemeal approach to deregulation, a failure to develop a well-thought-out overview of the regulatory system and what should be reformed. Its ad hoc tactics sometimes resulted in specialized "relief" for a particular economic sector rather than more permanent changes. Responding to the special interests and demands of the troubled automobile industry, for example, the administration in April 1981 announced a list of 34 regulatory actions it would take to suspend or revise some environmental and safety regulations affecting car manufacturers.

Others claimed that while efforts were being made to soften the burden of health, environment and safety regulation on industry, regulatory reform and deregulation actually had slowed in some economic sectors. The ICC for one was criticized for not moving quickly to implement the 1980 trucking deregulation act passed under Carter and for reinstating some controls.

Some regulatory experts attributed these conflicting actions to two divergent schools of thought within the administration. One who subscribed to that theory was Antonin Scalia, editor of *Regulation*, a well respected monthly magazine published by the non-partisan American Enterprise Institute for Public Policy Research. At a December 1981 seminar on regulation conducted by the institute, Scalia termed one group the "principled deregulators," who advocated market-based solutions where they could most efficiently achieve desired goals, application of cost-benefit analysis to existing and proposed rules, and, wherever possible, elimination of entry and exit barriers to enhance competition.

The other school, he said, included many business interests and "people who haven't given any systematic thought to regulation in general, but know that in the past few years things have gotten out of hand." That group called for health and safety deregulation, but paid scant attention to, and in some cases even supported, anti-competitive economic regulation, Scalia said. The consensus of most of the participants at the symposium was that because of these divergent pulls, the administration's record on regulatory reform during its first year in office had been mixed.

Moving to the Back Seat

By 1982 the high priority initially given by the administration to changing the regulatory landscape had taken a back seat to other, broader concerns such as getting the sluggish economy moving again, pushing budget cuts through Congress, enacting tax reform and beefing up the nation's defenses.

Meanwhile, the Senate in March 1982 passed omnibus regulatory reform legislation. A similar bill was reported by a House committee but still was pending in the full chamber at the end of September.

One controversial feature of both versions was the legislative veto under which Congress could turn down new regulations by a majority vote in both houses. The administration opposed the provision, and some critics said it would drown Congress in detailed and time-consuming review of rules.

"Part of the difficulty in judging what has been achieved [by the Reagan administration] stems from the very scope and diversity of regulation itself," wrote regulation specialists Marvin Kosters and Jeffrey Eisenach. "Unless carefully chosen to exhibit a common theme, a set of particular regulatory initiatives is typically so heterogeneous that it suffers either a piecemeal and opportunistic approach to reform or a lack of coherent direction. Another part of the difficulty is that it is far easier to state reform objectives than it is to apply realistic criteria to actual regulatory developments."

Whatever one's assessment of the actions taken by Congress and the Reagan administration in the arena of regulatory reform in the early 1980s, one aspect of government rulemaking seems clear. For all their independence and expertise, regulatory agencies are political entities subject to a tug of war between Congress and the White House. They must be sensitive to the public's perception of regulation and are influenced by a multitude of groups that include business, labor, environmentalists, consumers and a variety of special interests. Moreover, for all the criticism, government intervention in the American economy is not likely to go away any time soon. While most people agree that the system needs reform, few advocate dismantling an apparatus that has brought many benefits to the U.S. economy and society.

2

Development of Regulation

All industries are regulated at some level, whether it be federal, state or local. From taxicabs to nuclear power plants, every enterprise in some way affects the "public interest" and therefore is liable to some measure of public oversight. Even industries that normally are not thought of as being "regulated" must adhere to laws concerning their products and the manner in which they are produced and distributed. Such regulations affect not only the industries but the economy as a whole.

The legal authority for federal regulation is contained in the commerce clause of the Constitution, Article I, section 8, which empowers Congress "To regulate Commerce with foreign Nations, and among the several States...." Over the decades, the term "commerce" — which originally applied only to activities involving interstate transportation or foreign commerce — has evolved to include almost all forms of economic activity. But there still is no universally agreed upon definition of federal regulation. *(Expansion of the commerce clause, box, pp. 12-13)*

Defining Regulation

The narrowest definitions of regulation focus on the control of economic conditions, such as market entry and price. In the broadest sense of the term, regulation could include all federal government activity. Almost every federal agency regulates to some extent, if only by dictating the procedure to be followed by applicants for any kind of government aid program, including Social Security and grant programs. Moreover, all departments and agencies issue regulations dealing with their internal operations, such as budgeting and hiring practices.

Although conflicting definitions of regulation abound, political scientists and economists generally agree on two points. The first is that regulation transfers some amount of private discretion to the public sector. The second is that it entails sanctions to discourage undesired conduct.

According to Robert E. Cushman in his book *The Independent Regulatory Commissions*, an agency is regulatory "when it exercises governmental control or discipline over private conduct or property interests. This control may take different forms and use different methods, but there is always present an element of coercion." Political scientist Alan Stone defined regulation in his book *Regulation and Its Alternatives* as "a state-imposed limitation on the discretion that may be exercised by individuals or organizations, which is supported by the threat of sanction."

The federal government itself does not subscribe to any single description of what constitutes regulation. When President Gerald R. Ford asked his administration for a comprehensive listing of all federal agencies involved in regulation, the Office of Management and Budget (OMB) was hard pressed for an answer. "We went through a lot of soul-searching up here, trying to come up with a common definition," recalled one OMB official.

The Congressional Budget Office in 1976 defined regulation as those activities that (1) had an impact "on the operating business environments of broad sectors of private enterprise, including market entry and exit; rate, price and profit structures; and competition;" (2) affected "specific commodities, products, or services through permit, certification, or licensing requirements;" and (3) involved the development, administration and enforcement of national standards, violations of which could result in civil or criminal penalties, or which result in the types of impact described above."

The General Accounting Office (GAO) in a 1978 report on government regulatory activities put the number of independent and executive branch agencies engaged in regulation at 116. Admitting that the nature of the regulatory powers and activities exercised by the agencies it included was not uniform, the GAO focused on regulatory programs that "have an impact on the private sector without categorizing them by a specific regulatory definition." The report pointed out that some agencies were predominantly regulatory; others had regulatory as well as other program responsibilities; the regulatory activities of still others constituted a small portion of their congressional mandates; and still other agencies had only the power to investigate, make recommendations or set standards, with no authority to make or enforce their rules. Nevertheless, all these agencies exercised regulatory functions.

The following definition of a federal regulatory agency, written in 1977 by the Senate Governmental Affairs Committee, seemed to strike a balance between narrow and broad interpretations of the term. The committee (then named the Government Operations Committee) described a federal regulatory office as "one which (1) has decision-making authority, (2) establishes standards or guidelines conferring benefits and imposing restrictions on business conduct, (3) operates principally in the sphere of domestic business activity, (4) has its head and/or members appointed by the president ... [generally subject to Senate confirmation] and (5) has its legal procedures generally governed by the Administrative Procedure Act."

THE REASONS FOR REGULATION

Competition is the cornerstone of the American economy, and the basic purpose of regulation is to ensure the continuation of a competitive atmosphere. Regulation corrects market failures that occur when competition either does not exist in an industry or does not allocate resources efficiently.

Natural Monopoly

The most common economic justification for regulation is "natural monopoly," a type of market failure where economies of scale in an industry are so great that the largest firm has the lowest costs and therefore is able to drive its competitors out of the market.

The primary attribute of such a natural monopoly is that one firm can supply the entire market with a good or service more cheaply and efficiently than several smaller firms. The provision of local telephone service is a good example of a natural monopoly. Parallel distribution systems by several firms would involve wasteful duplication of facilities and probably result in higher prices.

However, unregulated monopolies have the potential to restrict output and charge elevated prices compared with those in a competitive market structure. It is that potential for abuse that is used to justify federal regulation.

Regulation of public utilities is the classic example of government controls on natural monopolies. A public utility commission determines what the single supplier (the monopolist) may charge for output, the minimum quality of the service and what profit the monopolist is entitled to earn.

Defining a natural monopoly is not always easy in practice, however, and what once seemed a natural monopoly may cease to be one with changes in the market or with the advent of new technology. Market growth and the appearance of substitute products or services can offset the tendency toward concentration in an industry, making the natural monopoly characteristics of an industry and the resulting regulatory justification obsolete.

The railroads, for example, were considered natural monopolies in the 19th century; as such, the rates they could charge as well as other aspects of their business were regulated. But with the development of other viable methods of transportation in the 20th century this natural monopoly rationale for government regulation ceased to exist. By deregulating the railroad industry, the 1980 Staggers Rail Act was intended to provide transportation users with the benefits of the competitive market system.

The telecommunications industry is a more recent example of a situation where changing circumstances may negate its classification as a natural monopoly and therefore the rationale for continued federal regulation. Given the sharp increase in demand for communications services,

evolving new technologies and reduced scale economies in the industry, deregulation and a more competitive climate might give consumers more benefits than the highly regulated market does.

Sometimes monopoly results from circumstances other than those due to scale economies. A company or a group of companies may take deliberate action to set prices or control supply and thus drive other competitors out of business. Since it enacted the Sherman Act of 1890 the government has made such combinations in restraint of trade illegal.

Destructive Competition

Monopoly is not the only economic justification for regulating. Economic failure in a given industry, such as banking, may be so costly to the public that it cannot be tolerated. Yet some experts have maintained that greater competition among banks ultimately would benefit the public, who could be insured in other ways against bank failures.

Destructive competition occurs when companies in a competitive situation operate at a loss over a long period of time. Vigorous competition among such companies can result in sharp price reductions and unrecovered total costs. Ultimately such activities lead to a deterioration in product quality, bankruptcy and monopoly.

The railroad price wars that raged in the 1870s and 1880s are a good example of the harm imposed by destructive competition. Prices and product quality fluctuated wildly, consumer demands went unsatisfied and industry planning became increasingly difficult. Both the railroad companies and their customers suffered from this instability. The ICC was created in 1887 in part to end the destructive competition.

Destructive competition entails more than just poor profit performance and the failure of firms per se. Situations as obvious as the railroad price wars rarely happen. Nonetheless, the fear of destructive competition is often used to support arguments for extended or continued regulation of an industry. The railroads used this argument when they sought federal regulation of the trucking industry in the 1930s.

Externalities

Another form of market imperfection involves what economists call "external diseconomies" or "externalities." Also known as spillovers or neighborhood effects, externalities develop when the production or use of a product has an unintended effect on third parties. Positive externalities are benefits enjoyed by third parties.

Negative externalities, on the other hand, are costs borne by third parties as well as by the producer and consumer. A company that gets rid of its used chemicals by dumping them alongside the roadway, causing the public to pay for cleanup, is externalizing part of its production costs.

Air pollution from automobiles, which harms the health of the public in general, is a good example of a negative externality. The driver pays for the car, including the costs of the control equipment that reduces the car's pollution, but does not incur the full costs or consequences of degrading the quality of the environment.

Nor do the auto manufacturers pay the full costs of air pollution. Although resources, such as clean air and water, in reality are scarce and exhaustible, manufacturers treat them as a "free" input in the production process, and consequently production costs do not include the expenses of the pollution. From a social point of view, therefore, the company's goods will not reflect the true costs of production. Those are shared by the public and the price can include illness and expensive health care.

Companies that take voluntary steps to absorb the full costs of negative externalities can find themselves at a competitive disadvantage. To continue the auto pollution example, John J. Riccardo, former president of Chrysler Corporation, noted: "A large part of the public will not voluntarily spend extra money to install emission control systems which will help clean the air. Any manufacturer who installs and charges for such equipment while his competition doesn't soon finds he is losing sales and customers. In cases like this, a government standard requiring everyone to have such equipment is the only way to protect both the public and the manufacturer."

Other Market Imperfections

Many other economic justifications are used to warrant government intervention in the marketplace. A regulatory agency may be needed to allocate limited space; this argument was used to justify regulation of the airlines and the broadcast spectrum. It is also the basic purpose behind traffic regulations — imagine the chaos if there were no rules to govern traffic speed or which driver proceeds first at an intersection.

The regulation of some natural resource extraction can be justified on two economic grounds. The first is on the basis of the existence of a natural resource monopoly. Without regulation, a single supplier with exclusive control over an important or essential raw material can set his own prices, lower output and charge monopoly prices. The Organization of Petroleum Exporting Countries (OPEC) is an example of a natural resource monopoly at the international level. The second reason involves efficiency and interdependency. If one producer's activities affect a second firm's access to a natural resource, efficient utilization of the resource may only be possible with government intervention.

The development of crude petroleum fields illustrates this kind of production interdependency. Too many wells in a single oil field and excessively rapid pumping will lower the field pressure and reduce the quantity of recoverable oil. Large oil fields are usually covered by many separate leases to different companies. Before government regulation was imposed, pumping was virtually a game of musical chairs; oil that one company was slow to extract was recovered by competing firms. All companies had an incentive to overpump and thus damage the oil field. To provide for efficient and stable recovery of the crude oil, the government stepped in to oversee industry operations.

A large and important part of government regulation is justified on the grounds that manufacturers do not provide adequate information about their goods and services. Many consumer product and occupational safety regulations fall into this category of economic justification. In certain markets — such as automobile insurance or medical care — the nature of the goods or services being bought is so complex that consumers may be incapable of making intelligent decisions without adequate explanatory information. Other kinds of information regulation warn consumers about potential health or safety hazards of a particular product or service.

Independent Commissions

Agency	Year Est.
Interstate Commerce Commission (ICC)	1887
Federal Reserve System (Fed)	1913
Federal Trade Commission (FTC)	1914
Federal Home Loan Bank Board (FHLBB)	1932
Federal Deposit Insurance Corporation (FDIC)	1933
Federal Communications Commission (FCC)	1934
Securities and Exchange Commission (SEC)	1934
National Labor Relations Board (NLRB)	1935
Civil Aeronautics Board (CAB) [1]	1940
Federal Maritime Commission (FMC) [2]	1961
Equal Employment Opportunity Commission (EEOC)	1964
Occupational Safety and Health Review Commission	1971
Consumer Product Safety Commission (CPSC)	1972
Commodity Futures Trading Commission (CFTC) [3]	1974
Nuclear Regulatory Commission (NRC)	1975
International Trade Commission (ITC) [5]	1975
Federal Election Commission (FEC)	1975
Federal Energy Regulatory Commission (FERC) [6]	1977

1. Successor to the Civil Aeronautics Authority, established in 1938.
2. Assumed the regulatory functions of the Department of Commerce's Maritime Administration, established in 1936.
3. Successor to the Agriculture Department's Commodity Exchange Authority, established in 1922.
4. Assumed the regulatory functions of the Atomic Energy Commission, established in 1946.
5. Successor to the Tariff Commission, established in 1916.
6. Assumed functions of the Federal Power Commission, established in 1930.

Social Regulation

Although market failure has been the primary justification for government regulation, it has not been the only one. Government has used regulation as a tool to achieve several broad social policy objectives. These have included:

- Redistribution of income within society to make it

more equitable; examples are Social Security, unemployment compensation and welfare programs.

• Preservation of national security; an example is the deregulation of the price of domestic oil to reduce the country's dependence on petroleum imports.

• Considerations of equity or fair play, such as government regulations to prevent employment discrimination.

• Protection of those who provide essential services to society, such as farmers who might be driven out of business without crop price supports and other farm subsidy programs.

• Allocation of scarce resources; gasoline rationing in emergency situations might illustrate this type of regulation.

• Protection of consumers from excessively high price increases; for example, the price of natural gas was regulated after consuming states complained about steadily increasing prices.

• Considerations of macroeconomic policy; imposition of wage and price controls to curb inflation is an example.

• Preserving property rights that resulted from earlier regulation; for example, broadcast licenses issued in the industry's infancy are worth much more in modern times. A change in regulation could diminish that value at great loss to the owners.

Regulation also may be imposed to guarantee service to remote areas that otherwise might be ignored. The Civil Aeronautics Board has compensated airlines that operate less profitable routes to smaller communities; railroads are not allowed to abandon service without approval from the Interstate Commerce Commission.

Political considerations may be as responsible as economic justifications for a significant portion of the government regulatory establishment in place today. At times regulation has been imposed in response to the requests of special interests and intensive lobbying campaigns. This was a factor in the imposition of controls in the 1930s on trucking, which directly competed with the heavily regulated railroads.

Likewise, Federal Communications Commission regulation of broadcasting was extended to cable television, even though cable transmissions presented no airwave interference problem, which was the original justification for regulating the broadcast industry. Proponents of cable regulation argued that, without federal controls, cable operations could force some broadcast stations out of business, leaving some markets unserved by either cable or broadcast transmissions. Instead of regulating trucks and cables, critics respond, the railroad and broadcast industries should have been partially deregulated to take advantage of the benefits derived from a more competitive market structure. In 1980 Congress removed most federal controls on both the rail and trucking industries. Deregulation of the telecommunications industry was being debated in 1982.

In some cases the economic reasons that justified regulation in the first place disappear but regulation continues because the regulated industry or others who benefit from the regulation want to preserve the status quo. Even though economic factors seemed to indicate that the industry and consumers would be better off under a more competitive industry structure, many of the powerful major airline companies opposed the 1978 airline deregulation legislation, arguing that federal controls brought needed stability to the industry.

Government regulation is not always the only option or the most appropriate tool by which to remedy market imperfections or achieve social goals. Alternative tools may be less costly or have fewer adverse effects on the economy. However, after a careful analysis of the federal regulatory system, the Senate Governmental Affairs Committee in its 1978 report *Framework for Regulation* concluded that "In general,...much of federal regulation is justified." It then added a note of caution: "Simply because a problem exists and, in theory, is remediable does not mean that regulation or other intervention is desirable, even on economic grounds. The potentially widespread indirect costs and consequences of regulation, subsidy, and other interventions are clear, and even direct costs are significant. In light of that burden, intervention should only be undertaken where there is a clearly identified problem, and where the potential achievements of Government action are substantial."

THE HISTORY OF FEDERAL REGULATION

Economic regulation is as old as human societies. The Old Testament cited business regulations, and the ancient Babylonian Code of Hammurabi established uniform weights and measures and limited interest rates. The decline of the Roman Empire brought imperial edicts fixing maximum prices for hundreds of goods.

Catholic sovereigns in the Middle Ages regulated commerce according to theological notions of "just price," and the church banned usury. The medieval feudal organization in Europe was superseded by the mercantilist system, under which governments strove to capture foreign markets. To ensure that their goods were of low cost and high quality, governments carefully regulated production, both directly and through corporations and trading companies.

The age of mercantilism came to an end after the publication in 1776 of Scottish economist Adam Smith's landmark book *The Wealth of Nations*, which is considered the foundation of modern economics. Smith attacked the mercantilist regulations and lauded the merits of laissez-faire competition in which every individual, in pursuing his own self-interest, was led as if by an "invisible hand" to achieve the best results for all. The competitive market system, in which prices and production rise and fall freely with demand, should be regulated only in those few areas where it might work against the consumer, such as certain banking practices that hindered trade and commerce, Smith said.

Britain and America in the 19th century came perhaps as close to this laissez-faire system as any other society, either before, during or after that era. Prior to the Civil War, the United States was a predominantly rural country with no large nationwide business enterprises. The federal government was more interested in encouraging exploitation of the nation's resources than in controlling their use. Federal influence on the economy was exerted through such actions as building public works projects, patenting inventions, granting public lands to homesteaders and railroads and imposing protective tariffs to nurture infant industries. It was an age not only of great economic development and material progress but also of periodic business crises, waste of precious natural resources and extremes of social inequity and corruption. Gradually, however, this system eroded as a few businessmen came to dominate certain industries. The marketplace no longer operated freely.

Such government regulation as there was in the 19th century was provided almost entirely by narrow statutes, usually at the state and local levels, and was enforced through the traditional machinery of the courts. But this system proved insufficient to deal with the complexities of a modern industrial economy and eventually gave way to a system of administrative controls, the predominant means of regulation in the 20th century.

As the regulatory process worked in the 1980s, the legislature provided only the broad mandate for a particular regulatory scheme, leaving a designated agency the authority to implement and enforce it. The agency often was given the power to prescribe regulations having the force of law, to police those subject to its authority and to decide cases involving possible violations — legislative, executive and judicial power in one body. In theory, at least, the agency would be able to provide the continuous supervision and expert knowledge that could not be expected of the legislature.

Early Federal Regulation

The federal government in its first 100 years established some agencies, most within executive departments, that performed regulatory functions. Designed largely to promote and develop the young nation and its industries, these agencies included the Army Corps of Engineers (1824), Patent and Trademark Office (1836), Comptroller of the Currency (1863), Copyright Office of the Library of Congress (1870) and Bureau of Fisheries (1871). Two other agencies, the Internal Revenue Service (1862) and the Civil Service Commission (1883), were established primarily to facilitate administration of the government itself.

But it was not until after the Civil War that the federal government began to exercise its constitutional authority to regulate interstate commerce. The watershed year was 1887 when Congress created the Interstate Commerce Commission (ICC) to regulate the railroad industry. Robert E. Cushman explained the importance of this event in his book *The Independent Regulatory Commissions:* "The crucial problem in 1887 was not whether railroads ought to be regulated; it was whether the time had come for the national government to take over the task of regulation. The Interstate Commerce Commission was an innovation not because it was endowed with a new type of power, but because it represented a new location of power in the federal system."

The ICC and its organizational setup were to serve as a prototype for regulation by independent commission as federal regulatory powers expanded into other areas of industry and commerce.

State Regulation of Railroads

The industrial revolution, with its new kinds of production processes and business organizations, fostered unprecedented expansion in the United States in the early 1800s. This in turn stimulated large interstate markets, which grew even larger as the country itself expanded and the railroad system developed. Initially, the federal government's role was one of promoting, not regulating, the railroads. Because railroads were considered essential to military and postal operations, Congress aided railroad development through charters, rights-of-way, land grants for the laying of track, and loans and subsidies to the railroad companies. In 1840 the "several states" were connected by 2,800 miles of railroad track. Within 40 years the rail system increased to 93,000 miles; in another 20 years it doubled to nearly 200,000 miles of track.

As the rail industry expanded, so did the abuses associated with it. The public was often the victim of bitter competitive battles among railroads. Railroad monopolies were able to influence the success or failure of communities, shippers and even entire industries. Cutthroat competitive practices included financial manipulations and rate abuses. At times, railroads lowered rates sharply to eliminate competition; as soon as that objective had been accomplished, rates went back up. Discrimination against certain types of customers became widespread, involving both freight and passenger service. .

Because the first railway lines were operated locally, most early regulation was left to the states. Although the states attempted in various ways to curb the railroad abuses, their efforts generally were ineffective. After the Civil War, however, customers organized to seek state regulation of the large manufacturing and railroad companies to curtail their power over the individual consumer. In many states it was pressure from farmers that resulted in the passage of state laws regulating railroad rates. Among the most successful of these organizations was the secret order called the National Grange, which won passage of laws in several states regulating how much railroads could charge farmers to carry their produce to market. Some states also regulated the rates that grain elevator companies could charge to store farmers' grain.

In 1877 the Supreme Court appeared to sanction such state regulation of these businesses with its decision in the *Granger Cases,* involving both railroad and grain elevator rate regulation. The court acknowledged that regulation of railroad and grain elevator rates fell within the purview of the federal power under the commerce clause of the Constitution. But, in the absence of federal regulation, the court held that the states could regulate these matters even if the state regulation affected interstate commerce.

The *Granger Cases* — especially *Munn v. Illinois,* upholding the right of a state regulatory commission to regulate grain elevator storage rates — implied a major grant of power to the states. To limit that grant, the court devised the concept of "public interest" to distinguish those businesses that might be subject to state regulation from those that could not be. "When private property is devoted to public use, it is subject to public regulation," concluded the court.

State regulation of grain elevators survived for several decades, but in 1886 the Supreme Court sharply limited the power of the states to regulate railroad rates. The business panics of the 1870s and 1880s and the westward expansion of the country had led to the consolidation of the railroads into vast interstate networks. In *Wabash, St. Louis and Pacific Railway Co. v. Illinois,* the Supreme Court ruled that the states could not regulate rates, even for the intrastate portion of a trip, of any railroad that was part of an interstate network.

Regulation of an interstate railroad by each of the states through which it passed would have a "deleterious influence upon the freedom of commerce among the States

Congress Expands Regulatory Role...

Congress has no explicit constitutional mandate to protect public health, public welfare and public morals. Such protections traditionally have been the responsibility of the states acting through their police powers. Nonetheless, Congress by the 1890s had begun to develop a federal police power to deal with a growing list of social and economic problems that were no longer local but national in scope.

This was the period of the progressive movement when farmers, laborers and consumers rose up against their exploitation by those who held the nation's wealth and power. Unemployment and poverty created by a series of economic depressions was widespread. Women and children worked long hours under wretched conditions for low pay. Immigrants and other poor people were crowded into filthy city ghettoes. Local governments were rife with corruption.

Samuel Eliot Morison, Henry Steele Commager and William E. Leuchtenberg described this period in *The Growth of the American Republic*: "Against the crowding evils of the time there arose a full-throated protest which distinguished American politics and thought from approximately 1890 to World War I. It demanded the centralization of power in the hands of a strong government and the extension of regulation or control over industry, finance, transportation, agriculture, labor and even morals. It found expression in a new concern for the poor and underprivileged, for women and children, for the immigrant, the Indian and the Negro. It called for new standards of honesty in politics and in business. It formulated a new social and political philosophy, which rejected *laissez-faire* and justified public control of social and economic institutions on the principles of liberal democracy."

The national legislature used its constitutional grant of authority over interstate commerce to justify much of its new regulation, claiming the power to regulate any matter that at some point was a part of interstate commerce. "Where the commerce power had previously been used primarily to regulate, foster or promote commerce for its own sake, . . . it now seemed that Congress might seek to regulate social and economic practices within the states, provided only that at some point they involved a crossing of state lines," wrote constitutional historian Robert K. Carr in *The Supreme Court and Judicial Review*.

Police Power Developed

Initial attempts by Congress to exercise a police power were largely unsuccessful. The Supreme Court ruled that such regulations could apply only in areas of the United States outside state boundaries, such as the District of Columbia.

In 1902, however, the court upheld a federal statute prohibiting the transportation of diseased cattle in interstate commerce. The following year the court sanctioned the federal police power in a controversial case of great significance, *Champion v. Ames (The Lottery Case).*

In that case, the court ruled that the power to regulate commerce included the authority to prohibit that commerce. "[W]e know of no authority in the Courts to hold that the means thus devised [prohibition of shipment] are not appropriate and necessary to protect the country . . . against a species of interstate commerce which . . . has become offensive to the entire people of the nation," the majority wrote.

This decision, historian Charles Warren wrote in *The Supreme Court in United States History*, "dis-

and upon the transit of goods through those states. . . ," the court wrote. "[T]his species of regulation is one which must be, if established at all, of a general and national character, and cannot be safely and wisely remitted to local rules and local regulations. . . ," the court concluded.

The following year, Congress enacted the long-pending legislation to create the Interstate Commerce Commission, beginning what would become extensive federal regulation of the nation's commerce.

ICC Established

Two approaches to federal regulation of the railroads had been debated in Congress for nearly a decade before the Supreme Court struck down state regulation. One approach was to prohibit unreasonable rates and unfair prac-

tices and give the Justice Department authority to enforce the prohibitions. The other approach was to give broader powers to a separate regulatory commission. According to Louis Fisher in his book *The Politics of Shared Power*, Congress chose the latter approach because a commission would: "provide flexible and expert administration of the railroad industry; serve as an expert body to aid Congress in formulating a railroad policy; protect the public and small shippers against the legal talents of the railroad corporations; serve as an arbiter for conflicting interests among the railroads; provide valuable expert opinion to the courts; and build on the successful model of state commissions."

The 1887 Act to Regulate Commerce was a landmark in American political history. In addition to punishing wrongful acts after they were committed, the government

...To Protect Public Health and Welfare

closed the existence of a hitherto unsuspected field of national power," and Congress was quick to take advantage of it. Between 1903 and 1917 Congress enacted laws prohibiting the interstate transportation of explosives, diseased livestock, insect pests, falsely stamped gold and silver articles, narcotics, prostitutes and adulterated or misbranded foods and drugs.

The Supreme Court sustained every one of these acts. The only exception was a federal law enacted in 1916 that set work standards for child laborers and banned the interstate shipment of goods made in factories that employed children under age 14. The court in the case of *Hammer v. Dagenhart* held that Congress had exceeded its power when it enacted the law.

The court did not rely heavily on the *Dagenhart* ruling as a precedent. In fact, the justices continued to sanction use of the commerce power as a regulatory tool when it was applied to universally recognized social evils. A few weeks after the child labor case decision, the court unanimously upheld the constitutionality of the Meat Inspection Act of 1906, which required local inspection of meat products and banned from interstate commerce meat that had been rejected or not inspected.

The Power Broadened

In 1941 the court overruled its decision in the Dagenhart case when it upheld the 1938 Fair Labor Standards Act, which applied minimum wage and overtime rules to most private manufacturers. "The motive and purpose of the present regulation is plainly to make effective the Congressional conception of public policy that interstate commerce should not be made the instrument of competition in the distribution of goods produced under substandard labor conditions, which competition is injurious to the commerce and to the states from and to which the commerce flows. The motive and purpose of a regulation of interstate commerce are matters for the legislative judgment upon the exercise of which the Constitution places no restriction and over which the courts are given no control," the court said in *United States v. Darby Lumber Co.*

That ruling not only affirmed Congress' police power, it further broadened federal power to regulate the manufacture as well as the shipment of goods. That broad construction continued into the 1980s. Not only was the commerce clause the foundation for ever more detailed supervision of the commercial life of the nation by Congress and executive agencies; it was used to prohibit racial discrimination in public accommodations and to justify federal regulation of environmental pollutants.

Only once since the New Deal era has the Supreme Court ruled that Congress exceeded the scope of its commerce power. Like the *Darby* and *Dagenhart* cases, this case involved fair labor standards, specifically the extension of minimum wage and overtime requirements to state and local government employees. The court struck down that law in 1976, ruling that Congress had interfered too deeply into the essential functions of state and local governments.

Five years later, the court in 1981 again affirmed Congress' broad powers to regulate to protect the public health and welfare. Federal strip mining regulations were an appropriate response to Congress' finding that strip mining often adversely affected commerce and the public welfare by destroying or diminishing the usefulness of the land and by contributing to floods, water pollution and property damage.

---

now assumed a major role in preventing their occurrence. The act stipulated that all rates be "reasonable and just" and prohibited certain railroad practices such as rate discrimination, price-fixing, rebating and pooling.

To administer the act, Congress created the Interstate Commerce Commission (ICC) to be headed by a commission of five members, no more than three of whom could be from the same political party. Appointed by the president with the consent of the Senate for staggered six-year terms, the commissioners could be removed from office only for corruption, negligence or malfeasance. As it finally evolved in the early 1900s, the ICC set the precedent for regulatory commissions to come: "independent, expert, nonpartisan agencies wherein the worlds of politics and industrial economics would be reconciled," as described by Louis Kohlmeier Jr. in his book *The Regulators*.

However, Congress apparently did not originally intend the ICC to be an *independent* commission. During congressional debate on the agency's creation, the word "independence" was not mentioned at all, and the issue of presidential influence was not discussed. In *The Independent Regulatory Commissions* Cushman wrote: "There was virtually no discussion of the commission's relationship to Congress. Congress was, of course, creating the commission and assigning it powers, but there is nothing to suggest that the legislative leaders looked upon the commission as having a relationship with Congress different from that of any other administrative agency."

Congress initially placed the Interstate Commerce Commission within the Interior Department. The ICC's budget, staff and internal management were subject to the approval of the secretary of the interior. Two years later, in

1889, Congress amended the original act to give the ICC sole authority over its own operations. It has been suggested that the Democrat-controlled House pushed the change through in an attempt to insulate the commission from the possible political influence of the incoming Republican administration.

The ICC's early independence — and regulatory effectiveness — was hampered because it lacked final legislative and adjudicative power. The ICC originally had no specific authority to set railroad rates or to adjust "unreasonable" rates and no coercive powers to enforce its rulings; it could issue cease-and-desist orders to halt any railroad determined to be in violation of the act's provisions, but the power of enforcement still resided in the judiciary. The courts insisted on reviewing commission orders to such an extent that, in effect, they substituted their judgment, which often favored the railroads, for that of the commission. Years of litigation were required before regulation beneficial to the public was realized, and the railroads soon saw that they could obstruct the ICC by court appeals.

Passage of the Hepburn Act in 1906 freed the ICC from its judicial straitjacket. The act:

● Expanded the commission's jurisdiction to include express companies, certain pipelines and sleeping car companies.

● Increased the number of commissioners from five to seven.

● Authorized the commission to adjust rates it judged to be unreasonable or unfair.

● Gave the ICC final ratemaking powers, subject to judicial review on complaint of the carriers; rates established by the ICC were to become effective immediately without the need for prior approval of the courts.

Renewed demands from the public and some of the railroad companies led Congress four year later to strengthen the ICC's enforcement mechanisms. The Mann-Elkins Act of 1910 authorized the commission to suspend and investigate new rate proposals and to set original rates. The large railroad companies challenged the act as an unconstitutional delegation of legislative authority, but the Supreme Court in 1914 held the contention was "without merit." The ICC's authority over the railroads and other forms of interstate transportation continued to grow steadily. The number of its commissioners grew as well, to nine members in 1906 and to 11 in 1920. In 1982 Congress reduced the number to five.

Piecemeal Expansion of Regulation

At first it appeared that the ICC might handle all federal regulation of commerce. When this proved impracticable, Congress created a series of new agencies, patterned on the ICC, beginning with the Federal Reserve System in 1913 and the Federal Trade Commission (FTC) in 1914.

Congress passed the Federal Reserve Act to bring some semblance of stability to the nation's financial system. The Treasury Department's Office of the Comptroller of the Currency (OCC) had been established in 1863 as the first federal agency to regulate banking activities. But the OCC by itself had failed to provide the essentials of a centralized commercial banking system. The banking industry, comprised of privately owned banks located mainly in New York, increasingly was characterized by inelastic currency and immobile reserves, causing the economy to fluctuate wildly and uncertainly in a cyclical pattern of booms and busts.

Relying on its constitutional powers "to coin money [and] regulate the value thereof," Congress responded to this economic chaos by setting up the Federal Reserve System as the nation's central bank. The Fed's primary purpose was to provide a flow of credit and money that would foster economic stability and growth, a high level of employment, stability in the purchasing power of the dollar and a reasonable balance in foreign transactions. It was set up as an independent regulatory commission with seven members, called governors, appointed for staggered 14-year terms.

Simultaneous with the increasing complexity of the financial system was the growth of powerful combinations, or "trusts," in many areas of business and industry. Formed to circumvent the vicious competition that so often resulted in bankruptcy, the trusts frequently eliminated most competition of any significance and drove smaller entrepreneurs out of the market. By 1901 trusts dominated the steel, oil, sugar, meat packing, leather, electrical goods and tobacco industries.

This threat to the traditional concept of the free enterprise system was not popular, nor were the unsavory methods frequently used by the trusts to gain control and enlarge their hold on the industry involved. Public outcry against the trusts led Congress in 1890 to pass the Sherman Antitrust Act, which made illegal "every contract, combination in the form of trust or otherwise, or conspiracy, in restraint of trade or commerce among the several states, or with foreign nations. . . ."

However, it soon became apparent that the act, which provided criminal as well as civil penalties for business practices such as price-fixing and monopoly, was inadequate to solve the problems of industrial concentration. The Justice Department's Antitrust Division, established in 1903, brought lawsuits to enforce the act, but courts responded slowly and often ruled in favor of the trusts. Another agency, the Bureau of Corporations, had been established in 1903 as part of what was then the Department of Labor and Commerce to gather data from businesses on their trade practices. The agency was a good fact-finding body, but it lacked the final authority of an independent commission.

Broad support for such a commission developed quickly. All the political parties involved in the 1912 election campaign endorsed the concept. ICC regulation of the railroads had proved satisfactory, and there was little doubt that another independent commission could monitor other industries just as successfully. Many also argued that an independent agency would be a more effective trustbuster than the Justice Department because its members would not be subjected to the political pressures faced by an executive branch agency.

Sen. Francis G. Newlands, D-Nev., emphasized that view in an address to the Senate on Jan. 11, 1911: "Had we submitted the administration of the [Sherman] antitrust act to an impartial quasi-judicial tribunal similar to the Interstate Commerce Commission, instead of the Attorney General's office, . . . we would by this time have made gratifying progress in the regulation and control of trusts, through the quasi-judicial investigations of a competent commission and through legislation based on its recommendations."

No serious obstacle blocked passage of the Federal Trade Commission Act of 1914. The wording of the legislation was intentionally vague, giving the FTC broad powers to define business practices that constituted "unfair methods of competition." The FTC was also made responsible for the 1914 Clayton Antitrust Act, which prohibited specific business activities, such as discriminatory pricing and tying agreements, that tended to lessen competition or to create monopolies.

Like its predecessor, the Bureau of Corporations, the FTC relied on voluntary compliance by businesses; but the new commission also had authority to investigate collusive or unfair business practices and order them stopped. The Justice Department's Antitrust Division retained complete responsibility for violations under the Sherman Act.

Between 1915 and the beginning of the New Deal, Congress set up seven more agencies and commissions that regulated aspects of the nation's commercial and financial systems. These included the Coast Guard (1915), Tariff Commission (1916), Commodities Exchange Authority (1922) and Customs Service (1927). In 1927 Congress set up the Federal Radio Commission to regulate the issuance of station licenses, allocation of frequency bands, assignment of specified frequencies to individual stations and control of station power. In 1930 Congress established the fourth independent regulatory commission — the Federal Power Commission (FPC) — to replace the ex-officio Water Power Commission, which had been created in 1920 to coordinate control over the growing nation's power resources and which had proven inadequate. And in 1931 Congress created the Food and Drug Administration to monitor federal laws ensuring the purity of certain foods and drugs.

New Deal Regulation

The Great Depression of the 1930s — and the Roosevelt administration's response to it — resulted in an unprecedented surge of administrative regulation. Most of the eight major regulatory agencies set up between 1932 and 1938 were created to alleviate the economic chaos that began with the stock market crash of October 1929. These agencies were designed to restore the securities markets, real estate and agriculture industries, and the banking and financial system in general, all of which had suffered tremendous losses during the Depression. But Congress also reorganized federal regulation of the rapidly expanding transportation system, increasing ICC jurisdiction and setting up agencies to regulate the maritime and air industries. And it consolidated interstate communications regulation into a new independent regulatory commission.

There is little evidence that Congress had any overall scheme in mind when it established these New Deal agencies. According to Marver H. Bernstein, author of *Regulating Business by Independent Commission*, the growth of regulation during the New Deal was "initiated by particular groups to deal with specific evils as they arose, rather than inspired by any general philosophy of government control."

The regulatory agencies geared toward restoring the economy were:

● The Federal Home Loan Bank Board (FHLBB), established in 1932 as an independent agency within the executive branch to regulate federally chartered savings and loan associations, which are the nation's primary source of private funds to pay for building and buying homes.

● The Federal Deposit Insurance Corporation (FDIC), created by the Banking Act of 1933 as an independent agency within the executive branch to be the primary regulator of state-chartered insured banks that were not members of the Federal Reserve System. The FDIC offers federally guaranteed insurance for bank deposits.

● The Farm Credit Administration, set up as part of the Agriculture Department in 1933 to supervise and regulate the activities of the cooperative Farm Credit System, which provided credit and other services to farmers and ranchers. (In 1953 the agency was granted independence from the executive branch.)

● The Securities and Exchange Commission (SEC), an independent commission set up in 1934 to protect the public against fraud and deception in the securities and financial markets. The SEC's mandate was expanded during the 1930s to include all investment companies as well as public utility holding companies.

● The National Labor Relations Board (NLRB), an independent commission established by the Wagner Act of 1935 to prevent "unfair labor practices" and to protect the right of employees to bargain collectively.

Transportation Regulation

Federal regulatory involvement expanded just as rapidly during the 1930s in the transportation sector as the needs of the nation increased and new methods of transportation evolved.

The Motor Carrier Act of 1935 brought the burgeoning trucking industry under ICC jurisdiction. The agency was authorized to regulate entry into the industry, commodities transported, rates charged, and acquisitions and mergers of trucking firms.

The 1935 law was enacted largely at the urging of the already regulated railroad industry. The trucking industry was cutting into the railways' freight business, and the rails wanted both transportation modes to play under the same rules. According to Peter Woll in his book *American Bureaucracy*, passage of the 1935 act "meant essentially that regulation in the public interest . . . became equated with regulation in the interests of the railroads. The shift also reflected changing patterns of political support, which led to commission reliance upon the very interests it was supposed to control for the necessary political support to maintain itself as an independent agency in the bureaucratic structure."

Paralleling this development was a sharp upswing in federal activities to promote a diversified transportation industry, including grants-in-aid for highway, airport and mass transit facility construction; subsidies for shipping and airline operations; and loan guarantees for new carrier equipment purchases. The Maritime Administration was created as part of the Department of Commerce in 1936 to promote the merchant marine and regulate the nation's ocean commerce. These functions were transferred in 1961 to the newly created independent Federal Maritime Commission.

At the same time, increased competition among airlines necessitated coordination of airline routes and regulation of flight operations. Because the Interstate Commerce Commission was already heavily burdened with increased responsibility for surface transportation, Congress in 1938 created the Civil Aeronautics Authority to promote and regulate the industry. Two years later it replaced that agency with the Civil Aeronautics Board (CAB), an independent commission.

The board assumed responsibility for the Air Commerce Act of 1926, which had imposed safety regulations but not economic ones. In 1958 CAB jurisdiction was broadened to include authority over the economic, routing and pricing practices of U.S. airline companies, including air carriers operating to and from the United States. Airplane safety functions were given to the newly created Federal Aviation Agency, which became the Federal Aviation Agency within the Transportation Department when that department was created in 1967.

At the urging of President Franklin D. Roosevelt, the independent Federal Communications Commission (FCC) was established in 1934 to consolidate federal regulation of all common carriers in interstate communications, at that time radio, telephone and telegraph. The FCC replaced the Federal Radio Commission, which had been created in 1927 to allocate frequency and control station power. But the 1927 law had left the Commerce Department with the authority to inspect radio stations, license radio operators and assign radio call signals. Furthermore, jurisdiction for telegraph operations had remained divided among the ICC and the Post Office and State departments.

Social Regulation

The New Deal era proved to be the high-water mark for creation of regulatory agencies intended to ensure certain economic goals. It also set the stage for the proliferation of non-economic, or social, regulation that characterized the late 1960s and 1970s.

The New Deal programs marked a fundamental shift away from the limited role that the federal government had previously filled in the nation's economic and social life. During the 1930s, the government first took on responsibility for managing the economy. The New Deal also produced a host of programs that redistributed the nation's wealth from one group to another and from some regions to others. After the Depression, the federal government continued to expand income transfer programs and take over more and more functions that states, local governments and individuals previously had performed.

Such programs, including many providing federal grants to state and local governments to fund specific projects, grew gradually in the 1940s and 1950s. Few new regulatory agencies were created in the first two decades following the New Deal. The major ones were the Atomic Energy Commission (1946), the Small Business Administration (1953) and the Federal Aviation Agency (1958).

Then, starting in 1965, under the direction of President Lyndon B. Johnson, the government launched a stream of Great Society programs that extended its role in providing medical care, education aid, regional development, nutrition, urban renewal, job training and other services for people and localities. During the 1970s, Congress enlarged most of these programs — and added a few new ones.

The federal bureaucracy needed to administer these programs grew just as steadily. Of the 13 Cabinet-level departments in existence in 1982, three had been formed since 1965: Housing and Urban Development (1965), Transportation (1967) and Energy (1977). Furthermore, in 1980, the Department of Health, Education and Welfare, which had been set up only in 1953, was split into the Department of Education and the Department of Health

and Human Services. Many of the social programs administered by these departments did not require regulation in the traditional sense, but the hundreds of rules relating to program eligibility and performance contributed to the public's perception that the government had too much control over everyday life.

The extraordinary social activism of the period, which began with the civil rights movement and grew to encompass the Vietnam War protests and the consumer and environmental movements, also led to another intense period of federal regulation. Although it had significant impact on the economy and specific industries in particular, this surge of regulation was intended primarily to achieve social goals, such as cleaner air and safer workplaces, which most businesses and industries were unlikely to provide on their own. The new surge of regulation also resulted in establishment of several new and far-reaching regulatory agencies.

One of the first of these was created by the historic Civil Rights Act of 1964, which prohibited discrimination in employment on the basis of sex, race, color, religion and national origin. The Equal Employment Opportunity Commission (EEOC) was created to enforce the ban. The EEOC was authorized to investigate complaints of employment discrimination and to settle those it could through mediation and conciliation. If conciliation failed, the commission could recommend that the Justice Department file suit to force compliance. In 1972 Congress amended the 1964 act to allow the commission itself to file suit in individual job discrimination cases and in cases where a general pattern of discrimination ran throughout an industry or large company.

Advent of Consumerism

The consumer movement, which reached its zenith in the early 1970s, made a deep imprint on American life and the marketplace. Consumers organized at the local, state and federal levels to demand safer and better quality products, goods that lived up to advertised claims and lower prices for food, medical care, fuel and other products.

Consumer protection laws were not new. Congress had enacted laws as early as the 1890s to protect the public against immoral or impure products. In 1895 a federal law banned the interstate shipment of lottery tickets; in 1906 Congress outlawed interstate sale and shipment of impure or unsafe foods and drugs; and in 1910 it barred transportation of prostitutes across state lines.

Since then, Congress has enacted numerous laws to keep impure or unsafe products out of the marketplace, but the breadth of legislation enacted in response to the modern consumer movement was unprecedented. Congress wrote more than a dozen consumer protection laws and created several regulatory agencies to ensure that consumer products from baby cribs to automobiles met health and safety standards and that consumers had the information necessary to make intelligent purchasing decisions.

The catalyst for the consumer movement was Ralph Nader, a lawyer who had long been interested in consumer problems. Nader's career as the nation's foremost consumer advocate began in 1965 with publication of his book *Unsafe at Any Speed*, which attacked the automobile industry for emphasizing profits and design styling over safety. Nader concentrated his fire on the Chevrolet Corvair, "one of the nastiest-handling cars ever built."

Final passage in 1966 of auto safety legislation was due in large part to Nader's activities. The new law established federal motor vehicle and tire safety standards and brought the automobile industry under permanent regulation for the first time. In 1970 the National Highway Traffic and Safety Administration was created within the Transportation Department with authority to set auto safety and fuel efficiency standards as well as standards for state highway safety programs.

In 1969 Nader founded the Center for the Study of Responsive Law, the staging area for the activities of "Nader's Raiders" — groups of young people who gathered in Washington to ferret information from the government and business groups for reports on antitrust enforcement, occupational safety and health, air pollution, airline safety and the like. The exposés of waste and inefficiency documented in some of these reports won Nader and his raiders the title of modern-day muckrakers. The successes of Nader's organizations helped the consumer movement to grow rapidly, and several national consumer groups, among them the Consumer Federation of America, National Consumers League and National Consumers Congress, actively lobbied Congress for passage of their legislative program.

Much of that legislative program concerned consumer protection in financial and banking matters. Between 1968 and 1977, Congress enacted the Truth in Lending Act, Fair Credit Billing Act, Equal Credit Opportunity Act, Home Mortgage Disclosure Act, Consumer Leasing Act and Fair Debt Collection Practices Act. Congress in 1975 also passed legislation strengthening regulation of consumer warranties.

Consumers also concentrated on product safety, winning passage of the Consumer Product Safety Act in 1972. That law established the Consumer Product Safety Commission (CPSC) as an independent regulatory commission to protect consumers against unreasonable risk of injury from hazardous products. The CPSC was authorized to issue and enforce safety standards for the design, construction, performance and labeling of more than 10,000 consumer products. The new commission also was given authority over several existing programs transferred from other agencies. These included the Flammable Fabrics Act, Hazardous Substances Act and Refrigerator Safety Act.

Other agencies created to protect consumers included the Federal Highway Administration (1966), which establishes highway safety standards; the Federal Railroad Administration (1966), which sets rail safety standards; and the National Credit Union Administration (1970), which regulates member credit unions.

But the consumer movement was unsuccessful in its quest to establish another independent commission — the Consumer Protection Agency — to represent consumer interests before other federal regulatory agencies. Repeated attempts to push such an agency through Congress failed as opposition by business groups and national discontent with "big government" grew. *(Public participation, p. 39)*

Environmental Movement

Paralleling consumer activism was an equally enthusiastic public voice calling for a cleaner environment. More and more people took seriously warnings from respected environmentalists that humans might be harming their surroundings irreversibly. And environmental disasters, such as the 1969 oil spill off the coast of Santa Barbara, Calif., illustrated the need for immediate action.

Popular interest in ecology snapped into focus on April 22, 1970, with the celebration of Earth Day. Millions of

Regulatory Agency Growth

The following chart shows the growth in expenditures and permanent, full-time personnel for 57 federal regulatory agencies for selected fiscal years. (Figures do not add due to rounding.)

	1970	1980	1981	1982 (est.)	1983 (est.)
Expenditures (in billions)					
Social Regulation					
Consumer health and safety	$0.4	$2.4	$2.7	$2.4	$2.5
Job safety, other working conditions	0.1	0.7	0.8	0.8	0.8
Energy, environment	0.1	1.9	2.1	2.2	2.0
Subtotal	0.5	5.1	5.6	5.3	5.3
Economic Regulation					
Finance, banking	$0.1	$0.3	$0.4	$0.4	$0.4
Other industry-specific	0.1	0.4	0.4	0.3	0.3
General business	0.1	0.3	0.3	0.4	0.3
Subtotal	0.3	1.0	1.1	1.1	1.0
Total	$0.9	$6.1	$6.6	$6.4	$6.3
Personnel (in thousands)					
Social regulation	9.7	66.4	63.6	57.1	54.8
Economic regulation	18.0	24.1	23.0	22.2	21.7
Total	27.7	90.5	86.7	79.3	76.5

Source: Center for the Study of American Business, Washington University.

Americans attended environmental teach-ins, antipollution protests and various cleanup projects, all under the green-and-white banner of the new ecology flag.

One of the results of the environmental movement was the consolidation of the federal government's widespread environmental protection efforts into a single agency. The Environmental Protection Agency (EPA) was created in 1970 with relatively little fuss as an independent agency in the executive branch; it was soon to become one of the most controversial agencies of the federal government.

The EPA immediately assumed the existing environmental responsibilities of other departments and agencies, including the 1948 Water Pollution Control Act, the 1955 Air Pollution Control Act and the 1965 Water Quality Control Act. During the next 10 years, the EPA's responsibilities and authority were broadened substantially with congressional passage of laws to set limits on air pollutants, control noise, control pesticides and other toxic substances, provide clean drinking water and clean up toxic contaminants spilled or dumped into the environment. *(EPA and clean air, p. 111)*

Other regulatory agencies established to protect certain elements of the environment were the Materials Transportation Board (1975), which regulates the transport of hazardous materials, and the Office of Surface Mining Reclamation and Enforcement (1977), which regulates the strip mining industry.

Workplace Safety

Safety in the workplace was the focus of another new regulatory agency that had an immense impact on U.S. business. The Occupational Safety and Health Administration (OSHA) was created in 1970 as an agency within the Labor Department to promulgate and enforce worker safety and health standards. The agency was authorized to conduct unannounced workplace inspections, require employers to keep detailed records on worker injuries and illness, and conduct research. Within one month of its creation, the agency adopted some 4,400 standards from existing federal regulations, industry codes and the National Standards Institute. The agency also was authorized to issue standards for health hazards such as inhalation of cotton dust and exposure to toxic chemicals.

Congress in 1973 established the Mining Enforcement and Safety Administration within the Interior Department to promulgate and enforce mine safety and health standards. In 1977 the agency was reorganized as the Mine Safety and Health Administration and placed in the Labor Department.

Energy Regulation

The other major area of expanded federal regulation in the 1970s was the energy sector — where the United States was repeatedly confronted with the twin problems of dwindling energy supply and soaring costs. The 1973 Arab oil embargo made energy a top national concern, jolting Americans into the realization that the nation was dangerously dependent on foreign sources for much — perhaps too much — of its energy supply.

As the failure of voluntary efforts to spread scarce fuel supplies evenly became obvious, Congress in 1973 insisted that the president impose mandatory controls allocating oil and oil products among different regions of the nation and sectors of the petroleum industry. Free market advocates maintained that consumption could be cut and production increased only by allowing prices to rise in response to changing conditions. (By the mid-1970s, Congress was already beginning to take steps toward the eventual phasing-out of federal price controls.)

Congress responded to the energy crisis by trying to put together a comprehensive national energy policy. Those efforts included a reorganization of the federal energy structure. In 1973 Congress set up the Federal Energy Administration (FEA) to manage short-term fuel shortages. In 1974 Congress abolished the Atomic Energy Commission, creating in its place the Energy Research and Development Administration (ERDA), which was authorized to develop nuclear power and new energy sources, and an independent Nuclear Regulatory Commission, which assumed the AEC's nuclear safety and regulatory responsibilities.

In 1977 the federal energy bureaucracy again was reorganized to consolidate the vast array of evolving energy powers, programs and agencies throughout the government. In what was considered a victory for President Jimmy Carter, Congress approved the creation of a Cabinet-level Department of Energy to assume the powers and functions of the Federal Power Commission, the FEA and ERDA, all of which were abolished.

Authority to set prices for natural gas, oil and electricity was given to the Federal Energy Regulatory Commission (FERC), an independent commission set up as part of the Energy Department. Authority to regulate the allocation of various oil and gas products and to plan for national emergencies was given to the Economic Regulatory Administration (ERA) within the Energy Department. The ERA, however, lost much of its authority in January 1981 when President Ronald Reagan lifted all controls on oil pricing under the Emergency Petroleum Allocation Act of 1973.

Regulatory Growth

The economic recession of the mid-1970s slowed the number of new consumer and environmental programs as legislators sought to balance the benefits of sometimes costly social regulatory programs with the need for a stable and productive economy. The loss of income resulting from higher energy prices, the slowdown in productivity, and spiraling inflation and unemployment all combined to make the late 1970s an "era of limits."

Nevertheless, the 1970s witnessed the most dramatic increase in federal regulatory activity ever. According to the Center for the Study of American Business: ". . . federal regulatory activities during the 1970s grew not only in absolute terms, such as costs and the number of agencies, but also in terms of government penetration into the daily decision-making activities of nearly all areas of management in the modern American firm. The growth of the federal regulatory establishment over the past 13 years has perhaps no counterpart in governmental expansion in the peacetime history of this nation."

This growth was reflected in the budgets and staff sizes of the regulatory agencies. The center estimated that the budgets for what it considered to be the major regulatory agencies skyrocketed from $866 million in 1970 to more than $5.5 billion by 1979 — a growth of 537 percent over the course of the decade. The year 1980 appears to have been the high-water mark for federal regulatory activities. According to the center, total budget outlays for 56 regulatory agencies in fiscal 1980 grew 18 percent (8 percent after inflation), the largest increase since 1974. The areas of consumer safety and health, energy and environmental regulation accounted for most of this increase. *(Regulatory growth, chart, p. 17)*

The number of government employees involved in regulation also grew. The Environmental Protection Agency, which employed 3,860 persons in 1970, had 10,678 employees in 1980. OSHA increased from 1,558 positions in 1972 to 2,799 in 1980. The older agencies had expanded as well. The ICC, which had 1,060 permanent positions in 1951, had 1,880 in 1980. During the same period, the staff of the Securities and Exchange Commission doubled, increasing to 2,000 employees.

Although the number of agencies created during the late 1970s diminished, the agencies already in place issued more rules and regulations than ever before. One measure of this growth was the size of the daily *Federal Register*, which publishes all proposed and final rules and regulations; it skyrocketed from 9,562 pages in 1960 to 74,120 pages in 1980.

Regulation Backlash

The surge of regulation in the 1960s and 1970s improved the quality of life for millions of Americans; it also raised protests that the federal government had grown too big and too intrusive. Companies complained that the benefits of many regulations did not justify the costs of compliance. Others complained that the government required the most expensive, but not necessarily the most effective, means of compliance. Some small concerns claimed that the high costs of compliance with federal regulations had forced them out of business. And everyone complained about the paperwork required by federal regulators.

Congress tried to ease some of that burden by cutting back on the paperwork and exempting small businesses from compliance with some regulations. And the Ford and Carter administrations made impressive strides toward deregulating the transportation and banking industries. *(Transportation deregulation, p. 89)*

Still Ronald Reagan seemed to reflect the mood of a great majority of the public during his 1980 presidential campaign when he claimed that excessive and needless federal regulations were overburdening the U.S. economy and undercutting the prosperity of the American people.

By late 1982 it was unclear how successful Reagan would be in fulfilling his campaign pledge to cut the size and influence of the federal bureaucracy. But it did appear that the regulatory zeal of the previous two decades had come to a halt. As Murray Weidenbaum, then chairman of the president's Council of Economic Advisers, wrote in the March/April 1982 issue of *Regulation* magazine, "Not a single major new regulatory law was enacted during [1981], nor was a major new regulatory program promulgated by a federal agency. It was the first year in several decades that the federal dog did not bark."

3

Approaches to Regulation

Regulation can take any number of approaches — from requiring producers to provide certain kinds of information about their products or services to imposing strict price, market entry and rate-of-return rules to setting performance standards that industry products and activities must meet.

The regulatory technique chosen depends on a variety of factors. Congress may have stipulated the regulatory method to be used. If the hazard is not too threatening, the regulation may leave decisions about compliance to the industry. If the hazard to be averted is potentially very serious, a rule may tell the industry exactly what it must do to achieve the desired goal. In extreme situations, a government might prohibit continuation of an activity it deems to be hazardous or ban production or sale of harmful products.

As the number of regulations — and the costs of complying with them — has increased, so have the demands that government select the regulation that is the most cost-effective. One approach to assessing cost-effectiveness is to weigh the benefits to be gained from implementing a particular rule against its costs. Such cost-benefit analysis can be used both to compare the relative merits of various regulatory methods and to assess a rule's indirect impact or "ripple" effect throughout the economy.

Advocates of cost-benefit analysis also say that the method is a useful tool for deciding the optimum level of regulation. In general, initial regulatory efforts tend to generate more benefits than costs. But at some point, the resources required to obtain additional benefits become disproportionately high, and eventually the additional benefits may even be less than the costs. For example, between 1970 and 1978, the pulp and paper industry spent $3 billion to comply with federal clean water standards and achieved a 95 percent reduction in pollution. But to achieve the Environmental Protection Agency's proposed goal of 98 percent reduction by 1984, the industry would have to spend $4.8 billion more — a 160 percent increase in costs to achieve a 3 percent improvement in water quality.

There are many who distrust the cost-benefit approach, contending that many of the benefits of regulation are intangible and thus not easily quantified. What price should be placed on a person's life, they ask. Nonetheless, Congress in recent years has more and more frequently directed that regulatory agencies subject their proposed rules to cost-benefit analysis. And in one of his first actions upon taking office, President Ronald Reagan required executive branch regulatory agencies to apply cost-benefit analysis to all rulemaking and adopt the least costly alternative.

The following pages discuss the major techniques of regulation and the debate over the cost-benefit analysis method of reviewing existing regulations and deciding whether to promulgate new ones.

TOOLS AND TECHNIQUES

Once Congress has determined which risks are economically or socially unacceptable, it can call for one or a combination of several different kinds of regulations. These include dissemination of information, such as health warnings on cigarette labels; imposition of mandatory standards coupled with penalties for non-compliance; and imposition of penalties and fines to deter the creation of unsafe conditions and the manufacture of unsafe products. Economic regulation frequently involves setting rates and controlling who may provide the service.

Regulatory agencies not only *control* the activities of individuals, groups and industries; they also *promote* the well-being of those they regulate through grants, subsidies, controls on competition and licensing. Non-enforcement of established rules or laws also can be used to regulate or promote certain activities.

Information Disclosure

One of the most common forms of government regulation mandates disclosure of consumer information that companies might not provide voluntarily. The kinds of disclosure required depend on the complexity of the goods or services being offered; the difficulty of making informed purchasing decisions without the information; and the magnitude of the potential harm that can befall a consumer who makes the wrong decision.

The government may require information disclosure in cases where consumers cannot readily evaluate the quality or content of a product or service. Government labeling requirements and grading standards are types of this kind of information regulation. For example, Department of Agriculture grading standards for meats and dairy products assure consumers that the products have met minimum government standards. The Food and Drug Administration (FDA) requires that ingredients and nutritional values be listed on a wide variety of foods. Such information is not only useful to the general public but also to people who are allergic to certain kinds of food.

Occasionally the federal government determines that a product is so hazardous to public health that it bans the product altogether. An example is Tris, a flame-retardant used in children's sleepwear. In 1977 the Consumer Product Safety Commission (CPSC) banned continued use of the product because of its carcinogenic properties.

Less drastic than an outright ban is a label warning consumers that the product may be hazardous to them. The cigarette warning label is perhaps the best known example. Congress historically has been unenthusiastic about forcing new labeling requirements on business, unless labels are seen by the affected industry as the lesser of two evils. For instance, when it mandated the first cigarette health warnings in 1965, Congress canceled much stiffer anti-smoking action by the Federal Trade Commission (FTC).

Industries targeted for new labeling requirements generally argue that they cannot afford to comply. They insist their trade secrets must remain secret. They also argue — and Congress usually agrees — that they should decide what information consumers need and how best to provide that information. For example, one of the reasons doctors, pharmacists and drug manufacturers opposed a proposed Food and Drug Administration regulation to require information inserts in prescription drugs was that the information might only confuse purchasers and that the doctors themselves were the best source of information. The rule was eventually abandoned.

The federal government also has required disclosure of information in situations where the complexity of the goods or service offered militates against the consumer being able to judge if he is being treated fairly. The Truth in Lending Act of 1968, for example, required lenders to disclose key information about credit transactions so that consumers might shop for the best deal and know if the lenders were taking advantage of them. Legislation passed in 1974 and amended in 1975 required bankers and mortgage lenders to provide home buyers with advance information on settlement charges.

Licensing

Mandatory licensure, the most extreme type of information regulation, requires a person or company to secure a license to operate. Failure to obtain the license may result in civil or criminal penalties. Licenses are usually required in situations where consumers on their own are unable to judge the qualifications of the persons offering the service. States, for example, require doctors and lawyers to be licensed and make the license conditional on passage of competency tests. Many other occupations — ranging from beauty salon operators to plumbers to taxi drivers — are also licensed.

A government may also require a license to perform certain activities such as the generation of nuclear power, which represents a great potential danger to the public. In that case, the federal government determined that it was

not enough simply to require that nuclear generators be safe. Instead nuclear power plants may operate only after receiving a license that certifies they have met certain technical and safety standards.

While it is generally agreed that licensing should be mandatory for certain operations and professions — nuclear power plants and doctors among them — it also has been argued that excessive licensing has adverse economic effects and reduces consumer choice unnecessarily.

"If consumers are unable to evaluate bundles of diagnosis and service, then arguably the government should step in and set minimum standards to ensure the competence and integrity of those who offer such bundles...," said then Federal Trade Commission Chairman Michael Pertschuk in February 1979. "But licensing is also a cause of misdiagnosis and over-prescription to the extent that it becomes a vehicle for a profession's legitimizing its monopoly on discovering and remedying needs, and enforcing its mystique by limiting access to special knowledge. Generally, it is the members of a particular occupation — not the public — that seek licensing....

"Study after study has shown that licensing results in higher direct costs to consumers and that indirect costs, in the form of foregone innovation and experimentation, are higher still.... [L]icensing boards rarely monitor quality. Most professionals, once licensed, are licensed for life. One needs periodic reexamination in most states to drive a car or pilot an airplane, but not to continue practicing as a doctor or lawyer."

As an alternative to licensing in those cases that do not present an overwhelming danger to the public, Pertschuk and others have recommended a certification process that would provide consumers with information about the seller's competence. Customers would be free to seek out those who were certified, but unlike mandatory licensing there would be no requirement that all practitioners be certified.

As the Senate Committee on Governmental Affairs pointed out in the sixth volume of its study on federal regulation (December 1978), there are many variations on licensing. If, for example, a license is considered essential, its conditions might not necessarily have to specify such factors as equipment design or personnel training. Rather, a license could be granted upon demonstration of the desired level of performance.

Registration is still another type of information regulation that is appropriate not so much to provide information about the qualifications of the provider as to prevent fraud and theft. Individuals or firms are required to list themselves in an official register if they intend to undertake a certain activity. The government cannot deny them the right to pursue that activity, but failure to register can result in civil or criminal sanctions. Stores that sell firearms, for example, are required to register themselves as well as each firearm sold.

Standards

In situations where full information cannot be supplied to consumers briefly or easily or where the severity of the risk involved is great and the potential harm irreversible, the government may impose compliance standards. Such standards mandate that the manufacturing process, the product itself or the service offered meet a minimum level of achievement. Environmental pollution, safety and health, product quality, employment practices and other business behavior are regulated by mandatory standards.

There are two basic types of standards. Performance

Product Liability Lawsuits

The growth of federal regulation to protect consumers from unsafe products has been accompanied by a substantial increase in the growth and success of product liability lawsuits. That, in turn, has created demands that Congress put limits on liability for damages caused by defective products.

Some experts on regulatory systems consider product liability lawsuits an alternative to government regulation of product safety. The threat of such lawsuits may serve as an incentive to companies to market safe products. And decisions in favor of injured consumers can help compensate for the damages incurred.

Limits of Lawsuits

But private lawsuits, even when they are class-action suits potentially compensating hundreds of consumers, have considerable limitations as a regulatory tool. And in some cases, companies are being held liable even when their products are not hazardous in and of themselves.

A successful liability suit depends on the worth of the company or individual being sued. A bankrupt firm may not be able to pay the full compensation awarded by the court. In some cases, as in the nuclear power industry, there are legal limits to the amount of compensation that can be paid.

Individuals injured by unsafe products may not file suit, even against an especially hazardous product, if the cost of the action is likely to be greater than the anticipated award. Moreover, class-action suits, in which several consumers similarly injured share the legal expenses involved in the suit, have been limited in federal courts; such suits may not be brought unless each party alleges damages above $10,000.

Determining that the product in question caused the damage may also be difficult to prove. It is generally agreed that cigarette smoking can cause cancer, but a lung cancer patient probably would be unable to prove that cigarettes were the only cancer-causing agent he had ever been exposed to.

Furthermore, consumers themselves — through negligence or improper use — may be partially responsible for the damage caused by the product but still collect damages. "A speeding motorist may recover full damages from an automobile manufacturer for injuries that he himself could have avoided by reasonable care. A plaintiff who is burned by throwing perfume upon a lighted candle can recover from the manufacturer or retailer of the perfume because they did not warn that perfume was flammable," wrote Richard Epstein, law professor at the University of Chicago, in the September/October 1977 issue of *Regulation*.

As political scientist Alan Stone summarized in his book *Regulation and Its Alternatives*, the "utility [of private litigation] is limited to traditional situations involving simple causation, harm done to one or a few persons or firms, instances in which litigation and investigation costs are low, and situations where there is a virtual congruence between the legal result in which one side loses while the other side wins and a sound economic result."

Limits on Liability

Questions of regulatory effectiveness aside, the number of successful product liability suits has increased, and manufacturers have turned to Congress for relief.

Business representatives argue that they are being economically hurt by high liability insurance premiums, demands for large cash awards, legal costs, differing state liability laws and the uncertainty of whether a product considered safe may later be deemed otherwise.

Congress in 1981 passed legislation (HR 2120 — PL 97-45) to ease the problems of obtaining insurance. The measure generally pre-empted state statutes that restricted the formation of business "risk retention groups" for self-insurance or "purchasing groups" to buy product liability insurance jointly at favorable rates.

Business associations and consumer groups had pushed actively for the legislation for several years. Companies feared they could go bankrupt if they were subjected to large court judgments and did not have insurance. Consumers feared they would not be able to collect if businesses were not covered.

But business and consumers were not in agreement on a measure being considered in 1982 by the Senate Commerce Consumer Subcommittee. That bill would limit the liability of companies for defective products by setting time limits within which damage suits must be brought.

Several business groups and trade associations supported the measure. "[P]roduct liability problems are being exacerbated by inconsistent state legislation and totally unpredictable case law decisions. This has created irrational and unnecessary impacts on legal and production costs which are passed on to people who buy products," said Victor Schwartz, spokesman for the Product Liability Alliance. The alliance represented more than 200 businesses and associations, including the National Association of Manufacturers, Business Roundtable, U.S. Chamber of Commerce and the National Association of Wholesaler-Distributors.

But consumer groups argued that the bill would limit unfairly the right of people to sue for damages when they are injured. Allied against the bill were the Consumer Federation of America, Congress Watch and the Association of Trial Lawyers of America.

standards require that certain minimum goals be met without specifying the means the industry must use to comply. Specification standards spell out exactly what the company must do to conform to the regulation. Such details can extend to equipment design and manufacturing processes. A performance standard would require a company to reduce to a minimum level the amount of a hazardous material its workers are exposed to; a specification standard would tell that company exactly what equipment it must use to reach that minimum level.

Federal regulators may modify either of these kinds of standards in a variety of ways. An agency, for example, might couple a minimum standard requirement with licensing, granting licenses only to those who met the minimum requirements. Or an agency might allow exemptions under certain circumstances. In recent years, the Environmental Protection Agency (EPA) has experimented with several variations on the traditional standards. One of these, for example, would allow a company to exceed its pollution levels at one factory so long as it reduced pollution levels commensurately at its other plants. *(EPA offsets, p. 116)*

Those being regulated generally prefer imposition of performance, rather than specification, standards. Performance standards allow companies to find the most cost-effective way of complying with the standard and encourage technical innovation. Standards that stipulate what technology must be used, on the other hand, tend to discourage innovation.

"In some cases, it can be legitimately argued that specific standards are easier to observe (and therefore easier to enforce) than performance goals," noted the Committee for Economic Development in a July 1979 report. "For example, it is cheaper to inspect a plant to see if it has a specific smokestack than to monitor the plant's air emissions continuously. However, economists have argued that the same results could often be achieved at less cost through greater reliance on economic incentives, by minimum performance standards and by relying on self-certification of compliance, with appropriate penalties for inaccurate certification."

Either kind of standard, however, is only as effective as its enforcement. If the penalty for failure to comply with the standard is significantly less than the costs of compliance, or if enforcement efforts are lax, companies may choose to ignore the standards. Similarly, if there is no penalty for failing to disclose required information companies are unlikely to comply, especially in cases where the cost of providing the information is high or time-consuming.

Taxes and Recalls

Penalties for non-compliance may be considered regulatory tools because they induce the regulated person or company to comply with the rule. Similarly taxes and recalls may be considered "negative incentives" to compliance.

Since the inception of the nation, Congress has used its taxing power as a tool of regulation as well as a source of revenue. The protective tariff placed on imported goods in competition with domestic products is an early example of a regulatory tax.

Congress at the turn of the century imposed a 10-cents-a-pound tax on oleo colored yellow to resemble butter, but only a ¼-cent-a-pound tax on uncolored oleo. The tax clearly was intended to remove the competition to butter by making it too expensive to manufacture colored oleo. The Bituminous Coal Act of 1937 imposed a stiff tax on sales of coal in interstate commerce but exempted those producers who agreed to abide by industry price and competition regulations.

As part of its 1978 energy policy package, Congress imposed a tax on cars that used fuel inefficiently to discourage manufacture and purchase. Starting with 1980 models, new cars getting less than 15 miles per gallon of gasoline would be taxed $200. The tax and mileage standards increase every year so that by 1986, cars getting less than 12.5 miles per gallon would be taxed $3,850, and all cars getting less than 22.5 miles per gallon would pay some tax.

Murray Weidenbaum of the Center for the Study of American Business suggested that taxation could provide automatic incentives for prevention, avoidance and conservation. For example, Weidenbaum wrote, "Rather than promulgating detailed regulations governing allowable discharges into the nation's waterways, the government could levy substantial taxes on those discharges. Such sumptuary taxation could be 'progressive' to the extent that the tax rates would rise faster than the amount of pollution emitted by an individual polluter. Thus, there would be an incentive for firms to concentrate on removing or at least reducing the more serious instances of pollution."

Congress has also authorized regulatory agencies to initiate recall campaigns for cars and other consumer products that have some major defect that could harm their users. Under most recall orders, the manufacturer is required to fix the faulty part or replace the product entirely.

According to *Consumer Reports*, the Consumer Product Safety Commission between 1973 and 1980 recalled more than 120 million products in more than 2,600 actions, averaging about eight recalls a week in recent years. Between 1966 when auto recalls were initiated and 1980, more than 86 million cars, trucks, motorcycles and other vehicles were recalled in more than 300 campaigns.

The effectiveness of recalls, however, depends not so much on their numbers and frequency as on how many of the products actually are corrected or removed from the market. And the record is mixed on that score. According to a 1978 CPSC study, in 15 recalls of 265,000 television sets, 75 percent were inspected and repaired. In contrast, in 36 recalls of nearly two-and-one-half million hair dryers, electric frying pans and other small household appliances, only 12 percent were repaired or replaced.

The low rate cannot be blamed solely on the manufacturers involved. According to an October 1980 CPSC study, "Hazardous products have not received the kind of media attention that the severity of the hazard would appear to require." There are also problems involved in contacting each consumer individually, particularly since most relatively inexpensive purchases go unrecorded with the manufacturer. As the January 1981 *Consumer Reports* observed, "[r]ecall campaigns are beset with troubles — non-existent sales records, apathetic owners, truculent corporate managers, quarrelsome government bureaucrats."

Economic Incentives

The government also may induce desired behavior by individuals and firms through positive economic incentives such as direct and indirect subsidies, tax concessions, insurance and loan guarantees. Such incentives may be promotional and are regulatory only in the sense that they attempt to change what otherwise would happen if there was no interference.

The range of federal subsidy programs is vast, encompassing price supports for agricultural products (notably grains and dairy products), housing assistance for low-income families, federal insured loans at low-interest rates for college students, and medical care to the needy and elderly. Direct subsidies can take the form of cash, credit or benefits-in-kind, such as food stamps.

Direct subsidies often are offered to induce companies to provide service that otherwise would not return a profit. Subsidies to the U.S. Postal Service pay a portion of the costs of delivering mail, for example. Subsidies are granted to airlines to continue service to small communities.

There also are numerous indirect or "invisible" government subsidies, including land grants to universities and market entry restrictions, for example. Since the federal government first gave land to the railroads, the transportation sector especially has benefited from indirect subsidies. User fees do not cover the full costs of building and maintaining the federal interstate highway system. Until 1980, barges did not pay fees for use of the nation's waterways that were made navigable and maintained by the federal government. Air traffic control in part is an invisible subsidy, because landing fees and fuel taxes paid by the airlines do not cover the full federal and local costs of providing the system.

Tax preferences — which can be defined as exempting a special category from paying a certain tax — and tax credits are also indirect forms of subsidy that can induce firms to take one action rather than another. Investment tax credits might encourage a firm to invest a greater proportion of its profits in new plants or facilities that could increase employment and productivity. Tax credits defraying the costs of home insulation can conserve scarce fuels.

Another form of subsidy is the federal loan guarantee in which the government guarantees to pay off lenders if the borrower defaults on his loan. A recent example of this occurred in 1979 when Congress authorized $1.5 billion in loan guarantees to keep Chrysler Corp. from going bankrupt.

Other Options

Desired economic and social goals may be achieved through policy techniques other than direct federal intervention. More widespread provision of information to consumers has been advocated to take greater advantage of the workings of market forces and to preserve private discretion in decision making. Insurance programs — in effect a form of economic incentive — have been proposed as a means by which risk can be spread and damages compensated for, at relatively low costs.

Increased use of the private legal system also has been suggested as an alternative to direct government involvement. But limitations inherent in the legal system make it unreliable as a regulator. *(Product liability, box, p. 23)*

A controversial regulatory technique receiving increased attention in recent years in the environmental protection area is the establishment of so-called "property rights" for pollution, in effect creating a "market for pollution" to limit overuse of scarce and exhaustible natural resources such as air and water. Under this regulatory approach, the government would detemine the allowable level of each pollutant and then would auction off to firms the rights to use the environment to pollute. These rights would be exchangeable, and, in theory, with rights for certain areas limited, the law of supply and demand would work to determine the costs of these rights to pollute and ultimately lower emission levels.

Establishing a market for pollution would provide incentives for firms to reduce pollutants and spur innovation to develop new technologies for its abatement. Firms with high abatement costs would be willing to pay more for pollution rights, whereas those with lower abatement costs would be able to sell off their extra rights. Such a market system for pollution, proponents say, would be able to handle and respond to changing conditions, which would take advantage of firms' built-in incentives to reduce costs and maximize profits.

The Environmental Protection Agency began experimenting with a policy similar to a property rights system in late 1979. Under some circumstances, firms were allowed to "bank" the difference between their (lower) actual emissions and the permissable level as determined by the agency, with banked rights usable at a later date. Some critics of Federal Communications Commission regulation have asserted that establishment of a property rights system for radio and television spectra could have avoided some of the problems and efficiency distortions caused by current licensing procedures.

WEIGHING COSTS AGAINST BENEFITS

While few persons advocate a return to laissez-faire capitalism in which government had little or no role in regulating corporate behavior, many by 1982 were arguing for a large-scale cutback in complex and sometimes conflicting federal rules affecting health, the environment and other areas. Business people said that their desire to ease government restraints was not selfish. The entire nation would benefit from the higher productivity and lower prices that a weeding out of regulations would bring, they said.

That some federal regulations were unnecessary and excessive was hardly disputed. "Virtually every study of regulatory experience indicates both needless expense and ineffective operations," said Weidenbaum, an acknowledged expert on federal regulation issues. The question then was how to determine whether the tangible and intangible benefits derived from the rule outweigh the direct and hidden costs of implementing it. Many experts advocated cost-benefit analysis.

"For each new rule they propose, the regulatory agencies should be required to demonstrate at least a reasonable relationship between the costs imposed and the benefits produced — and to demonstrate they have chosen the most efficient (least costly) method of achieving those benefits," Weidenbaum wrote in the November/December 1980 issue of *Regulation*, a magazine published by the American Enterprise Institute, a Washington, D.C.-based research center. Weidenbaum, a longtime advocate of requiring such an analysis, was chairman of Reagan's Council of Economic Advisers until July 1982 when he resigned to return to the Center for the Study of American Business at Washington University in St. Louis.

"Regulators, even those hostile to cost-benefit analy-

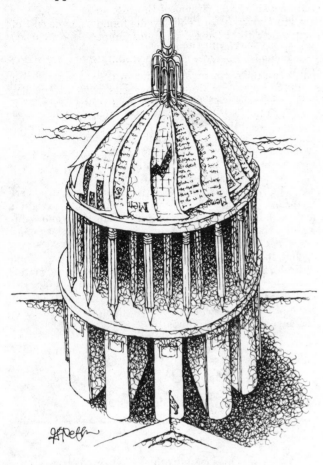

sis, inevitably use the technique, although frequently in a crude form," wrote Alan Stone in *Regulation and Its Alternatives.* "Not even the most zealous EPA administrator wants to reduce industrial emissions to zero, for that would mean the elimination of production as well. Nor would the most fanatic OSHA [Occupational Safety and Health Administration] regulator want to eliminate all risk in manufacturing plants, which would also bring activity to a standstill. In practice, regulators must consider costs and benefits. Why not do it in a precise, consciously conceived manner?"

Development of Cost-Benefit Analysis

Efforts to apply cost-benefit analyses to regulatory programs and rules are not new. They go at least as far back as 1902, when the Rivers and Harbors Act demanded that the costs of a water project be less than the benefits it would confer. More recently, the Defense Department in the 1960s instituted the "planning, programming, budgeting system" that applied cost-benefit analysis to national defense programs.

By the 1970s, criticism was mounting that government programs, in the words of Brookings Institution economist Lester B. Lave, had given "short shrift to economic efficiency, focusing instead on equity and due process." As a consequence, President Ford in 1974 directed agencies to prepare "inflation impact statements" to accompany their rules. The inflation impact statement program ran through 1976 and applied to all executive branch agencies. At the end of 1976, the program was extended and its title

changed to the economic impact statement (EIS) program.

Concern that government regulation was contributing significantly to rising inflation rates provided the principal impetus for the EIS project. But that was not the only motive for establishing the program. James C. Miller III, a former assistant director of the Council on Wage and Price Stability and chairman of the Federal Trade Commission in the Reagan administration, noted that: "[T]he officials responsible for the program were after more than a simple tracing through of the cost impact of proposed regulations and legislative recommendations. They wanted to use the requirement to improve agency decision making, and this meant getting the agencies to address the costs and benefits of their proposals. What program officials wished to avoid was the tendency for agencies to serve special constituent interests, often at greater cost to the general public; to view the objects of their regulations as natural enemies, to be dealt with punitively; to forge ahead with regulatory and legislative proposals without knowing enough about the problem being addressed or the effects of the proposed solution; and to resist suggestions for alternative, more efficient ways of dealing with economic problems."

The EIS program dealt only with major regulations that, in preliminary estimates, would have an impact on the economy of $100 million or more during the first year of operation. Each agency was responsible for making this determination and for preparing its economic impact statements, which were then forwarded to the Office of Management and Budget (OMB) and Council on Wage and Price Stability; subsequently, an agency had to certify in the *Federal Register* that the inflationary impact of the proposed rule had been considered and that an EIS had been prepared.

The program was not without its shortcomings. First, as Miller pointed out, it extended only to the executive branch regulatory agencies, not to the independent commissions such as the Federal Trade Commission and the Consumer Product Safety Commission. Second, the quality of the statements varied considerably. Although the cost estimates were reasonably accurate, the assessment of benefits was weak, as was the study of alternatives. On the other hand, the agencies themselves generally found the program useful in formulating their regulations and considered that the paperwork and time involved were not excessive.

President Carter gave strong support to the economic impact program. In an April 15, 1977, message on inflation he asked that full consideration be given to "the economic cost of major government regulations, through a more effective analysis of their economic impact." His Executive Order 12044, issued March 23, 1978, set criteria for identifying significant regulations requiring regulatory economic impact analyses.

In signing the order, President Carter said, "I will personally be involved in assuring that the executive order is carried out. And under me, the Office of Management and Budget will be working very closely with the heads of agencies and departments to insure that the spirit and the letter of the executive order is honored."

Carter also created a Regulatory Analysis Review Group (RARG), chaired by a member of the Council of Economic Advisers, to improve government cost-benefit analysis. During the first 18 months of its existence, however, the group had studied only eight regulations. Reagan disbanded the group when he came into office in 1981.

Former RARG Chairman George Eads offered an assessment of cost-benefit analysis during the Carter administration in the May/June 1981 issue of *Regulation*. Initially, Eads wrote, regulators prepared analyses designed to support options they had already chosen and to "prove their proposals." Gradually, they started to use analyses to help identify the likely impact of a range of possible regulatory actions. "Even so, by the end of the Carter administration, very few agencies were good at regulatory analysis and some did not yet understand what it meant," he said. "There is little reason to think this situation has improved since then, and some reason to think it has worsened: because of budget cuts and hiring freeze, a number of the best analysts have returned to the private sector."

The Carter administration "always took pains to stress that its requirements for regulatory analysis should not be interpreted as subjecting rules to a [strict] cost-benefit test," said Eads. "Hard and fast" requirements that agencies demonstrate that benefits would outweigh costs "are straitjackets which could paralyze the agencies."

In contrast, Reagan issued an executive order in February 1981 that *required* a cost-benefit analysis from agencies and gave OMB broad authority to review compliance. The order required that any proposed "major rule" be accompanied by a "regulatory impact analysis" that would assess "potential benefits," "potential costs" and "potential net benefits." Major rules were defined as those likely to have an annual effect on the economy of $100 million or more, lead to a major increase in costs or prices, or have "significant adverse effects on competition, employment, investment, productivity, innovation or on the ability of United States-based enterprises to compete with foreign-based enterprises in domestic or export markets." By mid-1982, it was still too early to tell exactly what impact the cost-benefit analysis requirement was having. (*Executive order text, p. 173*)

Assessing the Costs

Just what are the costs of regulation? According to the Center for the Study of American Business, the budgets of 57 federal regulatory agencies rose from $.9 billion in 1970 to $6.6 billion in 1981. That figure does not include the indirect economic costs to business of complying with regulations. In his book, *The Future of Business Regulation*, Weidenbaum estimated those costs to be $102.7 billion in 1979.

Among examples of reported regulatory costs:

• The Small Business Administration reported in December 1979 that paperwork requirements by regulatory agencies cost small businesses an average of $1,270 a year apiece.
• Data Resources Inc. estimated that the cost of meeting environmental regulations during 1979 was $12.3 billion, up from $9.6 billion in 1978.
• Louis Lasagna, a professor at the University of Rochester Medical Center, reported in the November/December 1979 *Regulation* that pre-market testing of new drugs required by the Food and Drug Administration cost up to $50 million.
• In January 1978, Dow Chemical Co. released a study showing that compliance with federal regulations cost the company $186 million, a 27 percent increase over 1975. The

study classified $69 million of the cost as "excessive."
• The University of Pennsylvania found that the cost of complying with 12 federal programs jumped from $350,000 in 1972 to $3.2 million in 1977.
• In March 1979, R. J. Reynolds Industries Inc. reported that it cost the company $29 million in 1977 to comply with regulations of nearly 40 federal agencies as well as regulations of various foreign, state and local regulatory bodies.
• Eli Lilly & Co., the pharmaceutical concern, reported that 50 cents of the cost of an average prescription went for compliance with federal regulations.
• According to estimates by Richard Posner of the University of Chicago, federal regulation of milk prices under the Agricultural Act of 1937 cost consumers an estimated 10 percent of their milk bills, or nearly $1 billion, in 1977.

Writing in the Summer 1980 issue of *Policy Analysis*, University of Virginia economist Roland McKean noted the high costs of enforcing environmental and safety regulations. He divided the related costs into three categories: avoidance costs on the part of the regulated parties (lobbying against a rule, concealing non-compliance, going to court to protest a rule); costs borne or imposed by the regulatory agency (inspections, recordkeeping, prosecuting violators); and costs incurred in the form of a reduction in benefits due to imperfect or incomplete enforcement.

McKean believed the third category was the most costly. He pointed to a number of factors that made a regulation difficult or expensive to enforce. There might be problems in identifying or measuring the behavior to be regulated; regulations might be ambiguous; there might be no consensus regarding the goals of regulation; and more than one agency might be involved, he said.

Weidenbaum Study

One of the most widely cited analyses of the costs of regulation was a study prepared by Weidenbaum for Congress' Joint Economic Subcommittee on Growth and Stabilization. The study, released April 8, 1978, was generally critical of the existing regulatory system. Among the areas Weidenbaum cited as being adversely affected by regulation were:

• Automobiles — Compulsory catalytic converters to reduce air pollution and mandatory seat belts added $666 to the price tag of a 1978 model. The converters increased national fuel consumption by approximately $3 billion a year.
• Housing — Inspection fees, building permits, environmental impact statements and delays in getting approval from myriad agencies hiked the cost of an average house by $2,000.
• Consumers — Manufacturers passed along the costs of complying with government regulations to consumers in the form of higher prices.
• Workers — The high costs of complying with environmental, safety and other regulations forced some businesses to close facilities and lay off workers.
• Investors — Weidenbaum estimated that $10 billion in new private capital spending was devoted annually to regulatory compliance rather than to profit-making programs.

Weidenbaum argued that one hidden cost of government regulation was its adverse effect on innovation. "The longer it takes for a new product to be approved by a government agency — or the more costly the approval process — the less likely that the new product will be

Improving Job Health and Safety ...

Behind all the arguments on legislation to preserve the environment or protect workers and consumers lies the basic question of cost. To some it seems crass to balance a dollar figure against the health or life of a human being. However, as Philip Handler, president of the National Academy of Sciences, told a scientific forum in 1973: "There is no escape from the need, somehow, to equate dollars and lives, to agree to the dollar value of an average human life in the population at risk. . . ." In a 1975 extension of his remarks, Handler said: "[W]hen the government contemplates regulatory activity to diminish the risk associated with some technology . . . an attempt is required to state both the cost and the benefits in quantitative form."

Defining the Risk

Since Congress first enacted the Occupational Safety and Health Act, the business community has complained that the Occupational Safety and Health Administration (OSHA) sets stringent health and safety standards without balancing the benefits to workers against the costs to employers. OSHA is authorized to limit workers' exposures to hazardous substances. Its decisions are based on the best available evidence about the health risks generated by the hazards. That evidence, especially when the diseases take a generation to appear, sometimes is skimpy.

When not enough is known about a substance in the workplace, OSHA has been forced to choose between holding back on regulation until more is learned or taking the maximum precautions. The agency most often has chosen the latter course, and critics have charged that OSHA has paid only minimal attention to how much it will cost the affected industries. "[T]he basic problem with the implementation of the act is that there is no fundamental agreement on the practical methods of balancing considerations of greater safety and health against considerations of cost," said Robert Stewart Smith of the New York State School of Industrial and Labor Relations at Cornell University.

Smith argued that "the government . . . should not force more safety and health on society than workers would choose for themselves if they had to pay the costs . . . . In their private lives . . . they smoke cigarettes, drive when they could walk, ski when they could read a book, and use power mowers when safer hand mowers would do."

The Supreme Court addressed the risk issue in July 1980 when it ruled in two cases that OSHA's benzene exposure standard was invalid because the rule was unsupported by sufficient evidence that it was necessary to protect the health of workers. A "safe" workplace need not be completely "risk free," the court declared (*Industrial Union Department, AFL-CIO v. American Petroleum Institute,* and *Marshall v. American Petroleum Institute*). By a 5-4 vote, the court found that OSHA had not provided substantial evidence to show either that workers exposed to benzene levels higher than OSHA proposed *would* contract cancer or that workers exposed only to the proposed level *would not* contract cancer.

Cotton Dust and Cost-Benefit

In 1981, the Reagan administration sought to reduce the federal presence in the field of occupational health and safety. Thorne G. Auchter took over as head of OSHA with the conviction that his agency had over-regulated industry. He also wanted to cut down on the number of OSHA inspections. Auchter, however, was not brought in specifically to

created," he wrote. "In any event, innovation will be delayed."

As illustration, he cited a 1973 study by Sam Peltzman of the University of Chicago of the 1962 amendments to the Food and Drug Act, which required manufacturers to prove that new drugs were effective as well as safe. Peltzman estimated that the amendments had delayed the introduction of effective drugs by about four years and had also led to higher prices for pharmaceutical products. Some highly effective but marginally profitable drugs were never marketed because the required testing would have made them prohibitively expensive, he said.

To back his claim that regulation impeded economic growth by claiming a rising share of new capital formation, Weidenbaum noted a study by Edward Denison of the Brookings Institution that appeared in the January 1978 *Survey of Current Business*. According to Denison, by 1975 output per unit of input in the non-residential business sector of the economy was 1.4 percent smaller than it would have been if business had operated under the regulatory conditions of 1967. Of that amount, 1 percent was due to compliance with pollution abatement regulations and 0.4 percent to employee safety and health programs.

Weidenbaum also observed that costs of complying with federal regulations fell disproportionately on small businesses. "Most of this impact is unintentional in that the regulations typically do not distinguish among companies of different sizes," he wrote. "But in practice, forcing a very small firm to fill out the same specialized forms as a large company with highly trained technical staffs at its disposal places a significantly greater burden on that smaller enterprise." Congress attempted to correct this problem in 1980 with passage of both the Regulatory Flexibility Act and the Paperwork Reduction Act. *(Details, p. 75)*

...Balancing Risks Against Costs

dismantle OSHA. Even OSHA's most vociferous critics generally conceded that in its 11 years of existence, the agency had increased the awareness of the country regarding occupational safety and health matters.

It was clear by the early spring of 1981 that President Reagan's desired emphasis upon cost-benefit analysis, expressed in Executive Order 12291, also had become Auchter's emphasis. The executive order, issued in February 1981, required federal agencies to assess the costs and benefits of major regulations.

In March 1981, OSHA announced that it would reconsider its controversial cotton-dust regulations with a cost-benefit approach in mind. OSHA said it would "use its re-examination of this particular standard to explore the usefulness of cost-benefit analysis in setting worker health regulations generally." It was "time to re-examine the traditional resistance to cost-benefit analysis," Auchter said. The Reagan administration then asked the Supreme Court to delay its ruling in two cotton-dust cases, which had been argued Jan. 21, while it reassessed the economic impact of the OSHA standards. The justices refused the request.

On June 17, 1981, the court rejected arguments by the textile industry that OSHA be required to demonstrate that benefits to workers outweigh costs to industry before promulgating a cotton-dust standard to protect textile workers against brown lung disease (byssinosis). By a 5-3 vote in the cases of *American Textile Manufacturers Institute v. Donovan* and *National Cotton Council v. Donovan,* the court upheld the stringent standards.

Writing for the majority, Justice William J. Brennan Jr. declared that economic and technical feasibility constitute the only limits on OSHA's power to adopt worker, health and safety standards. And in this case, OSHA found the cotton-dust standard feasible on both counts.

"Congress itself defined the basic relationship between costs and benefits, by placing the 'benefit' of worker health above all other considerations save those making attainment of this 'benefit' unachievable," Brennan wrote. He noted Congress had specifically required the use of cost-benefit analysis in certain other laws but did not include such language in the 1970 OSHA law.

The court did not rule out cost-benefit analysis as part of health standards but did say it was not specifically required by law. Only Congress could amend the law to require OSHA to conduct cost-benefit analyses of its health standards.

The court's cotton dust ruling was considered one of the most significant in the recent history of regulatory law. *Business Week* said on July 6, 1981: "The high court's review of OSHA's legislative history could spell trouble for the [Reagan] Administration's reliance on cost-benefit tests in other areas as well.... The Supreme Court's cotton-dust decision will almost certainly be used as a precedent by opponents of regulatory cutbacks, and the mere threat of such challenges could head off the use of cost-benefit tests in some areas."

But the decision did not appear to daunt Auchter. Following the decision, he said OSHA would consider four points in preparing regulations: whether a significant health risk existed; whether the proposed standard would protect workers from that risk; whether the standard was economically feasible for the industry affected; and whether the standard was cost-effective, that is, was the least expensive and most effective means to achieve a desired end.

Business Roundtable Study

Another major study of regulatory costs was released March 14, 1979, by the Business Roundtable, a group of the chief executive officers of approximately 190 major companies. The study showed that the regulatory policies of six federal agencies cost 48 major corporations operating in more than 20 industries a total of $2.6 billion in directly measurable effects in 1977. This compared with capital expenditures by the companies of $25.8 billion, research and development costs of $6 billion and net income after taxes of $16.6 billion. The agencies studied were the EPA, Equal Employment Opportunity Commission, OSHA, Department of Energy, FTC and the Labor Department's administration of the Employee Retirement Income Security Act.

The study, managed by the accounting firm of Arthur Andersen & Co., was distinguished from other regulatory cost studies by its specificity. It not only identified direct costs of regulation by general classification, such as operating and administrative costs, but also provided a breakout of costs of specific regulations. For example, 29 percent of the regulatory costs attributed to the EPA were related to water treatment regulations.

The Roundtable stressed that its study did not measure the cost of the regulations of all agencies, costs incurred by many industries or the costs of state regulations. It also omitted secondary costs of regulation, which it said were difficult to quantify. Examples of secondary costs were described as delays in construction of new plants and equipment, the misallocation of resources and the loss of productivity caused by regulation.

Overall, the study indicated that manufacturing companies bore the highest costs of regulation — $2.3 billion. EPA regulations imposed costs of $2 billion, 77 percent of the $2.6 billion total for all six agencies combined. OSHA regulations imposed costs of $184 million, a small portion of the participating companies' total expenditures for worker safety and health in 1977.

Regulation costs showed a wide variation among industries. As an illustration, the cost of complying with OSHA rules averaged $6 a year for each worker in the banking industry, but $220 a year for each worker in the chemical industry.

In addition, certain regulations were found to be especially burdensome, while others imposed relatively small costs. To illustrate the former, two regulations administered by EPA — Control of Air Pollution from New Motor Vehicles, and the National Ambient Air Quality Standard for Particulates — accounted for $900 million of regulatory costs in 1977.

The study also identified several attributes of regulation that resulted in especially high costs. These included continuous monitoring and periodic reporting of compliance activities, specific requirements for application of advanced technology and levels of compliance that were not achievable with available technology.

"Analysis of the costs of federal regulations is important if we hope to balance the impact of regulatory costs against intended benefits," said Frank Carey, head of the Roundtable's Task Force on Government Regulation and chairman of the board of International Business Machines (IBM). "Many regulations are necessary for the well-being of society. In many instances, they help business meet its obligations to society. Yet, the findings of the study show that expenditures for regulations may often be wasteful and non-productive."

Noting that the study did not measure the benefits of regulation or total regulatory costs, the business group urged legislation requiring economic impact analyses, congressional and agency review of regulatory programs on a systematic basis and greater flexibility for companies in meeting regulatory goals.

Quantifying the Benefits

In contrast to those studies that emphasized the costs of regulation, a 1980 analysis prepared for the Senate by the Center for Policy Alternatives at the Massachusetts Institute of Technology claimed that the American people saved billions of dollars each year as a direct result of federal regulation.

The report examined regulatory benefits for six major federal agencies — EPA, OSHA, CPSC, FDA, Food Safety and Quality Service and the National Highway Traffic Safety Administration.

The M.I.T. study found that effective health, safety and environmental regulations substantially reduced occupational death and injury rates, increased productivity of workers and consumers, fostered development of new and better products and processes and lessened abuse of the environment and other natural resources by the public. Releasing the report, Sen. Abraham Ribicoff, D-Conn., said, "At a time of soaring costs and double digit inflation, people are questioning what government can or should do. In that debate, let's remember the important achievements of federal regulation. That's what the M.I.T. report is all about — it's a reminder that regulation does more than cost money. It saves lives, avoids injuries and protects the public against marketplace failures."

The study's major findings included:

● Air pollution control benefits ranged from $5 billion to $58 billion annually — with automobile pollution controls alone worth $2.5 billion to $10 billion.

● Up to 60,000 lost workday accidents and 350 deaths were avoided in 1974 and 1975 because of OSHA rules on workplace safety — reducing the $15 billion society paid yearly for industrial accidents.

● Cleaning up water pollution resulted in a $9 billion gain due to increased recreational use — such as camping, fishing and vacationing.

● Crib safety standards reduced crib-related injuries to infants by 44 percent since 1974.

However, the report cautioned that not all regulatory benefits could be reduced to monetary terms or measured in any satisfactory way. The report stated that "There is no way to put a dollars-and-cents value on the costs of pain and suffering endured throughout a lifetime by a child who is the victim of a sleepwear fire."

Despite the contention that many benefits of regulation involve immeasurable or moral considerations, efforts have been made to quantify the benefits resulting from regulation and the costs that would be incurred without it. The EPA, for example, estimated that the cost of repainting surfaces damaged by polluted air was almost $650 million in 1970. A study for the EPA and the Council on Environmental Quality by Data Resources Inc. of Cambridge, Mass., concluded that environmental controls actually would decrease unemployment slightly (by 0.2 to 0.3 percent annually) and would result in only a tiny increase in the inflation rate (from 0.1 to 0.2 percent a year) over the next eight years. That study, while conceding that pollution controls would bring about job losses among production workers in industries such as steel and paper, concluded that such unemployment would be more than offset by hiring workers to construct, install and service mandated anti-pollution devices and sewers.

A report released in March 1981 by the National Commission on Air Quality estimated that the costs of installing, maintaining and operating pollution equipment were $16.6 billion in 1978. The benefits of air pollution control, including improved public health, reduced cleaning expenses, better vegetation, less damage to materials and higher property values were estimated at $21.4 billion. But the study said that the true benefits in 1978 could have been as low as $4.6 billion or as high as $51.2 billion, and it concluded that "the estimation of certain kinds of environmental benefits is still in need of much additional refinement."

One reason that it is difficult to measure costs and benefits is that they usually fall on different parties, the M.I.T. report noted. The benefits of regulation to one part of society can often exceed its costs to another. For example, air pollution regulation entails costs borne by the factory and, subsequently, the consumer. But depending on the nature of the pollutant, population density and type of surrounding development, the benefits of cleaner air could reach a great number of people. Moreover, it is often difficult to measure cause and effect. It may take years of exposure for a disease caused by a pollutant to emerge, and other factors may have contributed to its development. People tend to underestimate the costs of the consequences of a hazard until they have actually been affected by it, the report noted, and greatly underprotect themselves in low-probability, high-loss situations. For example, workers in hazardous industries make decisions to accept particular wages and face those hazards before they experience harm, rather than after they are injured or diseased and the costs of damage becomes apparent to them.

Costs, as well as benefits, are often difficult to quantify because they are not static. For example, in the area of pollution control, new regulations may give rise to technological developments that, in turn, dramatically reduce the cost of controlling pollution levels. Even without new technology, increased pollution control requirements may introduce economies of scale into the production of pollution abatement equipment.

Moreover, regulation may have unanticipated, but beneficial, side-effects on the economy. An article by Michael G. Royston in the November/December 1980 *Harvard Business Review* cited several instances in which pollution control efforts increased the productivity of regulated industries by reducing energy consumption through heat reuse, by encouraging recycling or by creating marketable byproducts out of materials previously regarded as process wastes.

Assessing the Approach

To many environmentalists and consumer advocates, much of the talk about the inflationary impact of regulation has been viewed as a ploy by business to trim its costs at the expense of human health and safety. Most of the information about the cost of regulation has been generated by business and, therefore, has been greatly exaggerated, they have argued.

For illustration they point to two contradictory studies on cotton dust. At the request of Congress, the Labor Department performed a cost-benefit study and estimated that 83,610 workers or 14 percent of those exposed to cotton dust could get brown lung disease (byssinosis). Under that study, OSHA's proposed brown lung standards were estimated to cost industry about $655 million to implement or about $8,000 per case avoided.

But the textile industry estimated that only 1 percent of the workers exposed to cotton dust were likely to contract brown lung and that implementation of the standards might cost $1.1 billion. By industry's analysis, each case avoided would cost more than $100,000.

Playing by Industry's Rules

A report by the House Commerce Oversight and Investigations Subcommittee accused industries of predicting "large compliance costs and major impacts ... knowing that such projections are likely to induce regulators or the courts to water down or delay ... a proposed regulation."

"We're playing by their rules," said Robert Stulberg, staff attorney for Public Citizen Inc. Health Research Group. "How can you possibly put a dollar figure on the cost of a human life? Why don't they carry out their computations to when a worker falls from a scaffold or dies in a grain shaft explosion? ... To attribute the inflation rate to few and meager health standards is fallacious. Take a look at what the inflation has been in companies' net profits."

Sen. Gary Hart, D-Colo., agreed with Stulberg that business' inflation argument was fallacious because the benefits of regulation to the nation are not part of the

equation. "Assume the cost to society of pollution damage such as respiratory disease is $1,000," he wrote in the January 1979 edition of the *EPA Journal*. "The $4,400 car with pollution control equipment is actually a new commodity which produces more net benefits to society than the lower-priced $4,000 car."

Workplace safety and health standards actually may help curb inflation, wrote John B. Ricker Jr., chairman and president of The Continental Corporation, in the Sept. 20, 1980, *New York Times*. "The soaring cost of health care has been a major contributor to the inflationary spiral .... To the extent that OSHA has helped to prevent accidents, it has thereby served as a check on inflation."

Mark Green, former director of Ralph Nader's Congress Watch, contested the argument of Weidenbaum and others that regulation impeded technological change. "Before the Food and Drug Administration banned spray cans using fluorocarbons, the industry said there was no alternative," Green wrote in the Jan. 21, 1979, *Washington Post*. "The day after the ban went into effect, the country had a new pump spray that didn't use fluorocarbons and that was *cheaper* than aerosol cans. After Washington imposed strict safety standards for car bumpers, auto engineers developed bumpers that are far stronger and lighter — and that save consumers an average $100 in repair costs."

Michael Baram, director of the government regulation program at the Franklin Pierce Law Center, summarized some of the advantages of cost-benefit analysis: "When used objectively, in good faith and with requisite analytical rigor, cost-benefit analysis provides a framework for the rational organization of multiple considerations. Determinations made from properly organized opinions and information can represent a logical process, which in turn promotes agency credibility and acceptance of agency decisions. Furthermore, cost-benefit analysis promotes the use of a consistent and predictable analytical structure for organizing data and opinions on the numerous issues involved in a proposed regulatory action."

However, Baram went on to say that cost-benefit analysis should not be applied to "persistent health, safety and environmental problems. It is a simplistic tool that reduces concern for the individual to a monetized balancing. Worse, it has become a self-serving numbers game obscuring arbitrary and subjective values and assumptions, while impeding real progress toward our espoused health, safety and environmental objectives."

In a March 20, 1981, letter to his Democratic colleagues, Sen. Thomas F. Eagleton, Mo., chairman of a Senate Democratic task force on regulatory reform, said Reagan's executive order requiring cost-benefit analyses could slow the regulatory process dramatically and could insulate administration decision making from public and congressional oversight. "At a minimum, these [cost-benefit] approaches could add needless delay and expense to the administrative process," he said. "Worse still, necessary regulations in such areas as nuclear safety and toxic waste protection could remain unissued merely because the value of avoiding atomic catastrophe or future genetic damage could not be precisely toted up in an accountant's ledger." Eagleton said there was consensus among the seven-member task force that some economic assessment of regulations should be made, but there was deep-seated concern about "mathematically strict cost-benefit analysis proposals that fail to recognize the imprecision inherent in the technique."

Eads, Carter's RARG chairman, also expressed concern about mandatory cost-benefit tests, contending they might "well be a hindrance to obtaining good analysis." Eads suggested it would be more sensible for agencies to identify "whatever costs and benefits they consider likely to flow from the proposed regulations."

Rebutting the Critics

"Critics of cost-benefit analysis tend to forget that it is a neutral policy concept and that it need not always be applied in dollar terms," wrote Weidenbaum in 1980. "Indeed, the costs as well as the benefits may at times properly be measured in terms of human life."

"Values play a role together with cost-benefit analysis not only in arriving at appropriate social decisions but in the process of engaging in cost-benefit analysis itself," agreed Stone. "One must not erroneously reject cost-benefit analysis simply because judgment must be used in such translations, for the cost-benefit technique at least compels us to frame a more precise question than would be the case without it. We can ask: How much additional cost would I be willing to incur to save a certain number of additional lives? Posing a question this way would allow most of us to conclude (albeit based in part on personal values) that the additional cost involved in requiring cars to be built as sturdily as army tanks is too costly relative to the addi-

tional lives that would be saved in automobile collisions."

"Wholesale deregulation of the entire government is not in the cards," said Weidenbaum. "The fact is, most Americans are concerned simultaneously about cleaning the environment and reducing the vast burdens of regulation."

Cost-benefit analysis "should be viewed as a tool for identifying the optimum amount of regulation rather than as a means of debating the pros and cons of regulation in general," he said.

Vice President Bush, chairman of Reagan's Task Force on Regulatory Relief, said, "What the president is attempting to do in this area is find a balance between safety in the workplace and environmental protection and, at the same time, eliminate from our economy unneeded regulations so that we can grow and increase our nation's productive capacity."

The administration's reform efforts "do not constitute a Neanderthal plea to ignore the real problems of pollution, discrimination and so on," said Weidenbaum. "Precisely to the contrary: They are offered in the belief that every task government undertakes should be performed ably and that the existing regulatory process simply is not working well. . . . In view of the magnitude of the resources devoted to regulatory purposes, the public deserves better than it has been getting."

4

Regulators and Rulemaking

Much of the debate on reforming the federal regulatory process centers on two important areas — the people chosen to direct the agencies and the procedures they use to regulate. Most regulatory heads are appointed by the president and confirmed by the Senate. But there are few guidelines for the selection process, and there is widespread belief that many federal regulators are not well-enough qualified for the job.

The basic procedures for writing regulations, setting rates or prosecuting violations of regulations are laid out in the Administrative Procedure Act of 1946. That act guaranteed public access to and due process in regulatory proceedings but added substantially to the time it takes for an agency to make a decision.

Both of these shortcomings have had substantial impacts on the regulatory process. Inept administrators have contributed to the low esteem with which much of the public regards the federal bureaucracy. Delays cost money to the companies involved and to taxpayers. Furthermore, a delay in promulgating a safety or health rule can mean unnecessary injuries, illnesses or even deaths.

Numerous experts, task forces and study commissions have examined the twin problems of quality of administrators and procedural delays and made hundreds of recommendations for improvements. But few of these recommendations have been implemented in any formal way and the debate on how to solve these problems is likely to continue.

THE REGULATORS: HOW THEY GET THERE

Most regulatory agency heads and commissioners are selected in accordance with Article II, section 2, of the Constitution, which states that the president "shall nominate, and by and with the advice and consent of the Senate, shall appoint Ambassadors, other public Ministers and Consuls, Judges of the Supreme Court and all other Officers of the United States...." Dividing the power of appointment between the president and the Senate was one of the checks the framers of the Constitution felt was necessary to ensure that one branch of government did not dominate the others.

The Constitution also permitted Congress to allow the president alone or his Cabinet secretaries to appoint "inferior Officers." Consequently, there are a few bureaus with significant regulatory functions whose heads are appointed by the secretary of the department in which the agency resides. The Food and Drug Administration within the Department of Health and Human Services perhaps is the most important regulatory agency whose head is not named by the president and approved by the Senate.

The Constitution also gives the president the power "to fill up all vacancies that may happen during the recess of the Senate, by granting commissions which shall expire at the end of their next session." Initially there was some question whether this authority referred only to vacancies that occurred during a Senate recess or extended to vacancies that had not yet been filled when the Senate recessed. It gradually became accepted practice that the president could make recess appointments to fill any vacancies no matter when they arose.

The president may remove for any or no reason heads of regulatory agencies that are within the executive branch. But independent regulatory commission members generally may be removed only for cause, such as inefficiency, neglect of duty or misconduct. Furthermore, once the Senate has confirmed a nominee and he has been sworn in, the Senate may not reconsider the nomination. *(President's removal power, box, p. 56)*

Statutory Qualifications

The Constitution does not specify any qualifications that a regulator must have. But it does place one limitation on appointments. No member of Congress may be appointed to another government position during a session of Congress in which that position was created or its salary increased. This "ineligibility clause" postponed the appointment of Charlotte T. Reid, a member of Congress from Illinois, to the Federal Communications Commission (FCC). President Richard M. Nixon apparently wanted to name her to the commission in 1970, but was barred from doing so because Congress had raised the salaries of top-level government executives, including independent regulatory commissioners, during the 1969-70 session of Congress. She was nominated and confirmed in 1971.

The only laws of general applicability to regulatory agency qualifications are those governing federal employment. They require that an appointee be a U.S. citizen, abide by federal employee retirement laws and not engage in other employment while serving in the government.

Congress, however, has required that appointees to particular agencies meet certain criteria. For example, the act establishing the Federal Reserve Board stipulates that members be chosen with "due regard to a fair representation of the financial, agricultural, industrial, and commercial interests and geographical divisions of the country."

Congress established more precise requirements for appointments to the Federal Aviation Administration (FAA). In addition to being appointed with "due regard for his fitness for the efficient discharge of the powers and duties vested in and imposed upon him," the FAA administrator is to "be a civilian and shall have experience in a field directly related to aviation."

The primary statutory qualifications involve conflict-of-interest laws. From 1963 on regulators were prohibited by statute from acting on any matter in which they or related persons had a financial interest. Related persons included spouses, minor children, business partners, organizations in which the regulator was an officer, director or trustee and anyone with whom the regulator discussed his future employment. In 1965 President Johnson issued an executive order that prohibited federal employees from having "direct or indirect financial interests that conflict substantially or appear to conflict substantially with their duties and responsibilities...."

The executive order also required presidential appointees to submit periodic confidential financial statements to the Civil Service Commission. But some critics charged that the order was not enforced effectively.

The Watergate scandal prompted new calls for better conflict-of-interest laws. When he took office in 1977 President Jimmy Carter issued the toughest financial disclosure guidelines ever required of executive branch appointees and many of them were enacted into law in 1978. That law (PL 95-521) required all executive branch employees paid at level GS-16 or above to file annual public financial disclosure statements, which had to include the source and amount of earned and unearned income; interests in property over a certain value; liabilities over $10,000 and gifts over a stipulated value. The law also defined the requirements for blind trusts and set strict new rules on former government employees representing private interests before their former agencies. *(Revolving door law, box, p. 42)*

There have been relatively few instances of outright conflicts of interest among regulatory commissioners. One example was uncovered during a 1958 investigation of regulatory agencies conducted by the House Interstate and Foreign Commerce Subcommittee on Legislative Oversight. FCC Commissioner Richard Mack admitted to the subcommittee that since his appointment in 1955 he had accepted loans totaling $2,650 as well as other favors from Thurman Whiteside, a Miami lawyer and close friend, who had contacted Mack in behalf of a National Airlines subsidiary that was seeking a Miami televison channel. Subcommittee members agreed that Mack's acceptance of loans and favors from Whiteside was improper, if not illegal. Mack resigned his commission March 3, 1958.

A more recent example occurred in 1975 when the Senate Commerce Committee rejected the reappointment of Isabel A. Burgess to a second five-year term on the National Transportation Safety Board. A committee staff report showed that Burgess had bought stock in an airline regulated by the board and had accepted free transportation, meals and lodging from other regulated companies.

Regulators and Industry

Whether commissioners should come from the industries they are to regulate is a question surrounded by controversy. Regulated industries are obvious sources of potential commissioners who are already expert in the matter to be controlled. By the same token, past association with an industry can open a commissioner to charges that he is biased in favor of industry interests to the detriment of the general public welfare.

The problem is not a new one. When it created the Federal Maritime Commission (FMC) in 1936, Congress prohibited appointment of persons who had worked for any water carrier within the previous three years. That restriction was deleted in later reorganizations of the FMC because it worked to disqualify most people familiar with the shipping industry.

More recently Calvin Collier, then Federal Trade Commission (FTC) chairman, commented on the issue in 1977: "Basically, the jurisdiction of the FTC covers every industry in the United States.... If appointments to the commission were restricted to those who had never been employed by, or served as counsel to, any entity subject to the agency's jurisdiction, the FTC would be foreclosed from the services of anyone who actually engaged as a participant in free market competition."

In 1949 the Hoover Commission suggested that "Where a particular nominee appears to be so closely allied with some part of the industry as to make his appointment unwise or undesirable, that can be handled more appropriately through refusal of the Senate to confirm." And that seems to be the tack that the Senate has taken in recent years.

In 1973, for example, the Senate refused to confirm Robert Morris to a seat on the Federal Power Commission (FPC) not because he was unqualified but because the Senate thought he was too close to the industry he would regulate as a commissioner.

Morris had served for 15 years as an attorney for the Standard Oil Co. of California. Opponents made clear that they found no fault with Morris' professional qualifications or integrity, only his past association with a major firm in an industry under the FPC's purview. Several senators argued that the seat should be given to a consumer-oriented person because all the sitting members of the FPC had been closely attached to the power industry prior to their appointments.

Shortly after Morris' nomination was rejected, President Nixon nominated James H. Quello to a seat on the Federal Communications Commission. Quello had been a Detroit broadcasting executive before his retirement in 1972, and his confirmation was opposed by consumer groups who argued he was too close to the industry he would regulate. Hearings on the nomination were delayed several months, but the Senate finally confirmed Quello in 1974.

Presidents frequently avoid the controversy by seeking expertise outside the ranks of industry in universities and the public sector. President Carter, for example, selected several key regulators who had worked for public interest groups or the government prior to their appointments. *(Carter appointees, p. 64)*

Administrative Procedure Act

The basic statute regulating the regulators is the Administrative Procedure Act (APA) of 1946, which spells out procedures regulatory agencies must follow in their rulemaking and adjudication proceedings.

The APA had its genesis in the proliferation of regulatory agencies during the New Deal. Having created more new regulatory agencies than any president before him, President Franklin D. Roosevelt became interested in the reform and control of the regulatory bureaucracy to make it more efficient. In 1939 Roosevelt asked Attorney General Frank Murphy to examine the agencies and to make recommendations for their improvement. The eventual result of this investigation was the APA.

Due Process

The act had two primary thrusts: to ensure that the parties affected by regulatory decisions had a role in making those decisions and to guarantee fairness. Upon enactment, Senate Judiciary Committee Chairman Pat McCarran, D-Nev., described the act as a "bill of rights for the hundreds of thousands of Americans whose affairs are controlled or regulated in one way or another by agencies of the federal government."

The APA divided administrative proceedings into two categories: rulemaking and adjudication. A "rule" is defined as "the whole or a part of an agency statement of general or particular applicability and future effect designed to implement, interpret, or prescribe law or policy or describing the organization, procedure or practice requirements of an agency." "Adjudication" is the process of formulating an order, which is defined as a "final disposition . . . of an agency in any matter other than rule making but including licensing."

The act established minimum requirements that all agencies must meet during rulemaking and adjudication proceedings. Based on these requirements, agencies have developed their own procedures. Major provisions of the act:

● Required agencies to publish in the *Federal Register* a description of their organization and rulemaking procedures and to hold hearings or provide other means of public comment on proposed rules.

● Prescribed standards and procedures for agency adjudications, including licensing and injunctive orders. One of the most important of these standards required separation of the prosecution and decision-making functions within each agency through a ban on investigatory or prosecuting officials deciding cases.

● Spelled out hearing procedures, including a requirement that the proponent of a rule or order carry the burden of proof. Directed each agency to appoint competent examiners to act as hearing officers and to make or recommend decisions.

● Provided that any person suffering legal wrong because of any agency action would be entitled to judicial review, except where statutes precluded judicial review or where agency action was committed by law to agency discretion, but required the aggrieved party to exhaust administrative remedies first. A court was required to overturn agency actions "unsupported by substantial evidence" and to review the whole record.

'Side Effects'

The act did provide uniformity and fairness to the regulatory process that had been missing before its enactment. But as Louis Kohlmeier Jr. wrote in *The Regulators*, "it also had unexpected side effects. The act forced the regulatory agencies to adopt more of the ways of courts and thereby slowed them down. It allowed more industries and companies to participate in formal agency hearings and permitted each party to have its full say. Thus it encouraged the delays for which the agencies are now famous, the arguments that go on for months and the case records thousands of pages long."

While there is near universal agreement that the APA has contributed significantly to the problem of regulatory delays, the basic provisions of the statute have never been revised, although the act has been amended. The first major amendment to the act came in 1966 with passage of the Freedom of Information Act (FOIA). That act required government agencies and commissions to make their documents available to "any person" requesting them, subject to certain exemptions. Exemptions included the disclosure of trade secrets, personnel or medical files, and other records that constituted "a clearly unwarranted invasion of personal privacy."

In 1974 Congress approved the Privacy Act, which gave individuals an opportunity to find out what files the government had about them and to challenge, correct or amend the material. Other provisions of the act were designed to protect individual privacy by preventing a person from looking at records involving another individual.

The 1976 Government in the Sunshine Act toughened the FOIA, making it even more difficult for government agencies to withhold their records. Meetings of multi-headed federal agencies were required to be open to the public, with certain limited exceptions. *(FOIA, Privacy Act, Sunshine Act texts, pp. 157, 159, 162)*

Political Balance

To ensure a degree of bipartisanship in regulatory decisions, Congress required that most independent regulatory commissions have no more than a simple majority of commissioners from the same political party. Frequently a president will circumvent the intent of this restriction by choosing members of the opposition party who nonetheless sympathize with his political views.

In its 1977 study of the regulatory appointment process, the Senate Governmental Affairs Committee (then named the Government Operations Committee) noted that Quello was nominated to the FCC as a Democrat even though he had contributed $1,100 to President Richard M. Nixon's 1972 election campaign. Elizabeth Hanford Dole, a nominee to the FTC in 1973 declared herself to be an independent even though she then served as deputy director of the Office of Consumer Affairs in the Republican White House.

The president is authorized to designate the chairmen of most independent regulatory commissions, and most presidents take this opportunity to name someone of the president's party. If there is no vacancy to fill, the president may designate one of the sitting commissioners as the new chairman. In that case, the former chairman is not required to leave the commission but may stay for the remainder of his or her term although many in fact leave.

Congress has provided fixed terms of office for some commission chairmen. For example, the chairman of the Federal Reserve's Board of Governors is limited to a four-year term, and the chairman of the Civil Aeronautics Board (CAB) must be named each year. To make the Consumer Product Safty Commission (CPSC) more independent of the president, the legislation creating the agency stipulated that the president was to designate one commissioner as chairman until his term as commissioner had expired. This meant that one person could serve as chairman for as long as seven years. A similar specification was included in the measure creating the Commodity Futures Trading Commission (CFTC). However, when those commissions were reauthorized in 1978, Congress amended their statutes to provide that the chairmen serve at the pleasure of the president.

Nominations

There is no established formal process for the recruitment and selection of presidential appointees although recent administrations have followed roughly the same procedures. Generally the president has an appointments adviser who is responsible for searching out, screening and recommending potential nominees.

The adviser may seek the opinion of any number of others both inside and outside the White House before making a recommendation. He may recommend just one person for the position or present two, three or more names to the president for selection. The president makes the final choice although in some cases, this simply may confirm the choice already made by the adviser and other presidential aides.

Indeed, one of the key variables is how much interest the president takes in the nominating process. While few presidents oversee the weeding-out process, some have been more involved than others in finding nominees. Gerald R. Ford, for example, met regularly with his appointments adviser who later said that Ford personally consid-

ered "virtually every appointment" to the regulatory agencies.

Patronage

The president and his advisers may consider several factors in deciding who to nominate to a regulatory agency. These can include the potential nominee's educational background and employment record, his familiarity with the matter to be regulated, his age, his health, and the region of the country he comes from.

But few people will be nominated who are not politically acceptable to the White House, and in some cases, politics and patronage may be the prime determinant in a person's selection. Powerful connections in the right high places often make a difference in the selection process. The authors of a report released in 1976 that studied appointees to the FTC and the FCC wrote that "many selections can be explained in terms of powerful political connections and little else."

In 1975 a nominee was forced to withdraw his name when charges of patronage were made against his appointment. President Ford nominated former New Hampshire Attorney General Warren B. Rudman to chair the Interstate Commerce Commission on Feb. 4, just four days before the 1976 New Hampshire presidential primary. Democratic and Republican opponents of the nomination claimed it was a tactic to boost Ford's chances in the primary. Rudman June 11 asked that his name be withdrawn. The charges apparently did not harm either man politically. Ford won the primary; Rudman was elected to the Senate in 1980.

One connection that has been useful to dozens of regulatory agency appointees is congressional sponsorship. In its study of 38 regulatory appointments to four agencies over a 15-year period, the Senate Governmental Affairs Committee found that congressional sponsorship was often an important, if not the predominant, factor in the selection process.

Among those who benefit from such sponsorship are congressional aides. Some of these staffers played a key role in creating the agencies they later served on. For example, CPSC Commissioner Stuart Statler, appointed by President Carter in 1979, had served as special assistant to the chairman of the National Commission on Product Safety, whose recommendations ultimately led to the creation of the CPSC.

The Senate Commerce Committee, which has jurisdiction over the confirmations of members of a number of the independent regulatory commissions, has placed several of its staff members on the independent agencies. A. Daniel O'Neal, once the committee's transportation counsel, was nominated to the Interstate Commerce Commission (ICC) in 1973 and became its chairman four years later. President Carter's choice for FTC chairman, Michael Pertschuk, was formerly the committee's chief counsel and was instrumental in developing laws strengthening the commission's control of unfair trade practices. President Ronald Reagan appointed Mimi Weyforth Dawson as an FCC commissioner. Dawson had been a personal assistant to Commerce Committee Chairman Bob Packwood, R-Ore.

Prior Consultation

Before officially submitting a nomination to the Senate, the president or, more likely, his advisers usually consult with key members of Congress and special interest groups in an effort to obtain informal clearance for the president's candidate. Because it is in the interests of the president to avoid a confirmation fight, serious opposition at this stage may lead him to choose another nominee for the post. As G. Calvin Mackenzie noted in his book *The Politics of Presidential Appointments:* "The president rarely announces a nominee without first assessing the sentiments of those individuals and interests most likely to be affected by the nomination."

Louis Kohlmeier Jr. commented on the pre-clearance by industry in his book *The Regulators:* "Every President in recent history has run some sort of check with industry before appointing or reappointing a regulator.... Almost no President has ever sent up for Senate confirmation a name to which industry takes vigorous exception.... All Presidents have run checks with industry before picking regulators, fundamentally because all have looked on regulation more or less as industry's preserve."

The White House usually seeks the opinion of the senators from the same state as the nominee and key senators on the committee that has jurisdiction over the nomination. The Reagan administration did not do this before it announced in 1981 that the president would nominate B. Sam Hart, a black Philadelphia radio evangelist, to the U.S. Commission on Civil Rights. Neither of the state's Republican senators, John Heinz and Arlen Specter, were notified in advance of Hart's nomination, and neither had ever heard of him. Heinz asked the Senate Judiciary Committee to put a "hold" on the nomination, saying Hart did not appear qualified for the post. Civil rights groups opposed Hart for his stands against school busing for desegregation, the Equal Rights Amendment and the concept of homosexual rights. He eventually withdrew his name from consideration.

Investigations

Hart's nomination also illustrated the embarrassment that can occur if a prospective nominee's background investigation is not thorough. In the days before Hart withdrew his name, news reports circulated that he owed $4,400 in back taxes on income, property and business, and rent payments on property his station used in Phoenixville, Pa. It also was disclosed that Hart had not registered to vote in Philadelphia until November 1980, the time that the White House notified some members of Congress that Hart was being considered for the post.

A thorough investigation of a prospective nominee typically does not take place until the final stages of the selection process. The FBI conducts a full-field investigation of the potential nominee's background and the White House usually conducts its own investigation to assure itself the nominee has no "skeleton in the closet" that might prove politically embarassing.

The FBI investigation looks into personal history, reputation and loyalty; its examination of the person's finances generally is limited, extending only to a check to see if income tax returns have been filed. Presidents usually do not allow Congress to look at these reports, but President Carter did grant access to the committee chairman and ranking minority member if they requested it.

In recent years, the White House has examined the financial backgrounds of possible appointees to weed out real and potential conflicts of interest. Occasionally these investigations do not eliminate later problems. An example concerned Donald L. Tucker, a Carter nominee to the CAB.

The Speaker of the Florida House, Tucker was the first major Florida politician to endorse Carter's 1976 bid for the presidency, and he was nominated to the CAB post in June 1977 after an interview with Carter friend and political adviser Charles Kirbo.

Sen. Howard W. Cannon, D-Nev., chairman of the Senate Commerce Committee requested Tucker's FBI report and on the basis of information there decided that the committee staff should conduct its own investigation, which reportedly linked Tucker to a series of questionable financial deals. Tucker's nomination eventually was withdrawn.

Confirmations

The Senate's advice and consent role gives Congress an important mechanism for monitoring the quality of regulatory agency appointments. Many have charged, however, that the Senate does not take full advantage of this power.

The Senate does not closely examine presidential choices for regulatory positions in the executive branch on the theory that the presidents should be allowed to choose their own staffs. A check of the candidate's basic qualifications, rather than a full-scale examination of his or her views, generally suffices.

Appointments to the independent regulatory commissions are a somewhat different matter. Until the early 1970s, presidential nominations to the independent agencies usually were confirmed routinely, without thorough investigation. After the Watergate scandal heightened sensitivity to potential abuses of government office, the Senate began to scrutinize nominations more carefully. More often than not, senators question nominees at length about their personal investments and financial background to ensure they have no interest in any of the firms or industries the agency regulates. In recent years, the Senate often has carefully examined a nominee's economic views and political philosophy as well.

The basic purpose of congressional confirmation proceedings is to determine the character and competence of the nominee: whether there is any conflict of interest — particularly financial — and whether the nominee's qualifications are deemed appropriate for the job. The committee holds hearings at which the nominee and others may testify. Most of these hearings are routine, although some have turned into grueling inquisitions. Quello, Nixon's nominee to the FCC, was subjected to eight days of hearings before his confirmation in 1974.

Once the committee has approved a nominee, his name is submitted to the full Senate. A pending nomination may not be put to a Senate vote on the day it is received or on the day it is reported from committee, except by unanimous consent. The Senate may approve, reject or recommit a nomination to the committee that considered it.

Controversial nominations may be debated at length, but few of them are brought to the floor if there is any chance the nominee will be rejected. Generally, a nominee facing that much opposition will withdraw his name before the appointment is considered by the full Senate. As Louis Fisher observed in *The Politics of Shared Power:* "Floor votes to reject a nominee are rare. Committees prefer to let the White House know that they will not support a candidate, forcing the president to withdraw the nomination."

The full Senate has rejected nominees to regulatory

agencies in only a handful of cases. Between 1950 and 1973 only two nominees were rejected.

In 1976 the Senate rejected a nominee to the Consumer Product Safety Commission only to reconsider its vote two days later and confirm the appointment. After the Senate disapproved the nomination of John S. Byington as chairman of the CPSC on a 33-37 vote, his supporters protested that too many members had been absent and forced a second vote. Byington was then confirmed, 45-39.

The full Senate may block a nomination without actually voting on it. In 1976 the threat of a filibuster by Democratic liberals during the waning hours of the session blocked Senate action on President Ford's nomination of George F. Murphy Jr. to a seat on the Nuclear Regulatory Commission. Murphy, executive director of the Joint Committee on Atomic Energy, was opposed by environmentalists and public interest groups. Some senators were also miffed because his nomination so late in the term left little time to explore his view on nuclear policies.

Postponing action on an outgoing president's nominees is a favorite way to preserve vacancies for the incoming president to fill, especially if the two presidents are of different political parties. Hoping to keep as many appointments as possible open for incoming President Reagan, Senate Republicans managed to defer action on many presidential nominations at the end of the 96th Congress in 1980. Except for some vacancies that Carter filled through recess appointments, 113 nominations were left unconfirmed by the Senate. Among these were appointments to the National Labor Relations Board and the Equal Employment Opportunity Commission.

Conflict-of-Interest Objections

Most rejections occur at the committee level for a variety of reasons. One of the most common objections is conflict of interest. In 1974 Ford nominated Andrew E. Gibson to be administrator of the Federal Energy Administration. His name was withdrawn, however, after publication of reports disclosing that Gibson had been promised $880,000 in severance pay from his former employer, an oil shipping company with interests related to matters Gibson would have had to handle as FEA head.

Potential conflicts of interest also have blocked some appointments. Robert Morris' nomination to the FPC was one example. Another occurred in 1977 with Carter's nomination of Kent Hansen as a member of the Nuclear Regulatory Commission. Sen. Gary Hart, D-Colo., chairman of the Senate Environment Nuclear Regulation Subcommittee, expressed concern about a "possible conflict of interest" because Hansen had acted as a consultant to Westinghouse Electric Corp. and General Electric Co. on nuclear issues.

In 1978 the Senate Agriculture Committee took the unusual step of recalling an already confirmed nominee for further hearings over a potential conflict of interest. During his confirmation hearings to a seat on the Commodity Futures Trading Commission, David G. Gartner, a former aide to Sen. Hubert H. Humphrey, D-Minn., voluntarily told the committee that over a period of four years, Minneapolis grain magnate Dwayne Andreas had given $72,000 worth of stock to Gartner's four children. The stock was in Archer Davis Midland Inc., a major grain dealer regulated by the CFTC and chaired by Andreas, a longtime Humphrey financial supporter. During questioning Gartner agreed to sell the stock and to disqualify himself from any CFTC decisions involving Andreas' firm. That promise satisfied the committee, and Gartner was confirmed.

However, criticism of the stockholdings and questions of conflict of interest re-emerged when Gartner took his CFTC seat. The Agriculture Committee called him back for more hearings, and President Carter, reversing course, decided Gartner had to go. On June 26 Carter and Vice President Walter F. Mondale, who had recommended Gartner for the post, took the unusual step of publicly asking Gartner to resign. Pointing out that he had sold the stock and put the proceeds in trust for his children, Gartner refused and remained a member of the commission.

Senatorial Courtesy

Influential members of Congress, especially committee chairmen, can wield significant power in the confirmation process. A senator may occasionally object to an appointee for patronage reasons — if, for example, he feels the interests of his state should be represented on a certain regulatory commission. A senator also may use the objection that a nominee is "personally obnoxious" to him or her. In that case, other senators usually join in blocking the nomination out of courtesy to their colleague. Senatorial courtesy played a role in the rejection of President Harry S Truman's nomination of Martin A. Hutchinson to a seat on the Federal Trade Commission in 1950. Hutchinson was opposed by Virginia's Democratic Sens. Harry F. Byrd and A. Willis Robertson because he was a foe of Byrd's political machine.

Sometimes the Senate refuses to support the reappointment of a commission member, frequently because of his past voting record on agency decisions. As a result, the administration usually does not ask for the reappointment of controversial officials. The Senate first refused a regulatory commission reappointment in 1920 when it would not confirm John J. Esch for another term at the ICC, due to a controversial vote he had cast in a case involving coal rates. In 1949 the Senate rejected the reappointment of Leland Olds as FPC commissioner. The opposition was led by Sen. Lyndon B. Johnson, D-Texas, and backed by oil and natural gas interests who wanted Olds out because he had played a key role in the development of federal regulation of the natural gas industry.

Generally, a nominee's political views are not a determining factor in acceptance or rejection by the Senate. However, in 1975 the Senate Banking, Housing and Urban Affairs Committee rejected former Rep. Benjamin B. Blackburn, D-Ga., to a seat on the Federal Home Loan Bank Board because of his opposition to civil rights legislation — including fair housing measures — during his years in the House. Blackburn had also made some public comments revealing attitudes toward blacks and public housing tenants that a majority of the committee found objectionable.

Question of Quality

The quality of regulatory commissioners has been at issue for many decades. "Good men can make poor laws workable; poor men will wreak havoc with good law," wrote President John F. Kennedy's regulatory adviser, James M. Landis, in 1960. Landis went on to attribute many of the agencies' shortcomings to "a deterioration in the quality of our administrative personnel" since World War II, "both at the top level and throughout the staff."

Broadening Public Participation

Although most federal regulation is undertaken in the "public interest," the public has not always been able to participate fully in regulatory agency proceedings or even to monitor those proceedings. In recent years there have been several attempts — not all of them successful — to ensure that the public was represented in regulatory agency proceedings and that such proceedings were open to public scrutiny.

One proposal that received widespread attention in the early 1970s was establishment of an independent consumer protection agency to represent consumer interests before regulatory agencies and the courts.

The Senate approved a consumer protection measure in 1970 and the House approved similar legislation in 1971 and 1974. Both houses finally agreed on and approved a bill in 1975, but it was never sent to the White House because President Gerald R. Ford threatened to veto it. Supporters in the House conceded they did not have enough votes to override a veto.

President Jimmy Carter supported creation of the agency in 1977 but it was too late to overcome the opposition that had been building for several years. The House defeated the measure in 1978 and no further attempts were made to create the agency. President Carter continued to press for more effective representation of consumer interests. On March 23, 1978, he issued Executive Order 12044, which, among other things, required executive branch regulatory agencies to afford members of the general public increased opportunity to participate in regulatory actions.

Reimbursement

Another approach to greater public involvement in regulatory actions was for the government to underwrite the costs of public participation in such proceedings. Legislation authorizing such funding was considered in 1976, 1977 and 1978 but was never approved.

A few individual regulatory agencies — including the Interstate Commerce Commission, the Consumer Product Safety Administration and the Food and Drug Administration — were authorized to establish their own programs to fund public participation. Most of these programs were experimental and their funding limited.

And by 1980 Congress had second thoughts about the public intervenor programs it had authorized. Congress restricted the Federal Trade Commission's program and prohibited public participation funding for the Civil Aeronautics Board, the National Highway Traffic Safety Administration, the Nuclear Regulatory Commission and the Federal Energy Regulatory Commission. It killed a $150,000 public participation program operated by the Environmental Protection Agency.

Sunshine Law

More successful was a four-year campaign to open the government to increased public scrutiny. In 1976 Congress enacted legislation requiring most federal agencies to open their meetings to the public.

Called the "Government in the Sunshine Act," PL 94-409 required for the first time that all multi-member federal agencies — about 50 of them — conduct their business regularly in public session. The unprecedented open-door requirements embraced regulatory agencies, advisory committees, independent offices and the Postal Service — almost all executive branch agencies except the Cabinet departments.

A separate section of the legislation placed a ban on informal — *ex parte* — contacts between agency officials and interested outsiders to discuss pending agency business. Calling that provision a sleeper, some Washington lawyers suggested that it could have a broad impact on what had come to be an accepted practice in regulatory proceedings.

The issue had first surfaced in 1958 when President Eisenhower's assistant, Sherman Adams, was forced to resign after congressional investigations disclosed his frequent interventions with the Federal Trade Commission, the Securities and Exchange Commission, and the Civil Aeronautics Board.

The final version of the bill represented a victory for advocates of tough open-meeting requirements. The definition of meetings included almost any gathering, formal or informal, of agency members, including conference telephone calls. Agencies were also required to keep transcripts of closed meetings. However, the bill did allow agencies discussing very sensitive matters, such as monetary policy, to keep either minutes or transcripts.

In 1982, however, at least one agency appeared to be trying to reduce its public visibility. The Health and Human Services (HHS) Department, which oversees Social Security, Medicaid and Medicare programs, in July 1982 proposed to eliminate public notices and comment procedures for certain rulemakings on the grounds that they led to procedural delays. The Food and Drug Administration, which is covered by its own rulemaking procedures, was exempted from the proposal.

Public participation advocates adamantly opposed the change. "They're trying to limit people's information on what they are going to do to them," said Eileen Sweeney of the National Senior Citizens' Law Center. "All the people who . . . benefit from the programs HHS administers stand to lose."

Studying the problems 17 years later, the Senate Governmental Affairs Committee did not find the situation much improved. "[T]here is something lacking in overall quality," the committee wrote. "It is not a matter of venality or corruption or even stupidity; rather, it is a problem of mediocrity." A committee survey of lawyers who practiced before federal agencies found that the quality of commissioners was cited as the second greatest problem, after procedural delay, with the regulatory system. The lawyers said they would not recommend reappointment of more than half the sitting commissioners.

While almost everyone agrees that the quality of federal regulators could be improved, there is little agreement on the reasons for the lack of quality and even less agreement on what should be done about it.

A Matter of Structure

Some have argued that the multi-member structure of the independent commissions contributes to the mediocrity of some of their members. This was the prime conclusion of a 1971 study by the President's Advisory Council on Executive Organization (commonly referred to as the Ash Report, after its chairman, Roy Ash).

"While we have found that the attraction and retention of highly qualified personnel poses a significant problem for the regulatory agencies, the inability of commissions to perform satisfactorily results more from their organizational structure than from defects in the recruitment process," the task force wrote. "Even if the best qualified person filled each position, the collegial structure would impede effective performance." The council recommended appointment of a single administrator serving at the pleasure of the president for every regulatory agency.

The Ash Report received comparatively little support and no action was taken on its recommendation. The Senate Governmental Affairs Committee said it was "convinced that highly competent men and women ... are willing to serve on a commission composed of multiple members...." The committee cited comments by former FCC Commissioner Glen Robinson, who wrote in 1973: "The large problem is to create a political environment in which the best men can and will be selected. The single administrator form of organization is not a solution to this problem."

A Matter of Selection

The selection process has taken much of the blame for the lack of qualified regulators in government service. Critics say it is haphazard and too often governed by factors other than a candidate's professional qualifications.

"All too often these posts have been parceled out as rewards for political service to president or party, as tokens of appreciation to favored segments of industry, or as booby prizes for inadequate officials ousted from other jobs or political candidates rejected by the voters," said Sen. Frank Moss, D-Utah, at Senate hearings in November 1975. In testimony during those hearings, David Cohen, then president of the citizens' lobbying group Common Cause, charged that the system for finding regulators "has produced commissioners who are more interested in maintaining political allegiances with the president than in effectively regulating private industry. And it has allowed many regulatory bodies to become dominated by commissioners with industry perspectives."

The Senate Governmental Affairs Committee report

Judging the Judges

Criticism of the quality of regulators has not been confined to the commissioners and administrators that head regulatory agencies. Administrative law judges (ALJs) have also come under fire.

ALJs serve as important figures in the adjudication process that regulatory agencies use to set rates, issue licenses, prosecute violations and the like. ALJs have the power to administer oaths and affirmations, issue subpoenas, rule on offers of proof and receive relevant evidence, regulate hearings, hold conferences to settle or simplify issues, handle procedural requests, make or recommend decisions and take other action authorized by agency rules.

Some agencies have only one or two ALJs; others have more, depending on their caseload. The 1946 Administrative Procedure Act required that each agency "shall appoint as many hearing examiners as are necessary for proceedings required to be conducted." In 1981 about 700 of the government's more than 1,100 administrative law judges were at the Social Security Administration, deciding on requests for disability insurance and other benefits such as black lung.

Under existing law, the judges did not have fixed terms and could be removed only for "good cause." Furthermore, the judges were not subject to performance appraisals as were other civil servants. A 1978 Government Accounting Office (GAO) report on the administrative law process criticized the "selective certification" process by which administrative law judges (ALJs) were appointed to the agencies and the lack of standards for assessing an ALJ's job performance.

To make the ALJs more answerable for their decisions, the Carter administration proposed seven-year fixed terms for the officials, along with periodic performance appraisals that could lead to their reappointment, removal and/or transfer. Those processes would be handled by the Administrative Conference of the United States a government panel that studied administrative procedure and suggested improvements.

Although the measure was reported by a House committee, it failed to clear Congress.

noted that regulatory commissioners have been chosen not on the basis of merit but of political palatability and connections, under Democratic as well as Republican administrations. The problem of upgrading the quality of commissioners, the committee said, was a "threshold issue" in regulatory reform. "No amount of improvements in organization, procedure or substantive mandate of the agencies can overcome regulatory problems if inadequate appointments are made ... in the first place."

Legislation introduced in Congress in 1975 — the "Regulatory Agency Appointment Reform Act" — proposed establishing a 15-member nominating board to screen and recommend regulatory appointees. It was never enacted, however, due to questions about the constitutionality of certain provisions stipulating that a majority of the board members be chosen by Congress and requiring the president to choose a nominee only from among those the board recommended.

The Senate Governmental Affairs Committee report offered 53 recommendations to improve the appointment process. Its suggestions to require public financial disclosure statements, to tighten blind trusts and to close the revolving door on later employment were enacted as part of the 1978 Government in Ethics Act. But several other major recommendations have not been acted upon. These include: making the membership of commissions reflect the composition of society; requiring commissioners to serve their full terms; and centralizing regulatory appointments in a single office in the White House, with opportunity for public participation in the selection process.

Advice or Consent

The Senate confirmation process has not escaped criticism, but, like the selection process, little formal action has been taken to improve it.

Part of the criticism stems from an ambivalence about the Senate's advice-and-consent role. Should the Senate use its power to try to affect policy or only to provide a screen for weeding out unqualified or corrupt appointees? One view holds that senators can and should inquire into the policy intentions and commitments of nominees before confirmation. But others have suggested that the president has the right to hire his own personnel and that the Senate should confine its role to determining that the people chosen are competent and of good character.

The Senate Governmental Affairs Committee in 1977 criticized Congress for acquiescing in the White House appointments process and for not exercising its oversight authority to ensure that well-qualified individuals were named. Common Cause in November 1977 published a report calling the confirmation process a "rubber-stamp machine." Based on an analysis of 50 Carter nominations, the report concluded that the Senate inadequately examined the background and qualifications of most nominees, failed to build an adequate public record for the confirmation decision and rushed to confirmation without any affirmative finding that the caliber of the nominees met the requirements of their offices. The study did, however, praise the Senate Commerce Committee for the tough procedures it had developed to examine nominees to the independent regulatory agencies. Common Cause cited the committee as evidence that an aggressive committee could do a thorough confirmation investigation if it wished.

Legislation proposed in 1977, but never enacted, was intended to standardize and centralize the Senate confirmation process. The measure was aimed at providing the Senate with the staff expertise and the time to conduct the complicated background work needed in the confirmation process. It would have created a Senate Office on Nominations to assume primary responsibility for conducting congressional background inquiries into a nominee's integrity and fitness for office.

The office was to have been empowered to demand detailed biographical and financial disclosure statements of nominees, which would be available for public inspection. It would also have had access to FBI summary reports and any other investigative reports prepared as part of the president's consideration of the nomination. The office was to compile a record on each nominee, identify any questions about his integrity, and report to the committee with jurisdiction. Critics of the legislation maintained there was little that the Senate committees already could not do to scrutinize nominees if they took the trouble to do so.

REGULATIONS: HOW THEY ARE MADE

Federal regulatory agencies use two procedures for writing and enforcing their regulations. The first is rulemaking, a procedure by which the agency writes a rule to regulate a specific activity no matter who engages in that activity. The second is adjudication by which the agency deals with the activities of a specific company or companies. The Federal Communications Commission is making rules when it sets up criteria for evaluating competing claims for a television license, adjudicating when it awards that license.

Regulatory agencies may undertake only those functions specified by the law creating them. Furthermore, rulemaking and adjudicatory proceedings must be conducted under the Administrative Procedure Act (APA). Enacted in 1946, that law established uniform and due process procedures to ensure fairness in making regulatory decisions. Since then each agency has supplemented the APA with its own internal procedures. (*Administrative Procedure Act, box, p. 35*)

Rulemaking usually is used to set general policy, with adjudication used to settle factual disputes. Generally, the traditional agencies — whose regulation is primarily economic — use adjudication more than rulemaking, while the newer "functional" agencies that regulate broader areas such as safety and health rely on the latter.

Initiating Proceedings

Every agency has some way, either formal or informal, of determining what matters or cases it will pursue and what priorities to assign them. Most regulatory agencies have the authority to initiate a case or rulemaking based on their own research or investigations. The Consumer Product Safety Commission, for example, uses this kind of "proactive" approach to regulation when it examines hospital records and uses statistics from its national injury information clearinghouse to launch an inquiry into the hazards of baby cribs or lawnmowers.

In a "reactive" approach, outside individuals or firms alert agency officials to possible violations of law or other complaints. Adjudicative proceedings at the FTC often arise from a complaint sent by a company alleging unfair trade practices by a competitor.

Who May Participate

Not everyone may participate in agency proceedings. The companies and industries affected by federal regula-

Revolving Door Rules Quickly Relaxed

In response to charges of "revolving door" practices between the federal government and companies doing federal business, Congress in 1978 passed the Ethics in Government Act (PL 95-521). The conflict-of-interest provisions of the law were aimed at breaking up what critics saw as a too-cozy relationship between agencies and former officials who had gone on to private employment. But less then a year after it had enacted the legislation, Congress relaxed it.

In his 1976 campaign, President Jimmy Carter had assailed "sweetheart arrangements between regulatory agencies and regulated industries" and strongly advocated that limits on the public-to-private-sector employment shuttle be written into law.

The 1978 law enacted at his urging barred former officials at the GS-17 level and above from any contact with their former agencies or departments for a period of one year following termination of government service. Contact was prohibited on any matter — new or old. A second provision prohibited these former officials — for a period of two years after leaving the government — from knowingly representing, aiding, consulting or assisting in representing any other person (such as a law partner) on any matter the former officials had dealt with while in government service. Maximum penalties for violations were two years in prison and a $10,000 fine.

The restraints almost immediately prompted a number of high-ranking officials in the Carter administration to threaten to leave government service before July 1, 1979, when the law was scheduled to take effect. They complained that the restrictions in the 1978 law would bar them from working in their fields for an unreasonable time after leaving government employment.

Mass Exodus Averted

To avoid what might have been a mass exodus from government service, Congress in 1979 quickly passed legislation weakening the controversial conflict-of-interest restrictions. Worried that it would be unable to attract top-notch talent if the curbs remained on the books, the Carter administration supported the measure.

As signed into law just days before the 1978 restrictions were to take effect, S 869 (PL 96-28)

● Clarified language in the ethics law on the two-year "assisting in representing" prohibition; the ban applied only to those matters that an official had participated in "personally and substantially."

● Permitted a former official to advise lawyers, colleagues and others representing his new employer on how to deal with his agency. The assisting-in-representing ban would apply only to personal appearances of the ex-official before his agency.

● Exempted from the one-year ban on contact with former agencies those former federal officials who went to work for colleges and universities, medical research and treatment facilities or state and local governments.

tions always have been well represented at agency proceedings.

But intervention by citizens and consumer groups in agency actions involves the question of standing — whether the petitioner has a legitimate right to be heard before an agency because his interests and well-being are affected. This has proved to be an ambiguous concept that the courts have interpreted in a number of more or less restrictive ways. While the right to appeal an agency decision before the courts is subject to limits imposed by the Constitution and court decisions, agencies enjoy broad discretion in setting and enforcing rules for participation in their own proceedings.

As a result, guidelines for intervention vary widely among agencies. They also tend to be general. For example, the Consumer Product Safety Commission has said that individuals and groups may participate if they will be "directly affected by the final order." The FTC rule provides that "any person, partnership, or corporation may make application, and upon good cause shown may be allowed by the commission to intervene and appear [in adjudicatory proceedings]." Rulings such as these have given the agencies much latitude in their decisions as to who can participate in particular regulatory cases. The result has been equally varied: open-ended rules on standing can either impede or facilitate representation by consumer and public interest groups.

The ability of groups other than the regulated industries to participate has been influenced by the regulatory system itself. Delay in the procedure is costly, and many small businesses and interest groups have found that they cannot afford to participate in a lengthy series of hearings and appeals. On occasion, there might not be adequate notice of a pending case. Although notice is required to be given in the *Federal Register,* unless a group has been following a particular issue closely, it may not be aware of a proposed ruling. In general, the regulated industries are better equipped to keep themselves abreast of forthcoming rules that fall within their interests.

A basic question that has been raised in recent years has been whether there is in fact a need to facilitate representation by consumer and citizen groups. It has been argued that their greater representation would provide the agencies with new or different information to enable them to make more informed judgments. Others have contended that because regulation exists to protect consumers and workers as well as industry interests, their views should be heard. But Congress repeatedly rejected creating an agency specifically to represent consumer interests before other regulatory agencies. And programs to reimburse citizens who take part in agency proceedings have met with mixed success and government support. *(Details, box, p. 39)*

Rulemaking

Rulemaking is the process regulatory agencies use to write standards and regulations for products and services. When an agency wants to propose a rule, it must give general notice in the *Federal Register*. The notice must give the time and place of any public proceedings and outline the proposed rule or the subjects and issues involved.

The agency begins gathering information on the case and invites all interested or affected parties to submit comments and data within a certain time period. The agency may decide to conduct informal legislative-type hearings, with oral presentations to supplement the written comments received. Unlike adjudicatory proceedings, administrative law judges do not have to preside over rulemaking hearings, and witnesses are not subject to cross-examination by the other parties involved.

The agency then reviews all the comments received, the hearing record and information the agency has gathered during its own investigation and re-evaluates the proposed rule, making any modifications it deems necessary. The final rule then is published in the *Federal Register*.

Any affected party has the right to petition to a federal appeals court if it believes that the record does not support the adopted rule. The court can accept, modify or return the rule to the agency for further evaluation.

'Offeror' Process

When it created the Consumer Product Safety Commission in 1972, Congress experimented with an innovation in rulemaking known as the "offeror" process, where interested and competent outside groups were invited to propose standards for the eventual adoption by the agency. It was thought the offeror process would provide high-quality information at cheaper cost than if the agency were to set up its own fact-gathering organization.

The standard offeror process usually began with a notice in the *Federal Register* that explained why a standard was needed in a certain area. Any person, consumer organization, government agency, association, institution or industry could offer to develop a standard. Offerors usually were professional testing organizations such as Underwriters Laboratories Inc. Offerors had to submit information that included evidence of technical competence, a time schedule and a plan providing for the involvement of all interested parties in standards development activities.

After the offeror submitted a proposed rule, agency officials reviewed it, assessing its impact on the product in question and whether it met the agency's intended goal. At that point the regular rulemaking procedure took over. The agency published notice of the proposed rule, asked for comments, perhaps held a hearing, evaluated the evidence and issued the final rule.

Congress in 1981 abolished the offeror process. It directed the CPSC to rely primarily on voluntary product safety standards. The few mandatory rules that CPSC

would write would be developed through traditional rulemaking channels.

Adjudication

In contrast to the more generalized and informal character of rulemaking, adjudication usually involves a more limited number of parties and is more judicial in nature. Formal adjudication involves either a formal trial in which the agency charges a named individual or firm with violating a law or regulation, or a proceeding to set rates or decide which of several parties will receive some benefit such as a license or permit to enter a market.

The Administrative Procedure Act outlined a strict format of notice, hearings, procedures, evidence, oral argument and formal judicial decision that adjudication proceedings must follow. Consequently adjudication is often a time-consuming and cumbersome process.

Enforcement proceedings begin when a possible violation has been brought to the attention of agency officials. The agency initiates an investigation, notifying the individual or firm under investigation. Agency investigators assigned to the case gather information by interviewing persons involved, subpoenaing documents and conducting preliminary hearings. The chief investigator then evaluates the record and makes a report recommending disposition of the case.

At this point the case may be closed if the investigator recommends that the evidence does not support the complaint, or it may be settled through a consent order. A consent order, which has no force of law, may be issued by the agency when a company indicates that it is willing to stop the practice allegedly in violation of the law without admitting any wrongdoing.

The agency writes a proposed order that spells out any corrective action — modifying its advertising, for example — that the company must take. The order is published in the *Federal Register* and is open for public comment (usually for 60 days). Comments received become a part of the record and are considered by the commission in deciding whether to issue the consent order in final form. At this point the commission may decide that the matter should go to adjudication or that the order should be revised before it is issued in final form.

Formal Adjudicative Trial

If a case is not dropped or settled through a consent order, the agency may initiate adjudicatory proceedings by issuing a formal complaint against the alleged violators. Formal adjudication is conducted in a manner very similar to a court proceeding. After the agency's complaint has been served, the charged party (the respondent) must provide a written response within a stipulated time. The case is assigned to an administrative law judge (ALJ) who presides over the trial. An informal pretrial conference usually is arranged between the litigating parties, at which oral arguments are presented and documents exchanged.

After the case has been narrowed to the substantive issues involved, the formal trial begins. The Administrative Procedure Act requires the agency to notify the affected parties of the hearing's time and place, the federal statute involved and the factual dispute to be decided. The parties may submit oral or written evidence, present a defense and rebuttal and cross-examine witnesses. The ALJ is prohib-

The *Federal Register:* Recording the Rules

The basic tool for finding out about agency rulings, proposed rules, meetings and adjudicatory proceedings is the *Federal Register*, which is published five days a week. The *Federal Register* system of publication was established by the Federal Register Act of 1935 and was enlarged and amended by the Administrative Procedure Act of 1946.

Contained in the *Federal Register* are federal agency regulations and other legal documents of the executive branch, including presidential documents. The rules and regulations that appear in the daily *Federal Register* are codified by subject title in the *Code of Federal Regulations*, which is updated annually.

Documents contained in the *Federal Register* are arranged under one of five headings: "Presidential Documents," "Rules and Regulations," "Proposed Rules," "Notices" and "Sunshine Meetings."

Rules and Regulations

Agencies are required to publish final rules and regulations in the *Federal Register* 30 days before they are to take effect. Exceptions to this requirement include "(1) a substantive rule which grants or recognizes an exemption or relieves a restriction; (2) interpretive rules and statements of policy; or (3) as otherwise provided by the agency for good cause found and published with the rule."

Each entry in this section usually contains a descriptive heading of the change, the type of action involved (i.e., a final rule, a termination of rulemaking or proceeding, a request for further public comment); a brief summary of the nature of the action; and the effective date. This is followed by supplementary information including the text of the change in the regulation. The supplementary information on final rules must summarize comments received about the rule, what action was taken on them and why.

Proposed Rules

The format for publishing a proposed rule is similar to that for final rules. The entry contains a brief descriptive title of the action; the nature of the action (proposed rulemaking, extension of public comment period, etc.); a summary of the proposed rule; the deadlines for receiving public comments and/or dates of public hearings; and a detailed supplementary section. Also included is the agency's "docket" number under which its files on the proposed action may be identified and examined.

An "advance notice of proposed rulemaking" is published in cases where a rule is being considered but where the agency had not developed a concrete proposal.

Requests may be made for an extension of the deadline for public comment but agencies are not required to grant them.

Notices

This section contains documents other than rules or proposed rules that are applicable to the public. Notices of hearings and investigations, committee meetings, agency decisions and rulings, delegations of authority, filing of petitions and applications, and agency statements of organizations and functions are examples.

Announcements of advisory committee meetings also are required to be published in the "Notice" section. Notices of filings of environmental impact statements are also included in this section.

Sunshine Meetings

Notice of open agency meetings are printed in the *Federal Register* in accordance with the provisions of the Government in the Sunshine Act. Each entry contains the name of the agency; time, date and place of the meeting; a brief description of the subject; and supplementary information. Agencies that have closed meetings are required to list them, citing the relevant exemption under the Sunshine Act. *(Sunshine Act text, p. 162)*

ited from consulting any party on an issue of fact unless all parties have a chance to participate. Generally, regulatory agencies are more lenient than law courts on the evidence that may be admitted; this leniency is based on the assumption that regulatory officials are experts in the matter and thus highly qualified to evaluate that evidence. But agencies must be careful that the evidence they do admit will stand in a court of law should the decision in the case be appealed.

The record is closed when the trial-type hearing ends. Each party to the case then submits a memorandum to the ALJ and responds to the other side's presentation. After reviewing the record, the ALJ issues a report explaining his decision with respect to the facts of the case and the applicable law. A proposed order to remedy any found violations of law is then issued and served on the involved parties.

Appeals

After an agency order has been served, the parties involved may appeal the decision of the administrative law judge to the full commission or the agency administrator in accordance with the particular agency's procedural rules. Upon completion of its review, which may range from cursory to thorough, the agency has the option of adopting the ALJ's decision, rejecting it or returning it for further consideration.

At this point the agency's determination of the facts of the case is considered final. But the affected parties have the right to appeal the case through the federal court system, starting with the U.S. Court of Appeals. The Administrative Procedure Act provides that "A person suffering legal wrong because of agency action, or adversely affected or aggrieved by agency action within the meaning of a relevant statute is entitled to judicial review thereof." The courts must rule on the basis of whether the agency decision has been "supported by substantial evidence" in the record.

The court may enforce the agency's order, return it to the commission for further consideration, make changes in the order or set it aside entirely. Aggrieved parties may appeal the court's decision to the U.S. Supreme Court. Some regulatory agencies, such as the Interstate Commerce Commission, have adopted specific appellate procedures limiting appeals to one mandatory initial review of a case and one administrative appeal, with decisions subject to appeal through the federal courts.

Problem of Delays

The complaint most often made about the federal regulatory process is that it takes too long for a rule to be issued or a case to be decided.

The problem of regulatory backlog has been recognized by lawyers practicing before the agencies as well as by the ALJs. In a survey of 1,157 lawyers conducted by the Senate Governmental Affairs Committee, undue delay was the most frequently cited problem in the process. Similarly, 67 percent of administrative law judges responding to the committee questionnaire ranked slow procedure as one of the three top problems.

Procedural delay is not a new problem. Railroad companies have repeatedly criticized the ICC for protracted delay in dealing with petitions for increases in freight rates. A Federal Trade Commission merger case passed on by the Supreme Court early in 1966 had been in the works for more than 13 years. A dispute at the FCC on how to allocate a certain radio frequency between radio station KOB in Albuquerque and WABC in New York took 36 years to resolve. And the Pennsylvania Railroad Co. and the New York Central Railroad Co. had to wait almost six years after filing joint merger applications with the ICC before the Supreme Court gave final approval.

According to statistics compiled by the U.S. Administrative Conference, administrative agency proceedings averaged more than 19 months for licensing, 21 months for ratemaking proceedings and over three years for enforcement actions. It took an average of 160 days for licensing and ratemaking cases to reach even the hearing stage and it took over a year before a hearing even was convened in enforcement actions. The study was based on all administrative agency proceedings that were referred to an ALJ and that were concluded in 1975.

"Many categories of important adjudicatory proceedings take an extremely long time," the Senate Governmental Affairs Committee noted in its July 1977 report on delay in the regulatory process. "For example, in fiscal year 1975, it took the ICC an average of 915 days to complete proceedings on approval of rail abandonments, mergers or securities issues by rail or water carrier or freight forwarders. It took the CAB an average of 908 days to complete merger cases, and it took the NRC [Nuclear Regulatory Commission] an average of 888 days to complete construction permit reviews."

Although some agencies have taken steps to streamline their procedures, long delays are still the rule rather than the exception. A 1980 Government Accounting Office study, for example, found that it took the Food and Drug Administration an average of 20 months to act on applications to market new drugs. Of 132 applications studied, only one was approved within the six-month statutory limit.

Reasons for Delay

Some observers believe that inadequate budgets have been responsible for at least some of these delays. Other reasons include inadequate leadership, insufficient staff, little or no establishment of priorities or deadlines, unnecessary layers of review and insufficient use of available incentives and penalties to encourage speedier proceedings. Externally, private individuals and groups may find it in their interests to delay a final decision in a case. For example, environmental groups opposed to nuclear power plants have attempted to thwart proposals to speed up the nuclear licensing process. Companies charged with alleged violations of a regulation have little incentive to see the case decided, particularly if the ruling is against them and they are required to pay a penalty. Or a company that competes with a company that is seeking a license may delay the proceedings to forestall the competition.

Rulemaking vs. Adjudication

Perhaps the primary reason advanced for excessive regulatory delays is the decision-making process itself. Numerous observers have said that the agencies tend to use lengthy trial-type procedures when instead they could use rulemaking.

The Senate Governmental Affairs Committee found that making decisions by rulemaking procedures was faster than by adjudication. After studying regulatory proceedings at six independent regulatory commissions during fiscal 1973 and 1974, the committee concluded: "At every agency but the [Federal Maritime Commission], it took at least one and a half times as long on the average to make a decision by going through the full process of adjudication as it did to make one through rulemaking."

Moreover, in a study on agency proceedings during fiscal 1975, the committee found that "for all agencies for which a comparison can be made, rulemaking is as fast or faster on balance than adjudication, and that this advantage holds even when an effort is made to compare the most important rulemakings with the most important adjudications."

Rulemaking is not always faster than adjudication. Each agency may set its own time limits for promulgating a rule. And regulators can take months reviewing comments or completing other steps, stretching the process out for years. Court challenges can also prolong a final decision on a rule.

And rulemaking may not always be substituted for adjudication. Ratemaking, one of the most complicated of regulatory proceedings, as well as merger and licensing cases, cannot be resolved by any other way but adjudication because the facts of each case vary extensively. Specific facts of actual cases — or disputes of fact — must be settled by adjudication. And sometimes an agency's congressional mandate leaves it no choice but to use trial-type procedures to set policy.

A number of observers, including the Senate Governmental Affairs Committee in its July 1977 report, have recommended greater use of rulemaking procedures where possible and have proposed a modified process for adjudicative proceedings that would eliminate cross-examination and would institute a legislative, instead of trial-type, hearing wherever feasible. A modified procedure used by the ICC for most motor carrier applications satisfies the due process requirements of the Administrative Procedure Act but does not require a trial-type hearing or an ALJ.

The Senate report suggested that such a modified procedure would be appropriate for most cases involving rates, permits, licenses, and market entry and exit. Moreover, the courts and Congress have begun to create a middle ground called "hybrid rulemaking" by imposing additional judicialized procedures on informal rulemaking.

Some procedural delay is unavoidable because agency officials are required to carry out their legislative mandates in a fair and orderly manner and due process takes time. As Alan Stone pointed out: "The U.S. system [of government] is based on the belief that any person who may be adversely affected by a decision must be afforded an opportunity to present his views, confront his accusers, and be given reasonable time to prepare a defense."

The Senate Governmental Affairs Committee agreed: "Regulatory proceedings are indeed lengthy and convoluted. However, understanding the problem requires a recognition that agencies must not act in a hasty or ill-considered fashion. Complex matters, often involving technical issues, do take time to resolve. . . . To some extent, delay is inherent in administrative action; and to the same degree, delays may be both appropriate and necessary. However, there is a difference between delay occasioned by careful consideration and a delay that results from inertia, inability or dalliance."

5

Independence and Accountability

Congress has established two kinds of regulatory agencies: independent commissions and agencies that fall within the executive branch. In general, what distinguishes "independent" from "executive" regulatory agencies is not the range of their powers but simply the organic statutes creating them as such and the means by which their heads are appointed and removed.

Executive branch agency heads serve at the pleasure of the president and may be removed for political reasons. Independent commissioners are appointed for fixed terms and can only be removed for specific reasons that Congress spells out in statutory form. In general, executive branch regulatory agencies are headed by a single administrator, whose nomination may or may not require Senate confirmation, while independent commissions are multimembered and always require Senate confirmation.

There are limits on independent and executive branch regulatory agencies alike. Many of those restrictions are spelled out in the 1946 Administrative Procedure Act. Regulatory agencies may not take actions that are "arbitrary, capricious . . . or otherwise not in accordance with law," or are "in excess of statutory jurisdiction, authority, or limitations, or short of statutory right."

Other limits are dictated by political sense. An independent commission that is not sensitive to the political tones of the president, Congress and the public is likely to find itself challenged on all three fronts.

"Each branch of the government exercises checks and responsibilities for the commissions, and those relationships define the true contours of independence," noted the Senate Governmental Affairs Committee in its 1977 study of regulatory organization. And though they are nominally responsible to the president, the same also could be said of the executive branch agencies.

The Independent Commissions

A comprehensive study of government organization by the Hoover Commission in 1949 concluded that the independent commission structure, unlike that of executive branch regulatory agencies, provided a means of "insulating regulation from partisan influence or favoritism, for obtaining deliberation, expertness and continuity of attention, and for combining adaptability of regulation with consistency of policy so far as practical."

In creating the commissions, Congress viewed them as an arm of the legislature and sought to insulate them from presidential control. For example, Congress in 1972 decided to establish the Consumer Product Safety Commission (CPSC) as an independent agency because it thought such an agency would be better able than an executive branch agency to "carry out the legislative and judicial functions contained in this bill with the cold neutrality that the public has a right to expect of regulatory agencies formed for protection. [The independent form] will tend to provide greater insulation from political and economic pressures than is possible or likely in a Cabinet-level department."

On the other hand, presidents traditionally have considered the same commissions to be adjuncts of the executive branch and therefore have argued that coordination and direction of the agencies should come from the White House. Many presidents have advocated a structural reorganization of the commissions to place them directly in the executive branch.

Conflicts over accountability have created a curious situation for regulatory commissions. As former Securities and Exchange Commission (SEC) Chairman William L. Cary described it in his book, *Politics and the Regulatory Agencies*, the commissions are "stepchildren whose custody is contested by both Congress and the executive, but without very much affection from either one."

In fact, both Congress and the president have considerable influence over the powers, composition and functioning of the commissions. Regulatory agencies are also accountable to the courts, which are empowered to review and enforce many federal rules and regulations.

In its December 1977 report on regulatory organization, the Senate Governmental Affairs Committee (then called the Government Operations Committee) pointed out that "there are a series of formal limitations upon the independent status of the commissions: Congress charts their regulatory mandate in the statutes; OMB [the Office of Management and Budget] and the president examine and typically revise their budgets, which in turn are subject to adoption by Congress; OMB also reviews their recommendations concerning legislative action; . . . the Justice Department coordinates, even conducts, their litigation; and the president with the advice and consent of the Senate appoints their commissioners."

Some critics have argued that the independent character of commissions hinders the political monitoring by the executive branch and Congress that would make the agencies more responsive to social and economic change. On the other hand, advocates of the independent regulatory structure contend that a certain degree of political insulation is necessary for commissions to perform many of their duties, particularly in the area of adjudication. Most observers would agree, for example, that partisan considerations should not color the awarding of licenses or the determination of rates. In addition, it is argued that independence contributes to continuity of policies and provides a buffer to changes resulting from congressional or presidential elections. The multi-member commissions and staggered terms serve as countervailants to presidential and congressional partisan influence. And the length of commission terms helps to develop the expertise that the legislative and executive branches lack.

"Much of the criticism directed at independent commissions is rooted in fundamental misconceptions," observed Louis Fisher, a specialist in American government at the Congressional Research Service. "Commissions are routinely attacked for being unresponsive to popular pressures, but they were made independent precisely to avoid abrupt policy swings that might otherwise occur from one election to another. It is inconsistent — indeed inconceivable — to expect a commission to be both independent and politically responsive.... We do not want commissions to accommodate each political whim and inclination," Fisher wrote in his book *The Politics of Shared Power.*

Political Vulnerability

Others have countered that the independent character of commissions has weakened the agencies by removing the benefits of presidential and congressional political support, thereby making them more vulnerable to pressures from the regulated industries. A 1950 Budget Bureau study concluded: "The absence of public support for regulatory policies places a premium on the ability of the commissions to live with the industries and trades subject to regulations. These factors help to explain the tendency of the commissions to become timid in defending the public interest and developing regulatory programs."

Conversely, some agencies have been accused of overzealously guarding consumer and public interests at the expense of business and industry. The Federal Trade Commission (FTC) serves as an example of the restraints that can be imposed on an agency when it is perceived to have gone too far in its efforts to protect the consuming public. Under intense pressure from the industries regulated by the FTC, Congress in 1980 trimmed the agency's authority and specifically instructed it to stop activities in certain areas. *(Details, FTC case study, p. 77)*

In another example, the American Trucking Associations (ATA) attacked the Interstate Commerce Commission (ICC) in 1978 for actions it took to reduce regulation of and increase competition in the trucking industry. The ATA, a powerful truck owners and operators lobbying group, claimed that ICC actions would greatly damage the economic stability of the trucking industry. Despite the group's opposition, Congress in 1980 enacted legislation deregulating the industry. *(Transportation deregulation, p. 89)*

Until the late 1970s the ICC long had been criticized for protecting and promoting the well-being of the truckers it regulated at the expense of would-be competitors and the general public. This charge has been made frequently especially against commissions such as the ICC that regulate a single industry. Such commissions may use their ratemaking, licensing and market-entry control authority to benefit that industry or individual companies in it. They are therefore susceptible to intense pressure from those industries.

In other cases such as the Environmental Protection Agency (EPA), FTC and CPSC, jurisdiction extends over a wide range of private sector activities, making it difficult for an industry to control regulatory activities of the agency. However, Murray Weidenbaum, former chairman of President Ronald Reagan's Council of Economic Advisers and professor of economics at the Center for the Study of American Business at Washington University in St. Louis, Mo., has observed that this kind of cross-industry regulation may have its own shortcomings:

"...[I]n comparison to the older agencies oriented to specific industries, in many important ways the newer federal regulators operate in a far narrower sphere. That is, they are not concerned with the totality of a company or industry, but only with the limited segment of operations which falls under their jurisdiction. The ICC, for example, must pay attention to the basic mission of the trucking industry, to provide transportation services to the public, as part of its supervision of rates and entry into the trucking business. The EPA's interest in the trucking industry, on the other hand, is almost exclusively in the effect of trucking operations on the environment. This restriction prevents the agency from developing too close a concern with the overall well-being of any company or industry. Rather, it can result in a total lack of concern over the effects of its specific actions on a company or industry.

"If there is any special interest that may come to dominate such a functionally oriented agency, it is the one that is preoccupied with its specific task — ecologists, unions, civil rights groups and consumerists. Thus, little if any attention may be given to the basic mission of the industry to provide goods and services to the public."

OVERSIGHT: KEY TO CONGRESSIONAL CONTROL

While Article I of the Constitution gives Congress the power to regulate commerce, the legislative branch has in turn delegated much of this power to regulatory commissions and executive branch agencies. Congress then uses its oversight powers to ensure that these agencies write and administer the regulations as Congress intended.

In its 1977 study of regulation, the Senate Governmental Affairs Committee listed six primary goals of congressional oversight. They were: 1) ensuring compliance with legislative intent; 2) determining the effectiveness of regulatory policies; 3) preventing waste and dishonesty; 4) preventing abuse in the administrative process; 5) representing the public interest; and 6) preventing agency usurpation of legislative authority.

"[O]versight is not simply hindsight," the report noted. "Oversight involves a wide range of congressional efforts to review and control policy implementation by regulatory agencies. Thus, oversight includes study, review, and investigations, but it also involves an active concern with the administration of policy *during* implementation. Congressional oversight thus includes both participation before agency action and review after the fact."

Methods of Oversight

The most fundamental method of congressional control over both independent and executive branch regulatory agencies is statutory — the passage of legislation establishing new agencies and commissions and spelling out their powers and limitations. Congress frequently assigns regulatory agencies additional regulatory responsibility after they are created. Congress substantially broadened EPA's responsibilities in the 10 years after it was created by passing noise, pesticide and toxic substances control measures that EPA was required to enforce.

Members of Congress also may have a hand in selecting nominees to both the regulatory commissions and many of the executive branch agencies. Presidents have customarily consulted members of Congress of their own political party on appointees from their states. But policy considerations, as well as political ones, often take precedence over this form of courtesy, and failure to extend the courtesy usually has not been the only factor in a nominee's rejection.

More important is the Senate's authority to confirm nominees to independent commission and many executive branch positions. The confirmation process provides a crucial means of oversight by giving senators not only a means to assess a nominee's qualifications but also to question his policy views. Nonetheless, senators on many occasions have been criticized for failing to utilize this means of oversight effectively. *(Details of selection, confirmation process, pp. 33-41)*

Once the agencies are established and their members confirmed, Congress has two principal tools — fiscal and legislative — to ensure that the agencies remain politically accountable to the legislative branch.

Congress also has a responsibility to investigate agency practices in light of possible abuses, costs and benefits of regulation, possible reforms and agency responsiveness to the elusive "public interest."

Appropriations

The appropriations process enables House and Senate Appropriations committees to scrutinize proposed agency budgets. Oversight through appropriations has been strengthened by the fact that the budgets of most regulatory agencies now are reviewed annually. In approving them, Congress may specify the purposes for which funds are to be used — a direct and unambiguous method of control. "The appropriations process is the most potent form of congressional oversight, particularly with regard to the federal regulatory agencies," concluded the Senate Governmental Affairs Committee in its 1977 report.

The committee then went on to note a significant drawback: "[G]iven their relatively small budgets, regulatory agencies do not get extensive consideration from the appropriations committees. Moreover, the appropriations process is an incremental one. Attention is normally focused only on requested increases to the previous year's budget."

There are other limitations to oversight through appropriations. These include backdoor spending authoriza-

Congress' Watchdog

Often referred to as the "watchdog of Congress," the General Accounting Office (GAO) is an arm of the legislative branch that was created to oversee the expenditures of the executive branch.

The agency is headed by a comptroller general and assistant comptroller general, appointed for 15 years by the president with the advice and consent of the Senate. They can be removed only by joint resolution of Congress, thus making the agency responsible to Congress.

Since it was established in 1921, the GAO's duties have been expanded from routine audits of the accounts of executive departments to analyses of program management and planning, and often to controversial investigations of how federal agencies are spending the taxpayers' money.

When Congress needs information about a program that will require additional funds, the GAO is contracted to conduct an investigation. When the Appropriations committees of the Senate and House are working on the annual appropriations bills, GAO staff members act as consultants. The GAO's management-analysis reports and audits may be used as reference material. If a government activity is of particular interest to a committee or member, the GAO may be asked to make a special investigation.

Many of GAO's investigations deal with the federal regulatory agencies. For example, in the four-month period from April through July 1982, GAO issued reports on pollution control laws, wastewater treatment regulations, federal maritime regulations, wetlands permits in Alaska, education program paperwork requirements, appliance energy efficiency standards and the Food and Drug Administration's (FDA) review of over-the-counter drugs.

In its 1977 study of the federal regulatory system the Senate Governmental Affairs Committee (then the Government Operations Committee) cited several instances in which GAO studies directly benefited the public. For example, the committee noted, the GAO reported that the FDA had permitted the use of the color additive Red Dye No. 2 for 15 years despite questions raised about its safety and in the face of a law requiring the agency to determine if the substance was safe. FDA banned the color additive shortly after GAO issued the report.

Some members of Congress have complained that occasionally GAO reports were of inferior quality, that the agency took too long to produce its reports and that the reports were bland and not always focused on the issues of most interest to Congress. Despite these shortcomings, Congress continues to expand GAO's oversight activities.

tions that allow agencies to spend money without regular appropriations, and permanent appropriations that provide funds without annual congressional action. At times Congress has been limited in its ability to make sure appropriated funds actually are spent. This issue surfaced during 1970-74, when the Nixon administration impounded (or withheld) funds for a number of agencies it opposed. The result was the 1974 Congressional Budget and Impoundment Control Act that required the president to obtain congressional approval to withhold funds. That act also strengthened the role of the General Accounting Office (GAO) in acquiring fiscal, budgetary and program-related information from federal agencies. *(GAO role, box, p. 49)*

In 1939 Congress restricted its own access to initial budget proposals by the independent commissions by enacting legislation allowing the Budget Bureau to review and change the requests before they were sent to Capitol Hill. However, initial agency budget requests may be submitted to Congress after the president's budget is proposed and in some cases must be transmitted simultaneously.

Authorizations

The appropriations review generally does not focus on the agencies' policies and goals. If it occurs at all, such scrutiny comes during the authorization process when Congress determines whether to continue the agency. A number of agencies have been given permanent authorization status, among them the Federal Communications Commission (FCC), the ICC and the EPA. Aware that permanent authorizations decrease its ability to oversee regulatory actions, Congress in recent years has required periodic authorization for some of the more controversial agencies, including the CPSC and the FTC. *(Authorizations, appropriations, box, p. 54)*

More often than not, Congress gives up some of its control by couching agency authorizing statutes in vague generalities, giving the regulators considerable leeway in the performance of their functions Occasionally agencies have taken actions that ran counter to congressional intent. In a few such cases, Congress then has felt obliged to narrow the agency's mandate.

An example occurred with the FTC. The Magnuson-Moss Warranty — Federal Trade Commission Improvement Act of 1974 expanded the FTC's power by allowing it to issue rules covering the practices of an entire industry. Before passage of the legislation the commission could proceed against abuses only on a case-by-case basis, and any ruling on an unfair or deceptive practice applied only to the company involved in that particular case, not to others guilty of similar practices. Six years later, after a prolonged battle over whether to extend the life of the agency, Congress wrote into the legislation specific limits on the commission's power to regulate children's advertising and agricultural cooperatives.

Congress sometimes shirks its responsibility to provide agencies with meaningful guidelines for political reasons. As Alan Stone wrote in his book, *Regulation and its Alternatives*, members may call for both cheap energy and a cleaner environment "without any disciplining agency — such as money — that compels them to consider tradeoffs." Legislators "have a strong incentive to demand the highest possible goal and leave the problem of means to administrators and regulated firms so that the latter can be blamed for failures," said Stone. "In so doing, legislators have an incentive to provide ambiguous, unclear — or even no —

information on the means by which to achieve policy goals."

Because members of Congress must contend with numerous interest groups, some with conflicting objectives, compromise on regulatory legislation usually is necessary. But compromise often is difficult (for example, finding a solution to aid the ailing auto industry while maintaining costly auto emission and safety standards), and inaction may result. Extension and revision of the Clean Air Act fell victim in 1982 to competing interests. And banking deregulation legislation was stalled by a lobbying conflict between banks that pressed for decontrols and savings and loan institutions that called for continued protection. *(Clean Air Act extension, p. 111; banking deregulation, p. 99)*

Besides these "formal" oversight powers, Congress has other tools at its disposal to regulate the regulators, among them hearings, informal contacts and directives contained in committee reports. According to Roger H. Davidson and Walter J. Oleszek in *Congress and Its Members* (1981), "non-statutory controls may be the most common form of congressional oversight. Administrators are well advised to consider carefully such informal instructions." A number of statutes require regulatory agencies to submit detailed reports to committees. Committee investigations also serve as a means to gain information and publicize the performance of agencies.

Shortcomings of Oversight

In the 1970s Congress began to express greater interest in oversight. Davidson and Oleszek attributed this to several factors, including widespread complaints from the public and industry that the federal regulatory bureaucracy had grown too big, too arrogant and too expensive.

Although the number of oversight hearings has been steadily increasing, the Senate Governmental Affairs Committee concluded in its report on regulation that "one of the most notable features of oversight by nonappropriating committees is its sporadic, unsystematic functioning.... Oversight tends to be done on a crisis basis only ... in response to a newspaper article, a complaint from a constituent or special interest group, or information from a disgruntled agency employee."

The committee detailed a number of major roadblocks to effective oversight, among them:

● Committee Structure. Because several committees usually share jurisdiction over an agency, oversight is fragmented, and coordination and cooperation among legislative panels is difficult to achieve, particularly among House and Senate committees. For example, 12 House panels and 29 of their subcommittees, and 10 Senate committees and 21 subcommittees had responsibilities over water programs in 1981.

At the same time it called for more coordination, the committee issued a caveat: "Just as monopolies are deemed to be undesirable in most other areas of society, congressional committees should not have a monopoly on oversight of a particular agency. Agency-committee relations may grow too cozy for effective oversight to flourish. Fresh perspectives may not have a chance to emerge."

● Access to Information. Committees sometimes have experienced difficulties and delays in obtaining requested information. Agencies may refuse to supply information, or they simply may not have it available. "Independent regulatory commissions are generally more responsive to committee requests for information than executive branch agencies; they do not have the power of the president to back up their denials of the information," noted the report.

Moreover, filtering most regulatory agency budget and legislative requests through OMB reduces the ability of Congress to obtain independent information. The OMB screening process "deprives Congress of a frank exchange of such agencies' views based on agency experiences, and agency decision making," said the Senate Governmental Affairs Committee. "It gives an unfair advantage to the executive branch in influencing any special position affecting independent regulatory agencies before congressional committees. It ignores the substantive and oversight capability of such committees to understand the effectiveness of independent agencies and to evaluate legislative recommendations from whatever source."

● Staff Resources. According to the Senate committee, the total number of professional staff members on legislative committees having oversight responsibility for the regulatory agencies was fewer than 200, reflecting the great disparity in size between congressional staffs and the agencies they oversee. Perhaps more important is the problem of developing the necessary staff expertise for effective oversight, the committee said.

The report noted several more intangible factors that hindered congressional oversight. These included the many demands on members' time and the belief that members gain more politically from sponsoring new legislation than from policing what has already been enacted. Finally, the committee noted that oversight was "inhibited by the alliance that often develops between the agencies and the committees.... Some committee members may have strong ties, as well, to the industry which is being regulated. These relationships may militate against vigorous oversight, especially when ineffective regulation may be in the industry's interest."

The Legislative Veto

One mechanism for achieving increased congressional oversight is the hotly debated legislative veto, the subject of numerous bills that have been introduced in recent years.

Although there are many varieties of legislative vetoes, also called congressional vetoes, all share a common purpose: to permit Congress to block an executive action — in some cases with, in other cases without, the president's approval. Regardless of the method used, the veto procedure forces the affected government agency to delay carrying out its regulation, usually for 30 or 60 days, while Congress considers the issue.

One form of congressional veto permits either house of Congress to block an executive agency plan or rule by passing a simple resolution of disapproval within a fixed period from the time of the agency's action. A variation permits a one-house veto if the second chamber does not overturn the first's action within a specified time.

Another common type of veto requires passage of a concurrent resolution of disapproval by both houses. A third form permits one or more congressional committees to block an agency action. Yet another type requires passage of a resolution approving a proposed rule or plan by one or both houses or one or more congressional committees before the plan or rule can be carried out.

In recent years, the number of congressional veto provisions in force has multiplied rapidly as Congress has

attempted to assert greater control over unelected bureaucrats, particularly those in regulatory agencies. By the end of 1981, about 200 statutes contained one or more legislative veto provisions, according to the Congressional Research Service. Of that number, at least a third had been enacted between 1976 and 1981. One law, the Energy Security Act of 1980, contained more than 20 veto provisions.

Efforts to win approval of a general legislative veto bill were intensified during the late 1970s. Those pressures came primarily from the House. In 1976 the House came within two votes of passing a sweeping bill that would have made most agency regulations subject to review and rejection. In 1980 Congress approved legislation that included a provision allowing a two-house veto of Environmental Protection Agency pesticide rules.

Attempts by Congress to pass a comprehensive veto measure as part of government-wide regulatory reform continued in the 1980s. In 1982 both chambers considered major regulatory reform bills containing legislative veto provisions. *(Details, p. 75)*

Although they had not reached their ultimate goal, veto proponents won a significant victory in 1980 when Congress passed the 1980 Federal Trade Commission Authorization Act (PL 96-252). That act was the first to give Congress comprehensive veto power over all regulations issued by a single agency.

The FTC's increasingly aggressive regulatory stance in the late 1970s mobilized the business community to lobby vigorously for a congressional check on the FTC. Congress appeared to be sympathetic to such pleas, but disagreement over how to proceed led to a prolonged funding dispute. In 1977 the agency's operations had to be funded through an emergency money bill when the regular authorization-appropriation process was blocked by the House's insistence on attaching a one-house veto provision and the Senate's objection to the provision.

The stalemate continued until 1980, when key House members announced they would not allow even emergency funding of the FTC until the veto issue was settled. In April 1980 the Senate finally gave in; FTC rulings were made subject to a two-chamber veto that did not require the president's approval. *(Details, FTC case study, p. 77)*

Controversy Threatens Independence Of . . .

The establishment and controversial history of the Consumer Product Safety Commission (CPSC) provide a dramatic example of how congressional and executive oversight can affect an independent regulatory agency.

The idea to create an agency that would monitor product safety was born during the consumer movement that swept the country in the late 1960s and early 1970s. The National Commission on Product Safety, a panel formed by President Lyndon B. Johnson in 1968, recommended in 1970 that such an agency be created. The task force had found that 20 million consumers were injured annually by consumer products, that approximately 110,000 of those were permanently disabled and that 30,000 were killed. Arnold Elkind, the task force chairman, told Congress that an effective agency could prevent as many as four million injuries and 6,000 deaths each year.

President Richard M. Nixon opposed the task force recommendations, preferring a voluntary and educational approach to combating consumer hazards through establishment of a consumer safety program within the Department of Health, Education and Welfare. Congress disagreed, and set up the CPSC as an independent agency in October 1972.

The CPSC was authorized to establish product safety standards, maintain a national injury information clearinghouse, ban consumer products if it determined they presented unreasonable hazards that could not be corrected by a standard, and required product manufacturers, distributors and retailers to repair or replace those hazardous products that did not meet standards.

To ensure that the administration could not undercut the new agency, the Democratic Congress required the commission to submit its budget requests and legislative proposals to Congress as well as to the president and the Office of Management and Budget.

From the beginning the Nixon administration showed little sympathy for the new agency. Nixon delayed naming any of the five commissioners for five months. The White House also insisted that non-career, high-level civil service appointees to the commission receive political clearance from the White House. The commission also clashed with OMB over opening budget deliberations to the appropriate committees of Congress. The CPSC wanted such meetings open; OMB did not. The agency finally prevailed.

President Gerald R. Ford apparently was no more enthusiastic about the agency than his predecessor had been. The commission's first chairman, Richard Simpson, wanted to be appointed to a second term when his first expired in October 1975. The date passed without a word from the White House and Simpson found himself in a sort of official limbo. He resigned at the end of the year.

Ford eventually nominated S. John Byington, a native of Ford's hometown of Grand Rapids, Mich., and a deputy special assistant to the president for consumer affairs, to take Simpson's place. But Byington was opposed by consumer and labor groups and the Senate Commerce Committee shelved his nomination.

Ford immediately renominated Byington, this time to an unexpired term of only two and one-half years. The committee approved Byington but the full Senate rejected him by a vote of 33-37. Sen. Robert P. Griffin, R-Mich., persuaded the Senate to reconsider its vote, and two days later Byington was confirmed, 45-39.

In addition, the CPSC's early years were marked by an unrelenting stream of criticism from consumers, businesses and Congress itself. The situation worsened under Byington, prompting a series of critical government evaluations:

● The General Accounting Office (GAO) July 26, 1976, criticized the CPSC for inefficient management, poor use of available resources and poor enforcement of its laws.

● The House Commerce Oversight and Investigations Subcommittee reported in October 1976 that the agency "has fumbled over arranging its priorities, run into complex problems in seeking to maximize

Presidential Opposition

The legislative veto has been a source of controversy since 1932, when Congress added to the fiscal 1933 legislative appropriations act a provision enabling either house of Congress to block President Herbert Hoover's anticipated executive branch reorganization proposal. The next year, when Hoover issued his reorganization order, the House voted to disapprove it.

According to Hoover's attorney general, William Mitchell, the attempt to give either house, "by action which is not legislation, power to disapprove administrative acts, raises a grave question as to the validity" of the 1932 executive reorganization act. (*Executive reorganization, p. 59*)

Although there was a record of executive acquiescence in legislation containing the veto, most presidents since Hoover have questioned the constitutionality of the procedure. Franklin D. Roosevelt, for example, signed the Lend Lease Act of 1941, which contained a veto clause, because he considered the act crucial to winning the war. But he then wrote to Supreme Court Justice Robert H. Jackson setting forth his constitutional objections to the provision.

...Consumer Product Safety Commission

public participation and delayed launching an effective enforcement program."

● A December 1977 GAO study criticized the slowness of CPSC procedures in using the "offeror" process to issue mandatory safety standards. The report noted that since it had been created, the agency had issued only three standards written by outside groups; they were for swimming pool slides, architectural glass and matchbook covers. Although by law an offeror was to take only 330 days to develop a proposed standard, the average for the three standards was 834 days. *(Offeror process, p. 43)*

Matters came to a head in early 1978 when Sen. Wendell H. Ford, D-Ky., asked Byington to resign. Ford's request followed release of a Civil Service Commission report alleging 30 cases of CPSC abuse of government personnel rules. Byington Feb. 8 announced his resignation, effective June 30, to "depoliticize" congressional hearings on extending the agency's authorization.

1978 Reauthorization

About the same time some of President Jimmy Carter's advisers were recommending that the agency be abolished. Initially it appeared that Carter might back such a dismantling effort. However, after vigorous lobbying by the commissioners, consumer groups and Esther Peterson, Carter's special assistant for consumer affairs, the president announced in April 1978 that he would support a three-year reauthorization.

Congress concurred, extending the agency through Sept. 30, 1981. It also agreed to some changes requested by Carter, including providing that the CPSC chairman serve at the pleasure of the president. Previously the chairman retained the post throughout his or her term.

In the three years following the 1978 reauthorization CPSC won increasing respect from industry and Congress. The agency worked more closely with private industry and trade groups to develop voluntary safety standards for the design and use of consumer products. It generally imposed mandatory

safety standards only for generic safety hazards and only if the voluntary standards proved inadequate.

The commission also was applauded for selective use of its regulatory tools. The CPSC attempted to target the most significant product hazards in a manner that least impinged on product utility, consumer demand, manufacturers' costs and competition in the marketplace. Furthermore, the agency undertook an ongoing process to review all of its regulations. In 1981, Murray Weidenbaum, then chairman of the Council of Economic Advisers, praised the agency for its use of cost-benefit analysis and for "trying to behave rationally."

1981 Reauthorization

Nonetheless, when the agency came up for review in 1981, its detractors, bolstered by the anti-regulatory mood of the country, again attempted to abolish it. In May Office of Management and Budget Director David Stockman announced that the Reagan administration wanted to dismantle the CPSC because it had "adventured too far in some areas of regulation."

Others wanted to reorganize it into an executive branch agency within the Commerce Department, where it would be accountable to the president. Consumer groups countered that folding the agency into the Commerce Department would blunt CPSC's effectiveness.

The result of the 1981 debate was legislation that continued the CPSC for two additional years but cut back on its independence and its budget. PL 97-35 allowed one chamber of Congress to veto CPSC regulations if the other chamber did not object. The measure also eliminated the agency's authority to issue safety standards containing product design requirements. And the legislation required CPSC to make detailed findings before it could issue mandatory safety rules. Congress agreed to Reagan's request of $33 million for the agency in fiscal 1982, a 30 percent reduction from Carter's recommendation. Since fiscal 1981 the agency had lost more than 200 full-time positions.

President Gerald R. Ford dramatized his objections in 1976 by vetoing a pesticides control bill solely because it contained a version of the veto. There was no attempt to override. That was one of the few instances in which a president directly challenged Congress on the issue. President Jimmy Carter said in 1978 that the veto infringed "on the executive's constitutional duty to faithfully execute the laws...." However, Carter did recognize the legitimacy of a one-house veto to disapprove presidential proposals to reorganize the executive branch. That type of veto "does not involve congressional intrusion into the administration of

ongoing substantive programs, and it preserves the president's authority because he decides which proposals to submit to Congress," he said.

It appeared initially that Reagan would be the first president not to oppose the veto. As a presidential candidate he had endorsed its use by Congress. But once in office he changed his position. Reagan's attorney general, William French Smith, announced early in 1981 that the administration considered the veto unconstitutional if it "intrudes on the power of the president to manage the executive branch."

Later the Reagan administration said it opposed legislative vetoes of executive branch decisions but would accept them for actions taken by independent regulatory agencies. And it agreed not to oppose them for executive branch actions when a veto required approval by both houses as well as the president's signature. However, in 1982 the Reagan administration gave its blessings to a regulatory reform bill approved by the Senate that contained a two-house veto provision without a presidential sign-off clause. The veto applied to all federal agencies except the Defense Department and the Internal Revenue Service and to all but a few types of regulation.

Pros and Cons of Veto Power

Proponents of the legislative veto said lawmakers should be able to block "bad" regulations. As the number of vetoes attached piecemeal to bills increased, the need for a uniform approach to reviewing all agency regulation also increased, they said.

Backers of the legislative veto argued that Congress must have the authority to overturn federal rules to keep overzealous regulators in check. They contended that the federal bureaucracy had become so isolated from the public as to be immune from normal political pressures. Supporters thus viewed the congressional veto as one of the few avenues left open to keep the government attuned to public sensitivities. They said that the veto would help rectify existing inadequacies in the oversight process by providing Congress with a clear-cut, rapid means of disapproving (or approving) a proposed regulation. Moreover, the threat of a legislative veto might make agencies more responsive to congressional sentiments, according to their view.

"The legislative veto will make certain that the people who are elected make the laws — not unelected bureaucrats who are obviously not accountable," explained Elliott H. Levitas, D-Ga., the chief House champion of the veto. Levitas introduced legislation in 1979, 1980 and again in 1981 that would give either house 60 days to pass a resolution disapproving an agency rule. Once invoked, the veto would become effective unless the other chamber acted within 30 days to block it.

To its opponents, the legislative veto was an unconstitutional encroachment on the authority of the executive branch. Moreover, they argued that the mechanism would result in additional delays in the regulatory process and that the 60-day waiting period would cause uncertainties for those within both the affected agency and the regulated industries. Congressional review of all federal rules would place an impossible burden on committees which would be forced to review some 10,000 regulations generated annually by federal agencies. And Congress already had ways to let agencies know when it felt a regulation did not reflect the congressional intent of the law, they said.

Levitas brushed aside arguments holding that legislative vetoes violated the separation of powers doctrine. "Regulation writers have the power to regulate only to the extent Congress delegates" that authority to them, Levitas said. Congress "can put any restraints [on rulemakers] we want," he added.

Levitas also dismissed the notion that Congress would be overburdened if it were forced to review all regulations. "Congress has the responsibility to supervise the law-making process," he said, adding that "any congressman who doesn't have time should not be in Congress."

Authorizations and Appropriations

Seven of the 13 major regulatory agencies have permanent authorizations. They are:

- Civil Aeronautics Board (scheduled to go out of existence in 1985),
- Equal Employment Opportunity Commission,
- Federal Deposit Insurance Corporation,
- Federal Energy Regulatory Commission,
- Federal Reserve,
- Interstate Commerce Commission,
- National Labor Relations Board.

The other six are re-authorized periodically by Congress. They are:

- Commodity Futures Trading Commission,
- Consumer Product Safety Commission,
- Federal Communications Commission,
- Federal Trade Commission,
- Nuclear Regulatory Commission,
- Securities and Exchange Commission.

Eleven of the 13 are subject to the annual appropriations process. The Federal Reserve and Federal Deposit Insurance Corporation are funded entirely through member fees. Three of the agencies — the Commodity Futures Trading Commission, Consumer Product Safety Commission and Interstate Commerce Commission — must submit their budget proposals concurrently to the Congress and the Office of Management and Budget (OMB). The remaining nine submit their requests to OMB, which may amend the requests before forwarding them to Congress.

But veto foes said unilateral congressional review of rules was unconstitutional. "We are invading executive functions," former Rep. George E. Danielson, D-Calif., said. "The Constitution provides that any bill ... must be submitted to the president before it can become valid." Moreover, said Danielson, "there is no way on earth [Congress] could handle the burden" of overseeing the thousands of regulations issued each year. "With our workload, we're scarcely able to function now," he added.

"Congress should not give itself broad, generalized veto power over the agencies' day-to-day rulemaking," concluded an editorial in the April 12, 1982, *Business Week*. "Congress is, if anything, less competent than the regulators to determine which rules make sense and which do not. A new veto power would simply open the doors to swarms of lobbyists arguing for and against all sorts of rules. Such a veto would make the staff experts on all sorts of congressional subcommittees de facto industry regulators. Finally, it would raise separation of power issues between the executive and legislative branches and could lead to endless court challenges."

The argument that the veto would invite industry lobbying surfaced during debate on a FTC proposal that would require used-car dealers to inform buyers of major known defects in autos. The used-car rule was the first to be reviewed under the 1980 FTC authorization veto provision. Dealers had urged Congress to reject the rule, contending that it would require expensive inspections to protect them from possible litigation, thereby adding to the cars' cost. FTC officials maintained the expense involved was minimal — about 18 cents for printing a disclosure sticker, plus the cost of filling it out.

Congress blocked the rule May 26, 1982, when the House voted 286-133 to approve a resolution of disapproval on the last day allowed by the law. The Senate had agreed to the same resolution May 18. During debate on the measure, Senate Commerce Committee Chairman Bob Packwood, R-Ore., and others argued that the possibility of a legislative veto encouraged special interests to lobby against resolutions they did not like, while the general public was not organized and was unable to counter the pressure.

"Even without the legislative veto, committees are already reviewing proposed regulations and using the regular legislative process either to delay the effective date of a rule or to prevent its implementation," wrote Fisher. He cited as an example 1978 legislation requiring the Department of Housing and Urban Development to submit a list of proposed rules to the banking committees of each chamber for review before publishing a regulation for notice and comment in *The Federal Register*. Once a regulation is published, either committee can delay the effective date for 90 calendar days by reporting out a joint resolution opposing or modifying the rule. "Use of a joint resolution does not constitute a legislative veto, since it is presented to the president, but the process demonstrates an ability and willingness on the part of congressional committees to evaluate proposed regulations," Fisher wrote.

Court Rulings

With so many constitutional questions raised by opponents of the veto, it was only a matter of time before the courts were asked to intervene. In October 1981 the Supreme Court agreed to decide whether a single house of Congress, could use a veto to nullify executive branch regulations.

The case before the court, *Immigration and Naturalization Service (INS) v. Chadha, U.S. House of Representatives v. Chadha, U.S. Senate v. Chadha,* arose after the House in 1975 vetoed an INS decision not to deport Jagdish Rai Chadha, a Kenyan student who had overstayed his visa. The House had acted under a provision of the 1952 Immigration and Nationality Act giving either chamber the power to veto an INS decision blocking an individual's deportation.

After he was ordered deported in 1976, Chadha appealed, challenging the constitutionality of the one-house veto. In December 1980 the 9th U.S. Circuit Court of Appeals struck down the provision and canceled Chadha's deportation. The court said the one-house veto conflicted with both the separation of powers doctrine and the constitutional requirement that both houses must act on legislation, in effect ruling that the veto was an unconstitutional

intrusion by Congress into the domain of the executive branch and the courts.

In a separate and considerably broader case, a three-judge panel of the U.S. Court of Appeals for the District of Columbia ruled on Jan. 29, 1982, that the legislative veto "contravenes the constitutional procedures for making law."

That ruling came on an appeal brought by consumer groups challenging a 1980 House veto of Federal Energy Regulatory Commission (FERC) natural gas pricing regulations. The veto was exercised under a provision of the Natural Gas Policy Act of 1978. In its opinion the appeals court said: "In effect, Congress is able to expand its role from one of oversight, with an eye to legislative revision, to one of shared administration. This overall increase in congressional power contravenes the fundamental purpose of the separation of powers doctrine. Congress gains the ability to direct unilaterally, and indeed unicamerally, the exercise of agency discretion in a specific manner considered undesirable or unachievable when the enabling statute was first passed."

If Congress decides it has given an agency too much power, the court continued, "it may by statute take it back or may in the future enact more specific delegations." The court acknowledged the ramifications of its ruling: "We are aware that our decision today may have far-reaching effects on the operation of the national government. Yet this cannot deter us from finding the one-house veto unconstitutional." The decision was expected to be considered by the Supreme Court, but not before a decision was handed down on the immigration case.

Sunset Proposals

Proposals to enhance congressional oversight through periodic review and reauthorization of federal agencies and programs enjoyed brief popularity in the late 1970s. Under various "sunset" plans, time limits would be placed on a program's existence; if, after a certain period, Congress found no justification for continuation, the program would be terminated.

The sunset mechanism has rarely been used. A 1976 study by the Congressional Research Service found that of the 235 agencies, boards and commissions created between 1960 and 1973, only 14 were created for a limited period of time. None of those 14 was a regulatory agency.

Advocates of sunset legislation argued that periodic review of agency statutes would require Congress to evaluate the need for and performance of the programs and eliminate wasteful expenditures. In addition, the threat of termination could pressure agencies to become more accountable to the legislative branch.

"A sunset law may be of particular value to regulatory agencies," observed the Senate Governmental Affairs Committee of its 1977 study on federal regulation. "The success of regulatory agencies depends largely on obtaining political guidance and support for their actions. . . . By requiring periodic renewal of agency statutory mandates, Congress will not only be forced to substantively evaluate the agencies, but those agencies that survive may benefit by a transfusion of political good will."

However, writing in the fall 1977 issue of *The Public Interest*, Robert D. Behm of Duke University's Institute for Policy Sciences delineated several problems with the

Court Limits President's Removal Power

"From a practical point of view the only way in which Congress can make the regulatory commissions independent is by limiting the discretionary power of the President to remove their members from office," wrote Robert E. Cushman in his study of the independent regulatory commissions. "If he can remove them at pleasure, he can control them; if he cannot remove them, he cannot control them."

After nearly 140 years of controversy over whether the president had the right unilaterally to remove government officials, the Supreme Court met the issue head on in 1926. The case involved a postmaster who had been removed from office by President Woodrow Wilson in 1920, without consultation with the Senate despite a 1876 law that stipulated: "Postmasters of the first, second and third classes shall be appointed and may be removed by the president, by and with the advice and consent of the Senate, and shall hold their offices for four years, unless sooner removed or suspended according to law."

In a 6-3 decision, the court upheld the president's unrestricted power of removal as inherent in the executive power invested in the office by the Constitution. "The provision of the law of 1876, by which the unrestricted power of removal of first-class postmasters is denied to the president, is in violation of the Constitution and invalid," the court concluded in *Myers v. United States.*

The FTC Commissioner

Nine years later, a unanimous court substantially modified that position. The 1935 case involved a federal trade commissioner, William E. Humphrey, whom President Franklin D. Roosevelt had tried to remove because, he told the commissioner, "I do not feel that your mind and my mind go along together on either the policies or the administration" of the Federal Trade Commission (FTC). The act setting up the FTC specifically prohibited the president from removing FTC members except for causes outlined in the act; political difference was not one of them.

In *Humphrey's Executor v. United States,* the court held that the FTC was "an administrative body created by Congress to carry into effect legislative policies" and thus could not "in any proper sense be characterized as an arm or an eye of the executive." The court continued: "Whether the power of the president to remove an officer shall prevail over the authority of Congress to condition the power by fixing a definite term and precluding a removal except for cause will depend upon the character of the office; the Myers decision, affirming the power of the president alone to make the removal, is confined to purely executive officers, and as to officers of the kind here

under consideration we hold that no removal can be made during the prescribed term for which the officer is appointed, except for one or more of the causes named in the applicable statute."

In ruling that Roosevelt had exceeded his authority in removing the commissioner, the court indicated that except for officials immediately responsible to the president and those exercising non-discretionary or ministerial functions, Congress could apply such limitations on removal as it saw fit.

The War Commissioner

In a 1958 decision in the case of *Wiener v. United States* the court built on its 1935 decision. The Wiener case involved the refusal of a member of the War Claims Commission appointed by President Harry S Truman to resign when the Eisenhower administration came to power.

Congress created the commission with "jurisdiction to receive and adjudicate according to law" certain damage claims resulting from World War II. The law made no provision for removal of commissioners.

Eisenhower removed Wiener, and the commission member sought his pay in court. The Supreme Court agreed with him. It noted the similarity between the *Weiner* and the *Humphrey's* cases: in both situations, presidents had removed persons from quasi-judicial agencies without showing cause for the sole purpose of naming persons of their own choosing. The court said it understood the *Humphrey's* decision to "draw a sharp line of cleavage between officials who were part of the executive establishment and were thus removable by virtue of the president's constitutional powers, and those who are members of a body 'to exercise its judgment without the leave or hindrance of any other official or any department of the government, . . . as to whom a power of removal exists only if Congress may fairly be said to have conferred it. This sharp differentiation derives from the difference in functions between those whose tasks require absolute freedom from executive interference." The court also noted the "intrinsic judicial character" of the commission.

As a result of these three cases, the rule has developed that a president can remove a member of a quasi-judicial agency only for cause, even if Congress has not so provided. Nonetheless, "we still lack a satisfactory theory on the removal power as applied to the independent commissions," wrote Louis Fisher in *The Politics of Shared Power.* "What we have is largely . . . a 'field of doubt' that occupies the territory between *Myers* (for executive officers) and the independent commissions covered by *Humphrey's.*" However, Fisher noted that presidents still are able to put pressure on commissioners to resign.

sunset concept. Besides being expensive, an effective evaluation would severely increase committee workloads. Moreover, Behm said, sunset laws, regardless of their other merits, could not be expected to change the tendency of members of Congress to bargain for support of their pet programs by agreeing to support those of their colleagues.

In remarks during June 1979 hearings on sunset legislation before the Senate Governmental Affairs Committee, Rep. James Blanchard, D-Mich., sponsor of a sunset bill in the House, said: "I think we would all agree that the present system has become burdensome and unmanageable.... Agencies have overlapping mandates; there has been little analysis of the costs and benefits, or the cumulative impact of regulations; and paper work requirements have mushroomed.

"It is no longer tolerable to allow this system to continue with no review. The question is whether we will turn to reviewing federal regulations one rule at a time, or establish a framework for a rational comprehensive review."

In contrast, Securities and Exchange Commission member Philip Loomis testified at the same hearings against the proposed legislation. Sunset provisions, he said, "are presumably designed to force the Congress and the executive to act promptly. But if for whatever reason this is not done, the consequences would be indiscriminately to destroy agencies and programs which happened to be next on the list when Congress became preoccupied with other matters...."

In 1978 the Senate overwhelmingly passed a sunset bill that established a 10-year reauthorization cycle for most federal programs. But the House never acted and the bill died. In 1980 the Senate Rules Committee voted to recommend a substitute measure that vitiated most of the strength of the 1978 proposal. But by then enthusiasm for the concept had faded and the bill never even reached the Senate floor. One reason for the loss of interest was that committee and subcommittee chairmen themselves had become increasingly concerned about the addition to the congressional workload that would be imposed by the bill. At the outset of hearings, Rules Chairman Claiborne Pell, D-R.I., warned against any measure that bound Congress to an inflexible review process at taxpayer expense without offering substantial promise of regulatory improvement.

ACCOUNTABILITY AND PRESIDENTIAL PRESSURES

"The notion of accountability to elected officials extends as well to the president, the only nationally elected politician," noted the Senate Governmental Affairs Committee in its 1977 report on regulation. "Efforts to improve congressional oversight do not diminish the president's responsibility for directing and controlling the bureaucracy. Increasing congressional control over the regulatory agencies should not diminish the effectiveness of the president, nor should increased presidential control alarm Congress."

Presidents have sought to exert control over the independent commissions almost from their beginning. In 1908 President Theodore Roosevelt urged that all independent commissions be placed in the executive branch under the immediate supervision of a Cabinet secretary. "It is unwise from every standpoint and results only in mischief to have any executive work done save by executive bodies, under the control of the president," he wrote.

A task force appointed nearly 30 years later by Franklin Roosevelt amplified that view "The President is held responsible for the wise and efficient management of the Executive Branch of the Government. The people look to him for leadership. And yet we whittle away the effective control essential to that leadership by parcelling out to a dozen or more irresponsible agencies important powers of policy and administration," the task force wrote in 1937.

In 1949 the Hoover Commission recommended that the "purely executive functions of quasi-legislative and quasi-judicial agencies" be brought within the regular executive departments. In 1971 the Ash Council, a task force set up by President Richard Nixon, proposed that rulemaking functions of the independent commissions be placed directly under the president. *(Details, p. 61)*

These proposals were ignored by Congress whose members consistently had sought to insulate the independent agencies from executive branch pressures. At the same time, Congress had to acknowledge some degree of presidential control; under the Constitution only the president may nominate federal officials.

Executive Controls

Appointments are a powerful means by which a president exerts influence over commissions and executive branch agencies. By choosing men and women who share his own political philosophy, a president may influence the course of federal regulation for years after he leaves office. Franklin Roosevelt had unprecedented opportunity to shape the federal bureaucracy. Five independent commissions and several more executive branch regulatory agencies were created during his tenure in office. He appointed members to all of them.

Likewise, the impact of Nixon's appointments to the regulatory agencies was felt for many years after the Watergate crisis forced him to resign the presidency on Aug. 9, 1974. Nixon appointees (or persons named by previous presidents whom he reappointed) dominated the 12 regulatory agencies then in existence. By the day of his resignation, Nixon had nominated every member of seven regulatory agencies.

Carter's appointments of Alfred Kahn to head the Civil Aeronautics Board (CAB) and Darius Gaskins to chair the ICC had a profound impact on the transportation industry, the principal area of Carter's deregulation drive. Both men were staunch advocates of decontrol. *(Transportation deregulation, p. 89; Carter appointments, p. 64)*

As of 1982, Reagan seemed to be making extensive use of the appointments process to cement his general philosophy and outlook about reining in regulation. Many of his appointments shared his aversion to regulation. Paradoxically, others, such as Reese Taylor of the ICC, were criticized for appearing to slow the pace of deregulation. *(Reagan appointments, p. 70)*

Heads of executive branch regulatory agencies serve at the pleasure of the president and this power of removal is another tool he can use to control executive branch actions.

The president is free to fire an agency head who disagrees with presidential policy. New presidents routinely replace regulatory agency heads with persons of their own choosing. The power to remove members of the independent commissions might have been equally forceful, but that authority was sharply limited by Supreme Court decisions that, in effect, allow removal of independent commissioners only for cause. *(Details, box, p. 56)*

Budget Proposals

Like Congress, one of the most important controls the president has over the regulatory agencies is budgetary. It is the president, and not the regulatory agency, who decides how much money to request from Congress and for what purposes. In this way the president can cut back regulatory efforts he disapproves and give a boost to those he favors. Although it is one of its main tools of oversight, Congress only infrequently changes significantly a presidential budget request for the regulatory agencies. One of the main weapons Reagan has used in his battle to cut the size and influence of the regulatory bureaucracy was the budget-cutting ax. *(Reagan budget cuts, p. 68)*

Since 1921 when the Budget and Accounting Act was passed, the president has had authority to review and revise budget estimates for all executive branch agencies before they were submitted to Congress. In 1939 that authority was extended to the independent regulatory commission.

Congress did not object to this executive control over the independent commissions' budgets until President Nixon created the Office of Management and Budget in 1970. Built around the nucleus of the old Budget Bureau, OMB was given new authority to coordinate the executive branch budget requests and legislative proposals. Unlike its predecessor, which had retained an image of neutrality, OMB was quickly identified as the president's agency, a tool the president could use to help push his budget and legislative proposals through Congress. The lawmakers were quick to challenge this new assertion of control as it applied to the independent commissions.

"The present budgetary procedure provides a dangerous potential for restraining the operational effectiveness of the major regulatory commissions," Sen. Lee Metcalf declared at 1972 hearings. "There is no more effective way of thwarting policy, as established by Congress, than through the budgetary process. As long as the regulatory agencies are under the thumb of the OMB, they will be reluctant to, or foreclosed from, asking for what they really need in money and manpower."

Presidents and their OMB directors disagreed, arguing that OMB review of independent commission budgets was necessary to a coordinated, well-balanced budget. "The budgets of individual agencies — including the independent regulatory commissions — have important relationships with those of other agencies and programs of the government," Bert Lance, Carter's OMB director, wrote to Metcalf in 1977. "Such relationships cannot be seen or evaluated until the entire budget picture is revealed when the president sends his budget message to Congress. Premature disclosure of individual agency requests could force the Congress to conduct a narrowly focused, disjointed consideration of such requests."

Statistics compiled by the Senate Governmental Affairs Committee showed that OMB consistently reduced requests for funding submitted by the regulatory agencies. Once the reduced request has been submitted to Congress, OMB insisted that the agency support the request.

Congress countered by authorizing some of the independent agencies to submit their proposed budgets to both Congress and OMB. When it created the Consumer Product Safety Commission in 1972 and the Commodity Futures Trading Commission in 1974, Congress required that the agencies submit their budget requests simultaneously to OMB and Congress.

Justice Department Supervision

Just as OMB has authority to review independent commission budgets and legislative requests, the Justice Department is empowered to act as attorney for the commissions. Most independent commissions are allowed to participate in judicial review of agency actions. But only a few can sue for enforcement on their own initiative without consulting with the Justice Department, and only one — the FTC — is allowed by statute to control and argue cases before the Supreme Court.

The Justice Department has consistently advocated a continuation of its coordination of litigation on the grounds that the department has greater legal expertise and is in a better position to assess a case in terms of the general welfare and overall government policy.

The regulatory agencies have argued just as vigorously that because they have the responsibility to implement policy, they should also have the authority to control their own cases. Supervision by the Justice Department undermines their independence and effectiveness, commissions argue.

It seemed unlikely that the situation would change in the near future. A Senate effort to give several of the agencies more authority to conduct their own litigation foundered in 1977.

Presidential Intervention

In addition to the appointments and budget powers, presidents are also free to issue directives and statements to the agencies telling them what to do. Although agencies are not required to comply with such orders, the president can often invoke public opinion to obtain the desired result.

"Such presidential directions must, of course, be kept at a safe distance from a commission's quasi-judicial work," noted Robert Cushman in his study of the independent regulatory commissions. "They should be kept clearly within the field of the broad policies which directly impinge on the realm of presidential duty. Public opinion would be likely to support an independent commission if it refused to comply with an objectionable or inappropriate order or instruction by the president. Since the president must depend upon public opinion to persuade the commission to comply with his orders or directions, the whole arrangement seems to carry with it its own protection against abuse."

The question of presidential direction or intervention is perhaps more pertinent when applied to the regulatory agencies within the executive branch. By the mid-1970s, Congress had given dozens of agencies *inside* the executive branch authority to issue regulations on a wide range of subjects — food safety to air quality, strip mining to export controls.

In some cases, such as the EPA, the administrator reports directly to the president. In other instances, such as the Occupational Safety and Health Administration, the administrator is responsible to the secretary of the department where the agency is lodged. The question has arisen whether these agencies are free to use their regulatory powers on their own or whether they are subject to presidential directives.

One school of thought holds that the president's power to appoint and dismiss Cabinet officers carries an implicit authority to direct actions by regulatory agencies within the executive departments. It is therefore inconceivable that the White House should be an outsider, or an adversary, in rulemaking procedures. Because the president is held accountable for his subordinates' actions, he should have some control over those actions.

An opposing school contends that these executive branch regulatory agencies are required by their authorizing laws to carry out their functions without being subject to presidential control. In promulgating their rules, they may accept White House advice but, ultimately, they are as independent as are the separate regulatory commissions.

The conflict between these two theories was brought into focus by a case involving OSHA, which in 1978 proposed a standard governing the permissible level of cotton dust in textile mills, where excessive levels had led to the occupational disease called "brown lung." The textile industry challenged the proposed levels because compliance would require costly new equipment which they said was of dubious technical feasibility. President Jimmy Carter's chairman of the Council of Economic Advisers Charles Schultze was also concerned that the measures would be inflationary. Schultze wrote to Labor Secretary F. Ray Marshall asking that the standards be modified. Marshall objected and the president himself reportedly intervened, calling a meeting of the two officials during which a compromise was reached that scaled down the cost and extended the deadline for promulgating the new regulations. Textile workers' unions opposed the compromise and appealed the cotton dust standards on numerous grounds, one of which was that the president's intervention was illegal because the OSHA statute vested the power to issue the regulation with the secretary of labor and the president could not lawfully instruct the secretary how to exercise his discretion. The courts, however, resolved the issue without addressing the question of presidential intervention.

Expressing his view about the propriety of presidential intervention, Lloyd Cutler, counsel to President Carter and himself an expert in regulatory agencies, wrote: "[T]he president does indeed possess the ultimate constitutional power over the content and the timing of regulations issued by executive branch agencies, so long as the action taken is within the agency's statutory authority. As a matter of political theory and policy, the president ought to assert such power whenever he deems it necessary to make an important balancing choice among conflicting and competing national goals. . . .

"The president is the elected official most capable of making the needed balancing decisions as critical regulatory issues arise within his own executive branch, while the most appropriate and effective role for Congress is to review and, where necessary, curb particular presidential interventions."

Presidential Review

In an attempt to gain control over the regulatory process and increase top-level coordination, Carter established the Regulatory Analysis Review Group (RARG) in January 1978. Composed of top administration economists, the group was to review 10 to 20 executive branch regulations a year for their potential to worsen inflation.

Creation of the review group did not go unchallenged. In February 1979 hearings before the Senate Public Works Committee, Sen. Edmund S. Muskie, D-Maine, charged that the White House had overstepped its authority. He accused the review group of "shadow rulemakings" and added that the procedures it used were illegal.

However, the American Bar Association (ABA) House of Delegates at its August 1979 meeting supported presidential efforts to coordinate actions of regulatory agencies, including independent commissions, with overall government policy goals. The resolution, purely advisory, was the result of a three-year study by the ABA's Commission on Law and Society, which found that the president was in a better position than bureaucrats to make "the needed balancing" decisions as major regulatory issues arose.

The debate on the legality of RARG was put to rest when President Reagan abolished the group in 1981, replacing it with an even more elaborate review procedure. In an executive order issued Feb. 17, 1981, Reagan gave OMB authority to require agencies to conduct economic analyses for any rule OMB considered "major" and to submit those analyses to OMB for review before publishing the rule. *(Text, p. 173)*

OMB's new authority, substantially broader than that vested in Carter's RARG, drew criticism on a number of fronts. Some opponents charged that the executive order circumvented the 1946 Administrative Procedure Act, which vested rulemaking authority within agencies and required that rules be based on the public record. They said that under the executive order, OMB actions could be influenced by behind-the-scenes industry lobbying and that a rule could be quietly killed before it was made public.

As evidence of special interest influence, critics pointed to a list OMB submitted to the House Oversight and Investigations Subcommittee in April 1981. Of 36 meetings OMB officials held with industry and consumer groups over a two-month period, all but four were with representatives from major industries and industry lobbying groups. The list did not include telephone conversations.

The executive order "has opened the way for unprecedented interference by special interests in the federal regulatory process and created the potential for corruption," charged the Alliance for Justice, a group of public interest lobbyists and lawyers, in an October 1981 report.

"The critical question," said Rep. Albert Gore Jr., D-Tenn., "is who makes the decision on the substance of a regulation? Is it made in the agency, where procedural safeguards are present, or is it made in OMB outside those procedural safeguards?"

Reorganization Authority

One vehicle for achieving control over regulatory agencies involves the president's reorganization authority provided by the Reorganization Act of 1949 and its extensions. This law permitted the president, subject to congressional veto, to make a wide variety of organizational changes. The process involved presidential submission to Congress of "reorganization plans," which took effect automatically in 60 days unless Congress specifically disapproved them. From 1949 to 1957 these plans could be blocked only by vote of a majority of the full membership of the Senate or House (a so-called constitutional majority), but in later years the law was changed to make congressional veto easier — only a simple majority vote of those present and voting in either chamber was required to kill a plan. Among the major agencies created by reorganization plans were the OMB and the EPA, both established in 1970.

Congress on occasion has disapproved proposed reorganization plans concerning regulatory agencies, generally on grounds they were attempted "power grabs" by the executive. This charge was made in 1961 after President John F. Kennedy submitted a number of reorganization plans to Congress that affected federal regulatory agencies. Both Congress and the president agreed on the need for reforms in the agencies. Nonetheless, Congress rejected three of the seven proposed plans. Members claimed that the administration planned to establish a "direct chain of political command" over the independent agencies.

Congress did not revive the president's reorganization authority when it expired in April 1973. President Carter successfully sought reinstatement of the authority in 1977, and during his four years in office submitted 11 reorganization plans. All but one, to create a Department of Natural Resources, were approved.

Two of Carter's plans affected regulatory agencies. The first consolidated most fair employment enforcement programs, previously scattered through several agencies, in the Equal Employment Opportunity Commission (EEOC). The second gave more authority to the chairman of the Nuclear Regulatory Commission, making clear that he was the principal executive officer and spokesman for the commission.

Executive Orders

Another vehicle for extending presidential control over agencies is change by executive order. During World War II, Roosevelt even created a number of agencies by that method.

Objecting to that use of the executive order, Congress enacted a law that prohibited appropriations for an agency established by executive order "if the Congress has not appropriated any money specifically for such agency or instrumentality or specifically authorized the expenditure of funds by it." Similar language has been contained in most subsequent appropriations bills.

Presidents more often used executive orders to review and coordinate the regulatory process. In September 1979, for example, President Carter issued Executive Order 12160 establishing a Consumer Affairs Council to provide leadership and coordination for government consumer programs. The council consisted of representatives of 12 Cabinet-level departments and 12 executive agencies.

As noted above, both Carter's establishment of the RARG and Reagan's designation of OMB as the chief regulatory oversight agency were accomplished by executive order. However, independent commissions were specifically exempted from the review. Reagan sought legislation that would extend general White House oversight to the independent commissions. *(Details, p. 67)*

Reforming Regulation

The rapid growth of government regulation has been accompanied by a surge of interest in reforming — or even doing away with — much of the regulatory apparatus. That interest was nowhere more evident than in the 1980 presidential race between Democratic incumbent Jimmy Carter and his successful Republican challenger, Ronald Reagan. Somewhat surprisingly, deregulation, generally considered a rather dull and politically uninspiring issue, emerged as a popular and prominent theme for both candidates. Carter pointed repeatedly to the deregulation measures passed during his presidency, while Reagan promised to mount a concerted attack on regulations across the board.

The "get-the-government-off-peoples'-backs" pitch was appealing, but there was no consensus on how the process should be changed and what should be regulated or deregulated.

Businessmen were disgruntled with what they considered unnecessary and costly aspects of federal regulations, particularly those aimed at cleaning up the environment, providing safer and healthier workplaces and protecting consumers from hazardous products. Industry spokesmen claimed that the costs of providing these protections interfered with capital formation and productivity and hurt the economy as a whole.

Consumer, labor and environmental groups, on the other hand, claimed that economic growth had not been stunted by such regulations and that relaxing them would be tantamount to turning back the clock. Some of these groups said that deregulation efforts should be geared toward those federal rules that protected some economic sectors from marketplace competition.

Despite these conflicting views concerning the merits of government-mandated controls, most of the people involved in regulation — and much of the American public — agree that something is wrong with the regulatory process, that it may be overloaded and that it may not be addressing the right priorities.

"People are fed up with regulations, but that begins to fall apart the minute you start asking about specific regulations," commented former Environmental Protection Agency Administrator Douglas M. Costle, in an interview in the Dec. 22, 1981, *National Journal.* "I don't see any support for the notion that the government should not be regulating to protect public health and safety. The more relevant question is whether we have selected the right tools of government policy to accomplish clean air or water."

Approaches to Reform

During the late 1970s and early 1980s regulatory reform proposals fell into three broad categories. One approach was designed to streamline the process and to review the justifications for existing and proposed rules. The idea that a rule should not be promulgated unless its benefits clearly outweighed its costs began to take hold.

Carter made this explicit by executive order. He required agencies to explain in detail why a proposed rule was needed, to estimate its impact on the economy by performing cost-benefit analyses and to outline alternative solutions. Reagan embraced the cost-benefit approach even more enthusiastically, and the concept was popular among members of Congress. *(Cost-benefit analysis, p. 25)*

A second approach emphasized making regulators more accountable to Congress, the courts and the executive branch. One of the most controversial proposals was the legislative veto that would allow one or both chambers of Congress to void proposed rules. Another proposal would give courts more power to review regulations. Still another would give the president increased controls over regulatory actions. For example, the Reagan administration, which had already taken steps to enlarge Office of Management and Budget (OMB) review powers over executive agencies, asked Congress to extend that review authority to independent regulatory commissions as well. The Senate in March 1982 approved legislation that contained these changes.

Proponents of a third approach argued that procedural reforms merely scratched the surface. What was needed, they said, was a broad-based attack on regulations themselves and on the statutes that gave agencies their rulemaking power. This argument surfaced during the prolonged controversy over renewal and revision of the Clean Air Act and reauthorization of several regulatory commissions.

Early Reform Efforts

The regulatory apparatus of the federal government has been the subject of numerous studies — in 1937, 1949, 1955, 1960, 1968, 1972 and 1977 — all of which found flaws in the system.

Most of the study groups commissioned by presidents to look into regulatory operations have recommended extending the president's influence over the independent agencies. For example, a committee appointed by President

Franklin D. Roosevelt in 1937 recommended placing the agencies within the executive branch, but Congress, concerned that such a move would give too much power to the president, rejected the proposal.

Congress did make one important change when Roosevelt was president. In 1939 the lawmakers amended the Budget and Accounting Act to authorize the budget office to review and revise the budgets for all executive offices and independent commissions before submitting them to Congress for approval. Previously the regulatory agencies submitted their budget requests directly to Congress.

Despite criticisms of the regulatory system, efforts since World War II to overhaul it have met with only mixed success. The Administrative Procedure Act of 1946 was designed to formalize the varied administrative procedures of government agencies and to set up uniform standards for judicial review. A major provision entitled any person suffering legal wrong because of agency action to seek judicial relief, provided he or she first exhausted administrative remedies. *(Text, p. 153)*

In 1947 Congress established a bipartisan commission, chaired by former President Herbert Hoover, to study the organization of the executive branch. Two years later the commission recommended that all regulatory agencies, including the independent commissions, be put under the jurisdiction of the Cabinet departments. Congress did not act on the recommendations.

Kennedy Proposals

One ambitious attempt to reshape the regulatory agencies took place shortly after John F. Kennedy became president in 1961. Kennedy had asked James M. Landis to study the agencies and submit proposals for improving them. Landis was a former Harvard Law School dean and one-time member of the Federal Trade Commission, Securities and Exchange Commission and Civil Aeronautics Board. His report noted the problems of delay, ethical conduct and quality of personnel and made 16 broad recommendations.

Among other things, the report called for extensive reorganization of most of the agencies; establishment of special offices in the White House to develop national transportation policy, telecommunications policy and energy resources policy; establishment by executive order of a federal employee code of ethics and limitation of off-the-record presentations in regulatory proceedings; and creation of a special office in the White House to oversee regulatory agencies.

Kennedy followed up Landis' report with a message to Congress in which he proposed that agency chairmen be given "broad managerial powers" to correct the existing, diffused authority of the commissions; that all agency chairmen serve in that capacity at the president's pleasure; and that a large proportion of agency responsibilities be delegated to inter-agency boards and hearing examiners to eliminate needless work on "unimportant details" at the top. Congress responded by reviving the Reorganization Act of 1949, which had expired two years earlier, so that the president could submit reorganization plans for the agencies.

Seven such plans were submitted, all of which had the basic aim of streamlining agency procedures. However, jealous of its authority over the agencies, Congress charged that the administration planned to establish a "direct chain of political command" over the independent agencies. It killed two of the plans, modified another and approved the other four.

Nixon, Ford Actions

Richard Nixon was equally interested in regulatory reform. In 1969 he established a President's Advisory Council on Executive Organization, chaired by Roy Ash, president of Litton Industries, to study and make recommendations on government organization. (Ash subsequently served as Nixon's director of the Office of Management and Budget.) In its 1971 report on regulatory commissions, the Ash council recommended several changes in the independent agencies, the most important of which was that they be headed by a single administrator appointed by and responsible to the president. The council envisaged a restructuring of agencies that would result in a type similar to the Environmental Protection Agency (EPA) established in 1970. Like earlier proposals Congress gave the idea scant attention.

On assuming the presidency, Gerald R. Ford declared revision of the regulatory apparatus a principal goal of his administration. Ford established a Domestic Council Review Group on Regulatory Reform that submitted a 72-page report in January 1977. Edward Schmults, who was deputy counsel to President Ford and chairman of the group, summarized the study as follows: "The report was not intended to be dogmatic or to give the view that we know the answers. It was intended to make people think and give the issues further study. There is an almost unlimited amount still to be done; someone will have to identify the areas where change will be helpful, put the data together, make the case for change and submit proposals."

Although his record in securing specific reforms of the regulatory statutes was limited, Ford succeeded in focusing attention at the highest levels on federal regulation and on its goals and achievements. It was the Ford administration that gave initial impetus to transportation deregulation, with proposals to decontrol the airline, trucking, rail and maritime industries.

Ford also sought to minimize the economic impact of regulation in general. In October 1974 he announced that he would require government agencies to assess the inflationary impact of their major proposed regulations and legislative recommendations. A month later, he established by executive order an Inflation Impact Statement (IIS) program that was to run through 1976 and apply to all executive branch agencies. At the end of 1976, Ford extended the program and changed its title to the more descriptively accurate Economic Impact Statement (EIS) program.

Congress and Regulatory Reform

Congress, for its part, studied and discussed the need for regulatory changes but was unable to pass any comprehensive reforms. A House subcommittee in 1976 released a study detailing the operations of nine agencies and recommending a restructuring of the system. In 1977-78 the Senate Governmental Affairs Committee (then named the Government Operations Committee) published a six-volume "Study on Federal Regulations," the most comprehensive study of federal regulation ever conducted by Congress. The study dealt with regulatory appointments, congressional oversight, undue delay, citizen participation, problems of organizational overlap and duplication, and substantive economic issues. The committee made numerous recommendations, some of which were put into effect in subsequent years.

In 1976 Congress enacted "sunshine" legislation requiring some 50 multi-membered federal agencies to open their meetings to the public (PL 94-409). Congress also toyed with various "sunset" proposals that would require periodic reauthorization of federal spending programs and timetables for review and renewal of regulatory agencies' mandates. And the House narrowly defeated a controversial proposal giving Congress the power to veto virtually every rule and regulation issued by federal agencies. *(Sunshine act, p. 162; sunset proposals, p. 55; legislative veto, p. 51)*

CARTER REFORM: A MIXED RECORD

President Carter took some executive actions to streamline the regulatory system and make it more cost-effective. But it was through the industry-by-industry approach that Carter scored his major successes in the area of regulatory reform, securing congressional passage of legislation deregulating the airline, trucking, rail and banking industries. Carter's other reform proposals, including legislation that would overhaul the entire regulatory system, met with less success.

At the same time that the Carter administration promoted deregulation of certain industries to improve competition, it promulgated dozens of rules and regulations providing new protections for consumers, workers and the environment. The administration launched a successful campaign to establish two new Cabinet departments, Energy and Education, to extend federal oversight into those areas. Both moves were criticized as unnecessarily adding to an already overblown bureaucracy. And during Carter's last days in office the administration issued more than 150 new regulations, many of them major.

Carter Executive Actions

Shortly after taking office in 1977 Carter asked that full consideration be given to the "economic cost of major government regulations, through a more effective analysis of their economic impact." In 1978 he took several executive actions to further that goal.

In January of that year he established a Regulatory Analysis Review Group (RARG) in an attempt to improve government cost-benefit analyses of existing regulations. The group included representatives of every Cabinet department, except State and Defense, and top officials in the OMB, the Council of Economic Advisers, the EPA and the White House Office of Science and Technology Policy. The RARG was to review 10 to 20 executive branch regulations each year for their potential inflationary impact. Only "significant" regulations, defined as having an annual economic impact in excess of $100 million, were subject to review.

The panel was praised as a first step toward increased presidential supervision of federal regulation and as an attempt to give more attention to cost-benefit analysis. But the group also was criticized because it reviewed only a small number of regulations and acted only after, and not before, they were put into effect.

In 1981, Reagan disbanded the group and turned over substantial regulatory oversight powers to the OMB, giving it authority to determine what regulations were "major" and to approve or disapprove proposed rules. *(Details of Reagan actions, p. 66)*

Agency Requirements

On March 23, 1978, Carter issued Executive Order 12044, which set criteria for agencies to follow in performing regulatory impact analyses. In addition to analyzing the expenditures the rules themselves would require, regulators in executive branch agencies were directed to give early consideration to several other factors. The analyses had to include "a succinct statement of the problem; a description of the major alternative ways of dealing with the problem that were considered by the agency; an analysis of the economic circumstances of each of these alternatives; and a detailed explanation of the reasons for choosing one alternative over the others." Agencies had to publish at least semiannually an agenda of significant regulations under development and review. The order did not extend to independent commissions. Nor did it require a strict cost-benefit analysis.

In September 1979 OMB issued a two-volume report on the regulatory performance of 58 agencies and departments in a first attempt to assess the effects of Carter's executive order. The report found that most agencies had difficulties foreseeing the effects of their actions and communicating in plain English. However, it said some progress had been made in streamlining regulatory processes. The results were mixed, OMB official Stanley Morris said when the report was released. "Once an agency has fought all the battles and cut all the deals to adopt a regulation in the first place, it's like poking a sleeping dog to get changes."

Critics of the order charged that it did not have enough "teeth" and needed to be revamped. In February 1981 President Reagan issued a new executive order that replaced Carter's with more stringent requirements for regulators.

Regulatory Council

In October 1978, Carter established a Regulatory Council composed of representatives from 18 executive branch agencies and 18 independent regulatory agencies and chaired by EPA Administrator Costle. The idea behind the council was to give the public, Congress, the president and the regulators themselves an overview of most of the major health, safety, environmental and economic regulatory actions being considered throughout the government.

In March 1979 the council issued its first calendar, a listing of 109 major rules under consideration by 20 agencies. The calendar, issued twice yearly, was designed to point out duplicative efforts and to describe the costs and benefits of the proposed actions. Each reporting agency summarized the principal regulations it was working on, the sectors of the population and industry affected, the alternative actions it could take, the statutory authority for the rule and the proposed timetable for promulgation. Of the proposals listed in the first calendar, 25 resulted in final rules by November 1979. Reagan abolished the council in March 1981 and phased out the calendar. The final edition was issued Jan. 13, 1982.

Reagan's first chairman of the Council of Economic Advisers, Murray Weidenbaum, suggested one of the reasons for terminating the council was that it had "become for the most part a protective association for the regulators (who constitute its entire membership). Its rhetoric and reports have served primarily to contain rather than to meet the pressures for reducing regulatory burdens."

An assessment in the March/April 1982 issue of *Regulation* magazine characterized the calendar as of marginal usefulness to private industry. By the time it appeared, many of the larger companies and interest groups already knew more about a listed regulation than the information was likely to provide. The article pointed out that the calendar was probably most helpful to agencies themselves to help them think through the effects of proposals. "If for the public the calendar was a catalog without prices, for the agencies it was an examination without grades," the article concluded.

Appointments and Procedures

Several of Carter's appointments to executive branch and independent regulatory posts reflected his interest in reducing the economic burden of regulations and in emphasizing a cost-benefit analysis approach. As chairman of both the Council of Economic Advisers and the Regulatory Analysis Review Group, Charles L. Schultze stressed the inflationary consequences of many proposed regulations and favored in some cases the use of taxation, rather than specific standard setting, as a cost-effective approach to compliance.

Alfred E. Kahn, who subsequently became the president's chief adviser on inflation, was appointed to head the Civil Aeronautics Board (CAB). Under Kahn the CAB gave the airlines more freedom to lower fares and expand charter flights. Kahn was a leading advocate of airline deregulation and helped push the bill through Congress. *(Details, transportation deregulation, p. 89)*

To chair the Federal Communications Commission Carter appointed Charles Ferris, who had been an aide to both Senate Majority Leader Mike Mansfield, D-Mont., and House Speaker Thomas P. O'Neill Jr., D-Mass., and general counsel for the Senate Democratic Policy Committee. Although Ferris had no specific experience with the communications industry he soon was arguing in favor of less protective regulation. Carter elevated another strong advocate of deregulation, Daniel O'Neal, to the chairmanship of the Interstate Commerce Commission.

Activists Appointed

Carter appointed a number of "activists" to head up major regulatory agencies involved with consumer protection and health and safety standards. FTC Chairman Michael Pertschuk was the former chief counsel for the Senate Commerce Committee where he was instrumental in developing the Consumer Product Safety Commission and laws strengthening the government's control of trade practices. Under Pertschuk, the FTC proposed bans on "unfair" (as opposed to "untrue") advertising, including restrictions on television advertising directed at children and automobile advertisements that encouraged more driving when gas supplies were short. At the same time, it lifted restrictions on advertising for a number of professions and products to provide consumers with more information in making their choices. Pertschuk's activism was a key factor in Congress' 1980 decision to impose restrictions on some of the FTC's operations. *(Details, p. 77)*

Joan Claybrook, named to head the National Highway Traffic Safety Administration (NHSTA), was formerly the director of Ralph Nader's public interest group Congress Watch. Claybrook long had advocated the mandatory installation of automatically inflating air bags in automobiles. It was during her tenure that the air bag rule, which the Ford administration had opposed, was formally proposed. Another activist appointed by Carter was Eula Bingham, director of the Occupational Safety and Health Administration (OSHA). Bingham, who was recommended by the AFl-CIO, once chaired the OSHA committee that developed controversial emission standards for coke ovens.

The president obtained a strongly consumer-oriented majority on the Consumer Product Safety Commission by reappointing its most activist commissioner, David Pittle, and adding Susan King and Edith Sloan, both of whom had backgrounds in public interest groups.

Reducing the Rules

Although some of Carter's agency heads wanted to expand some forms of regulation, many of them also took steps to streamline the internal operations of their agencies and to reduce regulations. In December 1977 Bingham announced that OSHA would abolish 1,100 of its more than 10,000 rules. Many of the abandoned regulations, such as the requirement that fire extinguishers in work places be hung precisely 39 inches above the floor, had been branded as nit-picking. During her tenure OSHA reduced by half the number of safety and health forms that employers had to fill out, virtually eliminating them for small businesses that employed 10 or fewer people. Inspections were concentrated on the industries with the worst safety records.

At the FTC, Pertschuk cited several examples of the agency's attempt to produce the most cost-effective method of regulation. These included extensive planning and budgeting processes through which key FTC personnel targeted areas that "promise the highest payoff for competition and consumers." The Food and Drug Administration moved to reduce the long delays before new drugs reached commercial markets. The Federal Communications Commission eliminated some barriers to entry into the telecommunications field. And the Interstate Commerce Commission took steps to speed up entry application proceedings for new trucking companies.

Other examples cited by Carter in his March 1979 reform message included the elimination of 300 pages of rules by the Department of Health, Education and Welfare and the cancellation of 145 rules by the FTC. The FCC rewrote in less complicated language its rules on citizens band broadcasting, and the Federal Aviation Administration reduced by more than two-thirds the hours small airlines had to spend filling out their forms. The EPA proposed procedures that would allow companies flexibility in meeting pollution standards.

Reforms of Major Industries

Carter's main regulatory effort, however, was to push for major overhauls in a number of industries, particularly

Lightening the Paperwork Load

Two years, 36 reports and 770 recommendations after it came into existence, the Federal Commission on Paperwork went out of business with a final report, issued October 3, 1977, urging a "less is more" approach to the problem of controlling government red tape.

The major thrust of the commission's findings was that government policy makers should take into account all costs of paperwork — including citizen frustration and administrative inefficiencies — as well as the substantial dollar cost. Private and public sectors spend more than $100 billion a year on paperwork — about $500 per citizen — the commission estimated. Information should be managed "as a resource, as we now manage money, personnel and property," it said.

The idea was a popular one. Three years later, in November 1980, Congress cleared the Paperwork Reduction Act (PL 96-511), probably the most significant of President Carter's government-wide regulatory reform initiatives to be signed into law. The statute was the first comprehensive mechanism for controlling paperwork since the Federal Reports Act of 1942, which directed agencies to obtain clearance from the Budget Bureau for any information form aimed at 10 or more respondents. The 1980 act took effect April 1, 1981, and $25.5 million was authorized for the Office of Management and Budget (OMB) to enforce it. *(Text, p. 167)*

Review System Created

The law attacked the paperwork problem by creating within the OMB a central Office of Information and Regulatory Affairs with authority to review all government requests for information from the public. The OMB director was instructed to make sure that the information requested was needed, that it was not available elsewhere and that it was collected in an efficient manner. The OMB was directed to design and operate a computerized Federal Information Locator System with a directory of information resources, data element dictionary and information referral service. The goal was to reduce the public paperwork burden by 25 percent three years after the legislation became effective.

The need for paperwork reduction was dramatized during hearings on the bill, when one attorney taped end-to-end the federal forms that had to be completed by anyone planning to start a small business. They stretched the length of the meeting hall. Classroom teachers complained that they had to spend, at a minimum, 26 working days of each year completing required paperwork. Local government officials, university presidents and community leaders estimated that 10 to 30 percent of federal grant money was wasted on paperwork.

A January 1981 OMB report said that Americans in 1981 would spend more than 1.2 billion hours filling out 5,000 different forms, averaging out to five and one-half hours per man, woman and child. If the work paid $10 an hour, the payroll would be more than $10 billion. The Internal Revenue Service accounted for about half of the burden, the Department of Transportation 20 percent and the Department of Agriculture 10 percent. It was expected that the new act would result in a 4 percent decline in paperwork in fiscal 1982.

In August 1982 the Reagan administration proudly claimed that that expectation had been exceeded. A White House fact sheet issued Aug. 4 said the administration had reduced the federal paperwork burden by 200 million hours during fiscal 1982 — a reduction of 13 percent from the paperwork in existence when President Reagan took office.

transportation. Proponents of deregulation scored a success in November 1977 when the president signed into law a bill (PL 95-163) removing most federal restrictions on airlines providing all-cargo service.

The next step was enactment of a measure decontrolling the airline passenger industry, legislation that had been advocated well before Carter took office. The 1978 law (PL 95-504), signed Nov. 24, 1978, phased out federal regulation of the commercial passenger airline industry and provided for the eventual abolition of the CAB. The act limited the CAB's authority to determine which airlines could fly which routes and the prices they could charge.

The administration then focused on surface carriers. First came deregulation of the trucking industry. Legislation (PL 96-296) enacted in 1980 lifted most anticompetitive, generally protective, controls. Regulated truck companies and the Teamsters union, which represents most truckers, wanted to preserve the regulations. They argued that excessive competition, unemployment and financial ruin for trucking companies would result if the bill became law. Backers of the bill maintained it would lower shipping costs for farmers, grocery stores and other users. It also would generate more business for some types of trucking companies, they predicted.

Enactment of the Staggers Rail Act (PL 96-448) followed on the heels of the trucking measure. Unlike trucking, rail deregulation had long been promoted by some, including railroad companies, as the key to saving an ailing industry from financial collapse. The railroad's problems stemmed from declining income, complex federal regulations, excessive trackage and management problems as well as competition from trucks. *(Details, p. 89)*

Banking Deregulation

The nation's financial industry was the second economic sector to be restructured during the Carter administration. The legislation (PL 96-221), which cleared Congress in 1980, removed many federal regulatory distinctions between commercial banks and savings and loan associations. The bill provided for phased deregulation of interest rates, less protection for certain privileged banking sectors, greater competition among the sectors and a more comprehensive national system of bank rules.

The sweeping bank deregulation measure also extended Federal Reserve Board power over the bank deposits that made up a large part of the nation's money supply. Treasury Secretary G. William Miller called the new law "the most important legislation dealing with banking and finance in nearly half a century."

The law's major innovations set the stage for broad changes in the nation's banking industry. Previously, banks provided most financing for business ventures and consumer purchases, while savings and loan associations specialized in home mortgage financing. However, the new law offered customers wider choices for earning larger returns on their savings and gave financial institutions more flexibility to compete for funds and adjust loan portfolios to inflation and wide interest-rate fluctuations. Since the mid-1960s, inability to make those adjustments occasionally had disrupted the flow of funds to housing, small business and other industries that depended on banks and thrift institutions for financing.

To ease those problems the bill permitted financial institutions to diversify the services they offered to attract deposits. The measure also set in motion a gradual lifting of the interest rate ceilings that prevented financial institutions from paying the going market rate on savings deposits. Finally, the measure dismantled federal regulations that had locked banks and thrift institutions into limited loan portfolios and kept them from competing effectively with high-yielding investment opportunities such as money market funds.

Despite the enactment of the legislation pressure continued into 1982 to decontrol the industry even further. The subject of an intense lobbying campaign was a bill that would allow mergers within the financial industry and relax some consumer protection rules. Commercial banks and savings and loan institutions were deeply divided on the issue. *(Details, p. 99)*

Other Attempts to Deregulate

Legislation to deregulate other sectors of the economy was not approved during Carter's administration. Bills were introduced in both chambers in 1979 to revise the 1934 Communications Act by loosening government controls in the industry.

However, strong opposition from the broadcast industry blocked action. Congress in 1979 also began a major review of federal food law, but no final action was taken before Carter left office.

In contrast to his efforts to deregulate major industries as a means to stem inflation, President Carter early in his administration proposed hospital cost regulation as the first objective in a drive to put the brakes on skyrocketing health care costs. But the legislation became mired in controversy and died at the end of the 96th Congress.

The bill would have provided for mandatory revenue controls beginning in 1980 if the industry as a whole failed during 1979 to hold revenues to a 9.7 percent rate of increase. However, approximately 57 percent of U.S. hospitals could have escaped the mandatory program under a variety of exceptions.

Substantively complex, the hospital cost control bill was difficult to sell. The benefits were relatively remote; moreover, many members of Congress were sympathetic to its target, hospitals. The bill also was hampered simply because it involved regulation at a time when members of Congress were quick to blame inflation and other economic ills on excessive government meddling in the private sector.

REAGAN PLEDGES AND PERFORMANCE

Armed with what he viewed as an election mandate Reagan began his attack on the regulatory maze as soon as he entered the White House. The new president concentrated on a series of executive actions that could be implemented more quickly than legislation. White House aides and congressional Republicans also were drafting bills to revamp basic agency laws, streamline the bureaucracy and make the executive actions part of permanent legislation.

All of Reagan's top economic advisers were on record as favoring deregulation. They included Vice President George Bush; Murray Weidenbaum, Reagan's first chairman of the Council of Economic Advisers (Weidenbaum resigned in 1982 and was succeeded by Harvard economics professor Martin Feldstein, who also had argued for a reduced government role in the economy); OMB Director David Stockman; James Miller, first the director of the Office of Information and Regulatory Affairs at OMB and subsequently FTC chairman; and Martin Anderson, Reagan's chief domestic policy adviser (Anderson resigned early in 1982 and had not been replaced as of September 1982).

Plans for the attack were developed before Reagan was inaugurated. Incoming OMB Director Stockman called for an "orchestrated series of unilateral administrative actions to defer, revise or rescind existing and pending regulations where clear legal authority exists."

"A dramatic substantial rescission of the regulatory burden is needed both for the short term cash flow relief it will provide to business firms and the long-term signals it will provide to corporate investment planners," he said in a November 1981 memo to the president-elect. "All told, there are easily in excess of $100 billion in new environmental, safety and energy compliance costs scheduled for the early 1980s."

Reagan's Executive Actions

Two days after he was sworn in as the nation's 40th president, Reagan Jan. 22, 1981, announced the creation of a Presidential Task Force on Regulatory Relief, chaired by Vice President Bush. The other members were Treasury Secretary Donald T. Regan, Attorney General William French Smith, Commerce Secretary Malcolm Baldrige, Labor Secretary Raymond J. Donovan, Stockman,

Weidenbaum and Anderson. Miller was the first executive director of the task force; when he moved to the FTC Miller was succeeded by Christopher C. DeMuth.

Reagan directed the panel to review major regulatory proposals by executive branch agencies; assess executive branch regulations already on the books; oversee the development of legislative proposals; and make recommendations on regulatory personnel and how to reform regulation through executive orders, agency actions and legislative changes.

Bush said the task force would be guided by three general principles:

- ● "Federal regulations should be initiated only when there is a compelling need."
- ● "Alternative regulatory approaches (including no regulation) should be considered and the approach selected that imposes the least possible burden on society consistent with achieving the over-all statutory and policy objectives."
- ● "Regulatory priorities should be governed by an assessment of the benefits and costs of the proposed regulations."

Weidenbaum said he expected the panel to be effective because it did not "have any interest group constituency to protect and defend. Its only constituency is the president and the president's program for rationalizing regulation."

"In other words," added Miller, "the very existence of the task force can stiffen the back of an agency head who's being pressured by a constituent. He or she can say: 'I'd like to do it for you, but there's no chance the task force members would go along — and they'd be right. The president set the principles and I've got to follow them.' "

OMB Powers Widened

Another early move to assert greater White House control over regulation came on Feb. 17, 1981. On that day, Reagan imposed strict new rules on Cabinet and agency regulators and gave OMB extensive powers over the regulatory apparatus. Executive Order 12291, which replaced Carter's Executive Order 12044, required executive agencies to prepare a regulatory impact analysis for all new and existing major regulations.

Subject to direction from the presidential task force, the OMB Office of Information and Regulatory Affairs was authorized to issue criteria for deciding when a regulation was "major" and could order an agency to perform an economic analysis for any rule. Regulatory analyses would have to be submitted to OMB for review 60 days prior to publication in the *Federal Register*. However, OMB was empowered to waive a regulatory impact analysis for any rule. Agencies had to apply cost-benefit analyses to all rulemaking and adopt the least costly alternative. Twice a year, they would have to publish a regulatory agenda of rules under consideration.

OMB was given authority to identify duplication, overlap and conflict in rules, which agencies then were required to rectify; develop procedures for cost-benefit analysis; recommend changes in laws authorizing regulatory activity; monitor compliance with the executive order; and schedule existing rules for agency review. The guidelines for preparing regulatory impact analyses noted that a dollar estimate of all regulatory effects was not required in an analysis but that all effects should at least be identified and, where possible, quantified.

The order applied only to regulatory agencies in the executive branch, but Reagan asked Congress to pass legislation applying it to the independent regulatory commissions. The Senate approved such an extension in March 1982 but the full House had not acted by the end of September.

Contrast With RARG

Reagan gave OMB much broader authority than that vested in Carter's Regulatory Analysis Review Group, which Reagan disbanded. The RARG studied only about 10 regulations a year and issued reports only after the proposals had been published in the *Federal Register*. Compliance with its recommendations was not mandatory.

Under Reagan's procedures, OMB reviewed regulations before they were published. The agency would have to delay action until the review was completed. The burden of proof that a regulation was needed, that the benefits outweighed the costs and that alternatives had been studied rested on the agency. A dispute between an agency and the OMB would be forwarded to the regulatory relief task force for resolution. The OMB was to monitor agencies' compliance with the order and report to the president. However, OMB was not given absolute veto power over agency decisions. According to C. Boyden Gray, counsel to Vice President Bush, OMB "could tell agencies to redo the analysis," which might cause some delays. "But they couldn't hold something off to displace the agency's decision-making authority," he said.

During 1981 OMB reviewed a total of 2,803 regulations proposed by federal agencies. Eighty-seven percent were found consistent with the economic principles outlined in Reagan's executive order, and the other 13 percent were revised, returned, or withdrawn during review. In the first seven months of 1982, OMB reviewed a total of 1,506 regulations, with the same percentage found in compliance with the executive order.

The executive order established the machinery "to make things happen," said Bush when he announced formation of the task force in February 1981. "There has been too much regulatory action which is adversely affecting our productivity in this country. It's gone to an extreme and we're seeking a balance."

Freeze and Postponement

The administration wasted little time in "making things happen" in its push to dismantle federal regulations. In the early months of 1981, scores of rules were revised, rescinded or postponed. The first of these actions came on Jan. 29, when the president put a freeze on 172 pending regulations. The freeze directed the EPA and all Cabinet-level departments except State and Defense to delay the effective date of any pending regulations and to refrain from issuing additional ones for 60 days.

Included in the freeze were more than 100 "midnight" regulations issued in the waning days of the Carter administration. Exempted were regulations with deadlines, set by statute or court order, that would fall within the 60-day period; those issued according to a formal rulemaking process; those affecting military or foreign policy; rules affecting agency organization, management or personnel; and regulations issued by the Internal Revenue Service.

Reagan's Feb. 17 executive order extended the freeze by directing that major new rules approved by executive branch agencies but not yet in effect must be postponed until agencies had completed regulatory impact analyses, subject to review by the OMB and presidential task force.

Reagan and the 'New Federalism'...

Reducing federal regulations was a principal feature of President Reagan's "New Federalism" initiative outlined in his January 1982 State of the Union message. Reagan proposed transferring many federal social programs to the states as part of a long-range plan to restructure federal-state relationships. The proposal called for a dramatic shift of some 40 social, transportation and community development programs — and revenues to help pay for them in the early phase — to the states. The president also proposed a "swap" of the three principal welfare programs for the poor.

The proposed program transfer encountered a mixed reception among governors and members of Congress, who charged it represented an abdication of federal responsibility. As a result the administration scaled back its proposal and no further action was anticipated until 1983 at the earliest. The Reagan administration nonetheless proceeded with its plan to reduce the federal regulatory burden imposed on state and local governments.

Deregulatory Actions

Soon after it was established the Presidential Task Force on Regulatory Relief, chaired by Vice President George Bush, solicited suggestions for regulatory reform from about 100 organizations representing businesses, consumers and state and local officials. By August 1981 it had received more than 2,500 responses, including requests from some states, cities and counties for specific changes in nearly 500 federal regulations. One month later, the task force announced 52 actions to relax some of the more than 1,200 regulations affecting state and local governments. Many of these were related to regulations written to administer federal aid, grants and entitlement programs affecting health, education and welfare.

A progress report issued in August 1982 by the task force claimed that various regulatory reform actions taken by the administration had saved state and local governments between $4 and $6 billion in total investment costs and $2 billion in annually recurring costs. Reductions in paperwork reporting requirements had freed almost 11.8 million work hours per year for state and local government employees.

The task force had targeted 27 regulations that it said placed an unreasonable regulatory burden on state and local governments. Of those 13 were revised and 14 were under review in August 1982. Among them were the national school lunch program, education grants, health care financing rules, community development programs and transportation grants. Those rules "have been the subject of frequent complaints from state and local officials," Bush said in a statement accompanying the report.

While spokesmen for state and local governments generally welcomed initiatives to do away with cumbersome regulations, they were more skeptical about proposals to transfer responsibility for programs and enforcement of regulations from the federal to the state and local level. Some questioned whether state and local governments would be able to bear the cost of administering the programs — even though the administration proposed transferring some federal funds to them — while others said the transfer was simply a reorganization that did not go to the heart of regulatory reform. Some of the officials said that the savings cited by the administration were inflated and that in any case, many of them, as revisions in environmental protection regulations, would accrue to business, not local governments.

On March 25, Vice President Bush announced that 63 health, energy, environmental and other rules would be modified or canceled, including 36 of the Carter administration's "midnight" regulations suspended in January. The other 27 were existing regulations that the administration planned to review and modify. On April 6 Bush announced the administration planned to ease, drop or postpone an additional 34 environmental and safety rules for automobiles and trucks. *(Details, p. 135)*

On Aug. 12 the task force issued a third list of regulations slated for review based on suggestions from state and local governments and the private sector. In February 1982 the task force announced it would review a number of regulations and paperwork requirements that particularly affected small businesses.

In other actions the administration rescinded the mandatory federal controls on building temperatures imposed by the Carter administration to conserve energy, revoked an order sharply limiting the export of hazardous products that were banned or restricted from use in the United States and postponed national energy efficiency standards for major household appliances.

The administration also moved to postpone, change or review a number of major environmental and health rules such as the Interior Department's surface mining regulations, the Labor Department's general rules governing exposure to chemical carcinogens in the workplace, EPA and OSHA noise control policies and regulations affecting toxic waste disposal.

Agency Budget Cuts

Among the weapons Reagan used to attack the federal regulatory bureaucracy, none was wielded more broadly

... More Power to the States

Congressional Objections

Moreover, Congress refused to approve some of the administration's revisions. It blocked a proposed rule, issued Aug. 4, 1982, that sought to remove many of the procedural and other requirements imposed on local schools under the 1975 Education for All Handicapped Children Act (PL 94-142). The draft regulations would have allowed states and local schools to set their own guidelines, standards and timetables in meeting the mandate of providing an "appropriate" education to the handicapped.

Congress also blocked proposed changes in regulations relating to education aid programs for disadvantaged children and to elementary and secondary education block grant programs. Members argued that some of the regulations violated congressional intent. They criticized the Education Department for seeking to exempt the two large programs from the General Education Provisions Act, which provides procedural protections for education programs.

Impact on Industry

Another aspect of Reagan's "New Federalism" would shift more of the burden for economic and environmental regulations to the states. While regulations at the federal level decreased during Reagan's first two years in office, the states became increasingly active in the areas of both social and economic regulation. As a consequence industries were turning their attention more and more to state and local actions.

The regulatory relief task force said that "differences in size, location, demographics, and economics mean that no two states or localities face the same set of regulatory problems. Even where the problems of two jurisdictions are roughly similar, local prefer-

ences are likely to result in different solutions. By its nature, federal regulation tends to ignore these differences, treating local problems and priorities identically across jurisdictions."

But some observers questioned the wisdom and appropriateness of decentralizing or eliminating federal regulations. "If you leave standard-setting to every single state, you are going to have 50 different sets of standards," said Douglas M. Costle, former administrator of the Environmental Protection Agency, in December 1981. "There aren't even a handful of states, however, that have the research capability to set their own [environmental] standards.... Also, how do you ensure the kind of national consistency to keep one state from creating a pollution haven in order to attract industry from another state that wants a relatively clean environment?... Pollution does not respect political boundaries."

A number of industry spokesmen expressed similar concerns. "[M]any business leaders are concerned that the New Federalism, along with the president's strong conviction that states should play a larger role in regulation and his decision to reduce federal agency staffs and budgets, could lead states to believe there is a regulatory vacuum to be filled," Jeffrey H. Joseph, Chamber of Commerce vice president for domestic policy, wrote in an issue of the chamber's *The Regulatory Action Network: Washington Watch.* The administration "must take the time to distinguish where New Federalism clashes with the interests of interstate commerce" and when the "national interest cannot be subject to the parochial interests of localities," Joseph said. If it does not, it "runs the risk of creating a bigger regulatory morass than the one it inherited."

than the budget-cutting ax. Although the fiscal 1982 budget for 57 regulatory agencies proposed minor cuts in real terms (about 4 percent), cuts actually ended up at around 10 percent, with a 9 percent reduction in staff, according to figures compiled by the Center for the Study of American Business. The fiscal 1983 budget requests continued the downturn in funding, calling for a spending cut of 7 percent and a staffing reduction of 3 percent.

Energy programs were scheduled for some of the deepest cuts. Reagan asked that the Commerce Department's energy regulatory programs be slashed to $14 million, from $46 million; and the Justice Department's petroleum regulatory programs to $21 million, from $46 million. The budget of the CAB, in the process of being phased out, was 32 percent lower than the fiscal 1982 level. The FTC was slated to take a 11.6 percent cut and the EPA a 6 percent cut.

Staffing reductions for some agencies were just as dra-

matic. The EPA was scheduled to have 2,762 fewer employees than it had in fiscal 1981. The Consumer Product Safety Commission was scheduled to lose 54 full-time positions, a reduction of about 235 full-time positions since fiscal 1981. The FTC would lose 145 full-time positions. Four of its 10 regional offices would be closed. (The EPA had 12,623 employees, the CPSC had 696 and the FTC had 1,622 employees as of June 1982.)

In another example, the administration reduced the number of authorized positions in the Interior Department's office of surface mining to 650 from 1,010; abolished its five regional offices; and reduced its federal inspection forces. The situation prompted *Washington Post* reporter Dale Russakoff to write: "Without changing a word of the tough federal strip mining law, the Reagan administration has systematically weakened the agency that enforces it."

Reagan's budget-cutting approach to deregulation was

criticized by some observers, among them former FTC Chairman Calvin Collier. Writing in the September/October 1980 issue of *Regulation,* Collier disagreed with the "belief that regulatory costs can be cut by cutting an agency's budget and the size of the *Federal Register.* . . . If the Republicans try to cut underlying compliance costs by slashing budgets, the result will be longer backlogs for permits, less research, less effort to improve existing rules and less use of techniques such as performance standards that really can cut compliance costs. . . . And if the GOP tells the agencies that regulatory reform equals fewer *Register* pages, they may just give the public less information."

Boyden Gray, counsel to Reagan's regulatory relief task force, agreed in part with Collier. "Too many people may gum things up, but too few can hurt, too," he said in 1981. "You can't build an industrial plant without an EPA permit, and if there are no people to process the permits, you're in trouble."

Some agency officials reportedly complained that they would not be able to carry out cost-benefit analyses and deregulation measures if their budgets and staffs were pared to bare bones. Meaningful regulatory review and reform is a monumental task that requires an adequate professional staff, they argued.

The Reagan administration's proposed cutbacks in research and development funds for the regulatory agencies also came under fire. Basic research was needed to avoid future technological inefficiencies in the means by which industries comply with regulations. Proposed cutbacks in research for the EPA came in for particular criticism by members of Congress and others. "If we don't focus on the right targets, then a lot of the money industry spends on pollution control will be wasted," said Brookings Institution economist Lester B. Lave in an interview in the April 10, 1982, *National Journal.* For example, "If we had known about acid rain in the early 1970s by spending more money on researching sulfur oxidation products, then we wouldn't have permitted the use of tall smokestacks that allow the sulfur dioxide to become acidified." *(EPA research cuts, p. 115)*

Reluctant Regulators

During his first months in office, Reagan seemed to be making extensive use of the appointments process to advance his plan to rein in regulation. Many of his appointments to executive branch regulatory agencies and independent commissions were people who shared the president's aversion to what he considered were excessive government controls. Among the appointments were:

● Thorne Auchter to head OSHA. Auchter was a Florida contractor who served on the task force for occupational safety and health for the state. "The question of the least costly approach [to health and safety standards] has an awful lot of merit," said Auchter soon after his appointment. "If we come up with a method that incurs lower cost, then that makes the most sense, provided we can reach the objective."

At Auchter's direction OSHA began to work more closely with industry. The agency should be a "partner lending assistance," to businesses, not a "policeman," he said. In June 1981 Auchter announced that OSHA would delegate more authority for regulating workplace health and safety to the states and would encourage employers to perform self-inspections of their work sites.

● Phillip Johnson, selected to preside over the Commodity Futures Trading Commission. A lawyer who had represented the Chicago Board of Trade before his appointment, Johnson had pressed for "self-regulation" for the futures industry.

● John Crowell, appointed to the post of assistant secretary of agriculture, where he was responsible for federal timber policy. Crowell had been the general counsel of a large timber products company and was an outspoken critic of existing wilderness preservation policies. His nomination became embroiled in conflict-of-interest charges, but the Senate ultimately confirmed him, 72-25.

● Raymond Peck, named NHTSA administrator. Peck had no background in auto safety but had held several other government positions where he advocated deregulation. Peck recommended suspension or revision of a number of auto safety regulations, including those related to passive restraints, bumper standards, hydraulic brakes and safety and wear performance standards for tires.

● Richard T. Pratt, former president of two companies that provide advice to savings and loan institutions and banks, named chairman of the Federal Home Loan Bank Board, which regulates the savings and loan industry.

● John S. R. Shad, chairman of the Securities and Exchange Commission, had been vice president of E. F. Hutton & Co., one of the nation's largest stockbrokers. Under Shad, the SEC adopted a sweeping package of disclosure rules to simplify filing of information required by corporations to market new securities. Shad's narrower view of SEC's role conflicted with the approach of the agency's traditionally independent and aggressive staff, which had sought to expand the agency's legal mandate through tough enforcement of disclosure requirements and anti-fraud provisions.

● Mark Fowler, chairman of the FCC, had practiced communications law, representing broadcast and private radio licensees before the FCC. He acted as communications counsel during 1979-80 for the Reagan for President and Reagan/Bush campaign committees. Fowler continued the overhaul of FCC regulations begun during the Carter administration. In early 1981 the commission eliminated regulation of radio broadcasting program content. The FCC also proposed to eliminate restrictions on subscription television service and moved to deregulate cable television. *(Broadcast deregulation, box, p. 72)*

"There's every indication that the agency leaders themselves will be very concerned with minimizing the burdens they impose," commented Weidenbaum in an interview published in the March/April 1981, issue of *Regulation.* "In fact . . . the first line of defense against overregulation lies in the agencies themselves."

However, at least in one case critics charged that an economic regulatory agency was re-embracing anti-competitive practices for the industry it regulated. A number of observers accused Interstate Commerce Commission Chairman Reese H. Taylor Jr., of slowing the momentum of trucking deregulation. "It's pretty plain that it's slowed down. Reese Taylor is a regulator. He doesn't approach things from a free market view," said Bob Ragland, director of regulatory reform for the National Association of Manufacturers, in early 1982. Taylor, who had served as chairman of the Nevada Public Service Commission, denied the allegations. "I didn't come to re-regulate," he said in early 1982.

Other appointees seemed to perceive regulatory reform as abolishing regulations altogether. Reagan nominated

Anne Gorsuch, a Colorado attorney and state legislator, to head the EPA. Gorsuch soon came under attack from all sides for administrative and budgetary actions taken to weaken environmental regulations and for what some considered her cavalier administration of the agency. "In the 10-year history of EPA, there have been periods of turmoil but none rivals what is happening now under the reign of Anne Gorsuch," said an article in the Oct. 12, 1981, *Automotive News*, a pro-business trade publication. "What was once a robust, dynamic entity has shriveled to a gray shadow of its former self, wracked by internal dissension, run by people with little expertise in environmental issues, and dogged by a paranoia that has virtually brought it to a standstill."

Finally, some agency heads simply lacked a program and direction. The CPSC is "in chaos," said W. Kip Viscusi, director of Duke University's Center for the Study of Business Regulation. "There is no clear vision from any of these people [at the commission] as to how they should change the agency."

During a December 1981 American Enterprise Institute seminar on regulation, George Eads, who served on Carter's Regulatory Analysis Review Group, expressed the opinion that "the administration is at war with itself. There are people in it who believe that better analysis and better attention to costs and benefits will produce better results. But there are a lot of other people who believe that regulation is inherently evil and that it doesn't really matter whom you appoint or how you instruct them. Regulations are going to mess things up so we might as well use regulatory appointments to pay off some political debts."

Assessing Reagan's Record

By the fall of 1982 some observers were giving the administration satisfactory marks for its regulatory actions, but others questioned the scope of the reform effort and noted a slowdown of momentum. They also pointed to lack of progress on reforming major regulatory statutes, such as the Clean Air Act.

In an Aug. 4, 1982, progress report, the Task Force on Regulatory Relief sought to refute those charges. It said that between 1981 and mid-1982, 111 existing regulatory programs had been designated by the task force for high-priority agency review. Fifty-one of those reviews resulted in final action to revise or rescind existing regulations, 35 reviews spurred the beginning of the revision process and 25 reviews were still pending in the agencies.

According to the task force, savings to industry derived from the 51 final revisions totaled at least $6.0 billion to $6.2 billion in annually recurring costs, and an additional $9 billion to $11 billion in one-time capital investment costs. The report noted that the figures were based on the best available agency cost estimates and included only decisions for which "reasonably accurate" estimates were available. The report claimed the administration had reduced the paperwork burden imposed by the government by more than 200 million hours. *(Paperwork reduction, box, p. 65)*

The number of final regulations issued by the Reagan administration in 1981 was about 22 percent less than during the final year of the Carter administration — down from a monthly average of 669 during the last year of the Carter administration to 519 during the first 17 months of

the Reagan administration. In addition, the number of proposed rules declined even more sharply — by 34 percent from 460 a month during the last year of the Carter administration to an average of 302 a month during the first 17 months of the Reagan administration. "Many of the proposed and final regulations issued by the Reagan administration have been to revise rules already on the books, rather than to add new ones," said the task force.

A Slowdown of Momentum

Some observers said it was hard to determine whether the decline in regulations reflected success in weeding out poor regulations. They speculated that the prospect of OMB review discouraged regulators from submitting proposals unlikely to survive scrutiny. Some also thought the slowdown was only temporary and that the number of rules would increase after agencies got their bearings under the new rules.

As Reagan's second year in office was drawing to a close, it appeared that the impetus for regulatory reform had weakened considerably after the initial flurry of activity. "I wonder whether other things are simply taking over the national agenda, or whether a Republican administration can really put together a coalition to deregulate when many of its constituents had a say in how those regulations were put together to begin with," said Robert W. Crandall, a senior fellow at the Brookings Institution, at a December 1981 regulation seminar sponsored by the American Enterprise Institute. "I get the feeling ... that we're losing momentum."

One indication of the administration's failure to develop a cohesive plan for tackling regulatory reform was its waffling on amendments to the 1970 Clean Air Act, up for renewal in 1981. Both environmentalists and industry spokesmen agreed that revisions needed to be made. But instead of taking a penetrating look at the act's accomplishments and shortcomings and then proposing comprehensive substantive revisions, the administration offered only a vague set of "principles" for rewriting the controversial legislation. Faced with the lack of a concrete administration position, Congress was reluctant to tackle the technically complex and politically sensitive act, and simply extended it while wrestling with a rewrite. *(Details, p. 111)*

The administration also softened its initial position on a rule requiring chemical manufacturers to label hazardous products in the work place. The original rule, issued by the Carter administration, had been withdrawn by Labor Secretary Donovan who then proposed a milder version. OMB had wanted to block even that rule, but pressure by interest groups, including the AFL-CIO, led OMB to agree to a compromise rule.

Court Challenges

A number of major administration actions were being challenged in the courts. For example, a federal appeals court in August 1982 ordered the Department of Transportation to reinstate a ruling requiring automobile manufacturers to install passive restraints in cars. The administration had withdrawn the 1977 ruling in October 1981. *(Details, p. 131)*

An administration rule revising enforcement of the Davis-Bacon Act also was under court challenge. The act required employers to pay the local prevailing wage on construction projects funded by the federal government. The effect often was to escalate the cost of federal con-

FCC and Broadcast Rules...

The Federal Communications Commission (FCC) in 1981 joined the list of independent regulatory commissions that have advocated some deregulation of the industries under their jurisdiction. Joined by the National Association of Broadcasters (NAB), the FCC proposed to abolish many federal broadcast regulations, contending that the federal government should not tell stations how they should program or run their businesses.

The FCC and the NAB also wanted Congress to kill the Fairness Doctrine and "equal time" rules required by law for controversial and political programming, and to ensure that FCC action to ease other regulations affecting broadcasters would not be reversed.

But such deregulation was strongly opposed by church groups, consumer advocates, labor unions and others who argued that it would give away control of the public's airwaves without ensuring a free flow of information.

The major support in Congress for broadcast deregulation came from the Senate, which on March 31, 1982, passed a bill that would give radio broadcasters more freedom to decide how much news and public affairs programming to air. The bill also would make it easier for radio and television stations to renew their licenses.

The Senate Bill

While Senate action occurred with little debate, there were strongly divergent views among influential members of the House. In 1981 House Energy and Commerce Committee Chairman John D. Dingell, D-Mich., and Telecommunications Subcommittee Chairman Timothy E. Wirth, D-Colo., blocked a bill similar to the Senate's, although they agreed to allow longer broadcast license terms.

The Senate bill would:

● Codify a decision made by the FCC in 1981 to eliminate rules on radio news and public affairs programming and commercial advertising.

● Bar the FCC from requiring radio broadcasters to survey the problems, needs and interests of its service area.

● Eliminate the existing license renewal procedure that required radio and television license holders to be compared with competing applicants.

● Direct the FCC to eliminate broadcast rules and policies that were unnecessary or that limited competition.

● Direct the FCC to encourage competitive and diverse programming.

● Require broadcasters to pay fees for FCC services, such as facility construction permits and station assignment and transfer.

"Deregulation benefits broadcasters not only in economic terms but helps preserve the First Amendment freedoms that belong to the press," Senate Commerce Committee Chairman Bob Packwood, R-Ore., said in urging the Senate to pass the bill.

He and others argued that federal regulation was no longer needed to ensure variety because the public had diverse sources of electronic and printed infor-

struction projects. The administration's rule would permit use of workers in federal projects at wages below those paid to journeymen, revise the method of computing the prevailing wage and reduce reporting requirements for contractors.

The administration was facing challenges from Congress as well. In August 1982 the Education Department backed away from some controversial rules that would rescind government regulations on education for the handicapped. But its revised draft proposal, which still would cut back the programs, encountered strong opposition by members of Congress and lobby groups. The result was adoption of language stating that the revised regulations should not take effect until Congress had a chance to vote on them. The administration bowed to that pressure in September, withdrawing six of the most controversial proposals and promising to reconsider the others.

The controversy over education for the handicapped was illustrative of both substantive differences over the need for tight federal regulation of social programs and the traditional institutional conflict over Congress' right to review executive department regulatory decisions. Similar issues involved administration proposals to loosen restrictions on employment of 14- and 15-year-olds and to change regulations affecting nursing homes. In both cases, members of Congress introduced bills to block the changes. "We cannot let this practice of regulations writers rewriting the law continue," said Rep. John N. Erlenborn, R-Ill., in August 1982.

OMB Role Questioned

Some observers expressed concern about the oversight procedures instituted by Reagan. The first was that there appeared to be no logical process for identifying which existing regulations should be reviewed. Some of the regulations singled out by OMB and the task force were relatively minor ones involving relatively slight costs and might not merit the time involved in scrutiny by a high level executive agency or panel. The small size of the OMB regulatory office and the fact that the staff did not have the expertise in specific areas of regulation available to the regulatory agencies themselves was another obstacle confronting OMB in its attempt to carry out its broad mandate.

...Deregulating Program Content

mation. They noted that no similar content restrictions were placed on newspapers and magazines.

Their critics, however, argued that there was not sufficient competition in broadcasting to justify removing federal oversight. And, they said, the airwaves were a scarce public resource, which distinguished broadcasting responsibility from those of the print media.

"I think it's an irresponsible giveaway," the Rev. Dr. Everett C. Parker, director of the United Church of Christ office of communication, said. The church was appealing the FCC's decision to deregulate radio programming.

Fairness and Equal Time

In addition to its administrative steps to deregulate broadcasting, the FCC asked Congress to repeal the Fairness Doctrine and equal time provisions of existing law. Under the equal time provisions of the Communications Act of 1934, if a candidate for public office used a station's airwaves, the station had to provide an equal opportunity to the candidate's opponents. The Fairness Doctrine, promulgated by the FCC after extensive hearings in 1949, required a broadcaster to present fair and balanced views on important community issues.

Congress in 1970 passed a bill repealing the equal time rules, but President Richard Nixon vetoed it and the Senate failed to override the veto. The Senate in 1973 added an equal-time repealer to its version of the campaign financing law amendments, but the provision was dropped from the final bill.

Packwood called for a constitutional amendment to extend First Amendment free speech protections to electronic communications; if adopted, such an amendment would eliminate the equal time and Fairness Doctrine rules. "Free expression, to be free, must be just that — free. And it cannot be free when government assumes for itself, or is granted, the power to regulate it in the name of technological necessity or for any other reason," Packwood said.

Dingell and Wirth, on the other hand, strongly opposed elimination of the two rules, contending that the government should ensure that diverse and controversial viewpoints would be aired. Some members of Congress favored retaining the equal time requirements because they feared their re-election efforts could be hurt by local stations favoring an opponent.

A coalition called Friends of the Fairness Doctrine was formed in 1981 to fight FCC and NAB efforts to eliminate the rules. The coalition included the United Church of Christ; Ralph Nader's National Citizens Committee for Broadcasting; Media Access Project, the public-interest broadcasting law firm; and the United Auto Workers.

While the administration generally backed broadcast deregulation, President Ronald Reagan's position on the Fairness Doctrine was unclear. He told the NAB in a letter that "it is essential to extend to electronic journalism the same rights that newspapers and magazines enjoy." However, the March 20 issue of TV Guide quoted him as saying "It seems to me there's a valid reason for the thing."

Another problem surrounding the new OMB role was one of accountability. Some members of Congress as well as others charged that giving OMB authority to review a regulation before it was made public jeopardized the independence the agencies needed, and were given by statute, to arrive at impartial decisions. They said OMB review subjected agencies to undue White House influence and weakened oversight by Congress and the general public. Behind-the-scenes and before-publication discussion of proposed regulatory actions might attract special interest lobbying as well.

In addition to skepticism about the ability of the OMB to perform its added regulatory functions, some critics questioned Reagan's overall approach to the issue. The administration was simply throwing out or postponing rules instead of taking an in-depth look at regulatory procedures, they said. Reagan may have cut down on regulations but the process that gave rise to the existing "overregulation" was still in place.

One example of this was discussed in a Nov. 6, 1981, General Accounting Office (GAO) report prepared at the request of Sen. Howard H. Baker Jr., R-Tenn., and entitled

"Improved Oversight and Guidance Needed to Achieve Regulatory Reform at the Department of Energy." The report concluded that among the principal causes underlying the Energy Department's inadequate regulatory analyses were failure to clearly identify who was to monitor the quality of analyses; the absence of minimum requirements on what critical issues the analyses were to address; and the limited amount of time given to prepare the analyses. The GAO recommended that someone within the office of the secretary should be given responsibility for overseeing regulatory reform.

Undercounting Benefits

Critics also questioned the manner in which the administration performed cost-benefit analyses, citing what they believed to be the scant attention paid to the benefits of regulation. One observer pointed to the fact that OMB regulatory analysis forms contained almost no space to list the benefits of a proposed rule. Some administration and agency officials acknowledged that many analyses needed improvement and that staff was not always skilled in performing the studies.

The OMB regulatory analysis guidelines, issued June 13, 1981, were of dubious assistance. They read, in part: "The monetary social cost should be subtracted from the monetary social benefit to obtain the monetary net benefit estimate (which could be negative). Any remaining nonmonetary but quantifiable benefit and cost information also should be presented.

"Then, nonquantifiable benefits and costs should be listed, in a way that facilitates making an informed final decision. Where many benefits are not easily quantified, the results should show the cost-effectiveness of the several alternatives." *(Cost-benefit analysis, p. 25)*

Some observers said that the administration was preoccupied with doing away with regulations and had not tried to change the regulatory responsibilities of the agencies themselves. However, the administration's philosophy was expressed in early 1982 by OMB information and regulatory affairs administrator DeMuth, who questioned the feasibility of the "statute-by-statute approach," and expressed "some skepticism about the possibilities for fundamental improvement in the regulatory statutes."

"This administration so far has shown little or no interest in statutory changes," said Eads, the former head of Carter's Regulatory Analysis Review Group. "But given the way they have created the appearance of change without statutory change, I don't see why they would want to take on the major statutes anyway. That's a big effort."

LEGISLATING REFORM: NO AGREEMENT REACHED

While a great deal of reform can be accomplished administratively through executive orders, the appointment of sympathetic individuals to important positions and streamlined agency procedures, it takes legislation to make orders permanent and to institute governmentwide reforms.

A Reagan administration budget fact sheet said: "Not all of our regulatory problems can be solved satisfactorily through more effective regulatory management and decisionmaking. Statutory constraints often preclude effective regulatory decisions." The administration pointed out that many laws were conflicting, overlapping or inconsistent.

It also complained that compliance deadlines established by law hampered effective rulemaking. "Where deadlines are unreasonable, changes will be sought," the report said.

Although many members of Congress and others agreed on the need to overhaul some aspects of the regulatory process, there was widespread disagreement over what should be done and how to go about it. Some of the legislative mechanisms proposed at various times to achieve reform include:

● "Sunset" legislation, which would require periodic congressional review of all government programs. *(Details, p. 55)*

● Comprehensive changes in the basic statutes of agencies and commissions.

● Legislation instituting industry-by-industry reforms, such as the air, trucking and rail deregulation acts; and

bills that would relax environmental and health controls, such as revision of the Clean Air Act.

● Legislative veto authority over regulatory agency and commission decisions. *(Details, p. 51)*

● Transferral of most of the independent agencies into the executive office and splitting their functions between planning and rulemaking, on the one hand, and adjudication on the other.

● Comprehensive regulatory reform legislation that would revise the 1946 Administrative Procedure Act to set new rules for selection and composition of regulatory bodies and the procedures they must follow.

Whatever the method of revision, there was no doubt that making the federal regulatory maze easier to navigate was a popular cause on Capitol Hill in the late 1970s and early 1980s. In 1979 alone, more than 150 bills had been introduced to straighten out the government's rulemaking machinery.

However, only a few received serious consideration and fewer still were approved and signed into law. While the most prominent proposals had many features in common, there were significant differences in several areas that proved difficult to compromise. The few bills that did pass addressed only one or two relatively narrow issues such as reduction of paperwork. Comprehensive reform proposals made little headway.

Carter Reform Bill

Reacting to complaints about the rising volume and compliance costs of federal rules, President Carter submitted his own comprehensive regulatory reform plan to Congress in March 1979. "Regulations that add needless costs add to inflation," Carter told Congress in a message accompanying his proposal.

Carter's bill proposed to strengthen the reforms introduced by his March 1978 executive order, make them permanent and extend them to the independent commissions. The bill would require a detailed economic analysis of each proposed rule containing a justification of why a regulation was needed, listing the alternatives and requiring that the least costly be chosen. If a more expensive rule was picked, the agency would have to explain why.

Twice a year each agency would be required to publish an agenda of major upcoming rules and when they were expected to be issued. To cut down on delays agencies would have to set completion dates for any rulemaking, licensing or adjudication. Once every 10 years an agency would be required to review existing regulations having an impact on the economy of $100 million or more. The agency would assess how well a rule had worked, whether the circumstances originally requiring it had changed, and if those affected by the rule understood it.

In the Senate, a bill similar to the administration proposal was introduced by Abraham Ribicoff, D-Conn., and Charles H. Percy, R-Ill., chairman and ranking minority member, respectively, of the Governmental Affairs Committee.

But efforts to enact a major overhaul of the regulatory system collapsed in controversy at the end of the 96th Congress. Although virtually all parties to the negotiations, including business lobbies, the AFL-CIO, the White House and Senate and House committees, eventually agreed to the heart of the bill, three peripheral provisions remained in dispute and eventually were responsible for the measure's demise.

Two of those would have given the courts and Congress new powers to restrain federal regulators. The "Bumpers" amendment, named after its Senate sponsor, Dale Bumpers, D-Ark., would have made it easier for individuals, companies and other groups to challenge regulations in court. And a legislative veto provision would have enabled Congress to knock down proposed regulations. The administration strongly opposed both provisions, saying they would erode the power of the executive branch.

The third proposal, a business-sponsored hybrid rulemaking process, would have given private groups an opportunity to make oral, as well as written, presentations to agencies considering new rules, and in certain circumstances to cross-examine experts relied on by the agencies. Government agencies and public interest groups saw the proposal as an attempt by business to complicate rule making unnecessarily, and thus choke off new regulation.

More Limited Measures

The most significant regulatory reform bill to clear the 96th Congress came in the closing days of the 1980 session, when Congress approved the Paperwork Reduction Act (PL 96-511). The act gave the OMB broad power to review all requests made by government agencies for information and reports from businesses and individuals. The Reagan administration pledged to enforce the act vigorously. *(Details, p. 65)*

Congress also approved a measure designed to relieve small businesses of some regulatory burdens. The Regulatory Flexibility Act (PL 96-354) required regulators to analyze a regulation's economic and paperwork impact on small business. The legislation was needed, the Senate Judiciary Committee said, because "uniform regulations often have a disproportionately greater economic impact upon small businesses and thus upon their competitive positions." Even if small and large companies bore exactly the same regulatory costs, small companies had fewer units of output over which they could spread that cost. Another problem was that small businesses could not take advantage of such corporate facilities as in-house data and accounting operations, but often had to hire outside help to provide those services.

During debate on the bill, Senate Small Business Chairman Gaylord Nelson, D-Wis., noted that the Small Business Administration had studied the burden of federal regulations on small businesses. The data showed that small operations dealt with a total of 350 million federal forms a year containing 850 million pages and 7.3 billion questions. That cost each small business an average of $1,270 annually for a total cost of $10 billion just to meet federal paperwork requirements.

An administration-backed "sunset" bill that would have required periodic review and reauthorization of all government programs was abandoned at the end of the 1980 session and had not been revived by 1982.

Another component of Carter's proposed regulatory reform package was a bill designed to make administrative law judges, the officials who presided over regulatory agency proceedings, more answerable for their decisions. Although the measure was reported by a House committee, it failed to clear Congress. *(Details, box, p. 40)*

Senate Reform Bill

On March 24, 1982, the Senate unanimously approved a wide-ranging regulatory reform bill that gave Congress,

Regulatory Activity

(Monthly averages)

	Proposed Rules	Final Rules	Federal Register Pages
1977-80	415	613	6,070
1980	446	647	7,251
1981*	276	471	4,856
Percent change, 1980 to 1981	−38%	−27%	−33%

* Data on monthly averages for 1981 exclude January. President Reagan on Jan. 29 instituted a freeze on 172 regulations pending from the Carter administration.

Source: Marvin H. Kosters and Jeffrey A. Eisenach, "Is Regulatory Relief Enough?" *Regulation*, March/April 1982, p. 22.

the president and the courts more control over the way federal rules are made.

The House Judiciary Committee reported a similar measure Feb. 25, but the legislation was stymied as of fall 1982 by the resignation in March of its chief sponsor, Rep. George E. Danielson, D-Calif., who accepted a California judgeship.

The Senate measure (S 1080), adopted 94-0, would tighten the reins on the bureaucracy by allowing Congress to veto most federal regulations, granting the president more authority to review the costs of new rules and making it easier to challenge regulations in court. According to Paul Laxalt, R-Nev., chief sponsor of the bill, the legislation would improve rulemaking procedures "so regulations will be more effective and less costly."

"After all the years of people talking about making government work better, we've actually sat down and done something that will," said Patrick J. Leahy, D-Vt., who with Laxalt led the bipartisan drive for passage of the regulatory relief bill.

"This is the kind of legislation that you wouldn't dare introduce 10 years ago," said Laxalt. "In those days all we heard was, 'How can you put a price tag on health and safety?'; but we must. Maybe we don't want to pay for 100 percent clean air. Maybe we just want to pay for 90 percent clean air."

As in previous years, one of the more volatile issues in 1982 involved a provision allowing a two-house legislative veto, without presidential review, of most regulations issued by executive and independent agencies. Although Congress had attached some form of legislative veto to other laws, the veto had never before been extended so broadly. The Senate measure would apply the veto across the board to all agencies except the Department of Defense and the Internal Revenue Service. Rules dealing with rates, wages, prices or mergers would also be excepted. The implementation of most rules would be delayed 45 days while congressional committees reviewed them. If a committee recommended disapproval of a regulation, each chamber would have an additional 30 days to act. A majority of both houses would have to reject the rule for it to be blocked.

Several provisions of the Senate bill, including a requirement for cost-benefit studies, already were in practice in executive departments under Reagan's executive order. The bill would codify some of those provisions and extend them to independent commissions.

The House version of the legislation would give OMB a mostly advisory role and would not give the agency more authority to ensure compliance with its procedures for cost-benefit tests. Moreover, the House measure would exempt 19 independent commissions from OMB oversight of the cost-benefit analysis.

The Senate legislation also included the Bumpers amendment, facilitating legal challenges to agency decisions by removing the benefit of doubt often given to agencies. Other major provisions of the bill would increase public participation in rulemaking and require a review of major rules every 10 years.

An Uncertain Outlook

By late 1982 the outlook for congressional action on comprehensive regulatory reform appeared uncertain. The administration had misgivings about some of the features of the bills under consideration, as did labor, consumer and environmental groups who opposed in particular the legislative veto, expanded court powers and strict cost-benefit analyses. The groups also were opposed to the administration's efforts to slash agency budgets and roll back health, safety and environment regulations.

One expert who questioned some of the proposals being aired on Capitol Hill was Antonin Scalia, co-editor of *Regulation,* who warned that "the imposition of new procedural impediments [by Congress] can only succeed, during the Reagan administration, in preserving the administrative decisions of the past." In particular, Scalia was critical of legislative veto proposals and a statutory cost-benefit analysis requirement. Such "executive enfeebling measures," he wrote in the January/February 1982 issue of the magazine, "do not specifically deter regulation. What they deter is change. Imposed upon a regulation-prone executive, they will on balance slow the increase of regulation; but imposed upon an executive that is seeking to dissolve the encrusted regulation of past decades, they will impede the dissolution."

A number of observers of the regulatory landscape have been critical of broad-brush regulatory reform. Among them was SEC Commissioner Barbara S. Thomas. "There is something ironic about this approach to regulatory reform; it bears a strong family resemblance to the techniques of regulation itself," she wrote in the June 3, 1981, edition of *The New York Times.* "These measures are little more than an attempt to 'regulate' the regulatory agencies into deregulation."

The FTC: A Regulated Regulator

Federal regulatory agencies — even those categorized as "independent" — are not entirely free to make and enforce rules as they see fit in the areas they are charged with policing.

First of all, each agency is created with a specific mandate that sets the bounds of its activity. The courts and Congress, through its oversight committees, see to it that the agency does not stray too far outside those boundaries.

Congress also views each independent agency as one of its arms, and each independent commission is subject to the authorization and appropriations process. Congress can, and does, cut or expand budgets, write in restrictions on agency activity, retain for itself a veto over regulations, and even rewrite the agency's basic law in extreme cases.

While the president cannot tell an independent agency what to do, he can appoint as members persons who share his regulatory philosophy. But the appointees must be able to pass another checkpoint — the Senate's confirmation power.

Finally, and perhaps most important, agencies are subject to public opinion. If the political climate favors strong regulatory action, an agency is freer to protect its constituency. If the mood of the country is anti-regulation, the agency's every move will be watched closely and protested quickly. Pressure groups dissatisfied with an agency's behavior can, in effect, go over its head and lobby Congress for legislative relief. *(Independence and Accountability, p. 47)*

Example: The FTC

Nothing better illustrates all of the tightrope-walking that a regulatory agency must do than the recent history of the Federal Trade Commission (FTC), one of the oldest and the largest of the independent agencies.

In the 1960s, if anyone mentioned the FTC at all it probably was with a yawn. At that time the commission was known as "the little old lady of Pennsylvania Avenue." Its gray headquarters building seemed to symbolize the agency — stolid, slow-moving, bureaucrat-ridden — better than the heroic statue outside of a man struggling with a horse (representing commerce).

On paper the leading consumer agency, the commission showed little awareness of consumerism. The movement's leader, Ralph Nader, wrote in 1969: "As the tide of consumer dissatisfaction rose in the 1960s, the FTC droned on, seemingly oblivious to the billions of dollars siphoned from poor and middle-class consumer alike by deceptive practices hiding shoddy and harmful products and fraudulent services."

Reborn in part because of that criticism, and wielding new powers handed it by Congress, the agency in the late 1970s again seemed to fall "out of sync" with the times. As the consumer movement slowed and the pendulum swung against regulation, the commission became more energetic than ever. Under an activist chairman, Michael Pertschuk, the commission began applying human and social values to its search for "unfair" or "deceptive" business practices.

The agency proposed to outlaw activity that in itself was more undesirable than evil, such as coaxing children to eat sugar-coated cereal or making claims that were not necessarily false but merely unproven.

Pressured by advertisers, undertakers and numerous other groups angered by the FTC, members of Congress began railing at "unelected bureaucrats" and "a rogue agency gone amok." Instead of prodding the commission to be more active, as it had a few years earlier, a wary Congress staked out certain areas where the FTC was forbidden to tread.

Balky Servant

With all the constraints upon it, how could the FTC appear to be so insubordinate and get away with it? One possible answer was offered by Yale University professor Robert A. Katzmann in a chapter he contributed to a 1980 book, *The Politics of Regulation.* Focusing on antitrust policy, Katzmann wrote that the FTC "is an agency that has struggled in the last several years to pursue actions in what it perceives to be the public interest, although it has not always been certain as to which policy course would best serve that interest. . . . The agency operates in a political environment — it must, therefore, not be unmindful of the actors (for example, Congress, the executive) who might attempt to influence antitrust policy. But the agency, while respectful of these elements, does not act as their servant."

This was particularly true during Pertschuk's tenure, when the FTC was anything but subservient to Congress. As general counsel of the Senate Commerce Committee, Pertschuk had helped write some of the legislation he was

FTC Chairmen, 1961-82

Name	Dates of Service	Party and State
Paul Rand Dixon	March 1961-Dec. 1969	D-Tenn.
Caspar W. Weinberger	Dec. 1969-Aug. 1970	R-Calif.
A. Everette MacIntyre (acting)	Aug. 1970-Sept. 1970	D-N.C.
Miles W. Kirkpatrick	Sept. 1970-Feb. 1973	R-Pa.
Lewis Engman	Feb. 1973-Dec. 1975	R-Mich.
Paul Rand Dixon (acting)	Jan. 1976-March 1976	D-Tenn.
Calvin J. Collier	March 1976-April 1977	R-Pa.
Michael Pertschuk	April 1977-March 1981	D-D.C.
David A. Clanton (acting)	March 1981-Sept. 1981	R-Va.
James C. Miller III	Oct. 1981-	R-Ga.

Source: Federal Trade Commission Public Information Office

charged with implementing when President Carter appointed him to the commission in 1977.

After the 1980 election, the FTC entered yet another era. At his first opportunity, President Reagan fired Pertschuk as chairman and installed someone more philosophically aligned with the administration's goal of reducing the regulatory burden on U.S. businesses. The new chairman, James C. Miller III, shared Reagan's belief that the consumer is best protected when the market can operate free of unnecessary government interference.

A former specialist in regulatory economics at the American Enterprise Institute for Public Policy Research, Miller had headed Reagan's regulatory transition team, which called the FTC a "consumer cop." Miller's first job in the administration had been in the Office of Management and Budget (OMB). (Biography, box, p. 85)

Robert Pitofsky, a Democratic commissioner, resigned in March 1981, giving the Reagan administration its longed-for opportunity to appoint a chairman with a similar philosophy on trade regulation. Miller was moved from OMB to take that assignment.

David A. Clanton, a Republican commissioner since 1976, served as acting chairman until Miller took over Oct. 5, 1981. While no longer chairman, Pertschuk remained a commissioner and from that vantage point continued to assail what he called the "sack of Washington" by the

"Visigoths of the Reagan Administration."

With Clanton and Patricia P. Bailey already on board, Miller's appointment gave the Republicans a majority on the five-member commission. Under the new leadership, the commission immediately set out to reorganize the agency and curtail some of its activities.

Miller became the first regulatory chairman in recent memory to ask Congress to withdraw some of his agency's enforcement powers. But when the Senate moved to exempt state-regulated professional groups — doctors, lawyers and the like — from the FTC's jurisdiction, Miller protested, describing such an exemption as a mistake "masquerading as de-regulation."

For a time after the term of former Chairman Paul Rand Dixon expired in late 1982, Pertschuk was the lone Democratic commissioner. President Reagan's first choice to fill the vacancy was F. Keith Adkinson, a former Senate Commerce Committee staffer who had been national chairman of Democrats for Reagan. The president withdrew the nomination after it became clear that Adkinson could not win confirmation.

In September 1982 Reagan announced that he would nominate a conservative Texas economist, George W. Douglas of Austin, to succeed Dixon in the second Democratic slot.

FROM 'PAPER TIGER' TO POWERFUL AGENCY

Among federal regulatory agencies the FTC has one of the broadest mandates: Nearly every business that participates in interstate commerce falls within its jurisdiction. The FTC is charged with prohibiting "unfair or deceptive acts or practices." It may act to prevent practices leading to monopoly or restraint of trade, such as unfair methods of competition (for example, false or misleading advertising), price discrimination, and stock acquisitions of competing enterprises. It also has power to investigate and to issue cease-and-desist orders, and it shares anti-monopoly responsibility with the Justice Department. (The FTC as Trustbuster, box, p. 82)

The legislation that created the FTC, the Federal Trade Commission Act of 1914, sought to make the new agency the federal government's chief trustbuster. The wording of the legislation was intentionally vague; section five of the act gave the FTC broad powers to define business practices that constituted "unfair methods of competition."

Also in 1914, Congress passed the Clayton Act (frequently referred to as the Clayton Antitrust Act) — a law prohibiting specific business activities that tended to lessen competition or to create monopolies. With these two statutes to guide it, the FTC began operation on March 15, 1915.

After active lobbying by consumer and women's groups, Congress in 1938 gave the commission additional authority by adopting the Wheeler-Lea Amendment to the original FTC Act. Designed to provide some degree of consumer protection to those who previously had been at the mercy of business interests, the amendment authorized the commission to prohibit "unfair or deceptive" business acts and practices. In this way the FTC could move against a business on behalf of consumers without first proving the existence of anti-competitive behavior.

During the 1940s the FTC dealt extensively with deceptive advertising and it gained new powers to regulate labeling of wool, fur, textile and flammable products.

In the 1950s and 1960s the FTC made few waves, except for a 1964 rule that would have required cigarette packages and all cigarette advertising to carry a health-hazard warning. Tobacco industry lobbyists circumvented that rule by working for enactment of the 1965 Federal Cigarette Labeling and Advertising Act, which required a health warning on cigarette packages but barred government agencies from requiring a similar message in advertising. The ban has since expired. Later legislation prohibited radio and television cigarette commercials and required health warnings in printed ads.

Congress gave the FTC jurisdiction over credit and debt collection abuses with the passage of acts in 1974 and 1977.

Nader Criticism

In 1969 seven students working for consumer activist Nader issued a study of the FTC, charging that the commission was steeped in trivial matters, that its reliance on case-by-case investigations slowed progress and that voluntary compliance was not stopping illegal or unfair business practices. In reaction to the Nader report, President Richard Nixon asked the American Bar Association (ABA) to appoint a committee to study the FTC. The ABA committee report also was critical of the commission.

The 185-page Nader report, made public Jan. 5, 1969, attacked members and staff of the FTC for "spectacular lassitude and office absenteeism, incompetence by the most modest standards, and lack of commitment to their regulatory missions...."

Despite rising consumer dissatisfaction and a growing population, the report said, the FTC's completed caseload dropped from 1,557 in 1964 to 1,058 in 1967. (The Nader group dealt only with the agency's consumer functions, not antitrust).

The report attributed the FTC's problems in part to what it said was the "well-known prejudice," one "deeply rooted in Southern populist tradition," held by Chairman Dixon, a Tennessee native. It said graduates of prestigious law schools such as Harvard and Pennsylvania had a poor chance of joining the FTC, compared with graduates of schools like Kentucky or Tennessee. (The seven "Nader's Raiders" who wrote the report held degrees from Ivy League colleges or were graduate students there. One of them, Princeton graduate Edward F. Cox, later became President Nixon's son-in-law.)

The report recommended that the FTC: seek the best available legal talent; ferret out consumer problems without waiting for letters of complaint; make greater use of its legal powers to halt unfair or deceptive practices, with less reliance on voluntary compliance; use publicity as a weapon against objectionable corporate behavior; seek more enforcement tools from Congress; and conduct more of its business in the open to "minimize behind-the-scenes whitewashing of agency reports."

As for Chairman Dixon, the report said his "chief and perhaps only contribution to the Commission's improvement would be to resign from the agency that he has so

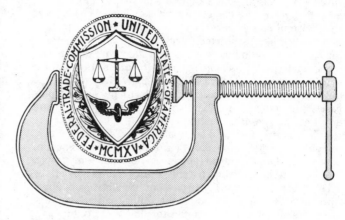

degraded and ossified."

Dixon, in an angry rebuttal four days later, called the authors of the report "young zealots" who had produced "a hysterical, anti-business diatribe and a scurrilous, untruthful attack on the career personnel of the commission." As evidence of what he called the students' "anti-business bias," Dixon cited a passage in the report calling for application of "'criminal sanctions to dishonest corporate behavior, for it [the report said] is far more damaging in contemporary America than all the depredations of street crime.'"

Dixon denied that he was prejudiced against prestigious northern law schools, a charge he said "galls me more" than anything else in the report. He said he consistently solicited all major law schools to have their graduates apply for FTC jobs.

Reappointed by Presidents Lyndon B. Johnson and Gerald R. Ford, Dixon remained on the commission until his final seven-year term expired in September 1981.

ABA Report

The ABA report corroborated many of the charges made in the Nader report. Sixteen lawyers and economists called the FTC "a failure on many counts." They said said there were "too many instances of incompetence in the agency, particularly in senior staff positions." The 119-page report was released Sept. 15, 1969.

The study group urged the FTC to devote more effort to retail consumer fraud and to set up pilot programs in major cities to detect and combat local frauds against consumers. The report recommended that Congress empower the agency to seek court injunctions against companies cited for unfair or deceptive practices.

Nixon's Response

While Nixon could have ignored the Nader, ABA and other criticisms, the reports made it politically advantageous for him to begin upgrading the agency. As Yale professor Katzmann observed in his 1980 study:

"... The pressure for change came from within and from without the agency; a consensus existed across the political spectrum that the agency had performed poorly. The new leadership proceeded swiftly; they installed mechanisms that centralized control of caseload decisions in the chairmen and top bureau officials and rid the agency of incompetent personnel. For the new administration, for those who wrote the ABA Commission's study of the FTC, as well as for Ralph Nader and his associates whose report called attention to the agency's ills, it seemed clear in 1969 and 1970 that a concerted effort to upgrade the recruitment system would have to be made. They correctly understood that the FTC could not hope to prosecute complex matters without attorneys of high caliber. Most staff attorneys in 1969 did not have the skills to pursue complex cases, and many did not have the inclination to investigate any but the simplest conduct cases."

In an attempt to change the agency's image, Nixon appointed Caspar W. Weinberger to the chairman's post in 1969. Weinberger stayed at the commission only seven months but began what became the revitalization of the FTC. Weinberger and his successors brought new staffers into the FTC, most of whom were young, activist lawyers. Commission rules were updated to allow more public participation and greater emphasis was placed on consumer affairs.

As a result the commission gained a favorable reputation among consumer groups as a willing partner in the consumers' fight for fairness and representation in the marketplace. On the other hand some business people charged that the commission became a close friend of consumers and ignored its responsibilities toward industry.

Magnuson-Moss Act

The push for improvements at the FTC culminated — after a five-year effort vigorously opposed by business groups — in passage of the 1974 Magnuson-Moss Warranty—Federal Trade Commission Improvement Act. The sponsors, Warren G. Magnuson, D-Wash. (1944-81), and Frank E. Moss, D-Utah (1959-77), were veteran proponents of consumer legislation in the Senate. For years Magnuson chaired the Commerce Committee, and Moss headed its Consumer Subcommittee.

The act expanded the FTC's power by allowing it to issue rules covering the practices of an entire industry. Until then the commission could proceed against abuses only on a case-by-case basis, and any ruling on an unfair or deceptive practice applied only to the company involved in that particular case, not to others guilty of similar practices. The legislation also established procedures designed to encourage greater public participation in the rulemaking process, including a program to reimburse individuals and outside groups who had a stake in FTC decisions but could not afford to participate in the agency's regulatory proceedings.

The warranties provisions authorized the FTC for the first time to spell out standards to be met by written warranties given by manufacturers or sellers of products priced at more than $5.

Political Climate

Passage of the Magnuson-Moss bill, which may have marked the last big legislative success of the consumer movement, was just one of several indications in the early 1970s that the public and its representatives on Capitol Hill still favored a vigorous Federal Trade Commission.

When oil company profits soared during and after the 1973-74 Arab oil embargo, congressional Democrats pressured the FTC to undertake an investigation of "Big Oil." Although Congress' ardor for the suit would soon cool, the FTC responded by launching an antitrust probe of the Exxon Corp. and seven other industry giants. Angry public reaction to the oil shortages and rising profits made it politically advantageous, at least for a time, for members to support the FTC action.

The FTC's activism was strongly supported by President Carter, who appointed consumer proponents to the commission. In particular Carter's appointee to the FTC chairmanship, Michael Pertschuk, had a strong pro-consumer reputation. Under Pertschuk, the FTC continued to push for consumer protection rules and regulations and took on some of the giants in the business and professional communities.

The FTC reached its peak size of about 1,800 employees during the Carter years. Reagan cutbacks lopped about 200 persons off the payroll. As of June 1982 the FTC employed 1,622 persons, a slight drop from the 1,661 employed in June 1975. However, the 1982 figure represented an increase of 40.2 percent from the 1,157 employed in June 1965. By contrast another big regulatory agency, the Interstate Commerce Commission, shrank 37 percent in the same period, from 2,427 employees to 1,530, largely as a result of federal deregulation of the railroad and trucking industries. *(Transportation deregulation, p. 89)*

Human Values

Besides using his own consumer sympathies and knowledge of Congress to help set the FTC's agenda, Pertschuk made an effort to cast the agency in his own image when it came to consideration of human, social and other non-technical aspects of the commission's work.

He raised eyebrows and some hackles in 1978 when he directed the agency staff to screen prospective candidates to replace retiring commissioner Calvin J. Collier. The unusual move was interpreted as an effort by Pertschuk to find a like-minded candidate and persuade the White House to appoint that person.

Business and legal groups were aghast at the procedure. "Mike wants a humanist FTC and the lawyers don't know how to deal with that," one consumer advocate was quoted as saying.

The person finally appointed, Robert Pitofsky, was reported to be satisfactory to Pertschuk as well as to business groups and antitrust lawyers. Pitofsky, a Georgetown University professor, formerly headed the FTC's antitrust unit, the Bureau of Competition.

SHIFT AWAY FROM CONSUMERISM

In the late 1970s, a decade after it had helped rouse the FTC from its somnolence, Congress began showing extreme irritation with the agency. It withdrew some of the agency's powers and imposed other sanctions, including the power to veto FTC actions it found offensive. Six years after it had empowered the FTC to move against industry-wide practices by passing the Magnuson-Moss bill, Congress wrote into law restrictions on the agency's authority to regulate children's television advertising, funeral homes and agricultural cooperatives.

What accounted for this turnabout? Had the FTC under Michael Pertschuk lurched out of control? Or had

Congress changed so that the FTC's activism no longer suited the temperament of its oversight committees? In a January 1982 study, Washington University economists Barry R. Weingast and Mark J. Moran suggested that the latter was the case.

Throughout the FTC's activist period in the 1970s, the study said, members of the Senate Commerce Consumer Subcommittee were more liberal than the Senate as a whole, as measured by their annual ratings from the liberal Americans for Democratic Action (ADA). The ADA scores of the men who chaired the subcommittee (particularly Moss') were even more out of line with the average senator's. During this period Magnuson was the Commerce Committee's chairman, Pertschuk was its counsel, and the FTC presumably was doing Congress' bidding as it went about enforcing the laws they were developing.

"The appointment of Pertschuk to the head of the Commission in 1977 seemed a natural culmination of this phase, not a coincidence," Weingast and Moran wrote. "The irony is that, just as he left the congressional domain to manage the FTC, the congressional support for FTC activism vanished."

The growing conservatism of both the Senate and its Consumer Affairs Subcommittee was documented by the declining ADA scores. In 1974, for example, the average senator had an ADA rating of 47.1 (out of a top score of 100), against 62.8 for the average consumer subcommittee member. By 1977 both groups had dropped to the same average rating — about 43. By 1979 the subcommittee membership's "liberal quotient" was markedly lower than that of the Senate as a whole, with an average ADA score of 26.4 against 37.5 for the average senator.

(In 1982 the Commerce Committee was headed by Sen. Bob Packwood, R-Ore., whose 1981 ADA score was 35, and the Consumer Subcommittee was headed by Sen. Robert W. Kasten Jr., R-Wis., with an ADA rating of 10.)

Commenting on Congress' imposition of sanctions on the agency, University of Houston professor Alan Stone said in his book *Regulation and Its Alternatives* that the FTC "failed to read the mood of Congress and thus almost invited Congress to 'clip its wings.' Agencies, including the FTC, do not usually respond this way. To the contrary, they are usually attentive not only to the general mood of Congress but also to the particular view, whims, and interests of the legislators, usually powerful figures on committees with jurisdiction over agency activities...."

Congress' increasing criticism of the FTC was consistent with its growing disenchantment with the whole consumer movement. Although Carter had installed consumer activists at other agencies as he did at the FTC, they were frustrated in their attempts to win passage of strong new consumer legislation. Their biggest setback came in 1978 when Congress killed the proposed consumer protection agency, despite Carter's all-out support for it.

At the FTC itself the decline of the consumer movement also affected the commission's efforts to attract and retain graduates of the best law schools. Many of the most promising new lawyers looked upon the FTC as a stepping stone in their careers. Katzmann of Yale said in a follow-up study that "Most analysts neglected to consider that the public interest fervor of the late sixties would not continue indefinitely or that the staff lawyer might be concerned not so much with the social or economic benefits of structural litigation as he would be with securing trial experience that would make him attractive to the private bar."

The 1980 election accelerated the movement to shorten the leash of regulatory watchdogs, especially at the FTC. With Reagan in the White House and the GOP in control of the Senate, Pertschuk-style activism became even more remote from the thinking then in vogue at the Senate subcommittee.

Source of Irritation

Many complaints about the FTC could be traced to two factors — the increased authority given the agency by the Magnuson-Moss Act to make industry-wide rules and Pertschuk's assertiveness in wielding those powers.

Supporters contended that the 1974 act was passed because business felt the FTC's action against individual companies was anti-competitive. While it allowed the commission to outlaw industry-wide practices, the act required due process hearings and cross-examination rights for affected parties.

Some critics complained that through these proceedings the FTC legislated more than Congress intended and that it had overstepped its authority. The broad discretion the FTC maintained in selecting its targets, without explicit direction from Congress, made its rulings more vulnerable to attack than those of other regulatory agencies.

Many observers said that under Pertschuk the FTC was more aggressive in confronting powerful corporate interests than it had been at any time in its 65-year history. Pertschuk defended the FTC's direction and accomplishments, saying, "Because we're an active agency and doing the job we ought to be doing, there are more groups into which the teeth of the commission are sinking now and more groups attacking [the rules] as they come to fruition."

Pertschuk conceded that in some cases "our economic analysis was not adequate, and the remedies were not thought out."

The Federal Trade Commission had initiated about 20 proceedings to regulate industries ranging from children's advertising to funeral homes since 1974. While most were initiated during the Republican administrations of Presidents Nixon and Ford, the proceedings were being completed under the leadership of Carter appointee Pertschuk, and he became a target of business displeasure over FTC actions.

Using its broad mandate to ferret out "unfair or deceptive acts or practices," the FTC antagonized, among others, the organized bar, health spa operators, mobile home salesmen, hearing aid counselors, the American Medical Association (AMA) and the insurance, television, advertising, automobile and drug industries.

Unfortunately for the FTC, some of its actions offended groups that can be found in any community — undertakers, used-car dealers, druggists. "People walk up to me out of the blue whenever I go home and tell me to get the FTC off their backs," one House member said.

'Kidvid' Furor

In one of its most celebrated cases the FTC angered grocery manufacturers, cereal makers, television networks, some members of Congress and others when it decided in 1978-79 to examine children's TV programs with an eye to regulating advertising aimed at the young audience.

For a time Pertschuk was barred from discussing the "kidvid" proposals after a federal district judge ruled that the FTC chairman may have pre-judged the issues in the case. Other regulatory agency members similarly involved in highly controversial matters likewise began hedging

The FTC as Trustbuster...

From its first year of operation in 1915 the Federal Trade Commission has had a dual role that some critics feel has impeded its performance in both jobs. Besides being a consumer protection agency, the FTC has shared responsibilities with the Justice Department's Antitrust Division, which has no other function.

The FTC drew many of its powers from the 1914 Clayton Act, which prohibited price discrimination, exclusive sales contracts, interlocking directorates and the acquisition of capital stock interests in a competitor firm.

Congress was concerned that the Justice Department, which had seen its enforcement of the 1890 Sherman Antitrust Act narrowed by court decisions, would be ill-equipped to enforce the new law. It also feared that the conservative federal judiciary would block its vigorous application. Consequently, Congress gave the FTC concurrent jurisdiction over the Clayton Act and exclusive responsibility to enforce the prohibition on "unfair methods of competition" contained in the Federal Trade Commission Act, also passed in 1914.

For decades the FTC showed more attention to fur, wool and textile labeling abuses than it did to anti-competitive business activity. Its role in antitrust, according to a 1982 study by Washington University economists Barry R. Weingast and Mark J. Moran, "was largely limited to such earth shattering cases as the monopoly in bull semen or the decline in competition among gift shops in the Virgin Islands. Indeed, the relatively innocuous character of the

FTC's caseload was the primary source of criticism of the agency during the 1950s and 1960s."

But once the FTC plunged into antitrust enforcement it gained a reputation of being somewhat more vigorous in that field than the Antitrust Division. The commission opened and won the battle in 1967 to keep the Procter & Gamble Co. from acquiring the Clorox Co., a bleach maker, on grounds that P. & G.'s economic power would have discouraged other companies from entering the bleach market.

FTC's general guidelines for mergers in the dairy industry were believed to have stopped some large dairies from becoming parts of existing conglomerates.

But taken as a whole the FTC's antitrust enforcement record has been a "dismal failure," in the view of University of Virginia law professor Ernest Gellhorn. Writing in the November/December 1981 *Regulation*, Gellhorn said that "Contrary to perceived wisdom, the FTC's basic deficiencies lie not in its people, the size of its budget, or its limited authority, but rather in the redundancy [with the Justice Department] of its antitrust assignment, the mingling of its consumer protection and antitrust responsibilities, and the degree of its vulnerability to interest group pressures."

Gellhorn noted that others shared his "gloomy evaluation." He quoted University of California at Los Angeles professor Wesley Liebeler as saying in a 1981 study, *The FTC Since 1970*, that the FTC " 'can be understood only in political terms' — namely, as a place where congressmen can lay the blame for any

their public comments, lest they be open to the same accusations.

The FTC contended that children's advertising was inherently "unfair" because pre-teens could not tell the difference between the commercials and the program. The rule under consideration would have banned all TV advertising for children under age 8 and all ads for "sugared products" aimed at audiences with a significant proportion of children.

Congress in 1980 placed restrictions on the children's advertising investigation, in effect forcing the FTC to suspend it.

Restrictions and Vetoes

Making clear its displeasure over FTC actions, Congress began chipping away at the agency's powers, sometimes granting exemptions to businesses and professions that protested the loudest about how they were treated.

In addition to suspending the "kidvid" investigation, Congress in 1980 imposed restrictions that virtually as-

sured a halt to an investigation the FTC had begun of insurance industry practices. The agency's study alleged that buyers were overcharged $1.3 billion for life insurance and that elderly men and women were being duped into buying health insurance that either duplicated their Medicare benefits or provided little extra protection.

Agricultural cooperatives and encyclopedia publishers were among other interests that obtained congressional action to keep the FTC off their turf. Some of the exempted groups — physicians and used-car dealers among them — were heavy supporters of congressional campaigns through their political action committees, prompting consumer groups to protest that the contributors in effect were buying protection from the FTC.

By 1980 Congress also was determined to trim back overall FTC powers, but disagreement over the best way to do it led to a prolonged funding dispute. Since 1977 the FTC had been funded by continuing resolutions, bypassing the normal authorization-appropriations process, because the House of Representatives had insisted on attaching to FTC authorization bills a provision allowing a legislative

... A 'Redundant Assignment'

and all ills of life arguably caused by the business community."

After examining the 44 FTC antitrust decisions made final in 1979, Gellhorn concluded that all of the vertical cases (involving companies controlling several steps in the production and marketing chain), most of the merger challenges, and many of the horizontal conspiracy complaints (those involving combinations at the same level of the distribution chain) were "unnecessary or counterproductive."

"In general," Gellhorn said, "the matter at issue in these actions was either a trivial event that could not have injured competition or an arrangement that would have made the firms more efficient. It seems clear the FTC pursued a highly interventionist antitrust policy, often grounded in a misunderstanding of how markets work and how individual firms operate in competitive markets."

Taking office in the midst of a merger boom (the FTC reported 1,083 pre-notifications of contemplated major corporate marriages in 1981), the Reagan administration quickly moved to soften federal antitrust policy — sometimes encountering FTC opposition.

For example, FTC lawyers opposed the Justice Department's 1981 decision to drop long-standing antitrust suits against American Telephone & Telegraph Co. and the International Business Machines Corp. But the FTC itself shelved antitrust cases that had been pending 10 years against the Big Three cereal makers — Kellogg Co., General Mills and General Foods Corp. *(Kellogg et al.)* — and eight years against the eight largest oil companies *(Exxon et al.).*

The cereal makers had been accused of maintaining a "shared monopoly."

In *Exxon,* the FTC staff reportedly concluded that the investigation, which the commission had launched under pressure from congressional Democrats in 1973, had dragged on too long in the pre-trial phase to warrant continuation.

The new FTC administration also cleared out other old cases, contending that their slow pace indicated the agency should not have undertaken them in the first place. In March 1982 the agency terminated an investigation of the automobile industry, halting a four-year effort to obtain thousands of documents from U.S. and foreign carmakers. Subpoenas already issued in the case were withdrawn. The commission said that economic changes in the auto industry made it difficult to find evidence of monopoly profits being made.

Reagan appointees to the FTC or its staff generally felt that bigness in itself was not harmful. Chairman James C. Miller III had been quoted as saying that the FTC should no longer "explore the frontiers of antitrust law."

Thomas John Campbell, tapped by President Reagan to head the FTC's Bureau of Competition, was a 29-year-old prodigy who had been the youngest student ever to pass the University of Chicago's doctoral exams in economics. Free-market economist Milton Friedman, for many years the dominant figure in Chicago's economics department, lauded the appointment. He had been Campbell's freshman adviser.

---

veto of agency actions. Both the Senate majority and President Carter opposed such an idea and argued that the legislative veto was unconstitutional because it encroached on the authority of the executive branch.

Some senators, however, supported the House position. "If the Congress is going to hand this kind of power to unelected bureaucrats, it is only reasonable that Congress retain the power to override agency regulations and rulings," said Sen. Harrison "Jack" Schmitt, R-N.M., in 1979.

The stalemate continued until 1980 when key House members announced that they would not approve any further funding for the commission until an agreement was reached on the veto issue.

On April 30, after having missed several self-imposed deadlines, House and Senate conferees eventually reached a compromise, but not before the FTC became the first federal agency to shut down because of a funding lapse. The closing lasted only one day, May 1, 1980. But the agency had to shut down again on June 2 and 3, 1980, when Senate procedural delays held up the FTC's 1980 appropriations until two days after its earlier funding had expired.

The compromise legislation that authorized FTC funding through fiscal 1982 also cut back the agency's powers and provided for a two-house veto of its rules. No final trade regulation rule could be implemented for 90 days, giving Congress that much time to overturn the rule. It was the first time Congress had given itself the power to veto actions of an independent regulatory agency without the approval of the president.

"This is indeed landmark legislation marking the first, major effort to recapture control of the government," said Rep. Elliott H. Levitas, D-Ga., a prime backer of the veto proposal. Congress made its first use of the authority two years later, in 1982, to block an FTC rule dealing with used-car sales. *(Used-car rule veto, below)*

Although he called the legislative veto provision "unwise and unconstitutional," President Carter signed the compromise authorization bill into law on May 28, 1980, because he said "the very existence of this agency is at stake." The Federal Trade Commission Improvements Act of 1980, as it was entitled, was not completely satisfactory to all parties but, according to then-Chairman Pertschuk,

"The most serious threats to the agency's ability to protect consumers have not materialized."

The act did not contain the far more restrictive provisions of the earlier House and Senate bills. No major FTC proceeding was terminated.

The act placed a three-year moratorium on existing FTC authority to promulgate rules for unfair commercial advertising, yet allowed the agency's rulemaking proceeding on television advertising aimed at children to continue. The legislation, however, demanded that the FTC would have to consider whether the children's advertising was deceptive, not merely unfair. This effectively stopped the "kidvid" study.

Similarly, the FTC technically was permitted to continue with its study of the insurance industry, but only if the House or Senate Commerce committee requested it. The study could take place only during the session of Congress at which it was requested, and it was limited to general review and analysis of issues.

The legislation permitted the agency to regulate agricultural cooperatives, but only if they exceed the protective limits of the 1922 Capper-Volstead Act, which gave farm cooperatives a measure of antitrust immunity. This provision allowed an FTC case against Sunkist Growers Inc. to continue. The agency charged that the cooperative unlawfully had monopolized western oranges, lemons and lemon products by engaging in anti-competitive practices.

The act also allowed the FTC to issue rules governing the disclosure of funeral home industry prices and service.

During the long and stormy deliberations that preceded final enactment, the Carter White House had indicated that it could accept some form of congressional veto only if no major FTC proceedings were terminated.

Among other things, the bill also tightened the trade regulation rulemaking process, increased restrictions on disclosure of information gained through mandatory reporting by corporations, and cut back the public participation program.

REAGAN-CONGRESS HARMONY ON FTC CUTS

Groups that had chafed for years under FTC restrictions saw an opportunity when the Republican Party took over the White House and Senate in 1981. They began pressing for congressional action to rein in the agency still further.

Associations of doctors, lawyers and other professionals, the Chamber of Commerce of the United States, dairy groups, advertising groups and the National Association of Manufacturers were among leaders of the curb-the-FTC movement.

With the FTC's authorization due to expire Sept. 30, 1982, the coalition launched a massive three-pronged attack that would:

• Renew and expand Congress' power to veto FTC regulatory actions.

• Eliminate or cut funding for "public intervenors," groups paid with federal funds to present testimony that otherwise would not be given in agency proceedings.

• Stop the commission from proceeding with regulatory actions, rulemakings, investigations and lawsuits against specific business interests.

The pressure group campaign fitted in neatly with the new administration's own plans to cut the budget of the regulatory agency and thus limit its activity.

At the same time, the FTC under Miller was acting from within to be more selective in its work. The consumer protection cases inherited from the Carter administration "were not always distinguished by the use of serious economic analysis," the agency said in a report covering the first six months of Miller's stewardship. The report said that the "enormous backlog" covered 1.5 million pages. Together with the antitrust Competition Bureau, the Consumer Protection Bureau dropped a fourth of the 962 matters that had been pending on Oct. 5, 1981.

Money factors became a key to deciding which cases to drop and which to pursue, enhancing the role of the FTC's Bureau of Economics. Miller ordered the antitrust and consumer bureaus to work closely with the Economics Bureau director in evaluating holdover and new cases.

Budget Weapon

However far-reaching Miller's changes may have been, they were mild compared with those he had advocated as the head of Reagan's regulatory transition team. The team's report called for cutting the FTC budget 25 percent by 1982.

Indeed, OMB Director David A. Stockman, the architect of Reagan's federal budget proposals, was reported to have told an interviewer in early 1981 that "the world would never know the difference" if the FTC were eliminated. The transition task force also offered the FTC little reason for optimism, claiming in its report that "A further narrowing of the agency's authority...is sorely needed."

By the spring of 1981 it seemed clear the agency would survive the anti-regulatory, budget-cutting mood of the new Republican administration. It appeared equally as clear that the agency would be subjected to the budgetary constraints to be placed on all federal agencies.

At one point early in the budget deliberations it looked as if the FTC's Bureau of Competition would be dismantled. Top Reagan administration officials split over that controversial move, however, and the proposal was abandoned.

In March 1981 Reagan trimmed the FTC's fiscal 1981 budget to $70.8 million, 4.7 percent less than Carter had proposed. Congress went along with the reduction.

For fiscal 1982, Reagan proposed to cut the agency to $69.4 million, 10.9 percent below Carter's request of $77.9 million. In the end, Congress approved a $68.8 million appropriation for the FTC for 1982, slightly less than Reagan requested but 11.7 percent under the Carter budget.

For fiscal 1983, Reagan proposed cutting the FTC to $60.8 million, or 11.6 percent below the fiscal 1982 appropriation. The cutback called for eliminating 145 staff positions and closing four of the FTC's 10 regional offices.

As of Sept. 23, seven days before the beginning of fiscal 1983, the FTC's new appropriation was still in doubt.

Regional Offices

Closing some or all of the commission's regional offices was a Reagan administration goal from the outset. Revitalization of the regional offices, begun under Weinberger, had continued under Pertschuk to the point where the

Miller: Preaching Reagan's
Regulatory Relief Gospel at the FTC

James Clifford Miller III, chairman of the Federal Trade Commission, grew up in Conyers, Ga., a town not unlike Plains, the hometown of President Jimmy Carter.

But despite their similar origins — and a shared commitment to deregulation — Carter and Miller brought entirely different influences to the FTC. Carter installed as chairman Michael Pertschuk, a consumer advocate and former Senate Commerce Committee counsel who raised the FTC to new heights of activity in patrolling the business community.

Miller, on the other hand, spent much of his first year in office undoing Pertschuk's handiwork, trying to rachet the FTC back to the pre-Carter days — and perhaps back to the pre-Nixon days when the FTC seldom antagonized anybody. To business Miller was a welcome relief from the gadfly Pertschuk. To consumerists he was a symbol of all that was wrong with the Reagan administration.

Regulatory Philosophy

Critics conceded that Miller brought style, grace and blue-ribbon credentials to his job. Even Pertschuk, who stayed on as a commissioner, said that "For the most part I don't agree with what he's doing. But obviously he's a man of integrity with a vision of the agency. I have a vision of the agency, too. Our visions are simply different, that's all."

Miller set forth his vision of what regulation should be in a September 1982 *Los Angeles Times* article explaining why he was "unalterably opposed" to congressional efforts to exempt the professions from FTC antitrust authority.

"That may strike you as strange, coming from a dedicated proponent of what I like to call the 'Ronald Reagan Regulatory Relief Religion,' " he wrote. "It's a gospel I have been preaching for a long time — as an academic, as the executive director of the Presidential Task Force on Regulatory Relief and now as chairman of the Federal Trade Commission. The heart and soul of regulatory relief is to lower prices for consumers — that is, I believe that eliminating unnecessary government regulation will reduce the cost of providing goods and services, with the savings passed on to consumers."

Summed up, that was the regulatory philosophy Miller honed over almost two decades of educational and government service. Born June 25, 1942, in Atlanta, Miller graduated from the University of Georgia in 1964 and received a Ph.D. in economics from the University of Virginia in 1969.

After teaching for a year at Georgia State University, he was a senior staff economist at the Transportation Department until 1972, when he served as a research associate at the Brookings Institution and the American Enterprise Institute for Public Policy Research (AEI) before becoming an associate professor of economics at Texas A&M University.

Miller returned to Washington in July 1974 as a staff economist for the White House Council of Economic Advisers, specializing in transportation, regulation and antitrust policy. He became an AEI adjunct scholar during 1975 and in October joined the Council on Wage and Price Stability as assistant director for government operations and research. At the same time he served on the Ford administration's Domestic Council Regulatory Review Group.

During the Carter presidency Miller was a resident scholar and co-director at AEI's Center for the Study of Government Regulation. He served on the editorial boards of AEI's *Regulation* magazine and *The AEI Economist*.

Five books list Miller as the editor or co-author: *Why the Draft: The Case for a Volunteer Army* (1968); *Economic Regulation of Domestic Air Transport: Theory and Policy* (1974); *Perspectives on Federal Transportation Policy* (1975); *Benefit-Cost Analyses of Social Regulation* (1979); and *Reforming Regulation* (1980).

Reagan Appointment

After the 1980 election Miller headed a Reagan transition team on regulatory agencies, including the FTC, and on Jan. 21, 1981, he became administrator for information and regulatory affairs at the Office of Management and Budget. He simultaneously was executive director of the regulatory relief task force, chaired by Vice President George Bush.

In July 1981, President Reagan appointed him to the FTC and, following Senate confirmation, he assumed the chairmanship on Oct. 5.

Miller and his wife Demaris have a son and two daughters. His mother, a real estate broker, and his father, a retired airline pilot, reside in Conyers.

For relaxation the Millers like to get away on weekends to their one-room log cabin in Virginia's Blue Ridge Mountains, according to a June 1982 profile in *Nation's Business*. Miller also likes to ride a motorcycle to work, a habit developed during his days at the Council of Economic Advisers.

"The other day, on Pennsylvania Avenue near the FTC building, employees arriving for work got a chuckle," the article said. "There was their boss, the stern Chairman Miller, putt-putting into the FTC garage driveway on his Kawasaki, a big grin on his face."

offices sometimes were an irritant to businesses in their areas.

Reagan's fiscal 1983 budget called for closing four of the offices without specifying which ones. Miller targeted the Boston, Denver, Los Angeles and Seattle offices for consolidation into the remaining six offices (New York, Atlanta, Cleveland, Chicago, Dallas and San Francisco). His goal was to accomplish the closings by mid-1982, but he held off in the face of congressional opposition, particularly from Sen. Lowell P. Weicker Jr., R-Conn.

But even though they remained open, at least for the time being, the regional offices lost some staff positions and came under tighter control from Washington headquarters.

Miller told a House subcommittee that the proposed consolidation would "improve efficiency, and make it easier for the bureaus and the regional offices to develop a coordinated, coherent approach to law enforcement." He estimated it would save $3 million to $5 million a year.

Even though he had "reluctantly acquiesced" in the commission's consolidation decision in April 1982, Commissioner Pertschuk fought the closings at subsequent congressional hearings. He said in House testimony that the effort to rejuvenate the offices had paid off. "In 1980, for example," he said, " with just 16 percent of the agency's total budget, the regional offices negotiated 61 percent of all the commission's consent agreements; litigated 52 percent of all its complaints issued that year; and obtained almost 100 percent of the $51 million in consumer redress won the by commission that year."

Pertschuk said it appeared there had been no cost-benefit analysis of the closings and that "From the very start they [the regional offices] were the intended victims of the administration's budget-slashing plans for the FTC."

Self-imposed FTC Curbs

While pressure was mounting outside for restraints on the FTC, the commission was reorganizing internally and taking a number of steps to reappraise whether it should get out of some troublesome areas. Among them:

● Deceptive Advertising. Shortly after he became FTC chairman, Miller told a press conference that the agency should review and possibly discard its 11-year-old rule requiring advertisers to substantiate their claims. He said the expense of proving such claims was being passed on to the consumer, who may prefer "cheap, unreliable products."

The FTC re-authorization bill approved by the Senate Commerce Committee May 11, 1982, would remove the FTC's authority to act against unfair advertising, but it would not prevent the agency from policing "deceptive" ads. Some FTC officials were concerned that this might restrict the agency's ability to require health warnings in cigarette ads.

● Over-the-Counter Drugs. On Feb. 11, 1981, the FTC unanimously rejected proposed restrictions on the advertising of over-the-counter drugs. Down the drain went more than five years of effort, including 19,058 staff hours, 4,230 pages of staff papers, 6,000 pages of documents from outsiders and testimony from 50 expert witnesses.

The aborted rule would have limited drug advertisers to the words the Food and Drug Administration (FDA) had approved for use in labeling the drug. Drug makers protested that in the vast majority of cases there would be no way of knowing if the advertising language was in compli-

ance, because the FDA had covered only a handful of categories in its effort (under way since 1972) to banish unsupported claims from drug labels. Advertising of the sometimes technical terms cleared by FDA, such as "hyperosmotic" or "antiemetic," might confuse the public and lead to the very kind of deception the FTC was trying to avoid, they said.

The commissioners agreed. Said Commissioner Pitofsky in announcing the rule rejection: "I am not convinced that FDA determinations with regard to labeling claims are always or even usually appropriate for drug advertising. There is a danger that a rigid approach which ties advertising to government approved words could restrict the dissemination of truthful and useful information."

Political considerations may have been a factor in the commission's decision. Writing in the July/August 1981 *Regulation*, Clemson University professor Bruce Yandle said that "One is left with the disturbing feeling that in 1975 the commission thought, based on staff recommendations, that the rule was a good idea, and that in 1981 the commission thought, based on policy problems apparent from the outset, that it was not. Interestingly, as a footnote that may reveal more about trends in opinion on regulation than about this decision, it is the second group of commissioners that seems the more liberal of the two. . . ."

Legislative Proposals

In 1982 Miller urged Congress to pare down the FTC's authority to correct unfair and deceptive business practices, limiting it to abuses that cause consumers "substantial injury." He said the agency should be required to determine through cost-benefit analyses whether a questioned practice did enough harm to justify the expense of trying to stop it.

"I see no reason to spend taxpayers' dollars unless consumers will be harmed," Miller told a House subcommittee. He said the FTC already had adopted such a policy, but he urged Congress to write it into law.

He asked Congress to define "deceptive acts or practices" as those that "mislead consumers, acting reasonably in the circumstances, to their detriment, or those that the perpetrator knew or should have known would be false or misleading."

Without a definition, said Miller's first six-month report, "the Commission has exceedingly broad discretion to find deception. Indeed, the agency could do nearly anything it has ever proposed to do under an unfairness theory under the current standard of deception as well. In many ways, the Commission has used its discretion in ways that actually harm consumers, by suppressing truthful and useful information."

He told the Senate Commerce Committee on March 18, 1982, that that the FTC should not be allowed to challenge the opinions in ads, even inaccurate ones, unless they caused economic damage to consumers. If the ads misled only a small group, such as children or the elderly, the FTC could not act under his plan unless it could show that the advertisers knew or should have known they were deceptive.

Commissioner Pertschuk and consumer advocates opposed the proposals. "It just makes the burden on the complainant just so much harder," said Jay Angoff of Congress Watch, a consumer advocacy lobby group.

The advertising industry asked Congress to go even

further, by exempting ads from the FTC's unfairness authority. The threat of prosecution, the ad agencies said, infringed on the right of free speech.

The Senate Commerce Committee's FTC re-authorization bill (S 2499), sponsored by Sen. Kasten, contained elements of Miller's economic test proposal for unfair practices, and it gave the advertising industry the unfairness exemption it wanted. But that was going too far, in Miller's view. He and the other FTC commissioners opposed granting any blanket exemptions.

The version of the bill approved by the House Energy and Commerce Subcommittee on Commerce, Transportation and Tourism would leave intact the FTC's powers.

Regulating the Professions

In line with his opposition to exemptions, Miller was sharply critical of proposals to curb the FTC's antitrust authority over state-licensed professional groups. Groups such as the American Medical Association had sought the exemption, arguing that they already were subject to state regulation.

"If professionals, immune from FTC law enforcement, are allowed to enforce restrictions that block free consumer choice, the evidence is strong that prices will be artificially raised and consumers will thereby suffer direct and tangible injury," Miller told a House subcommittee.

The dispute over professional regulation split the Senate Commerce Committee when it approved the FTC re-authorization bill. The vote was 11-3 for the bill, which would exempt 15 professional groups. Chairman Packwood, one of the dissenters, indicated he and House Commerce Committee Chairman John Dingell, D-Mich., would try to get less restrictive language on professional regulation in the final version of the bill.

Kasten defended the provision as "an appropriate balance between consumer interests and regulatory reform," but his House counterpart, James J. Florio, D-N.J., blasted it as "outrageous, a radical departure from the accepted perception of the public interest."

Nevertheless, there appeared to be strong sentiment in both chambers for at least a partial exemption for professional groups. In 1980 a similar move came within two votes of being approved by Congress. On Sept. 23, 1982, the Senate Appropriations Committee voted 14 to 5 for a one-year suspension of the FTC's authority over professions.

The proposed exemptions would undercut the FTC's efforts to ban medical profession rules against advertising by doctors, a move the FTC contended would widen consumer choice and perhaps result in lower fees. In a 4-4 decision March 23, 1982, the Supreme Court upheld the FTC's right under existing law to strike down the American Medical Association's advertising ban.

In 1978 the FTC lifted restrictions on price advertising by optometrists, opticians and opthamologists. That action, Miller noted in a September 1982 *Los Angeles Times* article, helped the price of contact lenses to drop from $256 in 1978 to $204 in 1982.

"The proposal for a special exemption is bad politics, bad economics and bad law," Miller wrote. ". . .I believe that no one should receive special treatment or special exemptions because of his or her status."

Used Cars and Funeral Homes

In two controversial areas — used cars and funeral homes — the new FTC administration went ahead in 1982 and asserted its regulatory authority over the businesses.

Making its first use of the power it gave itself in 1980 to veto FTC regulations, Congress promptly rejected the used-car rules, which would have required used-car dealers to inform customers of major known defects in cars and explain the extent of warranty coverage. The agency had issued the rule in 1981 after 10 years of investigations, hearings and deliberations.

Used-car dealers lobbied heavily for Congress to throw out the regulation. The Senate adopted the veto measure (S Con Res 6), by a 69-27 vote on May 18; the House followed suit, 286-133, on May 26. The dealers contended the rule would have forced them to pay for expensive inspections to protect themselves from lawsuits. But consumer groups noted that the measure did not specifically require dealer inspections.

The FTC fought the veto. Commissioner Patricia Bailey said that it would jeopardize other regulations the agency was considering, such as one requiring funeral directors to disclose price information. She said the used-car rule was "the major consumer protection measure that has been considered by the Congress during this session."

The congressional debate pointed up the disagreement over insulating regulatory agencies from outside pressures. Senate Commerce Chairman Packwood said the veto would encourage special interests to lobby against regulations they do not like, while the unorganized public would be unable to counter the pressure. The veto, Packwood said, would send a message that "We endorse shabby practices. We endorse cheating. We will take no action against those who would deliberately deceive."

But Sen. Kasten, chairman of the committee's consumer unit, said that the issue was one of state's rights. "I believe that we should not be afraid to use the legislative veto and other tools that are available to regain control of the government," Kasten said.

The Consumers Union of the United States planned to use the case to challenge the constitutionality of the legislative veto process, which already was awaiting Supreme Court review in another case. *(Legislative veto, p. 51)*

The funeral home regulations were the culmination of a seven-year study. Consumer advocates complained that the new rules were too mild, but funeral directors had lobbied Congress vigorously to head off any federal regulation.

As originally proposed in 1975, the rule would have barred 11 practices, such as requiring caskets for cremations. The pared-down version awaiting congressional review had four parts: 1) requiring undertakers to provide itemized price data, including replies to telephone queries; 2) prohibiting cremation except where specifically requested, with no casket required; 3) requiring written explanations of charges for items not selected and 4) blocking undertakers' efforts to discourage price advertising or the offer of low-cost funerals.

Outlook

As the FTC awaited approval of its authorization and appropriation for fiscal 1983, it was impossible to predict the outcome of the various battles at stake in that legislation. Among the possibilities was a congressional reversal of the two-house veto over FTC actions. The House Rules Committee on Sept. 16, 1982 struck that provision from the agency's re-authorization bill.

But it was unlikely that there would be any significant

change of attitude on Capitol Hill toward the agency, or any wholesale lifting of the 1980s restrictions placed on the commission.

For his part, despite his strong opposition to exemptions for specific groups, Miller was not backing down from his campaign to streamline the agency and return the case-by-case approach to its former high standing in FTC operations. He was making no apologies for that approach. "It is true that a lot of cases previous commissions would have taken on are not being taken on now," Miller told a *National Journal* interviewer. "And if that's the same as closing down the agency, I plead guilty.'

Transportation Deregulation

"One of my administration's major goals is to free the American people from the burden of overregulation," President Jimmy Carter said March 4, 1977, proposing legislation to deregulate the airlines. "We must look, industry by industry, at what effect regulation has — whether it protects the public interest, or simply blunts the healthy forces of competition, inflates prices and discourages business innovation. Whenever it seems likely that the free market would better serve the public, we will eliminate government regulation."

It was through the industry-by-industry approach, particularly in the transportation sector, that Carter scored his major regulatory reform successes, securing congressional passage of legislation deregulating airlines, trucks and railroads. A fourth measure, relaxing the tight government restrictions of the intercity bus industry, was enacted in 1982. Indeed, transportation, the first industry subjected to federal economic controls, became a testing ground for deregulation of a major industry.

The initial step in that dramatic reversal was taken in November 1977, when the president signed into law a bill (PL 95-163) removing most federal restrictions on airlines that provided all-cargo service. Under the new law, certain airlines already carrying cargo exclusively were entitled to all-cargo certificates giving them authority to operate nationwide. Most Civil Aeronautics Board (CAB) authority to control the rates set and routes flown by certified (that is, CAB-authorized) all-cargo carriers was abolished. A year after enactment, other carriers could apply for all-cargo certificates. The CAB would have to grant those certificates if the carrier proved itself to be "fit, willing and able."

Although the air cargo bill reformed a relatively small segment of the transportation industry, it provided some impetus for revising regulations for the large air passenger service industry, the next candidate for transportation deregulation. Initially opposed by most major airlines, the 1978 airline deregulation act (PL 95-504) instructed the CAB to stress competition in its regulatory decisions and ordered it to expedite and simplify its procedures. The act facilitated the offering of new services and routes by the airline companies and granted them a measure of flexibility in raising and lowering their fares. Following enactment of the bill, ticket prices fell as airline companies began competing with each other for new business. Instead of immediate disaster, as some airlines had predicted, the industry

prospered during the first year of deregulation as both ridership and profits increased. Although profits fell in subsequent years, many of the reasons for the airlines' financial troubles could be attributed to factors other than deregulation, according to many observers. *(Details of airline deregulation, p. 94)*

Buoyed by the passage of the airline bill, the Carter administration embarked on a vigorous campaign to revise controls over the two other major transportation industries — trucks and railroads — where, like airlines, the initial economic justifications for regulation no longer seemed applicable to the conditions of the late 1970s. The result was far-reaching deregulation plans submitted to Congress in 1979, one for an industry that wanted more freedom and one for an industry that was resisting it. Railroads had long been pressing for deregulation. They claimed that their financial straits stemmed in large part from excessive government restrictions on the way they were required to operate. Unless the federal government eased its regulatory grip, the railroads argued, the amount of subsidies it would have to pay out to prop up the railroads could be expected to grow in coming years.

The trucking industry, on the other hand, initially fought deregulation. Because Interstate Commerce Commission (ICC) rules limited entry of new competitors and kept rates high, existing firms were content with the status quo. The truckers argued that efforts to make their industry more competitive would result in poorer service and would harm the industry's economic stability. Further, the truckers claimed, somewhat ironically, that railroads as well as truckers could be harmed by trucking deregulation. Railroads and trucks compete for the same freight in many instances. Lower prices for the transportation of goods by truck could force the railroads to cut their prices, further depressing their already low earnings, to remain competitive.

In the end, both measures were enacted in 1980. The trucking bill (PL 96-296) and the rail measure (PL 96-448) gave individual truckers and railroads more flexibility to set prices. At the same time, the bills attempted to promote competition by removing most of the carriers' antitrust immunity that had permitted them to set rates collectively.

The airline, trucking and rail deregulation bills had several features in common. They represented attempts to eliminate what had come to be considered needless and damaging regulation. They signaled a return to relying on mechanisms of marketplace competition to achieve what regulation was intended to do in the first place. They were designed to promote the well-being of the industry as a whole and improve its services to the general public, the same goals that regulation initially was intended to achieve.

Three features were central to the bills: they granted price-setting or ratemaking flexibility; streamlined procedures for entry of new carriers; and facilitated abandonment of some non-profitable or circuitous routes by existing carriers. They also contained basic reforms of ICC and CAB powers, spelling out what was to be deregulated and establishing a timetable for accomplishing it.

However, although the measures reduced federal controls and altered the means of regulation, they were not what one might call total "decontrol." The bills revised, but did not entirely do away with, federal supervision of the industry. For example, the ICC continued to exercise the power to approve or disapprove trucking and rail rate schedules and to grant operating authority specifying the routes served and the types of freight handled. Likewise, the CAB retained some controls over airline tariffs and routes.

A remarkable feature of the move to deregulate transportation was the widespread support it received among Republicans and Democrats, consumers and business interests. Perhaps even more remarkable was that the commissions themselves had begun to promote deregulation. Even before the legislation was signed into law, the ICC and CAB had taken administrative actions to implement some decontrols over their respective industries. As it turned out, by endorsing the airline deregulation legislation, the CAB agreed to phase itself out completely.

One principal reason for the receptive political climate of the 1970s was the inflation-ridden economy. Inflationary pressures were particularly hard on what economists term "infrastructure" industries, such as transportation, whose well-being has a pervasive effect on the rest of the economy. In his book, *Regulation and Its Alternatives*, political scientist Alan Stone summarized the severe difficulties in economic performance confronting the transportation and other infrastructure industries. Among them were problems of supplying essential goods, such as fuel and food, where needed; deterioration of service, particularly in rail transportation; and inefficiencies caused by regulation, such as rules that prohibited truckers from carrying cargo on return trips. "But even more important than conspicuous resource misallocation," Stone wrote, "was the widespread view among economists and policy makers that regulation *per se* in transportation inherently led to inefficiency and that a movement toward market mechanisms would lead to greater efficiency and, hence, lower costs for both consumers and corporate purchasers of infrastructural services.

"Their message was that regulated infrastructural services tend to be wasteful, excessively costly, and inefficient.... [W]hen inflation magnifies each rate increase, regulation-induced inefficiencies are perceived to impose an intolerable burden.

"For this reason, the change in the public philosophy toward deregulation of the infrastructural industries drew enormous support from consumer and business interests and, to some extent from many of the regulated firms themselves who sought to adjust to new economic conditions and changed opportunities."

THE ICC, RAILS, TRUCKS AND BUSES

Like numerous other regulatory agencies, the ICC has been a constant target of criticism. Congress and the president never drew up a national transportation policy, let alone one that could respond to the substantial changes and developments in transportation industries. Thus the commission throughout its history promulgated regulations in a piecemeal fashion. *(Background on formation and early history of ICC, p. 11)*

This lack of regulatory coordination caused some serious problems. One of the most pointed examples was the anomalous relationship between the trucking and rail industries. Trucking's share of the nation's freight haul increased 20 times from 1929 to 1977. During the same period the railroads' share less than doubled. *(Chart, p. 92)*

Trucking

Trucking was first placed under federal regulation by the Motor Carrier Act of 1935, enacted in response to the rapid growth of the trucking industry and the depressed economic conditions that confronted it during the 1930s. By the early 1930s trucks were beginning to compete vigorously with railroads. As a result, the latter called for the imposition of controls over trucking. The truckers themselves also sought federal regulations.

Under the 1935 law, the ICC regulated entry into the industry, routes served, commodities transported, rates charged and the finances, mergers and acquisitions of the regulated firms. Exempted from controls were trucks owned by and serving the transportation needs of a single firm and trucks hauling goods such as unprocessed agricultural commodities and newspapers.

After the 1935 law was passed, the trucking industry experienced sustained growth. In 1940 there were about 5 million trucks carrying intercity freight; by the late 1970s that figure had grown to 25 million.

According to the House Public Works and Transportation Committee, the entire trucking industry generated about $108 billion in revenues annually, or 75 percent of all transportation revenues. Trucking regulated by the ICC accounted for $41.2 billion in revenues in 1979 and involved 17,000 firms.

Regulation Criticized

Criticism of the regulatory system grew along with the trucking industry. Critics charged that, under the protective shield of the ICC, new entry into the regulated trucking industry had become limited by the routine opposition of existing carriers to proposals for new or additional service — and by ICC acceptance of the existing carriers' arguments. They further argued that competition was limited by the consistent opposition of trucking companies to lower rates. It also was pointed out that empty "backhauls" were inefficient and seemed contrary to government efforts to conserve energy. ICC restrictions on regulated truckers' routes and commodities forced many firms that hauled goods from one market to another to return empty.

Faced with that situation, and to further his overall goal of relaxing federal regulation over the economy, President Gerald R. Ford in 1975 chose trucking as a major target for revision. His proposal met with immediate and vigorous opposition, particularly from the American Trucking Associations (ATA), representing the regulated carriers, and the International Brotherhood of Teamsters, representing 450,000 trucking employees. They warned that deregulation threatened to destroy what they considered to be the finely tuned balance of the nation's surface transportation system.

Ford did not see his proposal enacted while he was president, but when Jimmy Carter took office in 1977, he promised renewed efforts to ease regulation of the transportation sector.

While the administration was drafting its position on deregulation of the trucking industry, the ICC took steps on its own to deregulate the industry administratively. On Nov. 27, 1978, the commission rejected an application for a general rate increase proposed by the Southern Motor Carriers Rate Conference. The conference had argued that the rate increase was necessary to cover higher labor costs caused by its latest contract with the Teamsters. The ICC countered that industry profits already were too high. "We believe that the total effect of current regulation on motor common carriers of general freight has been to insulate them from price competition to a degree not found in industry generally," the ICC ruled.

The Carter administration backed the ICC move. At a November 1978 press conference Transportation Secretary Brock Adams characterized the ICC's deregulatory efforts as "good but not enough," adding that "the legislative route is preferable." But trucking company stocks tumbled and spokesmen warned that the ICC had endangered the industry's financial stability. Representatives of a number of companies urged members of Congress to push for curbs on the ICC's authority to deregulate the industry administratively.

The situation was further complicated by a selective strike in April 1979 by the Teamsters union and a subsequent lockout by the trucking companies over the Teamsters' wage demands for the next three years. On May 18 union members ratified a new contract that would increase wages and fringe benefits by more than 9 percent a year, according to union and trucking industry estimates.

Deregulation Proposed

On the same day, the Carter administration circulated on Capitol Hill a draft proposal for sweeping deregulation of the trucking industry. Joining Carter in support of the proposal was Edward M. Kennedy, D-Mass., then a likely contender for the presidency in 1980. Kennedy had pressed for deregulation legislation for two years, and his staff worked with the White House on the Carter proposal.

The Carter-Kennedy bill, which was formally proposed June 21, would have removed several ICC restrictions on truck routes and types of goods hauled, made it easier for new carriers to enter the market and given carriers considerable freedom to raise or lower their rates. The bill also proposed repeal of the Reed-Bulwinkle Act (PL 80-662), a 1948 law that permitted trucking companies to form "rate bureaus" to set prices collectively for their services without violating the antitrust laws. Such bureaus, which already existed for the railroad and ocean shipping industries, allowed individual trucking firms to band together on a formal basis to fix prices for their services. The bureaus

were needed, according to supporters of the 1948 act, to bring a measure of economic security and stability to the regulated carriers and to assure a continuity of service for shippers through periods of boom and bust.

Continued opposition from carriers and truckers made legislators reluctant at first to consider the legislation. But after the ICC threatened to take further decontrol steps, congressional leaders began to act. Senate Commerce Committee Chairman Howard W. Cannon, D-Nev., pledged to send a bill to the president by June 1980.

Fearing that agency deregulation would be more stringent than congressional deregulation, the ATA and Teamsters muted their campaign against the legislation, although they continued to oppose certain provisions of the resulting bill, which was signed into law on July 1, 1980.

The final measure created a zone of rate flexibility that provided individual truckers more freedom to determine their rates. The law made it easier for new trucking firms to enter the industry and ended some of the industry's antitrust immunity provided by the 1948 Reed-Bulwinkle Act.

In addition, the legislation outlawed "lumping," the practice of coercing a driver to pay for unnecessary loading or unloading assistance. Other major provisions included the elimination of gateway and circuitous route restrictions for hauling food, agricultural products and livestock; and less regulation of "piggyback" freight traffic, the carrying of truck trailers on railroad flatcars.

The Motor Carrier Act was expected to save consumers $5 billion annually in lower prices due to cheaper transportation costs. The ICC began implementation of the act immediately upon passage.

Writing in the January/February 1982 issue of *Regulation* magazine, Thomas G. Moore, a senior fellow at the Hoover Institution, termed the 1980 Motor Carrier Act "very successful," noting that it "had led to discounted rates, more trucks, improved service, service innovations and more Teamster concessions [concerning union wages]." But Moore went on to say that the Reagan administration was "backsliding" in the transportation deregulation effort. First of all, the administration had replaced Darius Gaskins, a Carter appointee and a strong advocate of deregulation, with Reese Taylor, a regulatory lawyer in private practice, as chairman of the ICC. Moore said Taylor had taken some steps to slow deregulation, such as increasing restrictions on new operating permits for truckers and rejecting some applications for rate reductions. Taylor denied the allegations. "I didn't come to turn the clock back. I didn't come to re-regulate," he said Jan. 22, 1982. "If there is to be a slowdown on the deregulatory approach or any advancement, it's up to Congress."

Nonetheless, criticism that the deregulation momentum had decreased significantly under Taylor came from some of the chief supporters of the 1980 legislation: Reagan's Council of Economic Advisers; the Joint Economic Committee (JEC), a bipartisan congressional panel; consumer advocacy groups; and segments of the industry and shippers. "The ICC under Chairman Taylor has abandoned the goal of a freely competitive trucking market and has moved to reverse the progress toward deregulation which has recently been made," the JEC said in a report released Feb. 3, 1982.

On the other hand, the ATA and Teamsters said the ICC was actually implementing the law more carefully and properly than its predecessor. "We think he's doing what the law requires," said Edward V. Kiley, senior vice presi-

Regulated Carrier Freight Revenue, 1940-1981

In dollars

Year	Air[1]	Rail	Truck
1981	$1,617,705,000	not available	$47,000,000,000[2]
1980	1,552,836,000	$26,756,612,000	43,000,000,000
1979	1,455,828,000	23,903,554,000	41,200,000,000
1978	1,326,842,000	20,610,292,000	36,500,000,000
1977	1,085,888,000	19,231,953,000	31,000,000,000
1976	932,958,000	17,706,608,000	26,000,000,000
1975	781,668,000	15,623,005,000	22,000,000,000
1970	498,322,000	11,124,128,000	14,585,000,000
1965	243,110,000	9,036,540,000	10,068,000,000
1960	118,873,000	8,151,706,000	7,214,000,000
1955	76,853,000	8,665,379,000	5,535,000,000
1950	44,583,000	7,933,764,000	3,737,000,000
1945	not available	6,617,213,000	1,406,000,000
1940	not available	3,584,201,000	867,000,000

[1] Airline statistics are for scheduled domestic operations, freight and express revenues.
[2] Estimate

Source: Civil Aeronautics Board, Interstate Commerce Commission, American Trucking Associations.

While revenues for both railroad and trucking companies increased since the Great Depression, trucking revenues claimed a higher and higher percentage of freight revenues. By 1980 when the two industries were deregulated, the trucking industry accounted for about 75 percent of all freight revenues. Trucking regulated by the Interstate Commerce Commission made up less than half of the industry's total revenues.

dent of ATA. "He's not dragging his feet," Roy Cayton, executive vice president of Overnite Transportation Corp. of Richmond, Va., asserted.

Some Office of Management and Budget (OMB) officials had been concerned about the ICC, but Christopher DeMuth, OMB administrator for information and regulatory affairs, said Taylor was "doing as much as he can."

Meanwhile, Taylor appointed a task force to review statutes with an eye toward asking Congress to eliminate some of the ICC's regulatory powers. The commission also was considering steps to further reduce regulation.

Railroads

While the trucking industry had criticized the ICC for moving too quickly toward deregulation, the railroad industry was concerned that the commission was moving too slowly.

Plagued by complex regulations, excessive trackage, management problems and other ailments, the railroad industry in 1970 had realized its lowest net income in 25 years. A decade later, the situation was no better, and many observers felt that fewer federal restrictions might help to solve the industry's problems.

'The Four R Act'

In 1976 Congress, seeking to ease the railroads' plight by allowing them greater authority to raise and lower their fares and to drop service on unprofitable routes, passed the Railroad Revitalization and Regulatory Reform Act (PL 94-210).

Implementation of the "Four R Act" was left to the ICC, and instead of acting quickly to transfer some of its pricing authority to the railroads, the commission interpreted the legislation conservatively and moved slowly. According to an October 1978 Transportation Department report, "A Prospectus for Changes in the Freight Railroad Industry," the potential benefit of the new law "was minimized by the ICC." While the Four R Act had reduced government controls, the report concluded, "the ICC still constrains the railroads' freedom of action."

As a result, Carter on March 23, 1979, submitted to Congress rail deregulation legislation that he said was needed to avert a "crisis" in the rail industry. "Though railroads still carry more than a third of the nation's freight and most of its bulk commodities such as coal, grain and chemicals," Carter said, "the industry is in a deep and dangerous decline. Year by year, the percentage of freight carried by the railroads has shrunk while profits have fallen and costs have soared."

If the railroads were not deregulated, Transportation Secretary Adams and chief White House domestic adviser Stuart E. Eizenstat said during a briefing for reporters the same day, the industry's declining economic health could cost taxpayers an estimated $13 billion to $16 billion in subsidies over the next five years.

"Catastrophic" railroad bankruptcies and service declines also might result if the railways were not deregulated, they maintained. "Simply stated," Adams said, "it is a bill to save the railroads."

The administration sought to minimize the possibility that deregulation of rail rate-setting might lead to rapid price increases, thus fueling inflation. Adams acknowledged rates were likely to rise for certain commodities and on certain routes where existing rates were being held to artificially low levels by government regulation. However, in other areas, where deregulation would result in increased competition between rail firms or between trucking and railroad transportation, lower prices would result, he said. While prices might go up overall in the first few years after the enactment of deregulation legislation, in the long run, said the secretary, "I would expect [the impact] to be deflationary."

ICC Chairman Gaskins explained the intent of the administration's proposal: "The key variable is rate competition in the market. Railroads will grow and prosper or shrink and go out of business on that basis."

Industry Support

The Association of American Railroads and railroad labor groups lobbied hard for the legislation, contending it was necessary to maintain an adequate rail network and prevent further bankruptcies. Opposing them were the coal industry, utilities that depended on coal, agricultural shippers, ports, other shippers and consumer groups. They argued that the legislation would permit railroads to raise rates excessively, especially for hauling coal, with little opportunity for federal review. Higher coal haul rates would result in higher utility bills, they said. They also warned that permitting carriers to abandon rail lines, would leave some shippers, especially coal shippers, "captive" to more costly forms of transportation.

But many of those critics withdrew their opposition after winning several concessions in Congress, including ICC review of rates under limited conditions, some protections against surcharges on joint rates (the rates charged when more than one rail carrier handled a shipment), and greater ability for agricultural shippers to negotiate rates with rail carriers.

The resulting compromise legislation, patterned after the earlier trucking deregulation measure, cleared Congress in September 1980 after months of controversy and an intensive lobbying campaign by the Carter administration. Entitled the Staggers Rail Act of 1980, the bill removed most of the railroads' ability to set prices collectively through rate bureaus, which previously were not subject to federal antitrust prosecution.

Like the Motor Carrier Act of 1980, the rail legislation created a regulation-free zone of rate flexibility within which carriers could annually raise or lower rates. The bill allowed the ICC to investigate a rate change within the zone of flexibility only if the increase resulted in a rate 20 percentage points above a stated threshold. If the ICC refused to investigate, it had to explain why.

In determining whether to take action, the ICC had to consider, among other factors, the impact of the rate on national energy goals and the carrier's mix of cargo to determine if one commodity was subsidizing the transportation costs of other commodities. A shipper challenging a rate below 20 points above the threshold would bear the burden of proving that the rate was unreasonable.

The rail law streamlined procedures for abandonment of service. If significant opposition to a proposed abandonment developed, the ICC could hold a formal proceeding; however, the commission was not required to investigate the case and a hearing was no longer mandatory procedure.

In his *Regulation* article, Moore termed the Staggers Act "generally successful. The rate freedom allowed under the act has permitted the railroads to pick up new business. The railroads and most shippers seem very happy. Only the coal shippers, who feel their rates have been increased too much, have been murmuring against the Staggers Act."

Intercity Buses

Intercity buses were the fourth transportation industry to undergo significant regulatory reform in as many years. Like railroads, trucks and airlines, bus deregulation, enacted in August 1982, allowed new bus companies to enter the industry, while existing firms could expand their operations or drop unprofitable routes with less government involvement than had previously existed. In addition, the bill gave companies more flexibility in raising or lowering rates without government interference. At the same time, like the legislation affecting the trucking and rail industries, the measure limited the companies' ability to set rates collectively through rate bureaus free of antitrust laws.

"Everyone who travels by bus and everyone who ships by bus can look forward to improved service," said John C. Danforth, R-Mo., chairman of the Senate Commerce Surface Transportation Subcommittee. The bill was supported by the American Bus Association, which represented the two largest companies (Greyhound Lines Inc., and Trailways Inc.), as well as small carriers; United Bus Owners Association, which represented mostly small firms; the Transportation Department; the ICC; and labor.

Bus companies had sought relaxation of government controls to allow companies to operate more efficiently and compete more vigorously with each other and with airlines and private cars. In particular, they sought freedom from some state regulation that had barred buses from picking up or dropping off passengers on intermediate points along routes. Industry officials also contended that state regulators had kept rates for service within a state unfairly low. The bill pre-empted some state regulation under certain circumstances.

One concern — which also had surfaced during debate over the airline, trucking and rail bills — was that service on less profitable, primarily rural, routes might be lost. "Many places are difficult to reach under present circumstances. Any decrease in bus service would only result in greater isolation for these communities," Senate Minority Leader Robert C. Byrd, D-W. Va., said during debate on the bus deregulation.

To alleviate those concerns the bill allowed the ICC to consider the effect of deregulation on services to small communities and whether a new service would impair the ability of any other bus carrier to continue a substantial portion of its regular-route passenger operations.

SUCCESSFUL TAKEOFF
FOR AIR DEREGULATION

"For the first time in decades, we have deregulated a major industry," declared President Carter Oct. 24, 1978, as he signed into law a bill that would end most federal regulation of commercial passenger airlines.

A top priority of the Carter administration, the legislation (PL 95-504) was intended to increase marketplace competition by phasing out over a seven-year period the federal controls that had been in place for 40 years. Substantially lower fares were expected as a result of the new pro-competition policies.

Even before Carter was sworn in as president, his advisers were urging him to declare his support for airline deregulation legislation. Because the issue already had been the subject of extensive hearings in the previous Congress, Carter's aides reasoned that the president could score a "quick hit" — an early legislative victory — by endorsing a measure already well on its way toward enactment.

But passage was neither quick nor easy. It took nearly a year for the bill to emerge from the Senate Commerce Committee and 10 weeks for companion legislation to clear the House Public Works Aviation Subcommittee. Once the bill reached the floor, it was entangled in a controversy over the separate issue of airplane noise, and it was not until the last day of its 1978 session that Congress approved airline deregulation.

Although Congress gave Carter all he wanted in a deregulation bill, the end product did not reveal the struggles along the way. Some airline companies favored deregulation, but most of them strongly opposed it. So did the airline labor unions, which feared deregulation would lead to job losses as the larger companies drove the smaller ones out of business. And small communities were concerned that increased competition would result in service losses to them as the airlines concentrated on the more lucrative major markets.

As proposed by the administration and cleared by Congress, the bill instituted an automatic entry program, whereby airlines would be allowed to enter new routes without needing to receive approval from the CAB, which regulated the industry. At the same time, an airline would be able to designate three routes to be protected from automatic entry by potential competitors during the period 1979-81. The bill also gave carriers a measure of flexibility in raising and lowering their fares.

To assure continued service to small communities, the bill guaranteed that "essential air transportation service" would be continued for a 10-year period. And the CAB was authorized to grant subsidies to airlines serving those routes. The bill also made airline employees eligible for compensation if they lost their jobs, had their wages cut or were forced to relocate due to increased industry competition brought on by enactment of the deregulation legislation. *(Provisions, box, p. 97)*

The sum of those provisions represented a philosophy diametrically opposed to that which produced the Civil Aeronautics Act in 1938. Ironically many of the arguments in favor of deregulation in the 1970s echoed arguments in favor of controls in the 1930s: concern for the health of the airline industry and a desire to enable it to meet challenges posed by the economic conditions of the time. And in both eras, those concerns were viewed as inextricably linked to the well-being of the consumers of air services. Nonetheless, in the space of 40 years the pendulum had come full swing.

Development of Airline Controls

The first general federal regulatory statute affecting civil aeronautics was the Air Commerce Act of 1926. That law imposed safety regulations but no economic restrictions on air carriers. Until 1938 any person complying with safety requirements was at liberty to operate an airline. As a practical matter, however, most conventional airlines were successful only if they held a mail contract with the U.S. Post Office Department. Those contracts were obtained through competitive bidding. Consequently the various airmail laws controlled to some extent the pattern of competition among carriers holding airmail contracts.

By 1938 there had developed two general categories of "air carriers." The first and economically most significant group was composed of the airmail contractors who flew over established routes and transported passengers, property and mail. The second consisted of so-called "fixed-base operators," most of whom operated airports, flying schools, crop-dusting planes and similar enterprises that carried passengers and property on a "fly anywhere anytime" basis in small aircraft, usually intended for other purposes.

The Civil Aeronautics Act of 1938, which replaced the Air Commerce Act of 1926 and the various airmail statutes, was enacted as much to promote the economic health of the industry as to regulate it. The 1938 act broadened the scope of safety regulation and subjected air carriers to the same type of economic regulation imposed on public utilities (except that it did not control issuance of securities). Carriers were given authority, in the form of certificates of public convenience and necessity, to transport passengers, property and mail only after the need for such service had been established in a public hearing. The act imposed controls over rates, routes and schedules.

"Grandfather" provisions gave certificates to most air carriers (the original mail contractors) then in operation. The holders of those certificates (American, Braniff, Continental, Delta, Eastern, National, Northwest, Trans World, United, Western and Pan American) became known as the "trunkline" carriers conducting long-haul passenger and cargo operations over the principal air routes. The certificate provisions also were used to authorize specialized carriers such as local service or "feeder" airlines, helicopter services and charter air carriers.

The 1938 law linked control over rates and entry to a federal subsidy program that provided payments for carrying mail. It was enacted when airlines were in their infancy and needed help to prevent destructive competition, particularly in the wake of the Depression. In Congress, debate did not concern the desirability of regulation so much as how it should be accomplished and who should do it (that is, whether the Interstate Commerce Commission or a new agency should have oversight responsibility).

Originally, the act was administered by three groups of officials: a five-member Civil Aeronautics Authority, a three-member Air Safety Board and an administrator of civil aeronautics. In 1940 the Air Safety Board was abolished and its functions transferred to the Civil Aeronautics

Authority which was renamed the Civil Aeronautics Board. The administrator of civil aeronautics was placed under the Department of Commerce as head of an agency called the Civil Aeronautics Administration (CAA).

Basically the CAB was responsible for economic regulation and route control, development of safety standards for aircraft and investigations of aircraft accidents. The CAA monitored airway operations and traffic control; policed the industry for compliance with safety rules, including recommending to the CAB that an air carrier's safety certificate be revoked; and developed safety standards for operations. The CAA also administered the Federal Airport Act, which provided airport development assistance to states and municipalities.

That structure was altered in 1958 with passage of the Federal Aviation Act, which overhauled the laws related to airline regulations and reorganized the responsibilities of the CAB. The CAA was abolished and replaced by the Federal Aviation Agency (then an executive agency, renamed the Federal Aviation Administration and incorporated into the Department of Transportation in 1967). The CAB retained all of its duties having to do with economic regulation, while all safety functions were transferred to the Federal Aviation Agency.

In effect, economic regulation meant that any carrier servicing more than one state had to obtain a certificate from the CAB before starting to operate and that CAB approval was needed to change any routes and to lower, as well as raise, air fares.

Road to Deregulation

By the beginning of the 1970s, the airline industry hardly could be recognized as the one addressed by the 1938 act. From an "infant industry" it had developed into a multi-billion dollar business with hundreds of aircraft and thousands of employees. It was no longer the struggling concern it had been when the CAB was created, and many observers were beginning to say the time had come to remove or relax the rigid economic regulation exercised over the air carriers.

CAB regulations made it difficult for new companies to begin operations and for existing companies to enter new routes. Federal regulation also eliminated most price competition among airlines. That meant the air transport industry was virtually closed to outsiders and, some argued, no longer served the best interests of its customers. As one observer noted, the CAB had come to pursue "zealously anticompetitive" policies that made the agency "vulnerable to charges that it was protecting the airlines at the expense of the traveling public."

"Between 1938 and 1974, the CAB generally placed its primary emphasis on sustaining 'sound financial conditions' for each of the certified airlines providing scheduled passenger service," wrote Bradley Behrman, in a study of the CAB in *The Politics of Regulation*. "It refused to allow new airlines to enter the industry or existing carriers to enter each other's routes when it appeared that new entry would harm the financial interests of an existing carrier." The CAB, he said, was in the position of managing an "imperfect cartel." The board "could keep newcomers out of the industry and could prop prices higher than they would otherwise be, but it could not prevent airlines servicing the same routes from competing with respect to various aspects of service quality," such as meals, frequency and timing of flights.

Intrastate carriers were able to charge lower fares

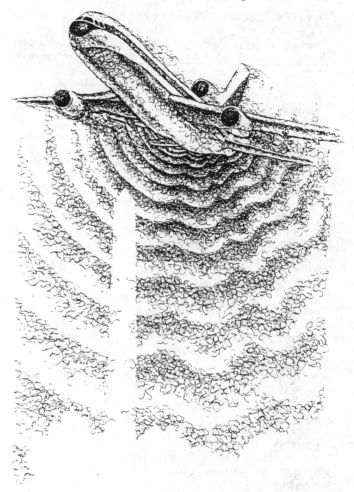

while at the same time realizing higher profits than the CAB-controlled and certified carriers. The smaller intrastate planes had proportionately more seats for their size and a higher percentage of those seats were filled. It seemed that many people preferred the low fare, "no frills" service.

Besides lack of competition within the industry, a number of other factors converged to make the mid-1970s ripe for airline deregulation. Following the 1973 Arab oil embargo, fuel prices soared. In response, the CAB let fares rise sharply and phased out some discount fares. The embargo was a major cause of America's general economic inflation, a situation that made many lawmakers more receptive to regulatory reform proposals and to decontrol of the airlines in particular.

But, somewhat paradoxically, it was the CAB itself that provided the principal impetus for the 1978 act — and its own eventual demise. That began when President Ford appointed John Robson a member and chairman of the CAB. Robson was initially noncommital about regulation, but under his leadership the CAB actively worked for airline decontrol.

Deregulation Enacted

"Few regulatory agencies — if any — have ever altered their policies as rapidly or radically as did the Civil Aeronautics Board between 1974 and 1978," wrote Behrman. "In 1974 the CAB was striving vigorously to protect the airline industry from competition and was regarded by many critics as the epitome of an agency 'captured' by the industry it regulates. In 1976 the agency unanimously endorsed legislation that would have substantially reduced its powers to restrain competition — legislation strongly opposed by the airline industry. By 1978 the CAB not only was supporting deregulatory legislation but also was doing everything it could (within legal and political constraints) to deregulate without even waiting for new legislation. When Congress passed the Airline Deregulation Act of 1978 — which [made] the CAB the first major federal regulatory agency ever to be abolished [by an act of Congress] — it did not so much *impose* reforms on the CAB as it *affirmed* policies that the CAB had been trying to implement for almost a year. In fact, the CAB's pursuit of deregulation played a prominent role in diminishing congressional opposition to the new legislation."

Indeed, the new competition in the airline industry was felt even before the deregulation measure went into effect. Under CAB Chairman Robson and his successor, Alfred Kahn, appointed by President Carter in 1977, the agency had acted administratively to inject an experimental dose of competition into the commercial passenger airline industry. Despite initial misgivings of many airline companies, passengers and profits increased during this trial period, and the airlines began to prepare strategies to capitalize on what they anticipated would be more extensive deregulation.

Even with CAB support, the fate of the deregulation law was in doubt until almost the last moment. Deregulation supporters feared the bill might die in the final days of the 1978 session because of attempts to hold it hostage to enactment of a controversial measure providing federal subsidies for airline noise abatement. To their relief, however, Congress decided to separate the two bills, and the deregulation measure cleared on Oct. 15, the last day of the session.

Four days before the bill was to become law, a line began to form outside the Washington office of the CAB. Soon, about 30 airline company representatives stood there, patiently waiting for Carter to sign the bill so that they could file for new routes under the liberalized conditions set by PL 95-504.

On Nov. 13, the CAB issued its first decision under the new law, awarding 248 new routes to 22 airlines. The routes were those on which only one company had provided a minimum level of service. Of the 22 airlines, six were intrastate carriers receiving their first interstate route awards.

At the same time, the CAB permitted nine airlines to retain 52 routes they were authorized to serve, but on which they were not actually operating plane service. Under the new law, the airlines were given 45 days to begin flying on the new routes and 30 days to serve routes they already were authorized to serve. If the companies did not begin service within the designated period of time, the routes were to become eligible for new applicants.

Before the act there were 36 CAB-certified airlines. By 1982 there were more than 90, according to a spokesman for the Air Transport Association (ATA), which represented major airlines. Among the new airlines were a number of smaller companies, such as Midway Airlines, which offered discount flights between Chicago's Midway Airport and other large cities; and Air New York, which offered low-fare flights on the East Coast, some between New York and Washington, D.C., in competition with the Eastern Airline shuttle.

At the same time, a number of airline companies announced merger plans. Among them were National Airlines and Pan American World Airways. North Central Airlines and Southern Airways united to form Republic Airlines. Some of the mergers, such as that between Western and Continental Airlines, were designed to strengthen relatively smaller and weaker airlines.

Although many of the smaller airlines initially feared they might be overrun by large carriers, they generally did well under deregulation. As the larger airlines dropped the short-haul routes, the smaller companies sometimes found themselves operating in near-monopoly markets. Their size made them well suited and cost-effective for the short-haul routes that the major airlines with larger planes could not operate profitably. "We have found niches," commented William Howard, president of Piedmont Airlines, during an ABC news program aired July 6, 1982. His company had chosen routes that passengers needed and had offered them new services, instead of "fighting for a share of the big pie."

Deregulation also meant that smaller airlines found themselves able to enter longer-haul routes more easily. "We certainly decided that we were going to come up with a program to run the airline as profitably as we could under deregulation, and that meant making necessary changes in the route structure that would benefit us," said Edwin I. Colodny, chairman of USAir (formerly Allegheny) in 1980. "We've simply continued to do what we had been trying to do for some years, namely expand our longer-haul flying to some markets such as Houston and Florida where we were able to capitalize on the more productive use of our aircraft plus improve our seasonality." (The airline previously had been concentrated in the Northeast, but with new services to the South, USAir enjoyed a profit in the first quarter of 1980 for the first time in its 43-year history.)

The deregulation act's provision for increased flexibility in setting air fares also had a beneficial impact on some airline companies, according to Colodny. "The ability to implement fare increases on a very timely basis to cover the very radical fuel increases of [1979] really has been very significant," he said. "Under the old system, we had tremendous lag in recovery of inflationary costs."

"The present trend is toward less concentration," said the CAB office of economic analysis in a June 1981 study. "Smaller airlines tend to be growing faster than larger airlines. The evidence suggests that there is little likelihood the industry will evolve into a highly concentrated oligopoly or monopoly. In some important ways, the air service network has become more integrated under competition."

Problems for Airlines and Airports

Despite the initial glow of deregulation, all was not well with the airlines. By 1981 the industry was showing an operating loss of $428 million, and ridership was down to 285 million passengers, from an all-time high of 317 million in 1979. Losses for the first quarter of 1982 were a record $600 million.

Beginning in the spring of 1979, the industry was socked by a surge in fuel costs. The average cost of a gallon of jet fuel jumped from 40 cents in 1978 to $1.05 in 1981. At the same time, the general economic recession cut into the number of discretionary fliers. And the industry was further dealt another blow in 1981 by the striking Professional Air Traffic Controllers Organization. According to ATA, the strike resulted in the imposition by the Transportation Department of restrictions at 22 major airports that initially cut airline operations in half. As of May 1982, the

Airline Decontrol Provisions

As signed into law, the 1978 Airline Deregulation Act (PL 95-504) contained the following major provisions:

CAB Policy. The bill changed the declaration of policy guiding the Civil Aeronautics Board (CAB) from one of promoting the nation's air transportation system to one of placing "maximum reliance" on competition in its regulation of interstate airline passenger service. The CAB would still be responsible for preventing anti-competitive and monopolistic industry practices and maintaining regular air service to small and isolated communities.

Other provisions of the bill were designed to speed up CAB actions; broaden the CAB's authority to prevent potentially anti-competitive agreements, mergers and other actions; and increase the board's discretion to grant exemptions from CAB regulation.

CAB Certification. The legislation ordered the CAB to authorize new services that were "consistent with the public convenience and necessity." The CAB was required to grant operating rights to any air carrier seeking to serve a route on which only one other carrier was actually providing service and on which other carriers were authorized to serve but were not providing a specified minimum level of service.

If two or more airlines actually were providing service on such a route, the CAB could allow additional service only if it determined such service was "consistent with the public convenience and necessity." The CAB could revoke the right of an airline that did not provide the specified minimum level of service.

Under existing law, the CAB was authorized to certify a particular service only if it was "required" by public convenience and necessity. According to the Senate Commerce Committee, the agency had used its discretion under the law "both to prevent any significant entry into the industry by new firms and to frustrate the expansion of existing firms." Between 1950 and 1974, the committee report stated, the CAB received 79 applications from new firms interested in serving domestic air routes, yet none was granted.

Automatic Market Entry. The legislation provided for an automatic market entry program, whereby airlines could begin service on one additional route each year during the period 1979-81 without formal CAB approval. Each carrier also was permitted to protect one of its existing routes each year by designating it as not eligible for automatic market entry by another carrier.

In its report, the Senate Commerce Committee said the automatic entry provision was necessary "to provide a meaningful threat of entry to insure that carriers will not fail to provide innovative or lower priced service in those markets in which it is economically feasible."

Small Community Service. To ensure that airline deregulation did not result in the loss of service to small communities and isolated areas, the legislation phased out over seven years the existing system of airline subsidies based on mail deliveries. This was replaced with a subsidy program designed expressly to preserve "essential air transportation" as determined by the CAB.

Charters, Commuters. The bill required the CAB to impose rules and requirements on charter airlines that were no more rigid than those it imposed on other classes of air carriers.

Commuter aircraft were required to conform to the safety requirements imposed on larger passenger aircraft "to the maximum feasible extent." Commuter aircraft weighing less than 18,000 pounds and carrying fewer than 56 passengers were exempted from most CAB regulation. (The Federal Aviation Administration — and not the CAB — was charged with regulating airline safety under existing law.)

Mergers. The bill required CAB approval of airline consolidations, mergers, purchases, leases, operating contracts and acquisitions. The burden of proving the anti-competitive effects of such actions was placed on the party challenging an action. Airline company acquisitions by non-airline companies were exempted from the CAB's authority.

All inter-company agreements affecting air transportation were required to have CAB approval, and the board was ordered not to approve any agreement reducing competition unless it found that the agreement served a "serious transportation need" or provided "an important public benefit."

Fares. The legislation established a zone of "reasonable and just" charges within which a carrier was free to set its fares without prior CAB approval. The zone ranged from 5 percent above to 50 percent below the "standard industry fare." This was defined as the fare in effect for a particular service on July 1, 1977, subject to semiannual CAB review and adjustment. The CAB still was authorized to disallow a fare if it considered it to be predatory.

Employee Protection. The bill made persons employed by an air carrier for at least four years eligible for compensation for a maximum of six years if they lost their jobs, had their wages cut or were forced to relocate due to increased airline industry competition brought on by enactment of the deregulation measure.

CAB Authority. The bill provided that, unless Congress acted to extend it, the board's authority over domestic routes would end Dec. 31, 1981; that its authority over domestic rates and fares, mergers and acquisitions would expire Jan. 1, 1983; and that the board would be abolished on Jan. 1, 1985.

airways system was operating at only 83 percent of the pre-strike level.

Rising fuel prices and declining traffic resulted in flight cancellations that affected nearly 400 localities in 1980. By 1982 about half of the nation's commercial airports had lost scheduled airline service as a result of those factors and the air controllers' strike. Many aviation officials in small and mid-sized cities feared that increases in air fares — due largely to rising fuel costs — would contribute still further to declining passengers and service. "We were far better off without deregulation," said Robert W. Ross, director of the Grand Rapids airport, in March 1981. "Cities like ours are hurt the worst; we're caught in the middle. Airlines are flocking to the big cities, and if we were smaller we could get subsidy. But the Civil Aeronautics Board tells us we're fine."

Albert J. Huber, general manager of Sandiford Field in Louisville, Ky., voiced similar sentiments: "Deregulation was touted as being beneficial to the consumer, bringing more service and lower fares. But that just hasn't happened. It's a rip-off. We don't have access to the deep discount fares that exist in New York, Florida and California, and we spend more time trying to get where we want to go."

With the airlines free to choose their routes, many began to adopt "hub and spoke" systems that usually meant fewer direct and non-stop flights between medium- and small-sized cities and more re-routing through larger cities. "I used to be able to fly up to Cleveland on an early morning flight, transact business and get on a return flight to Louisville that afternoon. Now, for the same amount of business, I must go up the night before, stay in an expensive hotel room and buy three restaurant meals," complained one Louisville businessman in 1981.

Operators of large metropolitan hub airports expressed concern about their ability to provide gate and ticketing facilities and necessary support space and service for the additional air carriers they handled. "Our terminals are saturated with people morning, noon and night, even though we just completed a 100 percent expansion program," said one airport executive, who was quoted in the Sept. 12, 1979, *Christian Science Monitor*. "Things are in a state of disarray, but we are simply not going to move beyond temporary solutions to today's problems until we find out whether this deregulation mess is temporary or permanent."

Despite the airlines' financial difficulties — dramatically illustrated by the 1982 bankruptcy of Braniff International — there appeared to be little interest in the early 1980s among members of Congress or the industry to reinstate federal controls. Key members of Congress, administration officials and industry spokesmen said Braniff's difficulties resulted largely from poor management, the economic downturn and high fuel prices, not deregulation.

Deregulation, they said, was doing what it was supposed to do — increase competition and allow management flexibility — and might even have helped some airlines weather economic problems better than they otherwise might have done.

"I don't think you can blame deregulation for the fact that in this case past management made bad decisions," Norman Y. Mineta, D-Calif., chairman of the House Public Works Aviation Subcommittee, said May 13, 1982, after Braniff began bankruptcy proceedings.

Paul R. Ignatius, president of the ATA, said most carriers believed it would be a mistake to re-regulate, even though they originally opposed deregulation. "It became the law of the land, and they're adjusting to it," he said.

Although there was considerable debate in Congress and the executive branch about putting the CAB out of business earlier than the deregulation act's 1985 deadline, no one agreed on when it should be done. The Reagan administration in 1981 proposed Sept. 30, 1982, as the last day for the CAB. The early sunset would eliminate the cost of operating the agency longer than necessary, said Transportation Secretary Drew Lewis. A CAB plan would terminate the board Oct. 1, 1983. Under a bill sponsored by Mineta, the CAB would cease to exist 150 days after the bill became law.

Disagreement about labor protection and other matters, as well as greater interest in enacting other aviation programs — including funds for airport development and air traffic control system modernization — effectively killed early sunset legislation for 1982. The administration measure, supported by the airlines and opposed by unions, would repeal labor protection measures such as giving employees laid off because of increased competition the right of first-hire by other firms.

As of 1982, little had been done to enforce the employee protection provisions of the 1978 law. The Department of Labor had not completed regulations that would allow unemployed workers to claim new jobs and file for benefits. Some observers said the administration was postponing action because the provisions would be expensive to implement. "Due to bureaucratic machinations in the government, our members are not getting the compensation that Congress provided for them," said James W. Johnson, staff lawyer of the Air Line Pilots Association, which represented 70 former Air New England pilots seeking compensation after the company folded in 1981.

"No institutional change of the magnitude of airline deregulation is going to please everyone," wrote James C. Miller in the March 26, 1980, *Wall Street Journal*. (Miller subsequently served as Reagan's director of the Office of Information and Regulatory Affairs at the Office of Management and Budget and then was appointed chairman of the Federal Trade Commission.) "Some have gained more than others, and some, at least for a time, may actually be worse off. But what is striking about airline deregulation is how limited and localized the adverse effects have been. And no program of publicizing horror stories is going to change that basic fact.

"The evidence thus far is overwhelmingly on the side of the proponents of deregulation. By 1984, when the CAB is scheduled for extinction, reasoned judgment may be on the other side. But that would happen only if in the meantime the industry experienced failures of disastrous proportions."

Banking Deregulation

In 1981 the public relations people at America's largest bank holding company, Citicorp, produced a tongue-in-cheek guidebook for bank robbers. Forget banks, the booklet advised; knock over a brokerage house, an insurance company, a retailer or a travel agent.

Citicorp was pointing to a revolution in the financial services industry, the aggressive entry of "non-banks" such as Merrill Lynch and Co., American Express Co., Prudential Insurance Co. and Sears, Roebuck and Co. into banklike business. These and other companies are the adoptive parents of money market mutual funds and similar devices that, free of the interest limits and other rules governing banks, have lured savings away from traditional depository institutions. "In Ma Barker's day Sears was 'Where America shops,'" jibed Citicorp. "Today, Sears is where America banks."

Citicorp and other major banks were pressing in 1982 for a measure of deregulation that would free them to fight back with mutual funds of their own. Like many of the non-banks, the banks envisioned a future in which most financial services — checking and savings, lending and investing, mortgages and insurance — would be handled by diversified, electronically sophisticated financial supermarkets.

This vision had some well-placed believers. Sen. Jake Garn, R-Utah, chairman of the Senate Banking Committee, in early 1982 vigorously promoted a first step toward massive restructuring of the financial industry. His bill was intended to dissolve some of the distinctions between banks and savings and loans (S & Ls), allow these traditional depository institutions into the blooming business of money market funds, ease mergers within the industry and relax various consumer protection rules. Garn stressed that his something-for-everybody bill could combine a variety of provisions.

The Reagan administration endorsed most of this, along with some longer strides down the same road. The administration was prepared to let banks loose in such forbidden territory as insurance and data processing, so long as they set up subsidiaries to run the new activities. Garn promised a full review of other major rules, including restrictions on interstate banking.

But a constellation of reluctant and influential lobbies, determined to protect their members and to avoid giving competitors an edge, stood in the way. Some of them feared that the decades of regulation they previously lobbied into

place to protect their pieces of turf could be rendered obsolete by the economy and non-bank enterprises. They also worried about getting trampled in the rush to deregulate. The ailing thrift industry, many smaller banks, the new money market funds, the real estate industry, home builders, and consumer groups all, for different reasons, saw deregulation as a dangerous proposition.

In search of compromise, Garn exhorted industry lobby groups to come together. He promised to address each faction's special problems, but only if it was willing to swallow some things it didn't like. "If the traditional depository institutions don't get their act together and stop the intramural warfare ... there won't be any legislation," Garn told the National Association of Federal Credit Unions Jan. 25, 1982, in what became his standard refrain.

The industry was listening. One noteworthy development was an unprecedented, closed-door summit meeting Jan. 14 and 15, 1982, of more than 75 officials from all of the major depository trade groups. While the meeting produced no consensus, participants emerged with informal proposals to take back to their respective organizations. Continuing through March, virtually every segment of this diverse industry held legislative meetings, with "the bank bill" at the top of the agenda.

"The signs are very good," M. Danny Wall, Garn's committee staff director, said early in the year. "There has been significant movement already." Privately, Wall added, the factions admitted they were closer to compromise than they appeared.

But the disagreements were of long standing and finally proved too difficult to overcome. In late July after it became apparent that he did not have the votes to push his deregulation package through the Banking panel, Garn agreed to strip the legislation of its most disputed provisions, leaving behind essentially an emergency bill to help the financially ailing savings and loans institutions and mutual savings banks.

The main thrust of the bill provided that if a federally insured thrift institution's net worth — the amount by which assets exceeded liabilities — fell below a certain level, the Federal Deposit Insurance Corporation or the Federal Savings and Loan Insurance Corp. would add to the institution's assets by giving it interest-bearing certificates. In return, the thrift would give the insurer a promissory note, which would be paid off later by returning the certificates.

The pared-down bill also made it easier for troubled S & Ls to merge and expanded their authority to make commercial loans. The bill authorized the Depository Institutions Deregulation Committee (DIDC) to phase out all interest rate differentials between banks and S & Ls by Jan. 1, 1985, and authorized commercial banks and thrift institutions to set up new short-term accounts that would be competitive with popular money market funds.

Chief among the provisions Garn had to jettison were changes backed by the banking industry that would have allowed commercial banks to offer mutual funds and underwrite revenue bonds.

The savings and loan industry was buoyed by approval of the measure. William B. O'Connell, president of the U.S. League of Savings and Loan Associations, called it a "major step forward in preserving and strengthening the savings and loan system." The commercial banking industry was not so thrilled. The American Banking Association (ABA) called it a "sweetheart savings and loan bill that leaves the commercial banking community at a greater competitive disadvantage than before. Little is left in this legislation which addresses the special needs of the banking industry."

As passed by the Senate panel, the bill was closer to two House-passed measures than the original Garn bill had been. One of the House bills would set up an $8.5 billion Treasury fund to be used to guarantee the net worth of any troubled thrift institution or commercial bank whose net worth fell below certain levels. The other measure, known as the "regulators bill," was aimed at easing emergency mergers of troubled institutions and providing an infusion of financial aid.

Garn's original, broader legislation had been the subject of intense debate throughout the early part of 1982, and the inability of the various participants in the debate to reach a compromise on it played a large part in the committee's decision to approve a less ambitious bill. The following case study sets out those issues and illustrates how disagreement within major segments of an industry can affect federal regulation of that industry, perhaps to the detriment of the industry itself.

The Thrift Problem

The most powerful motive for legislation was not Citicorp's passion to compete, but the wobbly condition of the thrift industry. The thrift industry includes S & Ls, credit unions and mutual savings banks — institutions designed to collect savings deposits and loan the money back out for non-commercial purposes such as home mortgages.

The economy had walloped the thrifts from two sides. Inflation-minded savers pulled out of low-interest passbook accounts in favor of better-paying money markets, certificates of deposit and other savings devices. Thus, the thrifts rapidly lost assets — and paid much higher rates for assets they had.

At the same time, many thrifts held portfolios of old, fixed-rate mortgages they made when interest rates were lower. Those mortgages had not produced income equivalent to what the companies had to spend to attract new funds. According to O'Connell of the U.S. League of Savings Associations, at the end of November 1981 S & Ls were paying depositors an average of 11.66 percent for use of their money but earning only an average of 9.92 percent on outstanding loans. The figures explain why that year the federal government was required to step in and arrange a record 23 mergers to prop up collapsing S & Ls.

On the part of the industry, O'Connell remarked in an interview that "we don't plan to stand aside and let the business be, in effect, semi-liquidated." In 1982 the thrift lobby advocated three steps to recovery:

● First, legislation to create an orderly merger process, so that the failing thrifts could be absorbed by more solvent institutions.

● Second, some sort of federal bail-out of their old, low-yield mortgages.

● Finally, once these measures had set them back on their feet, the thrifts sought legal authority to compete in new ways — some of the checking and commercial lending authority of banks, plus a crack at the new money market funds.

The 4,400-member U.S. League, the largest of the thrift trade groups, endorsed Garn's original bill because it was intended to help with the mergers and give thrifts new powers. Many of those features were retained in the version approved by the Senate Banking Committee. At the same time, the group and its allies pushed for a bail-out of low-yielding mortgages.

Various forms of bail-out were discussed, including tax write-offs or repackaging the old mortgages as collateral for new securities, but they all had the same basic result: The government would pick up the difference between the old, face value of the mortgages and their current market value. This proposition had many foes, including Garn and the Reagan administration. "We just feel that's too costly," said a Treasury Department spokesman. "We believe interest rates will come down, and that'll be the real solution."

The Bank Factions

Bankers — despite the poor-mouthing of Citicorp's booklet — had not done so badly due to their reliance on commercial loans for which interest rates are flexible. The industry generally had been profitable and, though some analysts in 1982 saw trouble ahead, there was less urgency about the banks' condition in Congress.

But the bankers themselves were divided deeply about reshaping their industry. Many big banks and bank holding companies considered the securities industry their competition. Relatively sanguine about competition from street-corner S & Ls, bankers were eager to diversify into innovative financial services. "We see the [original] Garn bill as an essential first step," said John S. Rippey, legislative director of the Association of Bank Holding Companies, whose 180 members included most of the companies salivating at the prospect of money markets. The association had its own draft of a proposed next step, which included letting banks operate across state lines. "Market forces should dictate where banks operate, rather than lines drawn in the 18th or 19th centuries," Rippey said.

On the other hand, many smaller banks, such as the 7,300 members of the Independent Bankers Association of America (IBAA), were suspicious of sudden change. One worry was that liberated big-city banks would gobble them up. Another was that if S & Ls gained commercial lending powers they would have built-in advantages; in some states, S & Ls had been allowed statewide branches while commercial banks had not.

IBAA favored the House regulators bill, and backed up the S & Ls in endorsing a bail-out of the thrifts. (Many small banks also were stuck with old, low-interest mortgages.) But IBAA lobbyists criticized Garn for holding thrift legislation "hostage" to win broader legislation. "The changes should be made carefully, so that as many people as possible can be survivors," said Jeanne Marie Murphy, Senate liaison for the IBAA.

The American Bankers Association, embracing 13,200 banks of all sizes, was dancing in the cross fire between big and small banks. Though eager to have its big members allowed into the money-market competition, the group hesitated to share its commercial lending authority with the thrifts, in deference to smaller members.

In informal negotiations, the ABA and U.S. League of Savings Associations focused on the new powers for thrifts. S & Ls indicated they would settle for limited power to make commercial loans — say, up to 20 percent of their assets. ABA still balked, preferring a different approach that would make it simpler for an S & L to change into a bank.

ABA does not take positions on legislation until it has reached a broad consensus through its "banking leadership process." The cumbersome machinery involves a committee of about 400 bankers, split into groups representing small, medium and large banks. At a meeting of the ABA in Washington on Feb. 10, 1982, the bankers agreed in principle to allow limited commercial loans by thrifts if the restrictions on interest rates imposed by Regulation Q were relaxed. *(Box, p. 102)*

Yet, according to Fritz M. Elmendorf of the ABA, such specific compromise terms were an expression of the increasing urgency felt by bankers for the long-term health of their own industry. The real terms of any trade off between deregulation for thrifts and banks would be left to comprehensive legislation.

Togetherness

A critical factor in the fate of Garn's original bill was his inability to weld the ABA and the U.S. League into a common front, yielding substantial political clout behind his legislation. Bankers and thrift executives alike had cultivated good relations with their hometown members of Congress. They tended to be civic leaders, chamber of commerce officials and campaign contributors — active in both state and federal politics. *(Bank political action committees, box, this page)*

Their trade groups had conducted a continual courtship of the bank-writing committee, both through routine lobbying and invitations to speak and socialize at conventions. (Usually for a price. Garn, for example, even before he became chairman in 1981, was collecting about $12,000 a year in honoraria for speaking to banking and related groups. The ABA consistently was among the dozen or so biggest honoraria spenders.)

When cued by ABA or the U.S. League, bankers and thrift executives made up an impressive lobbying machine. In 1981, for example, bank and thrift executives persuaded Congress to establish tax-exempt All Savers Certificates and to expand the use of Individual Retirement Accounts, two Treasury-subsidized efforts to win depositors back from the money markets.

But even if ABA and the league had reached accord, Garn's proposal would still have faced major obstacles. The independent bankers seemed adamant, and enough prospective opposition existed outside the industry to give skittish House members fits.

Bankers Deposit Big Political Money

As befit an industry whose business was money, banking and thrift executives were prolific donors to congressional campaigns. The financial world's two largest political action committees — the American Bankers Association (ABA) Bankpac and the U.S. League of Savings Association PAC — were expected to disburse more than $1 million between them for candidates in the 1982 elections.

Bankpac, with a spending goal of $650,000, was designed especially to cement the ties between lawmakers and their local bankers. While a portion of the money was used by ABA lobbyists for admission to Washington fund-raising parties, the bigger gifts were delivered in person by selected local bank executives back home. The U.S. League of Savings Associations expected to put about $400,000 into 1982 congressional races.

If the pattern of the 1980 political season held true, candidates were expected also to reap more than $100,000 from each of several other industry PACs, including those representing the Credit Union National Association, Inc., the Mortgage Bankers Association of America, savings and loan leagues in Ohio and Florida, California bankers, and Citicorp.

Another measure of the industry's campaign activities was the number of much smaller PACs that were organized, like branch banks, to help political candidates. A scan of Federal Election Commission (FEC) records disclosed more than 280 separate PACs affiliated with individual banks and thrifts, their state and national associations, or bank holding companies. Many of these planned to spend only a few thousand dollars on federal races, concentrating more on governors and state legislatures.

Depository institutions accounted for roughly one out of every seven corporate or trade association PACs registered to give money to federal candidates. The pervasive PACs, however, told only part of the story. Bankers were generous donors as individuals, especially to members of the banking, commerce or tax-writing committees. Many of them participated in the local fund-raising activities of their favorite candidates. And when a candidate needed seed money for a campaign or an extra boost in the closing days, he could go hat in hand to his local banker for help.

In 1982, according to the FEC, a bank or thrift institution could make unlimited loans to a campaign as long as it met the normal requirements for business lending.

Deregulation Committee Makes First Moves

In 1980 the bank overseers in Congress thought they had found a way to duck one of the fiercest intramural lobbying battles between banks and thrift institutions — the fight over Regulation Q, which limits the interest they can pay on deposits. Congress set up an independent panel of officials plucked from other financial regulatory bodies, called it the Depository Institutions Deregulation Committee (DIDC), and told it to phase out interest ceilings by 1986.

But far from bringing peace, DIDC itself became a second front in the battle over deregulation, with members of Congress continually drawn into the fray. On one side were commercial banks, urging a speedy end to interest ceilings so banks could compete with the high-paying money market funds. On the other side were the savings and loan associations (S & Ls), fighting to keep interest ceilings in place. They said raising the interest rates would force them to pay more for funds held in low-paying passbook accounts, without encouraging any inward flow of new deposits.

In 1981 the S & Ls successfully froze the deregulation process, primarily by doing just what they did before DIDC existed — bringing hundreds of local savings managers to Washington to appeal to Congress. In October, for example, a blitz by thrift lobbyists convinced DIDC to reverse itself and cancel a .5 percent increase in passbook interest rates that had been scheduled for Nov. 1. Then in November, with executives of the U.S. League of Savings Associations and the National Association of Mutual Savings Banks in Washington for a conference, the thrifts marched to Capitol Hill to assure that no deregulation would take place at a December DIDC meeting.

Several key lawmakers agreed to intervene on their behalf — including Senate Banking Chairman Jake Garn, R-Utah, and House Banking Chairman Fernand J. St Germain, D-R.I. — and DIDC deferred further action.

The bankers also put the squeeze on DIDC, though mostly on the defensive. While the S & Ls were derailing the December 1981 meeting, the American Bankers Association (ABA) was busy trying to make sure DIDC would not back away from an earlier decision authorizing new, unlimited-interest retirement accounts.

When more than 300 bankers came to Washington for a legislative meeting in November, the ABA had them bring copies of their local bank letterheads. The association sat the bankers down to write letters supporting the retirement account decision, collected the letters and delivered them to DIDC. DIDC stuck by its decision. "People at DIDC had said volume of letters did count," said ABA's Fritz Elmendorf. "So we gave them volume."

The pummeling of DIDC prompted hearings in a House Banking subcommittee, and left some DIDC members exasperated. William M. Isaac, chairman of the Federal Deposit Insurance Corporation and a DIDC member, sent Garn and St Germain a letter in December complaining of "conflicting signals, as evidenced by the scores of congressional letters received during the past week urging no action at the DIDC meeting." The substance of Isaac's message to Congress: Make up your mind whether you want deregulation or not.

In March 1982 the DIDC began to act on the original congressional mandate and instituted unrestricted interest ceilings on time deposits.

New Entries

One source of opposition was the securities industry, the proprietors of the booming money market mutual funds and other investments, whom Garn called "the new boys on the block." Two trade groups had been the principal guardians of this group's interests. The Investment Company Institute (ICI), representing 650 mutual funds, tried to protect the funds' hold on the money market business. The Securities Industry Association (SIA), representing 550 investment broker-dealers, placed more emphasis on keeping banks out of the business of underwriting municipal revenue bonds.

Both groups argued that banks have huge assets and that certain tax and legal advantages would make them instant goliaths in the new business. They warned that banks could end up using depositors' savings to bail out faulty investments — as commonly happened before banking and securities were separated by the 1933 Glass-Steagall Act. "The securities industry would probably applaud [Citicorp Chairman] Walter Wriston if he wanted to get rid of his bank and become a broker-dealer," said SIA's senior vice president Donald J. Crawford. "But not if he wants to enter the field with his $120 billion in assets."

Crawford also questioned the underlying assumption that the trend had been toward financial supermarkets. He said that may have been an overreaction to the heated climate of high interest and inflation. "Some of what is going on right now has a certain mob psychology to it," Crawford said.

The securities industry did not have the same strong, indigenous ties to members of Congress that banks and thrifts had, but brokers rivaled bankers for influence on Wall Street and in Washington. (In the Reagan administration, Treasury Secretary Donald T. Regan, the former chairman of Merrill Lynch, was perhaps the most prominent alumnus of the securities industry.) Moreover, computers — the nervous system of the securities industry —

made a dandy lobbying device, as the industry demonstrated in 1981.

In the spring of that year, congressional supporters of the depository institutions attempted to rein in the money market funds by requiring that money fund managers set aside large cash reserves. The U.S. League of Savings Associations and the ABA supported the effort. But, coached by the ICI, money market managers across the country sent their shareholders letters warning in dire terms that the assault would cut yields for savers. "The only way you can prevent this legalized theft from occurring is to write your senators and congressman and let them know what you think of this blatant piracy," said one letter from The Reserve Fund Inc., of New York City. "Politicians need two things to survive in office — votes and contributions. Bankers make contributions, but you have the vote."

The crusade was an enormous success — the proposal disappeared without a trace. Several congressional offices said the outpouring from constituents rivaled the flow of mail on President Reagan's economic plan. In addition, the victory convinced ABA and the savings league to shift strategy, from regulating securities to deregulating themselves.

Securities lobbyists doubted they could duplicate that success on an issue such as deregulation, since it was not a direct threat to their shareholders. Even some managers of money market funds were not enthusiastic about lobbying to keep banks out of the field. Thomas C. Miller, executive vice president of Government Investors Trust, a small mutual fund in Arlington, Va., said he felt his industry should accept competition from banks and focus on preserving its head start. To fight the entry of banks into mutual funds, he said, would be "illogical and contradictory for an industry based on the free market philosophy."

Yet if the securities lobbyists threw their weight against a deregulation bill, ABA's Elmendorf figured they would have a strategic advantage. "It's a relatively easy thing to *stop* a bill," he said. "You don't have to have the resources of the banks or thrifts to stop a bill." Garn added: "They don't have to oppose the legislation, because the banks and the thrifts have been doing such a good job of cutting each other up."

Remaining Difficulties

Another source of trouble for the Garn bill was the housing lobby. Realtors and home builders said they would support a bail-out of the thrifts, but not measures to let S & Ls turn their attention from mortgages to other investments. "It's almost as if they're all trying to walk away from housing," said Peter E. Knight, assistant director of mortgage finance at the National Association of Realtors. "I don't think we disagree that the Garn bill would make thrifts more profitable. But at what cost?"

The Garn bill drove two additional wedges between the thrifts and the housing lobby. The home builders were "unalterably opposed" to a provision that would let banks or thrifts get directly involved in development and real estate. And the Realtors worried that due-on-sale clauses would inhibit home sales. That issue was deflected somewhat in June 1982 when the Supreme Court overturned state laws barring due-on-sale enforcement by federally chartered savings and loan associations. The Senate Banking Committee bill widened that decision by extending it to mortages issued by commercial banks, mortgage banks and state-chartered thrift institutions. To appease the real estate industry the bill exempted mortgages originated or assumed during a specific "window period."

Consumer groups — supported by organized labor, state government groups and others — also had complaints about deregulation. Garn's bill, in the name of a free marketplace, would override a variety of state laws aimed at protecting consumers. Perhaps the most controversial provision would extinguish state usury laws that limit interest charges on consumer loans for cars, furniture and other purchases.

"We fondly refer to it as the loan shark revitalization act of 1982," said Ellen Broadman of Consumers Union. "The bill grossly intrudes on the ability of the states to protect the consumer in financing." Garn aide Wall countered that usury laws make it tough for consumers to borrow in times of high inflation. "The question is, do you want to be able to get a loan, or do you not?" he said.

John Brown, of Ralph Nader's Public Interest Research Center, said letting banks into the securities business would invite conflicts of interest, and would set a dangerous precedent for the ultimate unbridling of large corporations. "Garn and the administration have been very effectively stroked and fed information by the lobbyists for some of the big banks," Brown said.

While consumer groups may not have carried the weight of bankers and thrift managers, their message was one element of this complicated issue that may have had some appeal to the general public — and thus to the politicians. "This is an election year," noted Broadman, "and it is going to look real bad for people to be voting against laws that protect the consumer."

Food Safety

One of the most perplexing regulatory issues facing government officials is whether or when to forbid consumers access to potentially dangerous substances that nonetheless offer some apparent benefit or satisfaction. In the case of food additives, the question has been complicated by a federal law that tried to provide absolute safety.

The Delaney clause, enacted in 1958 as an amendment to the Food and Drug Act of 1938, prohibited marketing of any food additive found to cause cancer in humans or animals. That ban applied to any additive that caused cancer in test animals even if some putatively safe level for human food use could be established.

Much of the debate over the nation's food safety laws has centered on that clause. The arguments offered for and against adoption of the clause have not changed substantially since, but they have intensified. Opponents of the clause argue that it is too rigid and that even cancer-inducing substances should be usable if evidence indicates they are harmless for certain purposes or in certain quantities. Backers of the clause say it is unsafe to permit the use of any known carcinogen because there is no proven way to establish a threshold of danger below which a carcinogen would not cause cancer.

The debate over whether the Delaney clause is too restrictive has been reopened each time it has been applied. The clause has led to bans on one food coloring and an animal feed additive and was the basis in 1959 for a government warning against eating cranberries allegedly tainted with a cancer-causing pesticide. Its greatest impact, however, has been on artificial sweeteners.

In 1969, the Food and Drug Administration (FDA) ordered a ban on cyclamates, a class of artificial sweeteners used to flavor soft drinks and a variety of processed foods. Tests had shown that cyclamates caused cancer in laboratory rats. Manufacturers and consumers both protested the ban. They claimed that the tests were unsound because no human would ingest anywhere near the levels of cyclamates that had been given to the rats and that withdrawal of cyclamates from the market would deny a valuable product to diabetics who could not use sugar and to dieters seeking low-calorie foods.

Despite the protests, the ban took effect in 1970. Consumer complaints began to subside as manufacturers replaced cyclamates with saccharin, another artificial sweetener. Then in 1977 FDA proposed to ban saccharin. A

Canadian study had revealed that large quantities of saccharin fed to laboratory animals led to increased incidence of bladder cancer. Again consumers and manufacturers protested the ban. Because there was no readily available substitute for saccharin, their demands received more attention. Congress quickly passed legislation to prevent the proposed ban from taking effect. Congress' "ban on the ban" was extended several times, most recently in 1981 for two years through July 30, 1983.

In 1980, the FDA approved limited use of a new artificial sweetener. Called aspartame, it has been cleared for use only in dry foods, and is still undergoing extensive testing for hazardous health effects. It appeared on the commercial market in fall 1982. Meanwhile the debate over the Delaney clause continued with few signs that the questions it raised would be answered soon.

The Delaney Clause

Congress first authorized regulation of the food industry in 1906, following muckraking press reports of watered milk (with chalk added to restore white color), canned green beans whose color was maintained with copper, unsanitary meat processing and other disturbing food industry practices. Congress was also impressed by reports from the legendary "poison squad," which recommended stricter regulation of food and food additives. (Poison squad, box, p. 107)

The 1906 law prohibited manufacture of or interstate commerce in adulterated or misbranded foods. In 1938 it was the basis for the Food, Drug and Cosmetic Act, which tightened labeling requirements and broadened the definition of prohibited additives to any substance that was injurious to health. However, it was up to the federal regulators to find violators, gather evidence and initiate lengthy court proceedings to remove a hazardous additive from the market.

Not until 1958, 52 years after passage of the original law, did Congress require manufacturers to prove the safety of an additive before putting it into food. A law calling for mandatory pre-market testing for pesticides had already been enacted in 1954.

The 1958 act provided that no food additive could be

used unless the formula and a description of the proposed conditions of use had been submitted to the FDA and approved as safe for use under the conditions proposed. There were major exemptions to the pre-market testing requirements for two large groups of additives: those that had already been sanctioned for use by the FDA and those that were "generally recognized as safe" (GRAS), that is, they had been used for years with neither FDA sanction nor apparent ill health effects.

The Delaney clause was added to the bill at the last minute. It had been proposed by Rep. James J. Delaney (D-N.Y., 1945-47, 1949-78) who in 1951-52 had headed a review of pesticides and food additives. (The study group's recommendations for pre-market testing and FDA approval for food additives, coupled with growing public concern about the causes of cancer, had spurred congressional action on the issue.) The Delaney clause, however, was opposed by some scientists and food industry spokesmen and was not included in the version of the legislation as it was originally reported from the House Interstate and Foreign Commerce Committee. But Delaney used his position on the House Rules Committee to block floor action until the administration agreed to support the clause. The language was offered as a floor amendment in the House and it was quickly approved by both chambers.

Two years later, potentially cancer-causing color additives were also brought under mandatory pre-market testing and the Delaney clause in the Color Additive Amendments of 1960.

Cranberry Scare

Little more than a year after it went into effect, the Delaney clause became the center of a major controversy. In November 1959, the secretary of the Department of Health, Education and Welfare announced that part of the 1958-59 crop of cranberries had been contaminated by aminotriazole, a weed-killer found to cause cancer in laboratory animals, and ordered the tainted berries removed from the market. The government action was taken under the Delaney clause. Cranberry growers, who suffered severe financial losses even on untainted berries that stayed on the market, were outraged. They argued that the amount of aminotriazole on the berries could not have reached a level harmful to human health. They were later paid a $10 million indemnity for their losses by the government.

After the so-called "cranberry scare," questions arose as to whether the Delaney clause was a valid and workable rule in food additive regulation. President Dwight D. Eisenhower appointed a study group on the effectiveness of the clause in 1960. The group's report was the first of several to suggest that the FDA be allowed to exercise a "rule of reason" when applying the clause. However, Congress took no action on the panel's recommendations.

Red Dye No. 2

In 1976 the FDA banned Red Dye No. 2 after a study had found that the dye caused a statistically significant increase in cancer among test animals when administered in high doses. Products containing the dye already on the market were not recalled. Again, FDA action was taken under the Delaney clause.

As the most widely used artificial color, an estimated 1.3 million pounds of Red Dye No. 2 had been produced in 1975 and added to such foods as ice cream, processed cheese, cookies, and processed meats. The dye also had been added to lipsticks and pill coatings.

Opposition by the food-coloring industry was vocal, and again questioned the validity of banning a substance that "induced" cancer when administered in high doses. After the ban most food processors switched to Red Dye No. 40. This substance was developed by the Allied Chemical Corp. and was permitted to remain on the market after the FDA subjected it to a battery of tests.

DES Ban Attempt

In 1973, the FDA announced it would ban the use of DES (diethylstibestrol), a synthetic hormone used in cattle feed as a growth stimulant. DES had been found to cause cancer in test animals and in humans and the FDA had detected traces of the hormone in beef sold for human consumption. However, the ban was blocked in federal court on grounds that the FDA had not followed the proper procedure for issuing it. FDA persisted, and the ban finally was implemented in 1979.

Sweeteners Soured

The 1958 food additive amendments exempted from testing apparently safe additives that were on the market before 1958. Those generally recognized as safe (GRAS) substances included salt, sugar and common spices that had been used for centuries with no apparent ill effects. But food safety activists have charged that widespread and long-term use of a substance does not necessarily prove its safety; they point to cyclamates and saccharin, both on the GRAS list, as examples.

Cyclamates, made from cyclamic acid and its salts, were used as sweeteners in a wide variety of diet foods and drinks, as a cheaper substitute for sugar in processed foods and as a coating or sweetener for numerous drug products. The FDA had placed cyclamates on its GRAS list in the 1950s. However, subsequent tests found that the substances caused a high incidence of cancer in laboratory rats that were fed large daily doses of cyclamates.

The Cyclamate Ban

Citing the Delaney clause, the FDA banned cyclamates on Oct. 18, 1969. A schedule for phasing out cyclamates in foods and other substances was set, and on Aug. 14, 1970, a total ban went into effect.

The ban had a profound effect on cyclamate manufacturers who were forced to discontinue their production. The use of cyclamates had grown substantially during the decade preceding the ban. According to one report, consumption increased from five million pounds six years before the ban was announced to 17 million pounds in 1969. Production of at least 20 million pounds had been projected for 1970. The House passed legislation that would have allowed manufacturers to seek compensation for their losses but the Senate did not act and the bill died.

Although many food producers switched from cyclamates to saccharin the FDA periodically has been petitioned to lift the prohibition on cyclamates. An FDA administrative law judge last upheld the ban in February 1980, declaring that manufacturers had failed to prove that cyclamates are safe.

The cyclamate controversy prompted President Richard Nixon to order the FDA to evaluate the safety of all

'The Poison Squad': Human Guinea Pigs

In these days of extensive scientific experimentation with rats, it is difficult to believe that there was a time when human testing of food additives was federal policy.

Some time in 1902, a dozen young men in the Department of Agriculture sat down to the first course of what was to become a chemical "feast" that included saccharin, borax, sulphuric acid, formaldehyde and other proposed additions to processed food. Under the supervision of Dr. Harvey W. Wiley, chief chemist of the department's Bureau of Chemistry, these human guinea pigs were fed small doses of poisons similar or identical to substances found in then-common food preservatives.

The volunteers comprised an early food additive testing project, known officially as "the hygienic table." They quickly became a national sensation dubbed "the poison squad" by an enthusiastic press.

Later Food and Drug Administration officials have pointed out that, ominous as some of those early chemical entrees sound, they suggested the food industry was trying to respond to a real need for food preservatives.

"Just eating was hazardous to your health in 1900. People got sick and died from eating. They had diarrhea all the time from spoiled food," said one official. Part of the hazard, he added, was due to uncritical addition of chemicals and other supposed preservatives and colorings to food.

Experiments with human volunteers went on for five years. The poison squad ate its way to the conclusion that manufacturers should have to prove both the "need" and the "wholesomeness" of additions to food before they were marketed, according to FDA records. Wiley himself was convinced that chemical preservatives should be used in foods only when necessary to prevent spoilage and not just to enhance flavor or color.

The activities of the squad played a major role in passage of the 1906 Food and Drug Act, which prohibited marketing of adulterated or misbranded foods and drugs. Dr. Wiley's Bureau of Chemistry was in charge of enforcement. The bureau was reorganized in 1927 as a separate Food, Drug and Insecticide Administration, a name soon simplified to Food and Drug Administration. In 1940, the FDA was transferred to the Federal Security Agency, later to become the Department of Health and Human Services.

But it was not until 1958 that Congress acted on the poison squad's major recommendation. The 1958 amendments to the food and drug law required pre-market testing of all new food additives.

Although the poison squad's tests of saccharin convinced it that the sweetener should be banned, President Theodore Roosevelt, who took daily doses for unknown medical reasons, responded that anyone "who thinks saccharin is injurious to health is an idiot." In 1912 a saccharin ban did go into effect, but it was later lifted when sugar supplies shrank during World War I.

additives on the GRAS list. The study, undertaken for the FDA by the Federation of American Societies for Experimental Biology (FASEB), was completed in late 1980. The results, according to then FDA Commissioner Jere E. Goyan, were "generally reassuring to the American consumer." But the FASEB advised further safety studies or stricter regulation of some common and widely used additives, including salt, vitamins A and D, caffeine and the preservative BHA (butylated hydroxyanisole) and BHT (butylated hydroxytoluene).

The FASEB subsequently began an evaluation of items added to the GRAS list after 1958. Included were malt syrup and extract, collagen (a protein used in sausage casings) and char-smoke flavoring. Results of the second phase evaluation were expected by the end of 1982.

Saccharin Ban

When FDA officials announced in March 1977 plans to prohibit the use of saccharin as a food additive, they created a public uproar. After the ban on cyclamates, saccharin was the only artificial sweetener available, and reaction from diet food and drink manufacturers and the calorie-conscious American public was swift. According to some members of Congress, the ban provoked more mail and telephone calls from constituents than any other issue in recent memory.

The FDA decision was based on laboratory tests, conducted in Canada, in which rats fed large doses of saccharin showed an increased tendency to develop bladder cancer. Opponents of the ban ridiculed the Canadian tests, and claimed that a human would have to drink at least 800 12-ounce cans of diet soda daily to match the saccharin intake of the laboratory rats. The Calorie Control Council, an industry group, argued that banning the sweetener threatened the health of diabetics and people who needed to control their weight. People would brush their teeth less with unsweetened toothpaste, opponents warned, and children would refuse to take unsweetened medicines.

Besides arguments concerning public health, pressures on Congress to reject the FDA proposal also included economic contentions. Saccharin, with about 300 times the sweetening power of sugar, was cheaper for soft-drink manufacturers to use than its high-calorie counterpart, according to a Calorie Control Council spokesman. The no-calorie soft drink market, which accounted for the greatest percentage of saccharin consumption, had become a rapidly growing industry. Banning saccharin would be a costly measure and a burden not readily borne by soft-drink manufacturers.

Congress responded in November 1977 by adopting legislation ordering the FDA to postpone the ban for 18 months. The bill also asked the National Academy of Sciences to conduct an extensive study of saccharin and food safety policy.

Congress, however, let stand an FDA requirement that products containing saccharin carry a label warning: "Use of this product may be hazardous to your health. This product contains saccharin, which has been determined to cause cancer in laboratory animals." The FDA also required stores and vending machines to post warning notices next to products containing saccharin.

NAS Report Part I

The first part of the National Academy of Sciences report requested by Congress was released in November 1978. Saccharin, the report said, was by itself or in combination with other substances a relatively weak carcinogen in rats. Other findings of the report:

• It was scientifically valid to conclude that if a substance caused cancer in animals, it would cause cancer in humans, but animal tests could not be relied upon to gauge the risk of cancer in humans.

• There were no acceptable epidemiological (population) studies linking cancer directly to human consumption of saccharin, perhaps because investigatory methods lacked the necessary sensitivity to detect the incidence of cancer from a weak carcinogen or distinguish between the effects of saccharin and those of stronger carcinogens.

• The benefits of saccharin use by diabetics and the obese had not been determined in clinical studies.

• Although the cancer risk of saccharin was probably low, "even low risks to a large number of exposed persons may lead to public health concerns."

• Children and women of child-bearing age consumed more saccharin than other groups.

The saccharin-cancer link was disputed by three additional studies released in 1980. Prepared by the National Cancer Institute, the Harvard University School of Public Health and the American Health Foundation, the reports found little or no connection between saccharin and cancer and claimed that the dangers of saccharin use may have been overstated.

New Sweetener

When FDA proposed its ban of saccharin there was no available substitute. In July 1981 the FDA approved aspartame, a new artificial sweetener about 200 times sweeter than sugar for use in dry foods. Although the manufacturer received initial approval to market aspartame, FDA withheld final approval because the sugar substitute was suspected of causing brain damage. Subsequent tests conducted at the Massachusetts Institute of Technology found no link between aspartame and brain damage.

But the MIT study did state that the sweetener could pose a risk to persons suffering from phenylketonuria, an inherited illness characterized by an inability to correctly metabolize phenylalanine, an amino acid contained in aspartame. The FDA subsequently required the manufacturer to monitor aspartame consumption levels and mandated that aspartame containers bear the label: Phenylketonurics: contains phenylalanine."

Aspartame, which manufacturers began providing to the food industry by late 1981 and to consumers in tablet and granular form in 1982, is suited to replace saccharin only in certain cases. The new sweetener cannot be used for cooking or baking because it breaks down at high temperatures. After long-term contact with water, aspartame loses its sweet taste. Manufacturers, however, claim that it retains its sweetness for about as long as the average shelf life of low-calorie beverages. Beverages containing aspartame have been marketed successfully in Canada for several years. The initial application for approval in 1973 did not cover the use of aspartame in beverages, but manufacturers said they intended to file a petition to request FDA permission for its use in liquid products.

Scientific Testing for Safety

The limits of scientific knowledge have been a key topic in the debate on the Delaney clause. Pressures for decisions on saccharin and other additives pushed Congress and federal regulators into the murky world of scientific hypothesis where certainties are rare and almost always challenged.

Because ethics bar experimentation with potentially toxic substances on humans, food safety regulation has relied mostly on the results of large doses administered to laboratory animals. This has led to a problem of accuracy in testing. Drawing on animal data to predict human susceptibility to a carcinogen has consistently been an argument used by spokesmen for affected industries. They questioned the premise that producing cancer in animals was the same as producing it in humans. However, all but two substances known to cause cancer in humans similarly affect laboratory animals, according to researchers.

An additional problem facing cancer scientists is how to determine from animal test data the number of humans who might develop cancer from exposure to a carcinogen. Rats are smaller, their lives are far shorter and their cells multiply more rapidly than those of humans. But cancer researchers believe that the sizable doses administered to animals compensate for built-in shortcomings of animal tests. Even if test animals could perfectly duplicate human life span and size, no one could test a substance on 220 million animals, thus duplicating the size of the U.S. population. Therefore, according to the researchers, concentrated dosage is needed to reveal the probability of risk in smaller test "populations," and results from such tests are valid.

A second related testing issue involves the dramatic improvement of methods for detecting the presence of chemicals. Scientists can now measure quantities as minute as a nanogram — a billionth of a gram; a gram is about a thirtieth of an ounce. And detection techniques may be refined even further.

The capacity to measure ever-diminishing quantities means that scientists may never be able to rule out the possibility that a troublesome substance is present at very small, trace levels. Researchers refer to this as "the search for a vanishing zero." Scientists fear that they may be incapable of guaranteeing the total absence of harmful substances.

FDA: Regulating the Essentials

The need for regulation of the food, drug and cosmetic industry was recognized as early as the late 19th century, when Dr. Harvery W. Wiley of the Agriculture Department's Bureau of Chemistry began conducting experiments on preservatives in common American foods. Those experiments eventually led to passage of the Food and Drug Act of 1906 and creation of the forerunner of today's Food and Drug Administration (FDA). Although the agency has had its mandate broadened and undergone several reorganizations, its primary task is still to protect the public from unsafe foods and drugs.

FDA Responsibilities

The Food and Drug Act of 1906 called for the protection of the public from the potential health hazards presented by adulterated and mislabeled foods, drinks and drugs. Since then, Congress has added substantially to the agency's responsibilities, and in 1982 the agency was authorized to approve the safety of new human and veterinary drugs, certain medical devices, food additives and colorings before they are marketed. It licenses and inspects blood banks and the makers of vaccines, serums and antibiotics, sets standards for foods that are made according to a specific formula and tests products for compliance with those standards. The FDA establishes safety standards for products that emit radiation, such as microwave ovens, establishes regulations for the labeling of products and investigates consumer complaints about any of the products it regulates. The agency can prohibit the sale of adulterated and misbranded foods and drugs.

Several other agencies also have jurisdiction over various aspects of the food and drug industry. The Environmental Protection Agency establishes tolerances for the amount of pesticide residues left in or on food, the Department of Agriculture (USDA) monitors the safety of meat and poultry and the Commerce Department handles contaminated fish. Jurisdictions may overlap, which has caused confusion and regulatory oddities. For example, regular cheese pizza must adhere to the labeling requirements of the FDA, while a cheese pizza with sausage falls under the jurisdiction of the USDA, which has much looser labeling standards.

Agency Composition

The FDA is not an independent commission but a bureau within the Department of Health and Human Services (HHS). Unlike all other major regulatory agencies, the FDA commissioner is appointed not by the president but by the secretary of HHS. Senate confirmation of the appointment is not required. The FDA commissioner is assisted by eight associate commissioners responsible for agency policymaking. To monitor compliance with its regulations, the FDA employs inspectors and chemists who work out of the administration's regional offices. The inspectors are authorized to inspect factories; chemists analyze products to ensure that they comply with FDA standards.

When violations of the law are found, the FDA has several enforcement options. It can send an enforcement document called a "regulatory letter" to the top management of a firm, stating that legal action will be taken unless the apparent violations are corrected. A recall may be initiated by the FDA or the manufacturer to remove a defective product from the marketplace. If a voluntary recall is not effective, the FDA may initiate civil action against the individual or company involved seizing the goods in question.

Criticism of the FDA

Like most other regulatory agencies, the FDA has been criticized by both the public it protects and the industry it regulates. The laws FDA administers also have been challenged as inadequate. The Delaney clause, which requires that any food additive found to cause cancer be removed from the market, has been under especially heavy fire for its rigidity and both industry and consumers have called for its revision.

Industry critics have complained about the "drug lag" in the FDA's review process, especially in instances of obtaining permission to market new drugs. At the same time consumer critics have complained that FDA testing is inadequate and that the agency moves too slowly in removing potentially hazardous products from the market. They pointed to the case of the anti-arthritis drug Oraflex, which was linked to deaths from liver and kidney failure three months after its approval by the FDA in April 1982. The manufacturer voluntarily withdrew the drug in June.

Another criticism of the FDA concerns its standing as a regulatory agency. Because it is part of HHS it is accountable to the secretary and to the president. Following President Ronald Reagan's order to simplify the federal regulatory policy, Secretary Richard S. Schweiker issued a rule in May 1981 that "significant" FDA decisions would require his approval. Before that, FDA had been the only agency within HHS that could issue and approve its own regulations.

Schweiker's rule raised concerns among both the industries regulated by FDA, who feared the requirement would slow the regulatory process further, and consumer groups, who worried that the agency would become too political.

The problem of the vanishing zero can have devastating repercussions when applied to the Delaney clause which placed an absolute ban on any food containing any trace of a carcinogen. If the clause is applied consistently, the American population could be left with only a very limited larder of food available for consumption.

Revising Delaney

Some scientists and members of Congress found the risks of the artificial sweetener saccharin negligible, and its benefits to diabetics and dieters compellingly real. They called for a change in the Delaney clause so that the health risks or economic costs of a food additive could be measured against its benefits, case-by-case, substance-by-substance.

In the second half of its study the National Academy of Sciences urged a reform of food laws to do away with the restrictive Delaney clause. The NAS report recommended that Congress allow regulators to consider health or economic benefits when a ban on suspected carcinogens is under consideration. The NAS report said Congress should rewrite federal food laws to permit a variety of regulatory options for carcinogenic and other food additives, depending on how risky they were for human health. The FDA would be empowered to classify a substance as high-, moderate- or low-risk and fashion an appropriate regulatory action: outright ban, restricted sales, continued sales with warning labels, or no regulatory intervention.

Food regulators should have broad, discretionary power to decide how to deal with carcinogens and other health hazards, the panel said. According to the report decisions concerning classification and regulation of suspect substances should be based primarily on health considerations, but "perceived" benefits, such as those attributed to saccharin by diabetics, should be given due consideration.

In an unusual development, there was a minority report attached to the NAS study. Dissenting members of the study panel said in a strongly worded statement that there was still no "scientifically defensible way to divide carcinogens" or other substances with irreversible health hazards into different risk categories. The dissenters also believed that food regulation should be particularly strict, because of the "enormous" number of persons exposed to potential hazards and because the method of exposure — chronic ingestion — represented the "optimal" way to cause cancer.

The opinions in the NAS report summarized the tug of war over the Delaney clause. The food industry has lobbied for a revised clause that would allow regulators to consider any benefits provided by a suspect substance; public interest groups have requested that the loopholes in the Delaney clause be patched up and that the clause be extended to cover all additives. Consumers have taken an ambivalent position. They seem to want the protection afforded by Delaney so long as it does not affect products they consume.

Congress and the executive branch have been reluctant to meet these issues head on. A promised reform of food safety legislation by President Carter's administration failed to appear. The Reagan administration has been working on a proposal to relax the Delaney clause but by the end of September 1982 it had not made a formal proposal to Congress. Congress has discussed food safety reform for several years, but no cohesive legislative program has emerged, as legislators and regulators prefer to take what has been termed the "carcinogen of the month" approach to deal with such substances as saccharin.

One deterrent to congressional action is the continuing uncertainty of many parts of the food safety equation. For example, no one knows for sure:

• How environmental exposure, genetic makeup, the disease process and personal habits mix to cause the approximately 110 types of cancer.

• How to predict the magnitude of risk to humans from a substance that causes cancer in laboratory animals.

• How to set a safe level for consumption of, or other human exposure to, substances that cause cancer in laboratory animals.

Regulating the Environment

During its relatively short 12-year life span the Environmental Protection Agency (EPA) has evolved into one of the largest federal regulatory agencies (with 12,623 employees in June 1982) as well as one of the most criticized. The controversy stems partly from the fact that the agency administers a multitude of complex, far-reaching and costly laws. In most cases of EPA action or inaction to implement those statutes, environmentalists and industry representatives have squared off to fight for or against a deadline, a delay or a new standard. At times the agency has been the target of complaints from both supporters and opponents of the environmental movement. Nonetheless, it has been able to force significant reductions in the levels of pollutants in the environment.

Throughout most of its existence, EPA has been confronted with a dilemma. The sluggish economy that plagued the United States throughout the mid-1970s and into the early 1980s precipitated a jobs-vs.-environment controversy. Opponents of stricter environmental standards argued that the costs of complying with EPA regulation slowed industrial expansion. In some cases companies reportedly closed their doors rather than attempt to meet EPA-imposed standards.

Braking the Cleanup Effort?

After Ronald Reagan was elected president in 1980, Rep. Morris K. Udall, D-Ariz., prophesied that "it will be a long winter" for environmentalists. His prediction proved to be right on target.

Even before Reagan took office the announcement Dec. 22, 1980, that he was naming Colorado attorney James G. Watt as secretary of the interior sent shock waves through the environmental community. Watt was president of the Mountain States Legal Foundation, a conservative Denver public interest law firm specializing in representing pro-development interests; frequently, that meant opposing environmental protection.

Nor were environmentalists pleased with Reagan's selection of Anne M. Gorsuch to be EPA administrator. Gorsuch, a friend of Watt's, was an assistant district attorney in Denver and served in the Colorado House of Representatives, where she gained a reputation as a strong critic of environmental proposals. Gorsuch also served on Reagan's transition team advisory committee on intergovernmental relations.

Under Reagan and Gorsuch, the EPA in 1981-82 was engaged in increasingly heavy firefights with Congress on almost every front, with the latter resisting cutbacks in environmental programs. For example, Congress restored the administration's proposed EPA budget reductions for fiscal 1982. And the administration's legislative proposals for less federal policing of the environment were delayed, watered down, withdrawn, defeated or turned around to require more — not less — EPA activity. At the same time, EPA regulatory and administrative actions came under intensive scrutiny and frequent fire from Capitol Hill, especially in the Democratic-controlled House, where some members viewed the administration's environmental record as a choice target for campaign trail attacks during the 1982 election year.

Polls during 1981 and 1982 consistently found high public support for environmental protection, and many Democrats hoped to persuade voters that Gorsuch and Interior Secretary Watt were Trojan horses dedicated to destroying the very resources they were appointed to defend. *(Polls, box, p. 113)*

Moreover, the electoral clout of environmental groups was growing, according to Marion Edey, director of the League of Conservation Voters. The league's political action committee raised about $150,000 in 1978, but that figure had soared to $460,000 in 1980. As of the end of July 1982, the group had collected another $460,000 and hoped to reach $800,000 to $1 million by the end of the year.

Air Pollution Assignment

One of the most massive and costly tasks Congress gave to the EPA was administration and enforcement of the Clean Air Act, passed in 1970 and amended in 1977. The task of reviewing the 2,500-page landmark legislation was monumental, both technically and politically. The act had been due to expire in September 1981, but Congress kept it alive through continuing appropriations resolutions. At issue was whether the complex act, which affected virtually every industry, could be relaxed somewhat to stimulate factory building while still protecting the environment. The act explicitly prohibited any consideration of costs in setting national ambient air quality standards. The problem of rewriting the act was compounded by ignorance: Only a few experts and members of Congress understood the law and how it worked. The Reagan administration was of little assistance, offering only a set of rather vague principles, rather than concrete proposals.

The Senate Environment and Public Works Committee began marking up a reauthorization of the act in mid-November 1981 but did not report a bill until August 1982. In the House, the Energy and Commerce Subcommittee on Health and Environment held extensive hearings on the bill in 1981 but did not begin markup sessions until the next year.

Nowhere was the jobs-vs.-environment issue more hotly contested than with respect to the Clean Air Act's standards for auto emissions. Automobile manufacturers, representing the largest U.S. industry, blamed federal regulations for their financial ills, claiming that they were unable to meet EPA emission standards and still produce reasonably priced cars. To the dismay of environmentalists, the emission deadlines had been extended four times since their enactment in 1970. The extension granted in the Clean Air Act Amendments of 1977 (PL 95-95) delayed the deadline for an additional two years but tightened standards for 1980 and 1981.

During his presidential campaign, Reagan often attributed the serious problems of the automobile and steel industries to excessive government regulation. Soon after taking office, the administration in April 1981 proposed to eliminate or reduce 34 environmental and safety regulations for cars and trucks, including modification of some emission standards. And the administration supported legislation that cleared Congress in 1981 giving steel companies up to three extra years to comply with the Clean Air Act's 1982 air pollution cleanup deadline. According to the American Iron and Steel Institute, the economically depressed industry had spent $3.4 billion on pollution control between 1970 and 1980. Supported by the administration, the legislation (PL 97-23) allowed steel companies to negotiate until Dec. 31, 1985, on a case-by-case basis, extensions of the 1982 deadline for cleaning up air pollution emissions. Money saved by deferring pollution control expenditures had to be used to modernize older plants.

However, some observers blamed the problems of both the auto and steel industries on a host of factors other than regulation, including high wage rates and failure to modernize in the face of mounting foreign competition.

HISTORY OF EPA: AN AGENCY UNDER ATTACK

"Many of EPA's difficulties over the years can be traced to the fact that Congress loaded the agency with far more statutory responsibilities within a brief period of time than perhaps any agency could effectively perform," commented Russell E. Train, EPA administrator during 1973-77, in the Feb. 2, 1982, *New York Times*. When EPA came into being in 1970, it took over the air pollution, water pollution, solid waste, pesticide and radiation programs scattered around the federal government. Since then those programs have been broadened and improved, and Congress has heaped major new responsibilities on the agency.

The EPA was established at a time when the nation was becoming increasingly concerned about pollution, declining air and water quality and general deterioration of the environment. The dramatic blowout of an oil well off the coast of Santa Barbara, Calif., in late January 1969 focused public attention on the seriousness of environmental problems. Miles of beaches were covered with oil and thousands of fish and wildfowl were killed.

Pressure on Nixon

Four months after the Santa Barbara incident, on June 3, 1969, President Richard Nixon established by executive order a Cabinet-level Environmental Quality Council. Congress was not satisfied, calling the council formation a "patchwork approach" to environmental problems that was "little better than nothing." In December 1969 it passed the National Environmental Policy Act (NEPA), which made environmental protection a matter of national policy. The act required all federal agencies to submit environmental impact statements before taking actions or making recommendations that had environmental consequences. And it created a three-member Council on Environmental Quality (CEQ) within the executive office of the president to replace the environmental council. Many industry groups denounced NEPA, but conservation organizations such as the Sierra Club hailed it as "an environmental Magna Carta."

During its early days the Nixon administration was widely criticized for not displaying a strong commitment to environmental protection. As the pressure for corrective action mounted, Nixon in 1970 submitted to Congress a plan to consolidate the federal government's widespread environmental protection efforts into a single Environmental Protection Agency. There was little congressional opposition, and on Dec. 2, 1970, the EPA was created by executive order as an independent agency in the executive branch. Most existing environmental programs were transferred to EPA from other government departments. The first administrator of the agency was William D. Ruckelshaus, who served until 1973. Ruckelshaus proved to be a vigorous enforcer of water and air quality standards; he infused the EPA with an enthusiasm and sense of mission not unlike the Peace Corps'.

The Council on Environmental Quality continued to exist as an advisory and policy-making body. While EPA was charged with setting and enforcing pollution control standards, CEQ focused on broad environmental policies and coordination of the federal government's environmental activities.

Increased Responsibilities

Enthusiasm for environmental legislation continued throughout the early 1970s. Congress passed several laws designed to limit or halt the entry of pollutants into the environment, including the Water Quality Improvement Act and the Clean Air Amendments, both of 1970; and the Federal Environmental Pesticide Control Act, the Noise Control Act, the Marine Protection, Research and Sanctuaries Act and the Water Pollution Control Act Amendments, all of 1972. Responsibility for enforcing these laws was given to EPA.

The energy shortage created by the 1973 Arab oil embargo slowed the rush of environmental programs as legislators sought to balance the benefits of a sometimes costly anti-pollution program against the need for a stable and productive economy. Also, the environmental movement, which was the impetus behind much of the activity

The Polls: Clean Air a Sacred Cow?

A number of polls conducted in 1981 indicated that a substantial majority of Americans opposed weakening the Clean Air Act.

In a survey commissioned by the Council on Environmental Quality (CEQ), only 20 percent of the respondents agreed that "we must relax environmental standards in order to achieve economic growth," and 42 percent thought environmental problems "so important . . . that continuing improvement must be made regardless of cost." But only 27 percent agreed that economic growth should be sacrificed to protect the environment, compared with 58 percent in 1978.

A *New York Times*-CBS News poll found nearly two-thirds of adult Americans wanted to keep clean air laws "as tough as they are now" even if "some factories might have to close."

A survey by pollster Louis Harris also found deep, widespread support for the Clean Air Act across all age and political groups. Harris outlined his results before the House Commerce Subcommittee on Health and Environment Oct. 15, 1981.

In an exchange with Rep. Don Ritter, R-Pa., Harris said: "Mess around with the Clean Air and Clean Water acts, and you are going to get into the deepest kind of trouble. The Republican Party is at a crossroads on this . . . .

"I am saying to you just as clear as can be, that clean air happens to be one of the sacred cows of the American people, and the suspicion is afoot that there are interests in the business community and among Republicans and some Democrats who want to keelhaul that legislation."

"And people are saying, 'Watch out. We will have your hide if you do it.' That is the only message that comes out of this as clear-cut as anything I have ever seen in my professional career."

Harris found that 80 percent of the American public wanted no relaxation in existing federal regulation of air pollution. The largest single group, 51 percent, wanted no changes in the act, while 29 percent would make it even stricter. By a slightly smaller majority, 54-42 percent, respondents opposed postponing deadlines for meeting auto emission standards.

On the other hand, a November 1981 survey prepared for the U.S. Chamber of Commerce by the Opinion Research Corp. (ORC) found that people were quite prepared to see the act amended. While the poll showed there was "no question about the American public's desire for clean air and for continuing efforts to improve the country's air quality," ORC said, it also showed that "There is sizable support for reviewing the act in light of past experience and current technology. There is sizable support for administrative changes that do not affect standards."

On the issue of tradeoffs — environment vs. growth — 59 percent agreed with the statement that the nation could achieve the goals of environmental protection and business and new job growth at the same time. Twenty-two percent agreed that environmental standards should be relaxed to achieve business and new job growth; and 15 percent agreed that the nation should accept a slower rate of economic growth to protect the environment.

in Congress, had lost much of its momentum by the mid-1970s.

During this time, Train, a former tax lawyer and conservation advocate, took on a seemingly thankless job in September 1973 when he became the second EPA administrator. His low-key manner was a disappointment to some after the flair and imagination displayed by Ruckelshaus, but Train managed to run the young and controversial agency for three years under trying conditions.

Train broke openly with the Nixon administration over plans to weaken the 1970 Clean Air Act, impound federal sewage treatment grant money and cut funding for other environmental programs. He continued in his outsider role during the Ford administration, opposing other executive departments such as Commerce and the Office of Management and Budget (OMB) on environmental issues. He seldom won.

Train also was forced to defend his agency against a constant barrage of criticism and court challenges from the outside. Much of it came from the companies subject to the many regulations EPA issued to implement environmental laws. Industry spokesmen often portrayed the agency as a

bumbling bureaucracy manned by anti-business zealots. Environmentalists, meanwhile, prodded the agency regularly to take tougher stands on pollution control, criticizing Train's efforts to influence administration policy as too timid.

Nonetheless, EPA's responsibilities continued to expand in certain areas. The Safe Drinking Water Act of 1974 set standards for chemical and bacteriological pollutants in water systems. The Toxic Substances Control Act of 1976 gave EPA the responsibility for studying the risks attached to toxic substances and protecting the public from them. The Resource Conservation and Recovery Act of 1976 was intended to ensure that hazardous and non-hazardous wastes were disposed of in environmentally sound ways. During 1977 clean water standards were redefined and deadlines extended one year to 1984.

Additional responsibilities in the hazardous waste area were given to the EPA with the passage of the controversial "superfund" legislation in the waning days of the 96th Congress. In December 1980 President Jimmy Carter signed the Comprehensive Environmental Response, Compensation and Liability Act, which established a $1.6 billion emergency fund to clean up toxic contaminants spilled or dumped into the environment. The major part of the Hazardous Substance Response Trust Fund, 86 percent, would come from the chemical and oil industries; appropriations of general revenue in fiscal 1981-85 would provide the remaining 14 percent. EPA was given responsibility for administering the fund.

Under Administrator Douglas M. Costle, who had served on an advisory council that recommended establishing the agency, the EPA attempted to deal with the concerns of industry while continuing to protect the environment. Costle served as chairman of the U.S. Regulatory Council, an organization Carter established in 1978 to ensure better coordination of federal regulatory activities. Barbara Blum, deputy administrator under Costle, had announced in 1977 a plan to review all existing regulations for their inflationary impact. The EPA also had attempted to streamline its regulatory process and to be more cost-conscious in its enforcement procedures. For example, the innovative "bubble" and "offset" ideas were introduced during Costle's tenure in office. *(New concepts, box, p. 116)*

Congressional Concerns

Only months into the Reagan administration, a number of members of Congress, Republicans and Democrats alike, were voicing concern that the EPA was using deep budget cuts and regulatory "reforms" to retreat from its congressionally mandated pollution control duties. Members were especially concerned because the budget cuts were coming at a time when the agency was just starting to implement some of the laws Congress enacted in the previous decade, such as the 1976 Resource Conservation and Recovery Act controlling transportation of hazardous wastes.

An indication of congressional dissatisfaction with the EPA was the fact that between October 1981 and July 1982 agency officials had appeared before congressional committees more than 70 times; Gorsuch herself had been called to Capitol Hill to testify on numerous occasions since she took office in May 1981.

One appearance came July 22, 1982, during two days of "midterm exam" hearings held by four House subcommittees. The day before Gorsuch testified the panels heard members of Congress, state officials and the leaders of major environmental organizations criticize the agency's performance from many standpoints: protection of public health from toxic chemicals, budget adequacy, scientific competence, enforcement credibility, management effectiveness, support of state agencies, relations with regulated industries and openness to public scrutiny.

Gorsuch's backers as well as her critics bemoaned the breakdown of a dozen years of bipartisanship on the environment. Each accused the other of causing the polarization.

Agency Attacked

The Reagan administration made no strong public push for specific changes in environmental laws in 1981 and 1982, although it supported an industry-backed package of Clean Air Act amendments and sought relaxation of certain provisions of the Clean Water Act.

But Gorsuch's critics complained that she needed no legislative changes; she could get what she wanted through regulatory and budget decisions. "We are witnessing a wholesale dismantling of the environmental achievements and gains of the past decade and a half," said Gaylord Nelson, chairman of the Wilderness Society and a former Democratic senator from Wisconsin (1963-81). "It is being done by a series of executive and administrative actions, without review by Congress and beyond the view of the American people."

Some members of Congress apparently no longer trusted EPA to carry out the environmental laws passed in the 1970s. Sen. Patrick J. Leahy, D-Vt., who testified at the House hearings, accused Gorsuch of "severely damaging the EPA's ability to enforce the laws" and called her "incapable or unwilling to operate EPA under the prescribed acts of Congress." Rep. James H. Scheuer, D-N.Y., chairman of the House Science and Technology Subcommittee on Natural Resources, Agriculture Research and Environment, complained of Gorsuch's "reluctance to fulfill her statutory mandates." His panel was one sponsor of the hearing.

"Mrs. Gorsuch and the administration have used private meetings, reorganizations, budget cuts, and pledges of selective enforcement to emasculate the laws they are duty bound to faithfully execute," said Rep. Toby Moffett, D-Conn., chairman of the House Government Operations Subcommittee on Environment, Energy and Natural Resources, another sponsor of the hearings.

Gorsuch Responds

Despite the barrage of criticism, Gorsuch yielded no ground during her July 22 testimony. Indeed, she barely acknowledged the fire. "We are fully committed to a stronger, better directed, and more effective Environmental Protection Agency," she declared.

Gorsuch presented a 54-page statement attacking her critics and the Carter administration, listing her accomplishments and outlining her policy goals. "We have proposed changes, some basic, some structural, and some legislative, and we have done so in good faith," she said. "At every turn, these changes have been either ignored or misconstrued, often misinterpreted, and even misstated. Although it takes time to correct the problems of a decade, little attention is paid to those proposals likely to be popularly supported, or to the overall positive thrust of our programs.

"In order to improve the quality, quantity, and timeliness of EPA's activities, to move it from the areas where it was bogging down, and to carry out my mandate from the president, I determined to institute a number of reforms at the agency. These reforms included (1) providing a better scientific foundation for agency decision making; (2) the institution of regulatory reform measures to assist in supporting the president's economic recovery program; (3) the elimination of backlogs and delays in many of the agency's major programs; (4) strengthening of the federal-state-local relationships to support the president's 'new federalism' program; and (5) improved management and budget reduction measures at all levels of the agency." *(New federalism, p. 68)*

Gorsuch said both the nature of the nation's environmental problems and the response needed to deal with them had changed over the past decade. But the attitudes of some in Congress, she implied, had not kept pace. "In any society, there are those who oppose change," she said.

Budget, Staff Reductions

"Unable to repeal the country's environmental laws because the public would never stand for it, Reagan is gutting them through the personnel and budgetary back doors," said William Drayton, former EPA assistant administrator for planning and management and a member of Save EPA, a group comprised largely of former EPA officials.

Reagan requested $3.6 billion for EPA in fiscal 1983 — including $961.3 million to run pollution control programs, $230 million for cleaning up chemical dumps under "superfund," and $2.4 billion for sewage treatment plants. The $961 million operating budget request was down 29 percent from the $1.35 billion appropriated in 1981 for fiscal 1982 — and down far more once inflation was factored in. Under the budget proposal, the agency would have 1,176 fewer employees than in fiscal 1982, and 2,762 fewer than in fiscal 1981.

Many of the cuts could be accomplished without harming the environment, by reducing federal paperwork and bureaucratic requirements imposed on the states and by turning over more enforcement programs to them, said EPA chief of staff John F. Daniel in a Feb. 5, 1982, press briefing. Daniel also disputed accounts that the agency was suffering from low morale and that attrition was running at 2.7 percent a month, or 32 percent a year. Contrary to reports that employees were leaving the agency in droves, agency attrition was lower than usual in fiscal 1981 and 1982, Daniel said.

The 1983 budget request "is a product of intensive analysis and represents a trim and efficient EPA," said Gorsuch during her July appearance on Capitol Hill. She detailed $21 million worth of savings resulting from management improvements.

But her claims were disputed by Leahy, who had asked the Senate Appropriations Committee staff to analyze discrepancies between EPA budget documents submitted to the president's Office of Management and Budget and those given Congress. Leahy noted that Gorsuch had told Congress "that the very large EPA budget cuts can be accommodated by increased efficiency, increased delegation to the states, and because a large portion of pollution control is already accomplished." But he said that the staff study of the agency's documents "shows that, in over 70 instances, EPA told OMB, in plain English, that it was reducing its effort to stop pollution. This reduction of effort will affect control of toxic air pollutants, control of auto pollution, control of toxic water pollution and the assessment of health risks of high-priority drinking water contaminants."

Environmentalists and some members of Congress feared that the cuts could cripple the agency at a time when its caseload had nearly doubled. A 19-member task force formed by the House Democratic Caucus blasted the proposed cuts in a statement issued Feb. 2, 1982. Speaker Thomas P. O'Neill Jr., D-Mass., called them "a deceptive attempt to repeal indirectly laws that the administration knows the public would never allow to be repealed."

Earlier that day, the 4.5-million-member National Wildlife Federation released a study claiming that EPA needed an operating budget of $2.16 billion in order to carry out its legislative mandates.

Congressional committees refused to make the EPA cuts Reagan proposed, holding the line at fiscal 1982 levels, and Congress as a whole followed through in the first budget resolution (S Con Res 92), which basically froze all fiscal 1983 environmental and natural resources spending at close to 1982 levels — $9.5 billion rather than the $8.75 billion Reagan requested. In September 1982 Congress finally cleared legislation appropriating $3.7 billion for the agency, about $100 million higher than the budget request.

Research Cutbacks

Much of the concern among environmentalists and their supporters on Capitol Hill centered on EPA research efforts, which were hardest hit among major agency programs affected by the fiscal 1983 Reagan budget cuts.

Both the House and Senate required more research spending than the $215.88 million the administration proposed. In September Congress cleared a bill authorizing $282 million in fiscal 1983 and $298 million in fiscal 1984. Of that amount, $15 million each year would come from the "Superfund." Congress earmarked 20 percent of all EPA research funds for long-term research. Reagan, however, vetoed the bill Oct. 22. Congress could try to override the veto when it convened after the November 2 elections.

Science is at the core of many of EPA's most important regulatory decisions, such as the identification of dangerous chemicals and the determination of hazardous levels for air and water pollutants. Society considers it immoral to test toxic chemicals on humans. But industry has claimed that animal studies cannot "prove" a risk to humans. Scientific certainty is never absolute and results are always subject to further testing. While calculation of the odds in a particular chemical risk is a scientific judgment, pinpointing what level of risk is acceptable or worth trying to achieve is an ethical and political judgment.

Putting a price on life or health is an exercise that makes politicians very nervous. Congress in the past has set by law a very low allowable risk for toxic chemicals (for example, the Clean Water Act's prohibition on discharges of any amount of toxic wastes into waterways). Because near-zero risk is expensive to achieve, EPA has often delayed toxic rules, awaiting higher and higher levels of scientific certainty about the nature of the risk.

That situation led to charges that EPA rules were based on inadequate scientific research. Such allegations typically have been made by those, such as the chemical industry, that would bear large costs if required to meet tough EPA cleanup rules. "EPA's research program provides the information on which we base the clean air standards. It makes no sense to cut back on that information base at a time when we are bringing the standards under review," said Rep. Claudine Schneider, R-R.I., in 1981.

Gorsuch has acknowledged that EPA's science needs improvement. "One of the objectives of this administration is to improve the quality of the scientific basis underlying the regulatory decision-making process," she said at the July 22 hearing. She listed four ways EPA was seeking that improvement: a "quality assurance" program to improve the reliability and consistency of pollution measurements and laboratory data, a "peer review" program where EPA research projects are reviewed by non-EPA experts, a program of advance front-office review of all agency publications and a bigger role and larger membership for the agency's science advisory board. The decrease in the agency's budget request for research, Gorsuch said, "reflects the completion of efforts which will enable us to reduce our overall research component as well as invest in newer areas."

Pollution, Bubbles and Offsets...

Besides imposing regulations on industrial development in unpolluted areas of the nation, the 1970 Clean Air Act contained a different set of controls for companies building factories in urban areas where the national standards had not been attained for the pollutants those industries would emit. The complicated system envisaged a free market of offsets, allowing companies to buy, sell, trade and "bank" permission to pollute. This offset policy has been supplemented by the "bubble" approach aimed at reducing pollution within a single overall source or region. Both were innovative methods of getting private industry to comply with emission standards.

As provided in the Clean Air Act, here is how the system would work if a company wanted to build a factory emitting sulfur dioxide in a city that already had unhealthy amounts of that pollutant. Besides installing equipment that emits the least possible amounts of sulfur dioxide, the company must obtain a reduction in sulfur dioxide emissions from other plants in that city.

These reductions must *more than offset* the amount of sulfur dioxide the new plant will emit. That way, total sulfur dioxide levels will decrease, despite the addition of the new factory. Offsets are obtained by buying new pollution control equipment for an existing polluter, or by buying and closing down an existing plant that is too expensive to clean up. Or, an existing company that has earned "pollution reduction credits" by installing cleanup equipment can sell its credits to the firm wanting to build or modernize.

Creation of Pollution 'Banks'

To facilitate trading between two companies, the EPA encouraged the development of "banks" to buy, sell and broker pollution "credits." A company would be able to sell a credit for a certified pollution reduction to the bank, which in turn could sell that credit to a company that found pollution control economically unfeasible. The objective was to bring about an overall decrease in air pollution by making the buyers "pay" for more emission reductions than they could use. By 1981 three pilot pollution banks had been set up: Louisville, Ky.; San Francisco, Calif.; and Houston, Texas.

Congress devised the offset system so economic growth could continue as the air was being cleaned up. By creating market incentives, Congress hoped companies would devise new ways to reduce pollution. But industry complained that in practice the system did not work because offsets often were unavailable.

As of late 1981 only 26 offsets had been purchased by new companies from existing firms. One reason they were so scarce was that the clean air law required existing polluters in non-attainment areas to retrofit their plants with "reasonably available" pollution control equipment by July 1, 1979. Because a mandatory reduction did not qualify as an offset, the law eliminated most potential offsets new industries could have obtained.

Another reason offsets were hard to find was that existing factories were allowed to reduce their pollution and bank their credits for use in later expansion. But a bigger criticism was that the offset system put new companies at the mercy of existing firms. The system, in effect, gave "squatters' rights" to the very companies that had polluted the region and created the need for offsets, said critics.

Because they controlled the price and availability of offsets, existing industries could keep competitors from moving into an area and literally control the future economic growth of their region, opponents charged. Moreover, because new-source controls were more stringent than those on existing sources, companies had an incentive to maintain their older, dirtier plants.

Industry wanted to eliminate offsets and extend the 1982 deadline for achieving national standards if emissions in a non-attainment area showed improvement over the long term. Some industry groups also wanted to eliminate EPA's authority to impose construction bans in non-attainment areas that lacked approved state plans showing they could meet the 1982 attainment deadline. Industry complained that bans often applied to factories when automobile pollution was the real culprit.

The Bubble Approach

The Clean Air Act established national standards for major pollutants and required the states to impose technology-based standards to be met uniformly at every smokestack or other emission source. But the source-standards approach proved inefficient, and in 1978 the EPA endorsed an experimental "bubble policy."

Instead of determining emission standards for every process within a factory, the agency would put an imaginary bubble over the plant and set allowable standards for the entire operation. It was thought that this would give factory management a greater incentive to change basic plant operations rather than just add pollution control devices. Moreover, the EPA would consider placing a bubble over regional groupings of plants, allowing them to adjust their emissions to achieve the regional goal.

According to the final rule issued by EPA Dec. 11, 1979, "Sources will have the opportunity to come forward with alternative abatement strategies that would result in the same air quality impact but at less expense by placing relatively more control on emission points with a low marginal cost of control

... A New Approach to Regulation

and less on emission points with a high cost."

"This policy would mean less expensive pollution control, not less pollution control,"said EPA Administrator Douglas M. Costle. "There's no point in making a company spend $1 to control a pound of pollution if the same job can be done differently for 50 cents a pound."

Du Pont, Maloney-Yandle Studies

Based on material from a study conducted in 1976 by two engineers from the E. I. du Pont de Nemours Co., Clemson University professors Mike Maloney and Bruce Yandle concluded that when 52 Du Pont plants were placed under one regional bubble annual emission control costs were found to be 86 percent lower than the costs imposed by individual source standards. The findings, summarized in the May/June 1980 issue of *Regulation,* showed that under source-by-source standards the annual cost of an 85 percent reduction in emissions for all 52 plants was $105.7 million. When each plant was placed under a bubble and allowed to adjust emission control among sources within the plant, the annual cost for the same reduction in pollution fell to $42.6 million. Annual emission control costs for the regional bubble amounted to only $14.6 million.

But the authors cautioned that more data was needed on monitoring costs. It is easier to monitor compliance when industries are required to install designated equipment on each source of pollution. The bubble approach requires development of sophisticated monitoring techniques, they said.

Reagan Policy

The Reagan administration expanded the bubble and offsets programs in April 1982 when the EPA announced a policy to encourage the use of the bubble concept, including using it in areas where the air was dirtier than the standards permitted. Companies within a bubble in areas with dirty air would still be required to meet the act's pollution requirements, but once they reduced pollution below those limits they could sell or trade the "surplus" reduction, in effect giving other companies "permission to pollute." Previously, the bubble had been used only in areas where the air was cleaner than the law required.

The Reagan program would permit states to allow companies and regions to adopt the bubble approach without prior EPA approval. The agency would continue to monitor compliance. Another change concerned the time lag in applying offsets under the bubble. Previously, a company could get credits from EPA by closing a polluting facility and using those credits to legally maintain higher levels of pollution elsewhere within the bubble. However, those credits had to be applied when the plant closing took place. The new policy lifted the time-of-closure restriction. (In June 1982, Union Carbide Corp. became the first company to use the new "shutdown provision," when EPA said the company did not have to install $3.5 million in pollution control equipment at a plant in Texas City, Texas, because the company had closed an obsolete facility in the area four years earlier.)

EPA Administrator Anne M. Gorsuch said the policy could produce industry savings of more than $1 billion in equipment and operating costs by the end of 1982, "with equal or better air quality results."

"By harnessing rather than resisting natural market incentives, emissions trading will provide a more dynamic force for innovation in pollution abatement than the most ingenious technology-forcing standard anyone could write down in the *Federal Register*," said Christopher C. DeMuth, executive director of the Presidential Task Force on Regulatory Relief.

While industry groups generally welcomed the new policy, they had some misgivings about the control process. The procedures were complicated because regions are classified as attainment or nonattainment depending on whether they meet the national standards for a specific pollutant. Thus a city could be in an attainment area for one pollutant, but not for others.

As a result, in the same city a company could be subject to one set of requirements if it emitted pollutants for which the area was violating the standards, and to another set of regulations if it emitted pollutants for which the area was not in violation. Many companies recommended that EPA's industry-wide specifications should be imposed nationwide, regardless of where the plant was located.

Environmentalists criticized the bubble concept as a major setback for the achievement of clean air. Dirty air areas "are places where you need additional controls to reach the health standards of the act," said David Hawkins, an attorney for the Natural Resources Defense Council. But under the bubble concept "they are going to relax controls just because somebody is meeting emission limits." Hawkins predicted the policy would give rise to lawsuits and delays in cleaning up the air.

Indeed, lawsuits were not long in coming. The U.S. Court of Appeals ruled Aug. 17, 1982, that the EPA had acted illegally in extending the bubble concept to dirty air regions. Citizens for a Better Environment and Northwestern Ohio Lung Association had asked the court to review the regulation. Congress intended the Clean Air Act to "promote the cleanup of nonattainment areas," not simply to maintain the air quality, wrote Judge Ruth Bader Ginsburg. "We are therefore impelled" to hold that the change was "impermissible."

Sacrificing Quality?

Environmental groups and congressional critics, however, said EPA would need more research money if it was to have better science, and that it did not make sense for the administrator to be cutting funds most deeply in an area she said was one of her highest priorities.

One of the critics was Rep. George E. Brown Jr., D-Calif., chairman of the House Science and Technology Committee that has oversight over EPA research activities. Writing in the March 27, 1981, issue of *Science* magazine, Brown criticized the agency for neglecting long-term research. "What seems to happen over and over again in environmental programs," he said, "is that the policy makers run quickly through the 'packed down' knowledge existing in published sources and into areas of fundamental ignorance."

"Research as conducted by a regulatory agency is an extremely fragile undertaking," wrote Richard M. Dowd, former director of the EPA research office, and Terry F. Yosie, executive secretary of the agency's science advisory board, in the October 1981 issue of *Environmental Science & Technology*. "Congressional appropriation cycles for research impose time frames that often do not coincide with the research community's capacity to generate needed information.

"In addition, the tendency of regulatory agencies and congressional committees to exhibit a 'pollutant-of-the-year' syndrome results in continual redefinition of research priorities and the reprogramming of research budgets."

"Nowhere has low morale and the brain drain at EPA been more severe than among competent scientists and scientist-managers," said Audubon Society President Russell W. Peterson at the July 21 hearing. "Increasingly reliant on outside science, the administrator has shown her contempt for independent scientists who bring information which is inconsistent with the administration's political agenda."

Peterson, a former Republican governor of Delaware and CEQ chairman under Presidents Nixon and Ford, cited as an example a recent EPA-funded study on acid rain by the National Academy of Science. "The academy's preliminary report ... concluded that acid rain is real, that it is caused in large measure by industrial pollution, that it is increasingly destructive of aquatic ecosystems, and that we know enough to do something about it — now," Peterson said. "EPA did not like these findings and recommendations, and so — in a classic case of killing the messenger — Mrs. Gorsuch eliminated funding for any further acid rain research by the academy.

"As its own R&D program is being cut to the bone ... EPA is becoming more and more dependent on the scientific staffs of the industrial polluters. This seems to be a case of the regulator becoming captured by the regulated."

EPA's research program was identified as the top issue in a June 16 report entitled "State of the Environment 1982," by the Conservation Foundation, a private environmental think tank. The report was meant to replace a long-delayed annual report by CEQ, which also had been hit by drastic Reagan budget cuts.

"Because of budget cuts, the information base for environmental policy, always weak, is likely to be even weaker in the future," the report stated. "We will be less able to sort out important problems from unimportant ones, less able to tell which environmental programs are working effectively and which are not."

Adequacy of Enforcement

Another key area of concern to Congress was whether EPA was doing an adequate job of enforcing anti-pollution laws. Some critics said that if the administration was unable to rewrite environmental laws it would simply not enforce them.

In the regulatory arena, Gorsuch first abolished the office of enforcement, then reconstituted it with a much smaller staff, preferring to rely primarily on voluntary industry compliance. She reduced the number of enforcement cases earmarked for court action and began reviewing pollution control rules to ease regulatory burdens on industry.

"From an administration that quite rightly emphasizes the need for good management, what we are seeing at EPA is its very antithesis," wrote former EPA Administrator Train. Budget and personnel cuts had led to "demoralization and institutional paralysis. . . . Permits that businesses need do not get issued. Required rules and regulations do not get promulgated. Enforcement has ground practically to a halt. . . . Environmental protection needs are not going to lessen if EPA becomes ineffectual."

Gorsuch responded that "One of the primary methods [of protecting the environment] is strong enforcement of our laws and regulations. . . . Any violation of these provisions should result in quick and corrective action on our part. Where possible, we should remedy the violation at the lowest appropriate level. If an informal or administrative solution is not reached in a reasonable time, then we must take appropriate legal steps, including litigation."

She said results are the real question behind any enforcement effort and that "Measured by this standard, the enforcement effort existing at EPA prior to this administration was not particularly good."

Many agency critics, however, disagreed with Gorsuch's stress on voluntary compliance. One was Sen. Leahy, who presented a report at the July 21 hearing that was based on a study by his Appropriations Committee staff. "As a former prosecutor, I know that, unless the public believes our laws will be fairly enforced, against the powerful polluter as well as against the food stamp cheat, respect for government . . . will suffer," Leahy said. "This study has led me to conclude that the effectiveness of the enforcement division of the EPA was virtually destroyed by a combination of mismanagement and mixed signals."

Leahy said that between July 1981 and May 1982 the enforcement arms of EPA went through a major reorganization every 11 weeks. He also noted that there had been no overall legal director for EPA during six of the preceding 11 months, which he said resulted in two deputies feuding for control. According to the study, "one regional office with severe hazardous waste problems left all inspection to the states, while another region with relatively few problems led the nation in inspections." He called this a sign of poor priority setting.

"By any objective measure," Leahy's report concluded, "enforcement efforts have dropped by 70-80 percent." From 1977 through 1980, he said, civil actions sent by EPA to the Justice Department for action averaged 278 per year. In 1981 there were 78 such actions, a 70 percent drop.

Relations With Industry

Some House members questioned whether EPA's relations with industry were too friendly. Moffett, chairman of the House Government Operations Subcommittee on the Environment, called Gorsuch and other top agency officials on the carpet during 1981 oversight hearings to investigate meetings EPA had held with chemical industry representatives. The meetings reportedly concerned proposed regulatory actions affecting that industry.

The coziness issue surfaced again during the July 1982 hearings. Expressing concern over whether "special interests are calling the shots" at EPA, Moffett pressed the administrator about a Dec. 11, 1981, meeting between Gorsuch and representatives of Thriftway Co., a small New Mexico refinery. At the meeting Gorsuch allegedly promised not to enforce rules on lead in gasoline because she expected to revise them.

Moffett was joined by Rep. Bob Shamansky, D-Ohio, who asked Gorsuch a hypothetical question about the incident. "My answer is non-hypothetical," Gorsuch replied. "I did not recommend to anyone that they violate any of our environmental laws — nor will I." Gorsuch said she had been "exonerated" by an outside legal opinion requested March 19 by EPA Inspector General Matthew Novick and submitted on March 29. Moffett had asked Novick to investigate the matter March 2.

That outside legal opinion was the basis for a letter to the editor of *The Atlanta Journal* by EPA Public Affairs Director Byron Nelson claiming Gorsuch had been cleared. Moffett, however, produced a June 4 letter from Novick protesting that "The facts contained in Nelson's letter are absolutely false."

Moffett noted the outside legal opinion was submitted to EPA before Novick had concluded his own investigation. Novick's report, which drew no conclusions as to the propriety of the meeting, was dated April 5.

"If you don't feel the matter has been resolved," Gorsuch told Moffett, "I suggest you see the attorney general," adding that she did not intend to submit to "trial by Congress."

State Grants

Gorsuch acknowledged July 22 that a phase-out of all federal grants to help states run pollution control programs was an eventual administration goal.

States have responsibility for many aspects of pollution control programs required by federal law, such as writing permits under the Clean Air and Clean Water acts. While Congress originally legislated this planned delegation of responsibility to the states, the Gorsuch EPA pushed the process, arguing that under Reagan's "new federalism" policy, decisions should be made as close to the local level as possible.

Indeed, increased delegation was a justification for cutting EPA budgets and activities at the federal level. The states, however, while eager to get more flexibility and autonomy in environmental programs, said they could not afford to run all the programs Gorsuch wanted to delegate. Many states argued that the federal government had an obligation to help pay for programs it required. A May 1982 survey conducted by the National Governors' Association's Energy and Environment Committee found that in most states the 20 percent reduction in federal grants Reagan proposed for 1983 would require a proportionate curtailment of a number of environmental protection activities.

Generally, less than one-fifth of the states could make up any part of the cut with their own funds. Many were legally barred from charging fees for permits, one possible way to recoup lost funds. Some states already were talking of returning delegated programs to the federal government.

CLEAN AIR ACT: A CONTROVERSIAL LAW

Perhaps the most critical problem confronting the EPA is that it has to administer a host of highly technical and comprehensive laws, foremost among them the Clean Air Act. Up for renewal in September 1981, the complex act a year later still had not been rewritten or extended by Congress. (The legislation was kept alive through continuing appropriations resolutions.)

At issue was whether the act, which affected nearly all U. S. industrial, transportation, real estate and energy production activities, had to remain as stringent as it was to accomplish what most people agreed was a necessary goal. The act — by far the most costly piece of environmental and health regulation on record — expressly prohibited any consideration of expense in setting national ambient air quality standards.

As Congress reworked the Clean Air Act members had to decide whether to continue a decade-long commitment to protect all citizens equally from harmful air pollution, whether to accept a relaxation of clean air standards in the interests of economic development, or whether a healthy environment and economic growth could be achieved simultaneously.

Members also had to consider:
● Whether children, pregnant women and old people — who were the most vulnerable to air pollution — should have the same right to protection under the law as other persons.
● Whether the nation should continue trying to protect citizens from temporary episodes of watery eyes and difficult breathing, or if it could only afford to protect them from permanent lung damage.
● Whether to continue protecting unspoiled areas from encroaching air pollution.
● Whether energy development was so important that strip mining and belching smokestacks had to be allowed in clear view of national parks.
● Whether the government was using valid scientific data in setting the air pollution standards.

While trying to consider what impact these decisions would have in the future, Congress was looking back to see how well the Clean Air Act had worked in its first 10 years of operation.

Much of that assessment depended on how well the EPA had administered the law.

1970 Act and 1977 Amendments

The original 1970 Clean Air Act (PL 91-604) required the EPA to establish safe concentrations for major air pollutants and set a 1975 deadline for state and local governments to meet those national standards by whatever procedures proved necessary and acceptable. At the same time, emissions of certain pollutants were required to be reduced at the source, be they emissions from automobiles, other modes of transportation, industrial facilities or power plants.

Progress in reaching the goals of the Clean Air Act proved slower than expected, and in 1977 Congress enacted amendments modifying the 1970 objectives. The amendments relaxed several compliance deadlines but also tightened clean air legislation in several important respects. They established three categories of areas with air that is cleaner than required under national standards, specified to what degree levels of sulfur dioxide and particulates (fine particles) could increase in each category and required the EPA to propose regulations that would prevent the nation's air from deteriorating to a mediocre average.

Three kinds of clean air regions were defined. Class I includes all national parks and wilderness areas and may include other areas the states want to remain unsullied. No significant additional sulfur or particulate sources are permitted in Class I regions. Class II areas can have some industrial development, up to specified levels. Class III areas can have about twice as much pollution from additional sources, sometimes up to the minimum federal standards.

The amendments gave states until July 1, 1979, to complete their revised plans for attaining ambient air standards and required all plans to contain a permit program for major stationary sources of pollution. In "non-attainment" areas (areas not in compliance with ambient air standards), permits for new industrial facilities and plants would be granted only when additional emissions would be "offset" by reductions from other sources. States requesting extension of the deadline for compliance with ambient air standards from 1982 to 1987, because of severe auto-related problems, would be required to establish vehicle inspection and maintenance programs.

The 1977 amendments also extended until 1982, and in

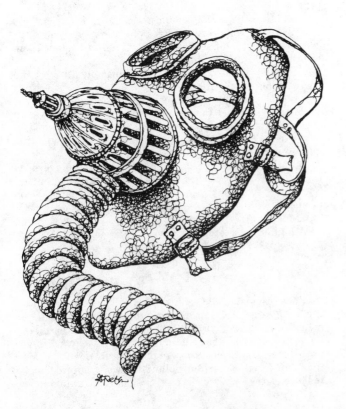

some cases until 1987, the deadline for cities to meet national air quality standards. The previous deadline was 1977. Most industrial polluters were given up to three more years to comply before facing heavy fines.

The most difficult task in writing the 1977 amendments concerned new standards and deadlines for three pollutants from automobile exhausts — hydrocarbons, carbon monoxide and nitrogen oxide. The lowest-level "statutory standards" under the 1970 act were to have been met by the 1975 model cars. But three postponements — two by EPA and one by Congress — delayed the standards until the 1978 model year. The 1977 amendments postponed existing standards for automobile emissions for two more years but tightened them for 1980 and 1981 model years.

The amendments also provided for the establishment of a National Commission on Air Quality (NCAQ), which would conduct a three-year study of national air pollution legislation and then recommend revisions to Congress. The commission originally was supposed to send its final report to Congress in August 1980, but did not complete its $9.5 million study until March 1981.

Key Issues in the Debate

The record of efforts to control pollutants regulated by the Clean Air Act was mixed. Nitrogen dioxide and ozone proved the most difficult to control. EPA figures showed particulates decreased 32 percent between 1960 and 1979. In urban areas sulfur dioxide decreased 67 percent from 1964 to 1979, and carbon monoxide dropped 36 percent from 1972 to 1979. But ozone remained constant, mostly because emissions from industrial processes increased while those from transportation sources were being controlled. Nitrogen dioxide levels increased 15 percent from 1975 to 1979, because of higher emissions from vehicles and factories.

Although progress had been made, the national commission's report said, millions of Americans still were breathing air that was dirtier than the national standards called for, and it said there were serious doubts that some regions would meet the 1982 and 1987 deadlines. At least four areas of the country — Los Angeles, Houston, New York and Boston — might never meet the national standards for carbon monoxide, according to the report.

NCAQ also warned that dangerous levels of carbon monoxide, nitrogen dioxide and cancer-causing formaldehyde could accumulate in well-insulated buildings and homes. And EPA was concerned about the increase of potentially carcinogenic diesel emissions as auto manufacturers were beginning to switch to diesels to meet mileage requirements.

Whether Congress should change EPA's way of setting national air quality standards was a key issue of the 1981-82 debate on extending and amending the act. Under existing law the EPA had authority to set standards to protect public health "allowing an adequate margin of safety" for vulnerable segments of society. Congress, however, gave little indication as to what it meant by "adequate."

The standards were the heart of the act because the rest of the law was designed to force the states to comply with them within certain deadlines. Environmentalists feared that significant changes could mean radical alterations in the act's basic thrust.

Critics of the existing legislation questioned the scientific validity of the data EPA used to set the standards — whether the pollutants were being measured accurately, whether the list should be extended beyond the original seven pollutants (sulfur dioxide, lead, nitrogen oxides, carbon monoxide, ozone, hydrocarbons and particulate matter) and whether the interaction between pollutants should be considered.

Industrial Growth

Industrial facilities and combustion account for nearly all sulfur oxide emissions, more than 80 percent of particulate emissions and over half of nitrogen oxide emissions. To control air quality, the act gave the EPA and the states power to review all proposed industrial construction and modernization to make sure major new facilities had the best possible pollution control equipment and would not cause air quality to deteriorate.

That construction-permitting process drew fiery industry criticism for being overly slow and duplicative. Before building a new plant in a clean air area, a company had to obtain a permit from the state air pollution board requiring the best possible equipment to control every emission source at that plant. In the case of a large petroleum refinery the permit could regulate more than 150,000 minor emission sources such as pumps, compressors and valves — not only large smokestacks. In certain dirtier areas the requirements were even tougher. Owners of new factories had to promise to install the best control equipment and clean up emissions at existing plants. In addition, all companies had to gather data on existing air quality where they wanted to build and then use computer models to predict how the air would change as a result of the new facility. The company also had to monitor emissions after a plant was built to show they did not exceed projections. The permit had to be approved by several entities, including the county, regional and state air pollution boards, the regional EPA office and EPA's Washington headquarters.

A study commissioned by the Business Roundtable found that the permitting process took three years or more and cost $250 million to $300 million per plant. Critics said the process had to be streamlined or it would impede industrial growth and modernization and stymie Western synthetic fuels development.

PSD Program

One problem Congress had to grapple with was how to prevent industries from fleeing to clean air areas of the South and West to avoid installing the expensive equipment required to clean up pollution at existing factories in dirtier Midwestern and Northeastern cities. Older Northern industries would have been at a disadvantage to new competitors in clean air areas.

To implement the non-degradation policy, the 1977 act outlined a highly complex system called the "prevention of significant deterioration" (PSD) program. By far the most controversial part of the act, the PSD program was so complicated that environmentalists and industry agreed it needed improvement. But industry wanted far more radical changes than environmentalists did.

Industry questioned the need for requiring cleaner air in PSD areas than the national standards, especially since the standards already ensured an "added margin of safety" for vulnerable persons. Critics also claimed the PSD system was designed to limit economic growth in the South and West to protect industries in the Northeast and Midwest.

Thus, the PSD debate threatened to turn into a Snow Belt-Sun Belt confrontation in Congress.

Industry and administration spokesmen were critical of the time-consuming process of meeting PSD requirements. "The average PSD permit takes nine months to process and approve in addition to the many months or even years required to prepare the application and conduct the monitoring," said Kathleen Bennett, assistant EPA administrator for air, noise and radiation. The delays cost millions of dollars, Bennett said. "In virtually all cases where the applicant has the necessary patience, the permit ultimately will be issued with little substantive change. High cost — little or no benefit," she added.

But environmentalists said any major PSD changes would mean dirtying up the nation's few remaining unsullied areas.

Although the National Commission on Air Quality found that the PSD program had not affected energy development, the report added the program had imposed more regulatory complexity on industry than could be justified by the benefits being achieved. The panel recommended retaining requirements that all new plants install the best available pollution control technology. But it recommended eliminating the system that allows pollution to increase only up to certain preset "increments," except in national parks and wilderness areas where both air quality and visibility would be protected.

Automobile Emissions

The act set limits for automobile emissions of hydrocarbons (HC), carbon monoxide (CO) and oxides of nitrogen (NOx), and required a 90 percent reduction from uncontrolled levels for HC and CO by 1982. NOx was to be reduced by 75 percent. The EPA could waive certain standards if public health did not require the statutory standards or if the technology to meet them did not exist.

The major auto manufacturers wanted the 1981 CO standard of 3.4 grams per mile to be relaxed to 7.0 grams per mile (the NCAQ also recommended a relaxation), and the 1.0 gram per mile NOx standard reduced to 2.0 grams per mile.

The proposal was tough to sell to Congress because it would mean removing equipment already on most cars and rolling back standards that already could be met. Nearly all 1981 cars met the NOx standard. For CO, the Carter administration had granted waivers to 30 percent of the 1981 fleet. When Reagan came into power his administration granted waivers to 70 percent of the 1982 fleet.

One reason industry wanted a weaker NOx standard was to allow production of more diesels. But environmentalists were concerned about the proliferation of diesels because their emissions were suspected of causing cancer. (Details on auto emissions controversy, p. 132)

State Implementation Plans and Delays

In its first 10 years the act resulted in cleaner air but progress was slower than hoped, partly because some industries resisted compliance, often in court, and partly because EPA was slow in implementing the act. In early 1981 EPA estimated that 93 percent of industry was in compliance. The companies still in violation were primarily power plants, steel plants and heavy metal industries.

Among the delays were those connected with State Implementation Plans (SIPs), which were to have been approved by July 1, 1979. As of June 30, 1982, only 18 had been fully approved.

EPA said the process had been slowed because states with severe automobile pollution balked at imposing transportation control programs required in the act. But state air pollution control agencies blamed the delay partly on the approval process, which they said was laborious. EPA also failed to meet the act's December 1980 deadline for reviewing the national air quality standards to ensure they reflected the latest scientific findings. And it was behind schedule in controlling toxic air pollutants, dangerous fine particles and short-term exposure to nitrogen dioxide.

Because of the problems facing many of the nation's largest industries, there was growing pressure to relax air regulations affecting industries and even to do away with the SIPs altogether. William Pedersen, a deputy general counsel with EPA under Carter, said in a 1980 paper distributed to agency officials that the clean air law "lacks any clearly defined mechanism for establishing with precision the sum total of requirements a given source must obey." He described the SIP process as overly cumbersome because it "requires affirmative action by at least two levels of government." Pedersen suggested scrapping most of the SIP process in favor of a simpler permitting system.

Many regulatory officials agreed that the procedures were awkward, but some expressed the view that the process of forcing all relevant interests to collaborate in preparing a clean air plan was valuable. Mark Pisano of the Southern California Association of Governments, which prepared the transportation parts of the clean air plan for the Los Angeles region, reported in late 1980 that the "full head of steam" that local organizations built up during preparation of the plan tended to dissipate because EPA took so long evaluating the plan. He went on to say that preparation of the plan otherwise represented a valuable experience for all involved.

EPA took its time with the California plan in large part because of the state legislature's refusal to enact a vehicle inspection and maintenance program, as required by the 1977 Clean Air Act Amendments. Generally the agency avoided imposing sanctions in connection with SIP approvals, but it insisted — as it must under the law — that states getting extensions on compliance deadlines implement inspection programs for cars.

Costs and Benefits

Underlying the debate over renewal of the act was the question of its costs and benefits. There were wide variations in estimates. The EPA put the total cost of implementing and complying with the act between 1970 and 1986 at $291.6 billion in 1977 dollars. According to figures compiled by the Council on Environmental Quality, the costs of complying with the Clean Air Act totaled $22 billion in 1979. That figure could increase to $38 billion annually by 1988. A report released in November 1980 by the Business Roundtable claimed that the law would cost industry $400 billion from 1970 to 1987 and recommended applying cost-benefit analyses in developing clean air standards. The report suggested that the standards, instead of allowing an "adequate margin of safety," should be set at levels to protect the public against "serious and irreversible threats to life and health." The National Coal Association and the Chemical Manufacturers Association as well as the Reagan administration recommended similar changes, which if enacted would mean that citizens would not be protected against temporary air pollution episodes causing

attacks of asthma, angina or minor discomfort.

However, the National Commission on Air Quality recommended continuing the existing method of establishing standards. The panel specifically rejected suggestions that the standards be based on cost-benefit analyses. The report recommended that EPA publish an analysis of the costs and benefits of a proposed standard but that the study should not be used to set the standard.

Opponents of the cost-benefit approach charged that it was nearly impossible to put accurate price tags on intangible benefits. The NCAQ report said that "unchallengeable estimates [of costs and benefits] are virtually impossible." Environmentalists said the cost-benefit argument was a smokescreen for cutting the heart out of the act.

Some critics also charged that the benefits of clean air had been underestimated. The commission's report, although warning of the difficulty in quantifying benefits, said that the savings of air pollution control — including improved public health, reduced cleaning expenses, better vegetation, less damage to materials and higher property values — were estimated at $21.4 billion. *(Commission study, box, p. 123)*

Another economic benefit of clean air has been the growth of the air pollution control industry itself. According to the Environmental Industry Council, an association of manufacturers of pollution control devices and systems, sales of equipment totaled $2.4 billion in 1981.

Action and Inaction

At first the Reagan administration saw renewal of the act as a chance to pare down the federal role in air pollution control, restricting it to advising the states on clean air standards. EPA Administrator Gorsuch disclosed this plan in a memo that Sen. Gary Hart, D-Colo., chairman of the NCAQ, made public in July 1981. Hart said the proposal would have repealed 51 provisions of the 1977 legislation and relaxed 64 others.

But then the administration switched its strategy entirely. Instead of proposing specific legislative modifications, Gorsuch at an Aug. 5 news conference presented the administration's position in a simplified, nine-point plan that indicated Reagan had second thoughts about defending complex new legislation on such a controversial issue. The principles were far more modest in scope and tone than the proposals contained in the earlier draft. The move was seen by many on Capitol Hill as a shrewd decision by the president not to stake his prestige on a bid for major revisions in the anti-pollution law in the face of polls showing massive public support for the act.

Principles, Not Legislative Proposals

The administration's principles would continue the nation's progress toward cleaner air, but "at a more reasoned pace," said Gorsuch. The principles, which called for relaxing pollution standards and delaying some cleanup deadlines, were met with enthusiasm by industry groups but with suspicion from environmental organizations.

Among the administration principles were:

● Continuing the current method of setting air pollution standards, without applying a cost-benefit test, so they provided an adequate margin of safety for public health. But the administration wanted the standards "based on sound scientific data" showing real health risks.

Report Cites Benefits of Clean Air Act

The fundamental purpose of the Clean Air Act was to protect the public from dirty air. To comply with that seemingly simple goal American industry was required to spend billions of dollars each year. Consequently, industry by 1981 was ready with a raft of amendments that it said would merely "fine-tune" the act to make it work better.

The National Commission on Air Quality, authorized by Congress in 1977 to provide information and proposals for revision of the act, agreed that some changes should be made, but it recommended against significant weakening of the 1977 standards. The commission, which released its report March 2, 1981, was composed of four members of Congress and nine private citizens named by President Jimmy Carter.

Commission Recommendations

Sen. Gary Hart, D-Colo., commission chairman, said the panel recommended "that Congress retain the current statutory formula for setting the national air quality standards. The standards should continue to be set at the level necessary to protect the health of the most susceptible people — the old and the infirm — with an adequate margin of safety. Only health considerations should go into the determination of the appropriate level of the standards."

The commission found that, on the whole, contrary to many industry claims, the Clean Air Act had not been an important obstacle to energy development and, in fact, allowed substantial increases in domestic energy production. Although the commission said costs should be considered in the development of air pollution control standards, it explicitly rejected setting regulations that were based on costs.

The commission did recommend that the Environmental Protection Agency (EPA) review certain air quality standards. It said that the standard for controlling airborne particles might be improved and it requested a review of ozone and carbon monoxide standards to ensure they adequately protected against long-term exposures.

It recommended that Congress keep existing protections for important national parks and wilderness areas designated before 1977, all national parks and wilderness areas protected against visibility impairment in 1977 and national lands that could not, under the existing act, be redesignated as Class III (wildlife refuges, national monuments, national recreation areas, national seashores, wild and scenic rivers and those national parks and wilderness areas designated after 1977). The report concluded that the "mobile sources" section had been the most effective part of the Clean Air Act, substantially reducing pollution from automobiles.

The most controversial of the commission's 433 findings and 109 recommendations was that Congress scrap the nationwide deadlines for cleaning up dirty air cities. A proposed change in pollution control for clean air cities was almost as controversial.

Commission Findings

Major commission findings were that:
- The nation's air was "measurably better" and was continuing to improve. In six or seven years, probably only eight metropolitan areas would fail to meet the national standards.
- Improved air quality had brought benefits worth from $4.6 billion to $51.2 billion per year, while costs of installing, maintaining and operating pollution equipment were estimated to have been $16.6 billion in 1978. The benefits included improved public health, reduced cleaning expenses, better vegetation, less damage to materials and higher property values. But the panel concluded that "the estimation of certain kinds of environmental benefits is still in need of much additional refinement."
- Air pollution controls had added about 0.2 percent to the annual inflation rate.
- Costs for air pollution control were likely to rise. One estimate was that about $37 billion (in 1978 dollars) would be spent in 1987 for construction, operation and maintenance of pollution controls.
- The law has not significantly inhibited economic growth.

- Continuing to have the federal government set the secondary standards, which protected crops, visibility and buildings from degradation due to air pollution.
- Continuing to protect the air in national parks from deterioration, but requiring uniform technology for factories in all other clean air areas.
- Establishing more effective controls on cancer-causing pollutants in the air.
- Accelerating research on acid rain — caused when sulfur dioxide and nitrogen mix with rain, sleet or snow — that alters the acidity of water and soil.
- Adjusting the deadlines for achieving national air quality standards "to reflect realities."
- Adjusting automobile emission standards to "more reasonable" levels, especially for carbon monoxide and nitrogen oxide.
- Eliminating requirements that emissions from new coal-burning power plants be scrubbed to reduce their sulfur content regardless of whether they burn low- or high-sulfur coal.

● Giving states a full partnership in carrying out the act, with the federal government monitoring their performance.

Under existing law EPA was required to set standards to protect public health "allowing an adequate margin of safety." The memo said the administration was considering eliminating that requirement and allowing standards to be set according to "a degree of significant risk" to public health.

Environmentalists said that some of the "minor adjustments" proposed by the administration would radically undercut the basic foundation of the law. They feared that, because the law was so complicated, major changes still could slip past the uninitiated. Their fears were heightened by the fact that 179 members — a third of Congress — had been elected since 1977 and had not dealt with the baffling legislation.

Moreover, some of the architects of the 1977 amendments to the act were not around in the 97th Congress to defend their handiwork. Sen. Edmund S. Muskie, D-Maine (1959-80), and Rep. Paul G. Rogers, D-Fla. (1955-81), who led the fight to protect the act in 1977, had retired.

1982 Congressional Action

Three months after the administration disclosed its "principles" Congress began work on the clean air legislation, but progress was slow. After nine months of markup sessions the Senate Environment and Public Works Committee Aug. 19, 1982, completed a rewrite that made only modest changes in the landmark anti-pollution law.

The House Energy and Commerce Committee, meanwhile, broke off work late Aug. 19 on a separate, industry-backed version (HR 5252) that made far greater modifications. In one key vote, the panel adopted a provision relaxing existing automobile emission standards, but not so much as U.S. automakers and their congressional allies originally wanted.

The two versions differed significantly. Environmentalists generally preferred the Senate bill, while the Reagan administration and industry backed HR 5252. The House committee had been bitterly divided during its markups, while the Senate panel achieved near-unanimity on virtually every element of the rewrite.

The Senate committee measure slightly relaxed the existing law but strengthened it in other respects, adding provisions designed to combat acid rain and to force the EPA to regulate hazardous air pollutants. Although the committee bill was a consensus product, it faced an uncertain future at best in the full Senate. Time was running out in the 1982 session of Congress, and Senate leaders were reluctant to call up such a complex and controversial bill.

Amendments Adopted

During its final markup session Aug. 19, the Senate committee made several significant decisions. The panel adopted an amendment on hazardous pollutants that would require EPA to decide within three years whether 40 pollutants should be listed as hazardous and subject to special regulation.

That was somewhat milder than the House committee's version, which applied to 37 pollutants EPA had identified as potential hazards. The bill automatically would list them as hazardous if EPA failed to act within four years. The 1970 act required EPA to identify such pollutants and set special emission standards, but as of

1982 the agency had taken no action on the 37 pollutants in question.

The Senate committee also adopted language that prevented any increase over existing levels of lead in gasoline. The provision bolstered EPA's decision to strengthen existing rules requiring a phasedown of lead in gasoline, and it was a rebuff to the Office of Management and Budget, which sought relaxation of those rules.

The panel rejected an amendment that would have eliminated the "percentage reduction" provision of existing law. That provision required utilities and factories to remove a certain percentage of sulfur oxides from their stack gases. The effect was to require installation of costly scrubbers, largely eliminating incentives to switch to low-sulfur Western coal.

The committee adopted an amendment requiring EPA to conduct research on indoor air pollution. Authorization for such research also was included in a House-passed bill.

The panel agreed to relax deadlines and technology requirements for non-ferrous smelters, a provision designed to help the copper industry.

Outlook Uncertain

Robert T. Stafford, R-Vt., chairman of the Senate Environment Committee, said the length of the debate over amending the Clean Air Act would depend on the lobbyists. "If those on all sides of the issue decide to take off their gloves and make this a major contest, rather than a cooperative venture, then we are going to be in for a long and difficult journey," he said. As of fall 1982 that appeared to be the case. "The odds are against our doing a clean air bill this year," said Rep. Henry A. Waxman, D-Calif., a member of the House Energy and Commerce Committee, on Aug. 11, 1982.

Whatever the outcome, revision of the act was being undertaken in a political context vastly different from the one that prevailed in 1977. A Republican administration dedicated to renewal of American industry was overseeing the legislative review, which took place against the backdrop of a troubled economy, amidst arguments that the act caused unemployment and hampered energy development.

Lobbying on the legislation was extremely intense. The American Petroleum Institute, the Chemical Manufacturers Association, the Iron and Steel Institute, the American Paper Institute, the American Automobile Association and countless other organizations pressed for modifications. So did four well-known business organizations — the Business Roundtable, the U.S. Chamber of Commerce, the National Association of Manufacturers and the National Environmental Development Association, composed of 34 corporations and the 17 members of the AFL-CIO Building and Construction Trades Department.

Arrayed against the industrial associations were a number of environmental, public health and "public interest" groups that would like to see the laws maintained in their essential features and, if possible, strengthened. The Sierra Club, the League of Women Voters, National Parks and Conservation Association, Friends of the Earth, the Natural Resources Defense Council and the Environmental Defense Fund were coordinating their efforts as members of the "Clean Air Coalition" founded in 1973.

"Members of Congress face a great temptation as they turn their attention to the Clean Air Act — the temptation to patch up the act with Band-Aids and baling wire," wrote David Harrison Jr. and Paul R. Portney in the March/April

1981 issue of *Regulation*. "If instead they rethink their present approach to air quality and face up to the shortcomings of the act, they will have helped to further both environmental and other important goals."

But others, among them Rep. Ron Wyden, D-Ore., warned against changing or weakening the act. Proposals to modify the PSD provisions "amount to playing Russian roulette with national treasures," Wyden said.

"The fact that the deadlines in the 1970 Clean Air Act have not been met does not mean that the act has 'failed,'" wrote Larry E. Ruff, a former economics professor and director of economic analysis-energy at W.R. Grace & Co., in a 1978 study for the Senate Governmental Affairs Committee. "Perhaps no realistic management system could have accomplished more in terms of reducing emissions and improving ambient air quality than the 1970 Clean Air Act (and its predecessors) has done.

"Where the 1970 Clean Air Act can be judged a failure is in its principal regulatory innovations, and in its simpleminded view of what solution of the air quality management problem would require. The rigid deadlines have not done what they were supposed to do, and may have been counterproductive in focusing attention on short-term fixes rather than longer-term solutions. . . ."

Where Clean Air Act requirements are enforced, they are expensive but effective, concluded Paul W. MacAvoy, professor of economics at Yale University and a member of President Ford's Council of Economic Advisers, in the Aug. 30, 1981, *New York Times*. "But they are so draconian in nature that they have not been enforced in the majority of the states, thereby producing expensive but inconsistent equipment installation with no substantial overall improvement in air quality."

The Washington Post, in an Aug. 30, 1982, editorial, said that "The health benefits of pollution control are unquestionable, but the law needs a better way to bring the costs into a more rational balance with them. There are areas in which the present rigid technical requirements are less effective in improving air quality than cheaper, more flexible rules might be.

"Congress also needs to pay a lot more attention to the actual administration of this law. Its congressional authors have tended to keep adding highly precise, and complex, standards as though they were self-enforcing. Between the excessive budget cuts and the general chaos that currently reigns within the Environmental Protection Agency, the whole process of enforcement is now sagging. Air quality monitoring is more perilously spotty than ever. The delays in reviewing and approving plans are endless."

As Congress wrestled with the legislation, it became obvious that cleaning the air presented ever-changing regulatory problems to which there would never be any permanent solutions. As consumption habits, lifestyles and industrial processes are modified, the sources of pollution change as well, and regulators must struggle to keep up. In the end, the future of such regulations could well depend on how strongly people felt about the air they breathe and on whether they were willing to make sacrifices to make it cleaner, rather than on elaborate, and perhaps inaccurate, cost-benefit analysis.

Regulating the Auto Industry

One of the facts of American economic life is the intrinsic antagonism between government regulatory agencies and the industries they oversee. Nowhere is the difference of opinion between federal regulator and regulated industry sharper than in the U.S. automobile industry. From a virtually unregulated condition less than twenty years before, American automakers by 1982 had become one of the nation's most controlled industries.

Almost everyone who drives or rides in cars is familiar with the emissions control devices and seat belts that must be installed in every new car. But federal auto regulations also affect industrial policy, fuel economy, consumer information and protection and fuel availability and pricing.

General Motors has estimated that the cost of complying with regulations totals $2.2 billion annually. That figure excludes development and installation of devices to meet emissions and safety standards. Those are the costliest regulations, but much of their expense is passed on to the consumer. Complying with regulations has required 26,000 full-time employees, according to the corporation. "When you are making $10 billion a year that $2 billion is one thing," said GM Chairman Roger Smith in an interview published in the Nov. 1, 1981, *New York Times*. "But when you are losing $700 million a year as we did in 1980, you look at it and say, 'that's the difference between losing money and making money.' "

Several federal agencies regulate the actions of auto manufacturers. And the impact of their rules on the design and performance of American cars is almost as great as decisions made in Detroit. The Department of Transportation's National Highway Traffic Safety Administration (NHTSA) oversees the industry's safety and fuel economy standards. The Environmental Protection Agency (EPA) monitors emission controls. The Occupational Safety and Health Administration inspects auto plants to ensure they are in compliance with federal workplace health and safety standards. Regulations issued by the Equal Employment Opportunity Commission play a major role in shaping hiring, firing and promotion policies in an industry with a 21 percent minority employment rate, compared with 11 percent for the total U.S. work force.

The automakers have complained loudly about the federal government's regulatory role since it first affected them. They argue that the rules are excessive, that they interfere with production schedules and industry growth and that they add to the price of the car. According to GM Chairman Smith, the added cost of government-mandated equipment for each car comes to about $1,125. Smith also cited the huge hidden costs exacted by regulations in the form of management time. Moreover, industry leaders say, because regulatory action hampers their efficiency, the American economy as a whole suffers.

The regulatory agencies have "worked toward their goals without respect to the impact their decisions would have on the ability of the industry to meet its other mandates," said Herbert L. Misch, a Ford vice president, in January 1981 testimony before the Senate Commerce Subcommittee on Surface Transportation. "It should surprise no one, therefore, that single focus agencies and the drive for maximum feasible progress [have] had a substantially adverse impact on the industry."

Disputing the auto industry's claims, environmentalists, consumer leaders, insurance groups and others point to the benefits derived from federal auto regulation. They say that regulations have saved lives, gasoline and air quality. These groups contend that regulation is not the major culprit behind the economic downturn sustained by the auto industry during the late 1970s and early 1980s. What is needed, they say, is cost control — particularly in wages, greater management efficiency and improved productivity. The industry's own complacency has been at the heart of the problems, they maintain.

About 3.6 million workers are dependent on automotive manufacturing, sales and service, and the industry's financial plight has not gone unnoticed in the White House or on Capitol Hill. The Reagan administration took several steps to ease the regulatory burden on the industry. And Congress in 1981 began working on revising the Clean Air Act, including provisions that placed controls on auto emissions.

Auto Industry Profile

At the turn of the century American automobile manufacturing was a cottage industry. For the most part, cars were produced by small, family-type operations on a made-to-order basis. Between 1900 and 1915 the fledgling automobile industry produced two million cars at an average price of more than $1,000 — a price well out of reach for the average American. Cars were viewed as an amusement for the well-to-do and were a curiosity for most.

By 1905 some 150 companies were making automobiles in the United States. One of the most influential auto manufacturers was Henry Ford, who set up the Detroit Motor Co. in 1903. Ford's first models were expensive and only moderately successful. The Ford Model T, introduced in 1908, was manufactured with standardized parts on an assembly line, a revolutionary concept in the auto industry. Some 15 million "Tin Lizzies" were sold, for as low as $290, before production of them ceased in 1927.

Ford's philosophy of automobile production was simple. He believed cars should be sturdy, plain, black and static in design. Ford also believed that car owners were entitled to reliable service. His company trained its own mechanics and dispersed them across the country as early as 1905. Ford thus created the modern corporation that would build, sell and service a product for as long as it lasted.

In 1908, the year Ford's Model T came on the market, William C. Durant, then head of the Buick Motor Co., formed the General Motors Co. Unlike Ford, Durant thought that once Americans became used to automobiles, they would demand more individuality in both styling and performance. He believed that the company should produce a variety of models, satisfying the tastes and needs of different levels of society.

By 1928 the number of companies producing automobiles in the United States had fallen to 44. The Chrysler Corp. was founded in 1925 by former GM Vice President Walter Percy Chrysler. With the acquisition of the Dodge Brothers Co. in 1928, Chrysler became the third largest auto manufacturer behind Ford and GM. Later Chrysler added Plymouth and De Soto to his line.

The Depression accelerated the trend toward mergers and the collapse of small automakers. Between 1925 and 1937, General Motors, Ford and Chrysler increased their combined share of the market to 85 percent from 63 percent. During that time, the position of the two leading manufacturers was reversed. In the early 1920s Ford produced almost half of all cars sold in America; General Motors was responsible for one quarter. By the mid-1930s, GM was selling twice as many cars as Ford.

Styling and Obsolescence

The emergence of the "Big Three" auto manufacturers affected both the competitive and price structure of the industry. It became virtually impossible for new manufacturers to market their cars and much more difficult for the smaller companies to survive. At the same time, the prices of comparable but rival models became almost identical. John Burby wrote in *The Great American Motion Sickness* (1971): "The industry's leaders were designers and salesmen, not engineers ... The styling concept of dynamic obsolescence was designed to make Americans feel ashamed of a car that was more than a year old."

According to automotive journalist John Jerome in *The Death of the American Automobile* (1972), the "golden age" of the automobile began when "the stodgy car died in 1955. All our clinging Calvinist sensibilities of practicality, economy, simplicity, all the cramped guidelines of American Gothic, were junked. We wanted more. We got it: bigger engines, more 'zestful' performance, more options, chrome, jazz, sex. This was the year the 'two-toned paint job' was finessed .... We were building automobiles for the new American voluptuaries."

The stress on change and styling came long before 1955, however. It is often traced to Alfred Sloan, who served as president of General Motors from 1923 to 1941. Sloan believed that continual changes in car design, luxury features and various options would persuade consumers to buy more cars more often despite large price increases. General Motors wrested the sales leadership from Ford in the 1930s at least in part by insisting on styling rather than pricing as the basis for competition. This emphasis reached the point of rococo excess in the late 1950s when tail fins and quantities of chrome adorned almost every new car.

By the late 1950s, however, the Big Three were concerned about competition from the compact and less expensive American Motors Rambler and from small foreign cars, notably the German Volkswagen, French Renault, Italian Fiat and English Ford. In the recession year of 1958, Rambler almost doubled its production and captured 4 percent of the domestic car market. Import sales had doubled each year between 1955 and 1958, and reached a record 614,000 in 1959. Confronted with studies showing that American consumers were attracted to smaller cars, the Big Three began manufacturing compacts in 1960.

A Troubled Industry

But Detroit continued to rely on bigger, highly styled cars, and by the late 1970s the American automobile industry, long a mainstay of the U.S. economy, was in deep trouble. Rising gasoline prices, along with occasional well-publicized fuel shortages, undercut sales of the large, inefficient cars. As a result American manufacturers lost market shares to foreign producers, especially in Japan, that exported smaller cars offering high mileage rates.

At the same time, inflation, government-mandated safety and pollution equipment and the cost of converting factories to make smaller cars pushed U.S. auto prices upward. Skyrocketing interest rates that increased the costs of financing car purchases also discouraged sales.

By 1980 even industry leader General Motors reported a $763 million loss for the year, while Ford Motor Co. also ran a substantial deficit. Chrysler reported a record $1.7 billion loss.

Chrysler, with only 9.1 percent of the domestic automobile market in 1979, was hit hardest by the industry's problems. Critics blamed Chrysler's financial straits on the decisions made by Lynn A. Townsend, corporation chairman during the 1960s. They contended that Townsend expanded the firm's overseas operations — building plants in South America, South Africa, Australia and Europe — at the expense of U.S. facilities. Townsend's successor John Riccardo took over Chrysler during the 1974 recession, cutting costs by stripping the engineering, style and sales staffs in a move that some experts suggested delayed Chrysler's development of smaller models.

Chrysler spokesmen blamed the company's problems on government regulations, especially federally mandated fuel mileage standards that forced expensive conversions to more efficient cars. Chrysler critics contended that the company simply misread the American car market by postponing investment in small-car facilities on the theory that consumers would return to larger automobiles when the gasoline shortages of the mid-1970s eased.

Congress in late 1979 approved $1.5 billion in federal loan guarantees for Chrysler. That pledge was part of a $3.5 billion package that staved off bankruptcy

Between 1980 and early 1982, the U.S. auto industry suffered massive losses of $5.5 billion, and there were predictions that it would lose another $1.4 billion in 1982. In the third quarter of 1981, General Motors reported losses of $468 million; Ford, $334.5 million; and Chrysler, $149.3 million. American automakers sold only 6.2 million cars in 1981, compared with the 1978 peak of 11.3 million. About 2.2 million imported cars were sold in 1981. Japan's share of the U.S. market increased to 21.8 percent from 12.1 percent in 1978. As of August 1982, 213,473 auto workers were on indefinite layoffs, and another 63,200 were temporarily unemployed.

At the same time, labor costs went up much faster in the auto industry than in manufacturing generally. Including fringe benefits, General Motors' workers earned 67 percent more than the average factory worker in 1979, and the gap widened in 1980. In contrast, according to an article in the Feb. 8, 1982, issue of *Fortune,* the Japanese were building a comparable subcompact car for about $2,000 less than U.S. manufacturers. By 1982 Japanese automobiles were competing in 60 percent of the U.S. market.

A 1980 Department of Transportation report said manufacturers would have to make approximately $70 billion in capital expenditures over the next five years to retool their facilities to keep pace with foreign competition.

Safety Regulation

Public concern over automobile safety arose as early as the turn of the century when autos began frightening horses, colliding with one another and killing pedestrians. In 1908 retired Supreme Court Justice H. B. Brown wrote in the *Yale Law Journal:* "Its great power, speed and weight have made it a veritable king of the highway, before whom we are all invited to prostrate ourselves. . . . Scarcely a week, sometimes a day passes without chronicling from one to a dozen deaths occasioned by the reckless driving of these machines."

As the number of cars increased, so did the number of accidents. Automobile fatalities jumped from just over 10,000 in 1917 to some 23,000 in 1926, prompting a nationwide call for traffic safety laws. The first uniform code for the regulation of traffic was enacted during World War I by the Council of National Defense, which was then engaged in an accident prevention program as a means of conserving the nation's manpower. Various states subsequently enacted their own traffic laws and regulations.

In 1924 a Uniform Vehicle Code was drawn up at a national conference convened for that purpose by Secretary of Commerce Herbert Hoover. The states began adopting various versions of the code in 1926. State laws set up motor vehicle departments with authority to administer drivers' licensing programs and to set up uniform rules of the road, including speed limits, reckless and drunken driving regulations and size and weight limitations. Federal regulation still lay decades in the future.

The Nader Factor

The movement to set up federal auto safety standards began in the late 1950s. John Keats raised the safety theme as early as 1958 in his book *The Insolent Chariots.* "Detroit sees itself as selling nothing but dreams of speed, sex, luxury and horsepower," Keats wrote. It would no more occur to automakers to sell safety, he added, "than it would occur to a fashionable restaurant to provide sodium bicar-

Fuel Economy Standards

One of the products of the oil shortage of the mid-1970s was a federal law requiring automobiles to meet fuel conservation standards. Title III of the Energy Policy and Conservation Act of 1975 mandated federal fuel economy standards for new automobiles manufactured or imported after model year 1977. The standards were intended to achieve an average fuel economy of at least 27.5 miles per gallon by 1985. The law and subsequent regulations promulgated by the NHTSA required that cars manufactured or imported after model year 1976 have labels indicating fuel economy performance.

The penalty for failure to meet the standards was $5 per 0.1 mile per gallon for every 0.1 mile by which a manufacturer's average failed to meet the standard, multiplied by the number of cars produced by that company. For manufacturers whose average fuel economy exceeded the standard credit was given to be applied forward a year or backward a year against any penalty assessed for failure to meet the standard. Automobile makers generally regarded the mileage standards as an economic burden, although they agreed that the United States needed to cut down drastically on its use of foreign oil.

President Carter in 1977 asked Congress to enact a "gas guzzler" tax — an excise on new cars and light trucks that did not meet the mileage standards set by the 1975 law. Congress complied the following year. Starting with 1980 models, new cars falling below 15 miles per gallon would be taxed $200 each. The tax and mileage standards would increase every year, to a maximum of $3,850 on vehicles that got fewer than 12 miles a gallon in 1986 or later. The Carter administration had tried unsuccessfully to persuade Congress to place a tax on 1978 models averaging 18 miles per gallon or less; it proposed first-year penalties ranging from $52 to $449.

The 1972 Motor Vehicle Information and Cost Savings Act authorized NHTSA to set fuel economy standards for cars after 1985. The agency issued an advance notice of proposed rulemaking exploring these standards in January 1981. However, because the auto industry was already exceeding all interim standards, the proposal was withdrawn as part of Reagan's auto industry relief package issued in April 1981.

bonate and a stomach pump with every place setting." Public pressure for safer cars increased in the 1960s as the number of traffic fatalities mounted and as auto defects received wide publicity.

The person who, more than any other, brought auto

safety to public attention was Ralph Nader, the consumer advocate. In his book *Unsafe at Any Speed* (1965), Nader accused the automakers of marketing vehicles they knew to be unsafe to get the maximum profit from the shoddiest materials. He contended that there was no economic incentive for the manufacturers to build in safety features because the costs and penalties of auto casualties were borne by the driver.

Nader attacked the accepted theory that the best corrective action was to study all elements of the safety problem — car, driver and road — instead of concentrating on the automobile. Nader argued that much could be done to make cars safer, whereas drivers would always be prone to error. He rejected the driver-at-fault theory on the basis that human failure could be offset through proper auto engineering and design.

Meanwhile congressional support was growing for passage of auto-safety legislation and Nader testified on behalf of such a bill early in 1966. On March 6, 1966, newspapers published Nader's complaint that he had been under investigation by private detectives hired by the auto industry. Three days later, General Motors conceded that it had initiated a "routine investigation" of Nader to find out if he had any connection with damage suits that had been filed against the company because of defects in its Chevrolet Corvair. (Some critics — including Nader — said the small car's design made it inherently unsafe. Several people injured in Corvair accidents were suing GM on that ground.)

In a nationally televised hearing on March 22, GM President James M. Roche told a Senate subcommittee that there had been "some harassment," and publicly

apologized to Nader. Final passage of the National Traffic and Motor Vehicle Safety Act of 1966 came five months later. House Speaker John W. McCormack, D-Mass., credited the final outcome to the "crusading spirit of Ralph Nader."

1966 Safety Acts

That act and a 1966 companion measure, the Highway Safety Act, brought the automobile industry under permanent federal regulation for the first time. The first law, known by its shorthand title of Traffic Safety Act, required the establishment of mandatory minimum safety standards for domestic and foreign vehicles and the development of safety and wear standards for tires. The Highway Safety Act required each state to set up a federally approved highway safety program by the end of 1968 or lose 10 percent of the state's federal aid for highways.

Together the two laws created the National Highway Traffic Safety Administration (NHTSA), which was directed to study consumer complaints and report its findings to the automobile manufacturers if a pattern of defects relating to safety was discovered. The manufacturers would then be instructed to notify owners, informing them of the nature and seriousness of the defects and advising them to return their vehicles to franchised dealers for inspection and repair.

As expected the agency soon found itself in disagreement with Detroit as to what safety requirements were needed and could be handled by the required dates. Auto manufacturers, backed by the United Auto Workers, complained that the standards for safety and engine reliability proposed by the agency put an economic strain on the industry. Both groups lobbied Congress to ease the standards and reduce the agency's jurisdiction.

But Congress retreated very little in subsequent amendments to the 1966 laws. Indeed, it added new safety restrictions. Amendments in 1969, for instance, required tire manufacturers to notify purchasers of safety-related defects. Until then, tire makers had not been subject to the same recall requirements that affected the automobile makers. Congress in 1974 required the manufacturers to repair safety-related defects free of charge; in the past only notification was required.

Recall Problems

Consumer confidence in automotive safety has been shaken by the growing number of recalls of privately owned vehicles by manufacturers to correct possible safety hazards. According to the NHTSA, between September 1966 and Aug. 31, 1982, domestic manufacturers were involved in 2,684 recall campaigns involving 82,078,500 vehicles; foreign manufacturers were involved in 664 campaigns involving 16,688,200 vehicles.

Auto recalls are troublesome and costly for everyone involved. Owners are obviously inconvenienced by having to take their cars to the garage for repairs. The dealers who have had to make the repairs see the process as robbing them of time that could be spent more profitably in private servicing. They also complain that the manufacturers are slow in reimbursing them for recall-related servicing. Finally, a recall means both negative publicity and a sizable repair bill for the auto manufacturer.

Although automakers generally have complied with recall campaigns, industry officials complain that the process of recalling entire lines of cars often has been wasteful, time consuming and less than totally effective in correcting defects. Detroit also says that it often has been difficult to trace older vehicles to their current owners. A title search might extend to three or four owners and an equal number of courthouse registers and end in a scrap pile.

Officials at Chrysler say that many of the recalls they were forced to make were not justified because no safety defects were involved. NHTSA, for example, asked Chrysler to recall one million vehicles which had a stalling problem that the company did not believe to be a safety hazard. The safety administration disagreed. "If you're entering a busy freeway from a ramp and your car stalls, you're in big trouble," an NHTSA official said.

The EPA, which began ordering large-scale recalls in 1974 for environmental reasons, asked Chrysler on April 20, 1978, to recall 77,000 1978-model cars because their carbon monoxide emission levels exceeded federal limits. In December 1976 EPA asked Chrysler to recall 208,000 cars for maintenance problems producing excessive air pollution. That request angered Chrysler officials, who said the company could not be responsible for the way people maintained their cars.

Ford and General Motors have had their own problems with recalls. The Supreme Court Jan. 16, 1978, left standing a lower court decision that GM must recall 1959 and 1960 model Cadillacs with a defect in the steering system. GM had argued that the recalls should not be required because there was no evidence that the defects had caused injuries or deaths. But the Supreme Court upheld the position of the NHTSA that a recall could be ordered if there was a reasonable chance that a defect could cause an accident.

Belts and Bags

Lap and shoulder belts, known in the industry as active restraint devices, have been required by law for all new cars since January 1968. Though it has been shown that the use of seat belts reduces deaths and injuries, it is equally true that many people do not buckle up.

The public's aversion to seat belts prompted Congress in 1974 to overturn a Department of Transportation regulation requiring manufacturers to install interlock systems that prevented cars from being started until the belts were fastened. At about the same time safety advocates began to lobby for regulations requiring automobiles to be equipped with passive restraint devices, such as air bags, which are activated without the occupant's having to do anything.

The automobile companies had been experimenting with automatically inflating air bags since the late 1960s. On front-end impact to the car the bags inflate within a fraction of a second to cushion the passenger.

President Ford's secretary of transportation, William T. Coleman Jr., announced in December 1976 that he would not order automakers to install air bags. That decision was overturned six months later by Coleman's successor, Brock Adams. In June 1977 Adams ordered manufacturers to phase in passive restraint systems over a three-year period, beginning with large cars in model year 1982, medium-sized cars in 1983 and small cars in 1984. Industry officials said it would take that long to make the necessary adjustments on the production lines.

The Department of Transportation estimated that if air bag restraints were installed in all passenger cars for the driver and front-seat passenger positions, there would be 9,000 fewer deaths and 100,000 fewer injuries on the nation's highways each year. A Gallup Poll conducted nearly a month before Adams' announcement showed that 46 percent of the respondents endorsed the installation of air bags while 37 percent disapproved.

Adams' decision gave auto manufacturers a choice between installing air bags or passive lap and shoulder seat belts that automatically encircled the passenger when the car door was closed. Such an automatic seat belt was already in use in the Volkswagen Rabbit. However, NHTSA studies indicated that 30 percent of those who bought VW Rabbits with passive belts disconnected them.

Rescission and Reinstatement

When Ronald Reagan came into office, his administration decided to delay the passive restraint order. Then, in October 1981 it rescinded the ruling. The administration estimated revoking the order would result in investment savings to the auto industry of $400 million and annually recurring savings of $1 billion.

NHTSA administrator Raymond A. Peck Jr. argued that the rule would not provide a significant increase in passenger safety. The companies had abandoned air bag development, he said, and the automatic seat belts they planned to use instead would not represent a major improvement over manual belts, particularly since, he predicted, many consumers would detach them. The ruling, he concluded, did not meet the Motor Vehicle Safety Act's requirement that standards be "reasonable, practicable and meet the need for motor vehicle safety."

But Peck's decision was overturned in August 1982, when a federal court ordered the rule reinstated. The court said the administration lacked evidence for the belt detachment forecast and termed the action "arbitrary and illogical." The court ruled that the standard would go into effect for all cars Sept. 1, 1983. However, NHTSA was given until Oct. 1, 1982, to develop information on whether manufacturers could meet the deadline. The agency still was free to seek additional comments, to conduct further "regulatory impact analyses" or to terminate the proceeding, the court said.

Rep. Timothy E. Wirth, D-Colo., chairman of the House Consumer Protection Subcommittee, called the order "a major setback for this administration's capricious attempt at deregulation for its own sake — without regard for its impact for the health and safety of our citizens."

Lowell R. Beck, president of the National Association of Independent Insurers, which represents more than 500 companies, was also pleased with the court's decision. "We are extremely gratified ... that the court properly recognized that the lives of thousands of American motorists hung in the balance," he said.

The automakers, predictably, were disappointed by the decision. Roger E. Maugh, automotive safety director for Ford, said that the "effect of the court order is to require us to divert scarce resources in an effort to meet a standard" that the company believed would be ineffective in enhancing safety.

Costs and Benefits

At issue in the debate was the difficulty of calculating costs and benefits of the passive restraint requirement; nobody knew for sure what the amount of usage, particularly of automatic seat belts, would be. NHTSA estimated that when non-automatic seat belts were used, fatalities were reduced by 49 percent and injuries by 66 percent. The agency said mandatory automatic seat belts would pay off only if usage was above 28 percent, the point at which benefits (reduced medical bills, lower insurance costs and so forth) equalled the costs of installing them.

Yale professor William Nordhaus, a former member of the Council of Economic Advisers, calculated that revoking the rule would cost $4.5 billion during the life of cars made in the 1982-85 model years in medical costs, insurance costs and lost wages due to death and injury.

In a submission to the NHTSA the Allstate Insurance Co. said that with the growing number of small, more dangerous cars "the automobile insurance affordability problem could well reach crisis proportions in the not too distant future" unless steps were taken to increase highway safety. The Nationwide Mutual Insurance Company estimated that annual insurance savings from air bags would total $2.499 billion, or $32.70 for each insured car.

"Time and again, the American consumer has said he wants and is willing to pay for safer cars," the Automotive Occupant Protection Association asserted in 1981. "Several foreign manufacturers intend to install air bags and automatic belts in some of their vehicles to be sold in the United States, allowing them to emphasize the safety of their cars as a selling feature.... If no air bags are manufactured, the consumer would be denied this proven safety system."

Wirth made a similar point. "I am concerned that a delay [in implementing the restraints] will only exacerbate the economic troubles of the American auto industry by encouraging them to defer safety improvements while their foreign competitors gain the edge once again by offering increased safety features," he said.

Industry spokesmen, however, expressed concern not only about the added cost of regulation, but consumer acceptance and possible problems of product liability. Air bags might encourage a sense of complacency that would prompt car owners to act rashly, some argued. "The possibility that the level of adverse reaction will approach the interlock is a consideration," agreed Peck in an interview in the June 27, 1981, *National Journal.*

"I believe this society, and this government and this Congress has to ask itself how far we want to go in forcing people to do what they would otherwise not voluntarily choose to do for themselves, how far we want to go in protecting people from themselves," said Lawrence J. White, professor at New York University's Graduate School of Business Administration, during January 1981 testimony before the Senate Surface Transportation Subcommittee. But subcommittee Chairman John C. Danforth, R-Mo., asked, "Are we throwing 9,000 lives a year into this sacrificial pit, in order to save $150 a car and therefore save the industry?"

Controlling Emissions

At the same time it was required to install new safety devices, the auto industry was directed to clean up car pollutants. Compliance with the interim emissions standards, written in 1970 and amended in 1977, had succeeded in reducing the level of noxious particles in vehicle exhausts. But the automakers continuously urged Congress to relax the final standards.

The problems of air pollution first were recognized during the 1940s. Beginning in the summer of 1943, Los Angeles County began to experience 10 to 20 days a year when "smog" — smoke plus fog, fumes and other pollut-

ants — irritated the eyes. Downtown visibility markedly decreased, crop damage was reported and possible health hazards were discussed. Early investigations revealed that the principal causes were oil refineries, fuel oil combustion, metallurgical industries and refuse burning. But the role of the automobile was increasingly mentioned.

The first federal research program on air pollution was initiated in 1955, and in 1958 the U.S. Public Health Service sponsored a national conference on air pollution that provoked increased public awareness of the problem. California in 1960 set state emission standards aimed at controlling fumes from both the exhaust pipe and the crankcase. American automakers responded in 1961 by installing "blowby" devices on all cars sold in California to return crankcase emissions through the engine for further combustion. But the industry's reluctance to place similar controls on all vehicles led Abraham Ribicoff, then secretary of Health, Education and Welfare, to warn automakers that he would seek federal legislation if they did not act voluntarily.

Setting Standards

Beginning in 1963, all new American-made, gasoline-powered vehicles were equipped with crankcase control devices. But with millions of old cars still on the road, the effect was hardly noticeable. In 1965 Congress enacted the Motor Vehicle Air Pollution Control Act (PL 89-272) to control air pollution caused by automotive exhausts. At first the Johnson administration opposed the measure, preferring to have the latitude to reach agreements with the automobile industry on control of exhausts. The administration also objected to the time schedule in the original version of the legislation. The president subsequently altered his position and supported the entire bill.

The final version directed the HEW secretary to prescribe emission standards for all new vehicles but contained no deadlines for implementation of the standards. During the next two years, limits were set for tailpipe, crankcase, fuel tank and carburetor emissions.

In 1966 a National Academy of Sciences study estimated that transportation accounted for 59.9 percent of the principal pollutants discharged into the nation's atmosphere each year.

Spurred by an increasingly serious national air pollution problem, Congress in 1967 enacted the Air Quality Act (PL 90-148) to strengthen federal powers to combat air pollution in the absence of meaningful state action. The bill earmarked $125 million for research on pollution caused by fuel combustion (including automobile emissions) and provided that exhaust standards could be issued only by the federal government, except for California, which was permitted to enforce its own, more stringent control standards.

The federal legislation that set strict and detailed deadlines for the reduction of auto emissions was the Clean Air Act of 1970. The act authorized the Environmental Protection Agency to set emission standards for all potentially dangerous pollutants from new motor vehicles and engines, and required the manufacturer to bear the costs of repairs to achieve compliance. The law also set yearly levels, through 1976, of carbon monoxide (CO), hydrocarbon (HC) and nitrogen oxide (NOx) emissions — the most harmful of the auto pollutants.

The automobile industry and the Nixon administration pressed Congress to make some provisions of the bill less stringent and to allow the EPA administrator more

1977 Clean Air Amendments

The most difficult task Congress faced in writing the 1977 amendments to the 1970 Clean Air Act concerned new standards and deadlines for the three major pollutants from automobile exhausts — hydrocarbons (HC), carbon monoxide (CO) and nitrogen oxide (NOx). But the act also required the auto industry to meet several other standards designed to protect the air and the public health.

Following are the provisions of the 1977 Clean Air Act Amendments relating to vehicle standards.

Auto Emissions. The following table shows the national standards in grams per mile and schedules for automobile exhaust pollutants set by the 1977 amendments.

Model Year	HC	CO	NOx
'77	1.5	15.0	2.0
'78	1.5	15.0	2.0
'79	1.5	15.0	2.0
'80	.41	7.0	2.0
'81 on	.41	3.4	1.0

However, the Environmental Protection Agency (EPA) could waive the CO standard for 1981 and 1982 up to 7 grams if public health did not require the statutory standard and if technology to meet it did not exist.

Other waivers were permitted for NOx. Small manufacturers, including American Motors Corp., that depended on emissions technology produced by other companies were given a two-year waiver until 1983 to meet 1 gram NOx. A waiver to 1.5 grams NOx for any four-year period after 1980 was permitted for certain innovative technology on up to 50,000 vehicles produced by one company. A four-year waiver to 1.5 grams NOx was permitted for light-duty diesel engines, but only for model years 1981-84.

High-Altitude Vehicles. Existing high altitude regulations were suspended until 1981. Models 1981-83 had to meet standards based on a percentage reduction no greater than those for all cars, based on emissions from 1970 cars operating at high altitudes.

For 1984 and thereafter cars had to meet statutory standards at all altitudes.

Trucks, Buses and Motorcycles. EPA had to set interim standards for HC and CO through 1982, with statutory HC and CO standards becoming effective in 1983 and statutory NOx standards in 1985. Statutory standards for heavy-duty vehicles mandated a 90 percent reduction from baseline for HC and CO, and a 75 percent reduction from baseline for NOx. Revision of any statutory standard required four years of lead time.

Tampering. The measure prohibited removal of or tampering with emission control systems by manufacturers and dealers, independent repair and service businesses, and selling, leasing, trading or fleet operations. Civil penalties of up to $2,500 per vehicle were authorized.

Warranties and Parts. The legislation set a performance warranty of 24 months or 24,000 miles, during which car manufacturers would have to bring into compliance with emissions standards any vehicle that failed an inspection and maintenance test. Catalytic converters, thermal reactors and other emission control devices had to carry warranties for five years or 50,000 miles. Within two years of enactment EPA was to provide regulations to certify parts made by other than the car manufacturer. Repairs and maintenance could be performed at any service shop using certified parts.

Fuels and Additives. The measure directed EPA to require manufacturers of fuels and fuel additives to test the potential health effects of their products, including the effect of a substance on emission control performance. Fuels or additives introduced into commerce or increased in concentration between Jan. 1, 1974, and March 31, 1977, had to be removed no later than Sept. 15, 1978.

The legislation relaxed standards on lead levels in gasoline produced by small refineries and directed EPA to set new standards for the period beyond Oct. 1, 1982.

discretion in setting deadlines. But their efforts failed. Some were inclined to attribute the act of Congress to an act of God: A weather pattern caused Washington, D.C., several days of choking air pollution in the summer of 1970 while the bill was being considered.

Automobile makers seemed reluctant to comply with emission controls. In May 1971 accusations surfaced that the industry had conspired during the previous two decades to suppress development and installation of control devices. In February 1973 Ford was fined $7 million for tampering with engines of certain cars to help them pass

federal air-pollution control tests. The company filed a no-contest plea in the case.

The companies successfully lobbied for postponement of the emission level deadlines. Two postponements granted by EPA and one by Congress delayed the standards until the 1978 model year.

In 1977 the manufacturers asked for another delay, saying they still could not meet the standards on time. As the 1978 model cars were readied for production in August and September 1977, industry leaders threatened to shut down the assembly lines rather than produce "illegal" cars subject to fines of up to $10,000 each.

President Carter then urged Congress to act to avoid potential damage to the nation's economy. Congressional leaders took steps to defer a planned recess of Congress until House and Senate conferees could resolve disagreements on separate versions of a bill dealing with the matter. The conferees, pressured by the White House and the auto industry, negotiated for eight days until they reached agreement in a seven-hour session lasting well past midnight. The bill that Carter signed into law Aug. 7 extended existing levels for the three main pollutants through the 1979 model year but set stiffer standards for 1980 and 1981 models. (Provisions, box p. 133)

EPA subsequently waived the carbon monoxide standard for 30 percent of the 1981 model cars, and about 5 percent of the fleet — primarily diesel powered cars — were exempted from the 1981 deadline for meeting the nitrogen oxide standard. The agency rejected most waiver requests; those it granted covered only about 28 percent of the vehicles scheduled for sale in 1981.

Debating Controls

Debate over auto emissions continued into 1981-82 as Congress considered revisions to the Clean Air Act. The controversy emerged sharply during the House Energy and Commerce Committee's work on an industry-backed version of modifications in the clean air legislation. By October 1982 the committee had been unable to reach agreement on a bill. The Senate Environment and Public Works Committee Aug. 19 approved a version that continued the emission standards in existing law.

"The auto emissions program has been the source of major controversies over the last decade, at least some of which could have been anticipated," noted David Harrison Jr. and Paul R. Portney, in the March/April 1981 issue of Regulation. (Harrison was associate professor at the J. F. Kennedy School of Government, Harvard University, and Portney was senior fellow at Resources for the Future.) "The combination of technology-forcing standards on a tight time schedule and draconian penalties for falling short virtually guaranteed showdowns between Detroit, EPA and Congress. The net result of each confrontation was to delay the standards. Penalties in gas mileage exacted by the technology used to control emissions placed the program in conflict with energy objectives. In addition, auto makers cite the emissions controls as among the causes of their current financial problems (although their foreign competitors must meet the same standards)."

Furthermore, Harrison and Portney said, most cost-benefit analyses showed that Congress had overregulated auto emissions. The authors recommended relaxing the standards and allowing for geographic variation. "If New York City, Los Angeles, Chicago . . . and some other metropolitan areas could impose stricter controls on autos than are applied nationwide, most of the benefits of reducing emissions would be captured while the residents of less polluted areas would be freed from substantial control costs."

Ford Vice President Misch also urged revision of the standards. "We believe the emission standards for passenger cars can be revised slightly with negligible impacts on public health, yet with savings of as much as $300 million annually to Ford customers," he told the Senate Surface Transportation Subcommittee.

"The pollution control requirements for cars and trucks . . . are too stringent," testified New York University professor White. "The small amounts of emission reductions which are being achieved by the 1980 and 1981 requirements do not appear to be worth the extra cost of doing so."

However, Henry A. Waxman, D-Calif., chairman of the House Health and Environment Subcommittee of the Energy and Commerce Committee, said the proposed relaxation of auto emission standards would neither create jobs for the auto industry nor increase sales. He quoted a General Motors spokesman who said it was a "phony issue" to link relaxing auto emission standards to the industry's economic health.

Waxman referred to a National Governors' Association study showing that if the CO standard were relaxed, some 38 cities would be unable to meet air pollution limits imposed by the Clean Air Act. And if the NOx standard were relaxed for autos, 11 to 14 cities might have to set new controls on factories to keep the air from exceeding the federal standards for NOx. "By giving Detroit this break, all we are doing is shifting the burden to another segment of our economy," he said during a March 23, 1982, committee session.

House Divisions

Throughout the House Energy and Commerce Committee's markup of the clean air legislation, the panel was split into two factions. One, headed by Waxman, wanted to retain the strict emission limits of the 1977 law. The other, led by committee chairman John D. Dingell, a Detroit Democrat, and James T. Broyhill, R-N.C., wanted those limits relaxed. A compromise was finally reached.

As originally written the committee bill would have doubled the allowable emissions of carbon monoxide and nitrogen oxide for gasoline-powered passenger cars, raising the CO standard to 7.0 grams per mile from 3.4 grams per mile, and raising the NOx standard to 2.0 grams per mile from 1.0. The compromise, offered by Philip R. Sharp, D-Ind., returned the NOx standard to the limit in existing law but kept the 7.0 grams-per-mile CO standard.

Waxman charged that Sharp's amendment went beyond temporary relief for the beleaguered auto industry. Arguing against the higher CO standard, Waxman said the committee had heard no testimony that automakers were having any technological trouble meeting the tighter 3.4-gram standard. He said the cost savings of a relaxed CO standard would be only about $30 a car.

Dingell and the industry set the figure higher. Automakers said that if both standards were relaxed, they could remove about $360 worth of pollution-control equipment, saving $60 on equipment to control CO and $300 on devices to control NOx.

Dingell, arguing in support of Sharp's amendment, said that 69 percent of the autos manufactured in 1982 had been given EPA waivers allowing them to emit up to 7.0 grams per mile of CO.

But Waxman quoted General Motors as saying that 70 percent of the cars with waivers met the tighter 3.4-gram standard anyway. Sharp defended the 7.0-gram standard, saying the existing level had caused driveability problems with small cars. His Muncie-centered district was dotted with auto-related industries, many of them hit by layoffs.

While environmentalists charged that the relaxed standards would worsen air pollution, auto industry supporters liked to put that increase in the context of the overall reduction achieved since the Clean Air Act was passed in 1970. Dingell noted that the 2.0-gram standard for NOx initially proposed in the bill required removal of 92 percent of the NOx in the uncontrolled emission — compared with the 96 percent removal achieved by the 1.0-gram standard.

Don Ritter, R-Pa., claimed that without controls CO emissions would total 88 grams per mile. A 3.4-gram standard would reduce the fleetwide average to 26.3 grams per mile, while a 7.0-gram CO standard produced a fleetwide average of 26.6 grams per mile, he said.

Emissions from old cars raised the fleetwide average emissions well above levels achieved by cars in the current model year. Dingell repeatedly pointed out that total emissions would continue to decrease as these old cars were replaced with new ones. Environmentalists, however, said that some of the problem was caused by newer cars whose pollution control devices did not work properly. They criticized several provisions in the committee bill that they said weakened programs to make sure pollution control devices continue to work.

Sharp's amendment also loosened NOx standards for light diesel cars and trucks by setting them at 1.5 grams instead of the 1.0 grams in existing law, and by allowing NOx emissions as high as 2.0 grams if particulates (another pollutant) were reduced. Sharp said the amendment, which was backed by diesel car manufacturers, would take advantage of a trade-off inherent in existing pollution control technology in which NOx reductions could only be achieved at the expense of particulates, and vice versa. But Waxman said newer devices could reduce both simultaneously.

Reagan Actions

The state of the automobile industry provided a significant test for the Reagan administration's "less is better" approach to regulation. On taking office the administration suspended numerous regulations issued in the waning days of the Carter administration. Many of the rules applied to the auto industry, including one that would have required car makers to provide crash-worthiness ratings on window price stickers.

In a further attempt to shore up the ailing industry and quell cries for auto import quotas, the administration April 6, 1981, proposed to eliminate or ease 34 environmental and safety regulations for cars and trucks. The administration claimed the actions would save industry $1.4 billion in capital costs and save consumers more than $9.3 billion over the next five years.

Among the actions were a delay in imposing the air bag standard, rescission of a proposed regulation on warning lights to indicate low tire pressure and suspension of the tire grading system. The administration further suggested a modification of the bumper standard regulation requiring front and rear bumpers to protect cars at speeds up to 5 miles per hour. The administration proposed reducing that protection requirement to 2.5 miles per hour.

The administration also supported a relaxation of the existing auto emissions standards. The change yielding the biggest consumer savings, and the one that generated considerable controversy, was a proposal to eliminate EPA regulations that would require all autos to meet emission standards designed to protect high altitude areas. Cars driven at high altitudes emit more pollution because of the way lower atmospheric pressure affects carburetion and combustion. Existing law required all cars to meet federal emission standards by 1984 regardless of where they were driven. That meant that 95 percent of all cars on the road and all new cars would need additional emissions control equipment. That change, which would require Congress to amend the Clean Air Act, would save consumers $1.3 billion over the next five years, according to the administration.

These and other Reagan proposals were criticized by some consumer and safety groups. "What bothers us is that there are no checks and balances here," said Clarence Ditlow, director of the Center for Auto Safety, in the Nov. 1, 1981, *New York Times*. "The White House and so-called regulatory agencies are working hand in hand to undo these protections built up over the years."

Responded NHTSA administrator Peck, "We are a safety agency, period. I don't talk to industry executives, except in formal hearings. I'm a regulator." Peck said his agency would focus on information programs and "behavior modification because it's cheap and it can work."

In the opinion of GM Chairman Smith, the administration's major achievement was not so much getting rid of the existing regulations as preventing new ones from going into effect. But many observers, including auto industry spokesmen, said Reagan's program had achieved few real savings. Moreover, progress was slowed by the fact that the Office of Management and Budget had to review all proposed regulatory actions, including those rescinding rules. (Details, p. 67)

As the complex and controversial Clean Air Act and its auto emission provisions remained stalled in the House committee in 1982 — and as controversy continued over the costs and benefits of safety regulations — auto manufacturers continued efforts to redesign American cars to meet the government's regulatory requirements, the public's demand for smaller, fuel-efficient cars and the challenge of foreign competition.

"It is in our national interest to find a means of strengthening the U.S. auto industry during this period of extraordinary conversion and record investment requirements," said Ford Chairman Philip Caldwell in an interview published in the January-February 1981, *Harvard Business Review*. While the Reagan administration and Congress concurred, there was no consensus on what should be done and what impact deregulation or regulatory changes would have on the industry.

Regulatory Agency Sketches

Following are brief sketches of the responsibilities delegated to the major independent and executive branch regulatory agencies.

Non-department Agencies

Civil Aeronautics Board (CAB) — Regulates routing and pricing practices of airline companies operating in the United States, including international carriers operating to and from the United States. Passage of the Airline Deregulation Act of 1978 greatly diminished the CAB's authority over pricing and set up a timetable to phase out the board entirely by 1985. Composed of five members appointed by the president and confirmed by the Senate; members serve six-year terms. Established in 1940 to take over the responsibilities of the Civil Aeronautics Authority, which had been created by the Civil Aeronautics Act of 1938.

Commodity Futures Trading Commission (CFTC) — Regulates futures trading on 11 exchanges and trading in commodity options and gold and silver leverage contracts. Composed of five members appointed by the president and confirmed by the Senate; members serve five-year staggered terms. Established in 1974 to replace the Agriculture Department's Commodity Exchange Authority.

Consumer Product Safety Commission (CPSC) — Establishes mandatory safety standards governing the design, construction, contents, performance and labeling of hundreds of consumer products; develops rules and regulations to enforce the standards. Composed of five members appointed by the president and confirmed by the Senate; members serve seven-year staggered terms. Established in 1972 by the Consumer Product Safety Act.

Environmental Protection Agency (EPA) — Regulates air, water and noise pollution; regulates waste disposal and specific chemicals considered hazardous to people and the environment; registers pesticides and regulates their use; administers cleanup of hazardous dumps; monitors other potential pollutants. Headed by an administrator who is assisted by a deputy and six assistants; all are nominated by the president and confirmed by the Senate. Established in 1970 by executive order.

Equal Employment Opportunity Commission (EEOC) — Investigates, conciliates and litigates charges of discrimination in employment on the basis of race, color, national origin, religion, sex and age; issues guidelines, rules and regulations to eliminate employment discrimination. Composed of five members appointed by the president and confirmed by the Senate; members serve five-year terms. Established by Title VII of the Civil Rights Act of 1964.

Farm Credit Administration — Supervises and regulates the activities of the member-owned Farm Credit System, which is designed to provide credit and closely related services to farmers, ranchers, commercial fishermen, persons who provide on-farm services, farm cooperatives and rural homeowners. Headed by a 13-member Federal Farm Credit Board; 12 members are appointed by the president and confirmed by the Senate, one is appointed by the secretary of agriculture and serves as the secretary's representative; members serve six-year terms and may not be reappointed. Established by executive order in 1933.

Federal Communications Commission (FCC) — Regulates all interstate and foreign communications by means of radio, television, wire, cable and satellite. Composed of seven commissioners nominated by the president and confirmed by the Senate; members serve seven-year staggered terms. Established by the Communications Act of 1934.

Federal Deposit Insurance Corporation (FDIC) — Insures funds of bank depositors up to a $100,000 limit; acts as the primary regulator of banks, including domestic and foreign branches, that hold state charters and are not members of the Federal Reserve System. Consists of a three-member board composed of the Comptroller of the Currency, who serves as an ex-officio member, and two others appointed by the president and confirmed by the Senate; appointed members serve six-year terms. Established by the Banking Act of 1933.

Federal Election Commission (FEC) — Administers and enforces the provisions of the Federal Election Campaign Act of 1971, as amended, which requires the disclosure of sources and uses of funds in campaigns for any federal office, limits the size of individual contributions and provides for partial public financing of presidential elections. Composed of six members appointed by the president and confirmed by the Senate; members serve staggered six-year terms. Established by the Federal Election Campaign Act Amendments of 1974.

Federal Energy Regulatory Commission (FERC) — Regulates the production, transmission and price of natural gas; the rate and service standards for the sale of electricity at the wholesale level; and the rates and practices of oil pipeline companies. Also licenses hydroelectric power projects. Composed of five members appointed by the president and confirmed by the Senate; members serve four-year terms. Established by the Department of Energy Organization Act of 1977 to replace the Federal Power Commission.

Federal Home Loan Bank Board (FHLBB) — Supervises and regulates savings and loan associations, supervises the Federal Home Loan Bank System and acts as the board of directors of the Federal Home Loan Mortgage Corporation. Headed by a board composed by three members appointed by the president and confirmed by the Senate; members serve four-year terms. Established by the Federal Home Loan Bank Act in 1933.

Federal Maritime Commission (FMC) — Regulates the rates charged for shipping in domestic and foreign commerce, licenses ocean freight forwarders, permits shipping companies to form rate-setting conferences that would otherwise be in violation of antitrust laws and investigates charges of discriminatory practices in ocean commerce. Composed of five members nominated by the president and confirmed by the Senate; members serve five-year terms. Established in 1961 by executive order to replace the Federal Maritime Board.

Federal Reserve (Fed) — Regulates the nation's monetary policy by controlling the amount of currency in circulation, fixing the discount rate that it charges member banks, controlling and regulating all extensions of consumer credit and setting the level of reserves that member banks must keep on deposit with the Fed. Acts as the primary regulator of state-chartered banks that join the Federal Reserve System. Administered by a board of seven governors appointed by the president and confirmed by the Senate; governors serve 14-year terms and may not be reappointed if they have served full terms. Established by the Federal Reserve Act in 1913.

Federal Trade Commission (FTC) — Promotes free and fair competition in interstate commerce through the prevention of trade restraints such as price-fixing, boycotts, illegal combinations of competitors and simi-

lar unfair practices; protects the public from false and deceptive advertising and unfair trade practices, regulates the packaging and labeling of consumer products to prevent deception. Composed of five members nominated by the president and confirmed by the Senate; members serve seven-year terms. Established by the Federal Trade Commission Act of 1914.

Interstate Commerce Commission (ICC) — Regulates trucks, buses, barges, coastal and Great Lakes ships, freight forwarders, express companies, transportation brokers and pipelines carrying commodities other than oil, water and natural gas. The Motor Carrier Act of 1980, the Staggers Rail Act of 1980 and the Household Goods Transportation Act of 1980 deregulating the trucking, railroad and moving industries respectively reduced ICC's authority over those industries. Composed of six members (to be reduced to five in 1985) nominated by the president and confirmed by the Senate; members serve seven-year terms. Established by the Interstate Commerce Act of 1887.

National Credit Union Administration (NCUA) — Supervises and regulates all member credit unions; membership in the NCUA is mandatory for all federal credit unions and optional for state-chartered credit unions that meet minimum requirements. Charters federal credit unions, examines federal credit unions to determine financial condition and administers insurance and emergency loan funds. Governed by a three-member board whose members are nominated by the president and confirmed by the Senate for six-year terms. Established by a 1970 amendment to the Federal Credit Union Act of 1934.

National Labor Relations Board (NLRB) — Acts to prevent employers and unions from engaging in unfair and illegal union organization activities and unfair labor practices; conducts elections to determine if workers want to be represented by a union. The board may act only if requested to do so by employers or employees. Composed of five members appointed by the president and confirmed by the Senate for five-year terms and a general counsel who serves a four-year term. Established by the National Labor Relations Act (Wagner Act) of 1935.

National Mediation Board — Mediates disputes over wages, hours and working conditions that arise between rail and air carriers and organizations representing their employees; determines who represents the employees. Composed of three members nominated by the president and confirmed by the Senate for three-year terms. Created in 1934 by an amendment to the Railway Labor Act.

National Transportation Safety Board — Investigates, determines cause, makes safety recommendations and reports the facts and circumstances of catastrophic transportation accidents, including all civil aviation crashes; many railroad, pipeline, and marine accidents; and selected highway accidents. Publishes recommended procedures for accident investigations, establishing regulations governing the reporting of accidents. Composed of five members appointed by the president and confirmed by the Senate for five-year terms. Created by the Department of Transportation Act of 1966 as an autonomous agency within the department; granted independent status by the Independent Safety Board Act of 1974.

Nuclear Regulatory Commission (NRC) — Licenses the construction and operation of nuclear reactors and other facilities; licenses the possession, use, transportation, handling and disposal of nuclear materials; develops and implements rules and regulations governing licensed nuclear activities; licenses the export of nuclear reactors and the export and import of uranium and plutonium. Composed of five members appointed by the president and confirmed by the Senate for five-year terms. Established by the Energy Reorganization Act of 1974 to take over the nuclear regulatory and licensing activities of the Atomic Energy Commission, which was abolished.

Occupational Safety and Health Review Commission — Rules on contested Occupational Safety and Health Administration citations alleging health and safety standards violations in the work place. Composed of three members appointed by the president and confirmed by the Senate for six-year terms. Established by the Occupational Safety and Health Act of 1970.

Pension Benefit Guaranty Corporation — Ensures that participants in the federally regulated private pension plans it ensures will receive their benefits in the event the plan does not have sufficient funds to pay. When an insured plan cannot pay benefits, the corporation makes up the difference in assets, administers the fund and distributes the basic benefits. The corporation may also force a plan to terminate if the agency determines the plan is in financial trouble; the corporation then takes over the plan to assure continued operation. A non-profit corporation wholly owned by the federal government and administered by a board of directors composed of the secretaries of labor, commerce and the Treasury. Created by the Employment Retirement Income Security Act of 1974, which established federal regulatory control over private pension and welfare plans.

Postal Rate Commission — Makes recommendations to the United States Postal Service on postage rates, fees and mail classifications. Schedules public hearings on rate changes, soliciting comments and publishing proposals in the *Federal Register*. Composed of five members appointed by the president and confirmed by the Senate for six-year terms. Established as an independent agency by the 1970 Postal Reorganization Act.

Securities and Exchange Commission (SEC) — Regulates the trading in securities on the nation's 13 national securities exchanges and in the over-the-counter markets, including activities of securities brokers, dealers and investment advisers; investigates securities frauds and other violations of securities laws and enforces sanctions against such actions; requires disclosure of facts concerning offerings of securities. Composed of five members nominated by the president and confirmed by the Senate for five-year terms. Established by the Securities Exchange Act of 1934.

Small Business Administration (SBA) — Promotes the interests of small business concerns through loans and other kinds of assistance; licenses, regulates and makes loans to small business investment companies that provide venture capital to small concerns. Run by an administrator appointed by the president and confirmed by the Senate. Established by the Small Business Act of 1953.

United States Postal Service — Regulates all aspects of the mail, including rates and rate classifications; sets standards for several areas related to mail delivery, including the size of individual pieces of mail, bulk mail and postal meters. Administered by an 11-member board of government; nine members are appointed by the president and confirmed by the Senate for nine-year terms. The nine select a tenth member who serves as postmaster general. The 10 members then select a deputy postmaster who fills the last slot on the board. Established by the Postal Reorganization Act of 1970 to replace the Post Office Department.

Department Agencies

Agriculture Department

Agricultural Marketing Service — Supervises marketing and regulatory activities for several segments of the agriculture industry including: cotton; dairy products; fruits and vegetables; livestock; poultry; grains and seeds; tobacco; warehouses; and packers and stockyards. Headed by an administrator appointed by the secretary of agriculture.

Agricultural Stabilization and Conservation Service — Administers programs that help assure an adequate and reliable supply of food, feed and natural fibers for domestic and export needs at prices fair to the producer and consumer. Administers various voluntary land-use programs to protect, expand and conserve farm lands, wetlands and forests. Headed by an administrator appointed by the secretary of agriculture.

Animal and Plant Health Inspection Service — Responsible for programs to eradicate diseases and pests that affect plants and animals; regulates the entry of agricultural products into the United States. Headed by an administrator appointed by the secretary of agriculture.

Commodity Credit Corporation — Administers programs designed to stabilize the supply and price of farm commodities. A wholly owned government corporation headed by a board of directors. The secretary of agriculture serves as chairman of the board; the other seven board members are appointed by the president and confirmed by the Senate.

Farmers Home Administration — Provides credit for individuals living in rural areas who are unable to obtain credit from other sources at reasonable rates and terms. Regulates the terms of the financial assistance offered; prescribes the terms of the loans, grants and agreements; and requires that the borrowers adhere to various federal regulations and guidelines. Headed by an administrator appointed by the president and confirmed by the Senate.

Federal Grain Inspection Service — Establishes federal standards for grain and undertakes inspections to ensure compliance. Headed by an administrator appointed by the president and confirmed by the Senate.

Food and Nutrition Service — Administers the food stamp program; national school lunch program; food donation program; special supplemental food program for women, infants and children; and programs that grant funds to certain non-profit organizations that provide food services. Headed by an administrator appointed by the secretary of agriculture.

Food Safety and Quality Service — Regulates the meat, poultry and egg industries for safety and purity by inspecting all meat, poultry and eggs shipped in interstate and foreign commerce; administers truth-in-labeling laws for these products. Headed by an administrator appointed by the secretary of agriculture.

Foreign Agricultural Service — Administers import quotas when they are imposed on certain items, including beef and dairy products; serves primarily as an information and promotion agency to expand the export market. Headed by an administrator appointed by the secretary of agriculture.

U.S. Forest Service — Manages the national forests and grasslands and regulates forest activities, which include lumbering, road construction, mining, farming, grazing and commercial enterprises. Administered by a chief appointed by the secretary of agriculture.

Commerce Department

Economic Development Administration — Regulates the administration of loans, grants and technical assistance to firms and communities adversely affected by imports. Headed by the assistant secretary of commerce for economic development, who is appointed by the president and confirmed by the Senate.

International Trade Administration — Works to expand exports, improve enforcement of U.S. trade laws and upgrade government trade activities; implements trade agreements; imposes countervailing duties and embargoes and conducts anti-dumping and national security trade investigations. Supervision is vested in the under secretary of commerce for international trade who is appointed by the president and confirmed by the Senate.

National Oceanic and Atmospheric Administration — Explores, maps and charts the global ocean and its living resources; issues licenses for ocean thermal energy conversion projects and deep seabed mining projects; assists in licensing deepwater ports; develops policy on proper ocean management and use along the U.S. coastline. Headed by an administrator appointed by the president and confirmed by the Senate.

Patent and Trademark Office — Issues patents on new, useful and non-obvious inventions and registers trademarks used with goods and services in interstate commerce. Headed by a commissioner appointed by the president and confirmed by the Senate.

Defense Department

Army Corps of Engineers — Regulates all construction projects, transportation and dumping of dredged materials in the navigable waterways of the United States; develops, plans and builds various structures — dams, reservoirs, levees, harbors, waterways and locks — to protect areas from floods, supply water and hydroelectric power, create recreational areas, improve water and wildlife quality and reduce transportation costs. Headed by a chief engineer appointed by the president from recommendations made by the secretary of the Army and confirmed by the Senate.

Education Department

Office of Civil Rights — Administers and enforces civil rights laws related to education and the handicapped; such laws apply to federally assisted programs and to employers with government contracts. Headed by an assistant secretary of education who is appointed by the president and confirmed by the Senate.

Energy Department

Office of Conservation and Renewable Energy — Formulates and directs the Department of Energy's energy conservation program. Headed by the assistant secretary of energy for conservation and renewable energy, who is appointed by the president and confirmed by the Senate.

Economic Regulatory Administration — Administers oil import, natural gas import and export and electricity import programs; supervises mandatory conversion from oil and gas fuel to coal and other abundant fuel resources. Headed by an administrator nominated by the president and confirmed by the Senate.

Health and Human Services Department

Food and Drug Administration — Regulates the purity and labeling of food, drugs, cosmetics and medical devices to protect the public against potential health hazards from those products. Headed by a commissioner appointed by the secretary of health and human services.

Office for Civil Rights — Responsible for ensuring that discrimination based on race, color, national origin, sex, age or physical handicap does not occur in any program or facility receiving funds from the department; institutions subject to regulation by the Office for Civil Rights include hospitals, nursing homes, home health agencies, day care centers, medical laboratories, and various governmental agencies receiving assistance from the department. Headed by a director appointed by the president and confirmed by the Senate.

Office of Human Development Services — Operates grant programs and coordinates governmentwide services for several specific groups of people — children of low-income families, people with mental or physical handicaps, runaway youth, older persons and Native Americans. Consists of four agencies under the authority of an assistant secretary for human development services who is appointed by the president and confirmed by the Senate.

Public Health Service — Promotes health standards to assure that the highest level of health care is available; assists states and communities in developing local health resources. Consists of six operating agencies under the authority of the assistant secretary for health: The Alcohol, Drug Abuse and Mental Health Administration; Centers for Disease Control; the Food and Drug Administration; the Health Services Administration; and the National Institutes of Health.

Social Security Administration — Administers the Social Security and Supplemental Security Income programs; regulates eligibility requirements for Social Security retirement benefits and disability payments, Supplemental Security Income programs, aid to families with dependent children and income maintenance programs in Puerto Rico, Guam, Virgin Islands and Northern Marianas. Headed by a commissioner appointed by the president and confirmed by the Senate.

Housing and Urban Development

Office of Fair Housing and Equal Opportunity — Administers the federal fair housing program; coordinates, plans, monitors and reviews programs to increase training, employment and business opportunties for low-income and minority group residents of HUD-assisted housing programs. Headed by the assistant secretary for fair housing and equal opportunity, who is appointed by the president and confirmed by the Senate.

Interior Department

Bureau of Indian Affairs — Administers 53 million acres of land held in trust by the government for Indian tribes and individuals; provides a variety of services and programs for approximately 700,000 Indians and Alaskan natives. Headed by an assistant secretary appointed by the president and confirmed by the Senate.

Bureau of Land Management — Manages resources on more than 350 million acres of federal lands; resources include timber, minerals, oil and gas, geothermal energy, wildlife habitats, endangered plant and animal species, range land vegetation, recreation areas, lands with cultural importance, wild and scenic rivers,

wild horses and burros, designated conservation and wilderness areas, and open space lands. Headed by a director appointed by the president and confirmed by the Senate.

Bureau of Reclamation — Responsible for water and power resource development in the 17 western states; programs include municipal and industrial water services, hydropower generation, flood control, river regulation, outdoor recreational opportunities, fish and wildlife enhancement and water quality improvement. Headed by a commissioner appointed by the president and approved by the Senate.

Office of Surface Mining Reclamation and Enforcement — Establishes minimum national standards for regulating surface effects of coal mining and assists the states in implementing strip mine regulatory programs. Headed by a director appointed by the president and confirmed by the Senate.

United States Fish and Wildlife Service — Regulates the development, protection, rearing and stocking of wildlife resources and their habitats; protection of migratory birds, game birds, fish and wildlife; endangered and threatened species; enforcement of regulations for hunters of migratory waterfowl; and preservation of wetlands as natural habitats. Headed by a director appointed by the president and confirmed by the Senate.

United States Geological Survey — Classifies and manages mineral and water resources on federal lands, including the Outer Continental Shelf; surveys, investigates and researches topography, geology, the Outer Continental Shelf, the identification of potential natural hazards such as earthquakes, and geothermal energy. Headed by a director appointed by the president and confirmed by the Senate.

Justice Department

Antitrust Division — Investigates possible violations of federal antitrust laws, conducts grand jury proceedings, prepares and prosecutes antitrust cases, prosecutes appeals and negotiates and enforces final judgments. Headed by the assistant attorney general for antitrust appointed by the president and confirmed by the Senate.

Civil Rights Division — Enforces the federal civil rights laws that prohibit discrimination on the basis of race, color, religion, sex or national origin in the areas of voting, education, employment and housing; in the use of public facilities and accommodations; and in the administration of all federally assisted programs. Also responsible for protecting the constitutional rights of the mentally disabled, state prisoners and psychiatric hospital patients. Headed by an assistant attorney general appointed by the president and confirmed by the Senate.

Drug Enforcement Administration — Enforces federal narcotics and dangerous drug laws; regulates the legal distribution of narcotics and dangerous drugs used for experimental and medicinal purposes. Headed by an administrator appointed by the president and confirmed by the Senate.

Immigration and Naturalization Service — Administers federal immigration and naturalization laws; guards against illegal entry into the United States. Headed by a commissioner appointed by the president and confirmed by the Senate.

Office of Justice Assistance, Research and Statistics — Assists state and local governments to improve and strengthen law enforcement and criminal justice. The aid includes grants to the states for community anti-crime programs, juvenile justice and delinquency prevention activities and law enforcement personnel training programs; provision of criminal justice statistics; and research on criminal justice issues. Headed by a director appointed by the president and confirmed by the Senate.

Labor Department

Employment Standards Administration — Develops minimum wage and overtime pay standards; requires registration of farm labor contractors; determines prevailing wage rates on government contracts and subcontracts; prevents discrimination against women, minority group members, veterans and handicapped workers on government contracts and subcontracts; supervises workers' compensation programs for federal workers. Headed by a deputy under secretary of labor for employment standards, who is appointed by the secretary of labor.

Employment and Training Administration — Funds and regulates training and employment programs administered by state and local agencies. Headed by the assistant secretary of labor for employment and training, who is appointed by the president and confirmed by the Senate.

Labor-Management Services Administration — Regulates the activities of labor unions and the activities of individuals who administer private pension plans. Headed by the assistant secretary of labor for labor-management relations, who is appointed by the president and confirmed by the Senate.

Mine Safety and Health Administration — Develops and promulgates mandatory safety and health standards, ensures compliance with such standards, proposes penalties for violating standards, investigates accidents and cooperates with the states in developing mine safety and health programs. Headed by the assistant secretary of labor for mine safety and health who is appointed by the president and confirmed by the Senate.

Occupational Safety and Health Administration — Develops and enforces mandatory job safety and health standards; maintains reporting and record-keeping procedures to monitor job-related injuries and illnesses; imposes temporary emergency standards when workers are in grave danger due to exposure to new toxic substances or hazards; grants variances for special circumstances; provides consultation services to small businesses. Headed by the assistant secretary of labor for occupational safety and health, who is nominated by the president and confirmed by the Senate.

State Department

Office of Munitions Control — Licenses all commercial export of defense articles and services; registers persons who manufacture and export arms, ammunition and other weapons; investigates reports of violations. Headed by a director who is responsible to the director of the Bureau of Politico-Military Affairs.

Passport Office — Oversees and issues passports in accordance with regulations and policies of the secretary of state; makes determinations of U.S. citizenship under appropriate statutes. Headed by the deputy secretary of state for passport service who is appointed by the president and confirmed by the Senate.

Transportation Department

Federal Aviation Administration — Establishes and enforces rules and regulations for safety standards covering all aspects of civil aviation; develops air traffic rules and regulations and allocates the use of U.S. airspace; promotes the expansion and modernization of the nation's airports. Headed by an administrator appointed by the president and confirmed by the Senate.

Federal Highway Administration — Sets functional safety standards for the design, construction and maintenance of the nation's highways; establishes safety standards for commercial motor carriers engaged in interstate or foreign commerce; administers the federal aid highway program. Headed by an administrator appointed by the president and confirmed by the Senate.

Federal Railroad Administration — Regulates the safety aspects of all rail transportation in the United States; administers federal aid programs for the National Railroad Passenger Corporation (Amtrak), railroads experiencing economic difficulty and state railroad safety programs, conducts rail transportation research and operates the Alaska Railroad. Headed by an administrator appointed by the president and confirmed by the Senate.

Maritime Administration — Administers programs that develop, promote and maintain the U.S. merchant fleet; provides several types of financial aid to the shipping industry. Headed by an administrator appointed by the president and confirmed by the Senate.

Materials Transportation Bureau — Develops and enforces equipment and operating safety regulations for the transportation of all materials by pipeline; designates substances as hazardous materials and regulates their transportation in interstate commerce.

Headed by a director appointed by the secretary of transportation.

National Highway Traffic Safety Administration — Develops mandatory minimum safety standards for domestic and foreign vehicles sold in the United States; establishes fuel efficiency standards for vehicles; supervises administration of the maximum federal speed limit (55 miles an hour); develops safety and wear standards for tires; enforces laws prohibiting tampering with vehicle odometers. Headed by an administrator appointed by the president and confirmed by the Senate.

St. Lawrence Seaway Development Corporation — Operates and maintains the section of the St. Lawrence Seaway within U.S. territorial limits, between Montreal and Lake Erie; with its Canadian counterpart, develops safety standards and sets rates for vessels using the seaway. Headed by an administrator who is appointed by the president and confirmed by the Senate.

United States Coast Guard — Regulates vessels, sets and enforces safety standards and prescribes license requirements for merchant marine personnel. Directed by a commandant appointed by the president and confirmed by the Senate.

Urban Mass Transportation Administration — Assists in developing improved mass transit facilities; establishes safety and design standards for equipment and structures built with agency funds; investigates possible safety hazards in urban mass transit systems and may withhold funds until a corrective plan is approved or implemented. Headed by an administrator who is appointed by the secretary of transportation.

Treasury Department

Bureau of Alcohol, Tobacco and Firearms — Imposes and collects taxes on manufacturers of alcohol and tobacco products; supervises and licenses the manufacture of alcohol and tobacco products, including industrial alcohol and gasohol; promulgates packaging and labeling requirements for alcoholic beverages; and regulates the possession and use of firearms, destructive devices and explosives. Headed by a director appointed by the secretary of the Treasury.

Comptroller of the Currency — Grants charters to national banks; generally supervises and examines nationally chartered banks; regulates the foreign activities of national banks and bank holding companies; issues charters to foreign banks that want to operate branches in the United States if those branches operate like national banks. Headed by the Comptroller of the Currency who is nominated by the president and confirmed by the Senate for a five-year term.

Internal Revenue Service — Enforces internal revenue laws except those administered by the Bureau of Alcohol, Tobacco and Firearms; determines pension plan qualifications and rules on the tax status of exempt organizations; issues rules and regulations to supplement the Internal Revenue Code. Headed by a commissioner who is appointed by the president and confirmed by the Senate.

United States Customs Service — Assesses and collects the duties imposed on imports and enforces customs and related tariff laws; enforces statutes and regulations concerning copyrights, patents, trademarks and quotas and more than 400 regulations relating to international trade on behalf of 40 other federal agencies. Headed by a commissioner of customs who is appointed by the secretary of the Treasury.

Oversight Agencies

Administrative Conference of the United States — Makes recommendations to improve the legal procedures used by government agencies to administer regulatory, benefit and other federal programs. The chairman of the conference is appointed by the president and confirmed by the Senate for a five-year term; the 10 other members of the Administrative Council are appointed by the president for three-year terms.

General Accounting Office — Makes written reports to Congress and its committees on the effectiveness and efficiency of federal government programs and agencies; has several other significant oversight and accounting responsibilities it exercises in behalf of Congress. Directed by the Comptroller General of the United States who is appointed by the president and confirmed by the Senate for a 15-year term.

Office of Information and Regulatory Affairs — Within the Office of Management and Budget, this office is primarily responsible for the development of regulatory reform proposals. It also works to expand interagency coordination and to reduce unnecessary paperwork and excessive reporting requirements of federal agencies. Under Executive Order 12291 issued in February 1981, the office was given additional responsibility to review all major proposed rules and regulations. Headed by an administrator appointed by the director of the Office of Management and Budget.

Task Force on Regulatory Relief — Formed by President Reagan in January 1981, the task force is the primary oversight body with regard to executive branch regulatory policy. The task force is to provide regulatory relief by developing ways to apply cost-benefit analysis to proposed regulations, reviewing "regulatory impact analyses" submitted by agencies proposing major new regulations and overseeing a cost-benefit review of rules currently in effect. The task force is chaired by Vice President George Bush and includes several Cabinet members and aides to the president.

Legislative Briefs

Following are brief descriptions of major regulatory legislation enacted by Congress between 1970 and 1981. The chronology does not include measures that set eligibility and other regulations for federal aid programs.

1970

Bank Holding Companies (PL 91-607). Removed a major exemption from the 1956 Bank Holding Company Act by extending federal regulation under the Federal Reserve Board to holding companies controlling a single bank.

Cigarette Advertising (PL 91-222). Banned all cigarette commercials on radio, television or on any other medium of electronic communication regulated by the Federal Communications Commission, effective January 1971; also required stronger wording for mandatory health warning labels on cigarette packages.

Clean Air Act (PL 91-604). Set specific deadlines for the reduction of certain hazardous automobile emissions and strengthened air quality standards; authorized a noise pollution study.

Environmental Protection Agency (EPA). Established a new executive branch agency to administer all major federal programs to combat pollution; EPA assumed some of the functions of the Federal Water Quality Administration, the National Air Pollution Control Administration, the Environmental Control Administration, the Food and Drug Administration, the Atomic Energy Commission and other offices.

Fair Credit Reporting Act (PL 91-508). Regulated credit information reporting and usage; established strict guidelines for furnishing credit information; authorized civil and criminal penalties for violations.

National Oceanic and Atmospheric Administration (NOAA). Established through a reorganization plan, NOAA assumed the functions of the Environmental Science Services Administration in the Commerce Department, and some of the functions of the Bureau of Mines, Bureau of Commercial Fisheries, Bureau of Sports Fisheries and Wildlife and other offices within the Army, Navy and Transportation Department.

Occupational Safety and Health Act (PL 91-596). Gave the Labor Department authority to set and enforce federal safety and health standards for the protection of workers; covered about 55 million industrial, farm and construction workers; created a three-member commission to enforce the standards; established the National Institute for Occupational Safety and Health in the Department of Health, Education and Welfare to conduct job safety research.

Poison Prevention Packaging Act (PL 91-601). Required special packaging of potentially dangerous household goods to protect children from serious injury or illness resulting from handling, using or ingesting such substances (including polishes, cleansers, drugs and common toxic household goods).

Postal Reform (PL 91-375). Reorganized the Post Office Department and the U.S. Postal Service into an independent government agency, the U.S. Postal Service; authorized the new agency to set postage rates and issue revenue bonds; established an independent Postal Rate Commission to make recommendations on rates, mail classifications and services.

Railroad Safety (PL 91-458). Standardized federal railroad safety rules in an attempt to reduce railroad-related accidents, especially those involving the shipment of hazardous materials; gave the states and the Transportation Department power to prescribe safety regulations and conduct research in all areas of rail safety.

Securities Investor Protection Act (PL 91-598). Insured customers against losses incurred when brokers become insolvent; established a private non-profit Securities Investor Protection Corporation (SIPC) and an insurance fund financed through a combination of existing stock exchange trust funds, assessments and lines of bank credit. Stockholders were insured against losses of up to $50,000 in cash and securities left on deposit and lost when brokerage houses failed.

Tire Safety (PL 91-625). Extended the National Traffic and Motor Vehicle Safety Act of 1966 for three years, through June 1972; new provisions required manufacturers of auto tires to notify purchasers by certified mail of safety-related tire defects and authorized the Transportation Department to set standards for equipment intended to safeguard motor vehicles and their passengers.

Wage-price Controls (PL 91-379). Gave the president descretionary authority through Feb. 28, 1971, to freeze wages, prices, rents and salaries at levels not lower than those prevailing on May 25, 1970. The controls allowed the president to seek injunctions to enforce the freeze and imposed civil penalties for violations. The Economic Stabilization Act was extended four times: through March 1971, April 1972, April 1973, and April 1974.

Water Quality Improvement Act (PL 91-224). Authorized the federal government to clean up disastrous oil spills that seriously jeopardized the nation's waters and beaches, with the polluter paying the costs; placed new controls on sewage coming from vessels which fouled many of the nation's marinas, harbors and ports; created the Office of Environmental Quality to act as a staff for the President's Council on Environmental Quality.

1971

No major regulatory legislation was passed during the first session of the 92nd Congress in 1971.

1972

Bumper Standards (PL 92-513). Required the Transportation Department to establish front and rear bumper standards for passenger motor vehicles to reduce low-speed collision damage; made it unlawful to disconnect or alter the odometer of any motor vehicle; authorized automobile owners to sue manufacturers in federal court if damages to their cars resulted from non-compliance with the federal standards established by this law.

Consumer Product Safety Commission (CPSC) (PL 92-573). Established an independent five-member Consumer Product Safety Commission (CPSC) to protect consumers from unreasonable product hazards; authorized the commission to conduct safety studies

and tests of consumer products and to promulgate mandatory safety standards, warnings and instructions to prevent or reduce risk of injury associated with domestic and imported consumer products; permitted the commission to ban hazardous products for which safety standards could not be written; provided for judicial review of commission safety standards.

Equal Employment Opportunity Commission (EEOC) (PL 92-261). Strengthened the enforcement powers of the EEOC by authorizing the agency to take cases of employment discrimination that could not otherwise be settled to federal district court for a further finding of discrimination (this authority was transferred to the EEOC from the Justice Department); extended coverage of Title VII of the 1964 Civil Rights Act to businesses and labor organizations with 15 or more employees or members, to state and local government employees (excluding elected officials) and to employees of educational institutions; authorized the Civil Service Commission to enforce the equal employment opportunity policy within the federal bureaucracy.

Noise Control Act (PL 92-574). Gave the Environmental Protection Agency authority to regulate and enforce standards limiting certain commercial sources of noise, such as construction and transportation equipment, motors, engines and electric or electronic devices; directed the EPA to propose noise standards for aircraft but gave the Federal Aviation Administration final authority to review and reject aircraft noise standards that it found unsafe or impractical.

Ocean Dumping (PL 92-532). Authorized the Environmental Protection Agency to issue permits for the transportation out to sea and dumping of waste materials if it would not unreasonably endanger human health and welfare or the marine environment; banned the transportation out to sea or ocean dumping of radiological, chemical or biological warfare agents or high-level radioactive waste products; set civil and criminal penalities of up to $50,000 for each day of a violation.

Pesticide Regulation (PL 92-516). Gave the government broader authority to control the vast array of pesticides and other pest killers by requiring that all pesticides in U.S. commerce be registered with the Environmental Protection Agency; authorized the EPA to suspend registrations of pesticides that presented an imminent hazard to health or the environment.

Water Pollution Control (PL 92-500). Gave the Environmental Protection Agency enforcement powers to regulate water pollution; gave the agency emergency powers to bring suit in federal district court to stop water pollution presenting an imminent health or welfare hazard; required waste treatment management plans and practices that applied the best practicable technology; made the discharge of any pollutant by any person unlawful except as authorized by a discharge permit.

1973

Highway Speed Limit (PL 93-239). Lowered the maximum speed limit on the nation's highways to 55 miles per hour until June 1975. In 1974 Congress made the 55-mile-an-hour speed limit permanent (PL 93-643).

1974

Antitrust Procedures (PL 93-528). Amended antitrust law to require the filing and publication of a proposed consent decree at least 60 days before its effective date, accompanied by a competitive impact statement; strengthened penalities for persons and corporations violating the antitrust laws.

Atomic Energy Reorganization (PL 93-438). Abolished the Atomic Energy Commission; transferred its nuclear power development responsibilities to a new Energy Research and Development Administration; transferred nuclear safety and regulatory responsibilities to an independent Nuclear Regulatory Commission.

Clean Air Act Amendments (PL 93-319). Extended Clean Air Act authorizations for one year, through June 1975; relaxed emission requirements for another year; required electric power plants that could burn coal to do so through 1978; authorized the Federal Energy Administration to order other fuel-burning plants to convert to coal.

Commodity Futures Trading Commission (CFTC) (PL 93-463). Established the independent five-member CFTC to strengthen and expand federal regulation of commodity futures trading; authorized the commission to seek injunctions against trading abuses and to intervene directly to protect traders against market manipulations or other emergency situations; directed the commission to establish regulations governing options trading in commodities where the practice was not already banned.

Employee Retirement Income Security Act (ERISA) (PL 93-406). Established minimum federal standards for private pension plans; did not require firms to provide pensions to their employees, but those that did or were planning to had to adhere to the federal rules; required that all employees 25 and over would have to be enrolled in the plan after one year of employment; stated that the employer could choose one of three alternative vesting formulas that guaranteed an employee at least part of his pension benefits after he had served for a certain period of time, even if he did not work for the same company until retirement; contained minimum funding standards and established a federally run pension plan termination insurance corporation to guarantee the payment of benefits in the event of bankruptcy; allowed an individual not covered by a pension plan to establish his own retirement account that could qualify for special tax treatment.

Equal Credit Opportunity Act (PL 93-495). Prohibited discrimination in the granting of credit, based on sex or marital status; gave enforcement to the Federal Reserve Board.

Fair Credit Billing Act (PL 93-495). Set up a system to protect consumers against billing errors; set standards for credit cards; amended the Truth in Lending Act of 1968 to exempt creditors from liability when making good faith efforts to comply with regulations of the Federal Reserve Board; included the Equal Credit Opportunity Act.

Federal Energy Administration (FEA) (PL 93-275). Created as part of President Richard Nixon's plan to reorganize the federal energy structure. Granted the agency authority to develop plans for dealing with energy shortages, to prevent unreasonable profits in the energy industry and to impose mandatory energy saving measures; gave FEA the functions of the offices of petroleum allocation, energy conservation, energy data and analysis, and oil and gas in the Interior Department.

Federal Trade Commission (FTC) Authorization (PL 93-637). Strengthened FTC regulation of consumer warranties; required manufacturers who issued written warranties on products costing more than ten dollars to label each warranty as "full" if it met federal minimum standards or "limited" if it failed to meet those standards; allowed a consumer to file suit in state or federal courts for damages from failure to comply with a warranty; enlarged the FTC's jurisdiction to cover activities "affecting commerce" as well as "in commerce"; expanded the commission's authority to protect consumers.

Freedom of Information Act Expansion (PL 93-502). Strengthened the 1966 Freedom of Information Act to make it easier for the public to get access to information on government actions. The legislation was intended to remove some of the obstacles the federal bureaucracy had erected to thwart effective citizen utilization of the 1966 act such as bureaucratic delays, the cost of bringing suit to force disclosure, and excessive charges levied by the agencies for finding and providing the requested information.

Hazardous Materials Transport (PL 93-633). Authorized the Transportation Department to issue regulations for the safe shipment of hazardous materials (excluding pipelines) and to prohibit the transportation of radioactive materials in passsenger airplanes (excluding short-lived materials used for medical treatment or research); removed the National Transportation Safety Board from the Transportation Department, making it an independent agency to investigate aviation, highway traffic, rail transportation and pipeline accidents.

Interstate Commerce Commission (ICC) Appeals (PL 93-584). Eliminated the right of persons and parties to appeal decisions of the ICC to three-judge panels from which there was a right of direct appeal to the Supreme Court without going first to courts of appeals; under the new procedure, the Supreme Court had more discretion to turn down such an appeal.

Privacy Act (PL 93-579). Designed to give citizens some protection from invasions of their privacy by the federal government; permitted individuals for the first time to inspect information about themselves contained in federal agency files and to correct or amend that material; prevented an agency maintaining a file on an individual from using it without the individual's consent. Law enforcement, Central Intelligence Agency, Secret Service and certain other government records were exempted from the disclosure requirements.

Real Estate Settlement Regulations (PL 93-533). Required mortgage lenders to give homebuyers 12 days' advance notice of settlement charges, such as real estate commissions, title insurance and attorneys' fees; imposed criminal penalties for kickbacks paid between those in the real estate industry for minor services; limited the amount of property tax payments a bank could collect in advance from a homebuyer and hold in a non-interest-bearing escrow account. This bill was substantially modified in 1975, and the 12-day disclosure requirement was repealed.

Safe Drinking Water Act (PL 93-523). Authorized the Environmental Protection Agency to establish national standards for drinking water, setting maximum allowable levels for certain chemical and bacteriological pollutants in some 240,000 water systems; directed EPA to require specific treatment techniques for each contaminant and to establish secondary standards governing the taste, appearance and odor of drinking water.

Seatbelt Regulations/School Bus Standards (PL 93-492). Overruled a Transportation Department regulation that required auto manufacturers to install interlock systems that prevented cars from being started until seatbelts were fastened; allowed owners of cars with such equipment to have the devices dismantled; required the Transportation Department to promulgate safety standards for school buses.

1975

Fuel Efficiency Standards (PL 94-163). Required that the average fuel economy for passenger cars manufactured or imported by any one manufacturer in any model year after 1977 be no less than 27.5 miles per gallon by 1985; set fines for failure to comply.

Pesticide Regulations Extended (PL 94-140). Extended the Environmental Protection Agency's pesticide regulation program through March 1977.

Real Estate 'Red-lining' Disclosure (PL 94-200). Required lending institutions within standard metropolitan statistical areas to disclose the number and total dollar amount of mortage loans they made each fiscal year within tract areas used by the Census Bureau for statistical purposes; required disclosure by zip code area if the Federal Reserve Board determined that disclosure by census tract was not feasible.

1976

Antitrust Procedures (PL 94-435). Authorized state attorneys general to bring antitrust suits (*parens patriae*) on behalf of citizens; required large companies to notify the government of planned mergers; strengthened federal antitrust investigatory powers in the Justice Department and the Federal Trade Commission. This act was nullified by the Supreme Court in the 1977 case of *Illinois Brick Company v. Illinois*.

Consumer Product Safety Commission (CPSC) Amendments (PL 94-284). Reauthorized the CPSC for two years; authorized the CPSC to conduct its own civil enforcement actions if the Justice Department did not object within 45 days of notice; confirmed the commission's authority to develop product safety standards or contract for third parties to develop standards.

Equal Credit Opportunity Act Amendments (PL 94-239). Extended Equal Credit Opportunity Act protections to applicants who received public assistance or had brought a credit discrimination enforcement action; allowed creditors to extend credit to special groups such as elderly citizens or young couples under "affirmative action" programs without violating the discrimination law.

Federal Rail Safety Regulation (PL 94-348). Extended rail safety programs for two years through fiscal 1978; set penalties for safety violations; establishd a number of new safety standards governing operations and working conditions.

'Government in the Sunshine' (PL 94-409). Required all multiheaded federal agencies — some fifty of them — to open their meetings to the public unless a majority voted to close a meeting; exempted those meetings convened to discuss national defense, confidential information, trade secrets, and court proceedings of personnel problems.

Grain Inspection Act (PL 94-582). Amended the Grain Inspection Act of 1916; brought grain inspection under greater federal control by establishing a federal grain inspection service within the Agriculture Department; authorized the inspection service to set standards for the quality and condition of grain and for accurate weighing and weight certification procedures; required federal inspection at export port locations (except where qualified state inspection agencies were already in existence). This act was relaxed in 1980.

Hazardous Waste Standards (PL 94-580). Required the Environmental Protection Agency to define the term hazardous waste and list specific hazardous wastes; required the EPA to set safety standards for producers and transporters of hazardous wastes and for operators of hazardous waste treatment, storage and disposal facilities.

Medical Devices Safety (PL 94-295). Established the federal government's authority to oversee the safety and effectiveness of medical devices ranging from crutches to kidney dialysis machines; prohibited the sale of most life-supporting devices and devices implanted in the body prior to approval by the Food and Drug Administration; authorized the FDA to ban risky devices, to set performance standards for less risky devices and to exert general controls over all devices.

Rail Reorganization Act (PL 94-210). Authorized federal money for the modernization and revitalization of the country's depressed railroads; eased somewhat federal regulation of the railroads; gave the railroads greater flexibility in setting freight rates under Interstate Commerce Commission supervision.

School Bus Safety (PL 94-346). Postponed the effective date for new federal safety standards for school buses to April 1977.

Toxic Substances Control Act (PL 94-469). Expanded federal regulation of industrial and commercial chemicals and for the first time required pre-market testing for potentially dangerous chemicals; directed the Environmental Protection Agency to require testing of chemical substances, establish standards and, if necessary, ban or restrict certain chemicals.

Vitamin Regulation Ban (PL 94-278). Narrowed the federal government's authority to regulate vitamins and minerals; barred the Food and Drug Administration from regulating the composition or maximum potency of vitamins, minerals, or combinations of these substances unless they were toxic, habit-forming or needed to be administered by a doctor; permitted the FDA to continue to impose such restrictions on vitamins or minerals used in dietary treatment of certain diseases, intended for children under age 12 and taken by pregnant or lactating women; gave the FDA the authority in certain circumstances to seize or take other enforcement actions against vitamin and mineral products if they were falsely advertised.

1977

Anti-Arab Boycott (PL 95-52). Prohibited American firms from refusing to trade with Israel or other American firms as a precondition for trading with an Arab state.

Cargo Airline Deregulation (PL 95-163). Removed many federal restrictions on airlines providing all-cargo service; abolished most CAB authority to control the rates and routes of certified all-cargo carriers; certain airlines already carrying cargo exclusively were entitled to all-cargo certificates giving them authority to operate nationwide.

Clean Air Act Amendments (PL 95-95). Amended and extended the 1970 Clean Air Act; delayed existing standards for automobile emissions for two more years but tightened standards for the 1980 and 1981 models; set new standards to protect clean-air areas, such as parks; extended the deadline for cities to meet national air quality standards until December 1982; directed the Environmental Protection Administration to review criteria for air quality standards every five years; established a National Commission for Air Quality to study clean air legislation.

Clean Water Act Extended (PL 95-217). Extended authorization for water treatment programs through fiscal 1980; authorized the Environmental Protection Agency to develop water treatment, conservation and pollution control programs and to provide grants to states for enforcement; clarified state jurisdiction over water rights and authorized EPA to report on coordination of water resources management and pollution control.

Debt Collection Regulation (PL 95-109). Established a nationwide system of controls on the activities of agencies that collected other companies' overdue bills; limited the procedures a debt collector could use to collect his fees.

Department of Energy (DOE) (PL 95-91). Created a new Cabinet-level Department of Energy to assume the powers and functions of the Federal Power Commission, the Federal Energy Administration, and the Energy Research and Development Administration; gave the department responsibility for fuel supply and leasing procedures, research and development, environment, international energy policy, national security, nuclear waste management and energy conservation; required the president to submit to Congress a biennial energy plan outlining the nation's goals for energy production and conservation.

Mine Safety Standards (PL 95-164). Toughened mine health and safety standards, applying a single statute — the Federal Coal Mine Health and Safety Act of 1969 — to both coal and non-coal mines; repealed a more lenient 1966 law covering metal and mineral mines; transferred regulatory authority over all types of mining activities from the Department of the Interior to the Department of Labor.

Saccharin Ban Delay (PL 95-203). Delayed for 18 months a proposed Food and Drug Administration ban on the sale or distribution of the artificial sweetener saccharin or any product containing it; required a warning label on any food product containing saccharin, which had been linked to cancer in laboratory testing.

Safe Drinking Water Act Extension (PL 95-190). Amended and extended the Safe Drinking Water Act through fiscal 1979; granted a waiver of the law's requirement that states must assume primary enforcement responsibility for public water systems; provided for Environmental Protection Agency grants for state and local water systems development, underground water source protection, special emergency assistance and the study of rural drinking water supplies.

Surface Mining Control and Reclamation Act (PL 95-87). Established federal control over surface mining practices; authorized the setting of national standards to protect the land and eliminate environment and competitive advantages or disadvantages in interstate commerce among sellers of coal; established an Office of Surface Mining Reclamation and Enforcement in the Interior Department to administer the act's regulatory and reclamation programs, approve state programs and provide grants and technical assistance to the states.

1978

Airline Deregulation (PL 95-504). Increased marketplace competition in the airline industry by phasing out federal controls over a seven-year period; phased out the Civil Aeronautics Board — the independent agency that regulated the airline companies — by 1985 unless Congress acted to extend it; exempted interstate airlines from state regulation of rates and routes; ordered the CAB to authorize new services that were "consistent with the public convenience and necessity."

Bank Agency Audits (PL 95-320). Directed the comptroller general of the General Accounting Office to conduct audits of the Federal Reserve Board and its member banks, the Federal Deposit Insurance Corporation and the Office of the Comptroller of the Currency.

Banking Regulations (PL 95-630). Extended the authorization for the U.S. Export-Import Bank for five years; included provisions that spelled out consumer safeguards in electronic fund transfer systems; tightened federal bank regulatory agencies' power to deal with "problem banks" in shaky financial condition.

Cable TV Pole Regulation (PL 95-234). Gave the Federal Communications Commission power to set the rates utilities could charge cable television operators for using their utility poles; gave the FCC authority to regulate rates, settle disputes and levy fines for violations where states did not do so; states could reclaim authority over pole attachments from the FCC if they adhered to federal regulations.

Coal Conversion (PL 95-620). Required new industrial and utility plants to use coal or a fuel other than oil or gas; required existing utility plants using oil or gas to switch to other fuels by 1990. The Energy Department had the authority to order some industries, on a case-by-case basis, to switch fuels; the department could also exempt utilities and companies from the requirements if certain problems, such as an inadequate supply of coal, existed.

Commodity Futures Trading Commission (CFTC) Extension (PL 95-405). Extended the agency through fiscal 1982; provided the chairman would serve in that position at the pleasure of the president; suspended trading on most options until the CFTC could show congressional Agriculture committees that it could regulate responsibly.

Consumer Product Safety Commission (CPSC) Extension (PL 95-631). Extended the CPSC for three years; provided that the chairman would serve at the pleasure of the president; permitted the commission to develop its own mandatory safety standards under certain conditions; required manufacturers to give the CPSC advance notice of the export of any product, substance or fabric not in compliance with an existing safety standard.

Energy Conservation (PL 95-619). Required utilities to give customers information about energy conservation devices such as insulation and storm windows; authorized the Department of Energy to provide grants to low-income families for the installation of energy-saving "weatherization" devices; required the Government National Mortgage Associaton (GNMA) to direct low interest loans for home energy conservation improvements.

Foreign Bank Regulation (PL 95-369). Subjected foreign banks operating in the United States to the federal bank regulatory system; gave the Federal Reserve Board some additional powers to oversee foreign bank operations in the United States; empowered the Federal Reserve Board to set reserve requirements for federal and state branches of foreign banks with $1 billion or more in worldwide assets.

Fuel Efficiency Tax (PL 95-618). Imposed a "gas-guzzler tax" on the sale by the manufacturer of passenger cars that used fuel inefficiently; graduated the tax so that the most inefficient cars paid the highest amount; by 1986 cars getting less than 12.5 miles per gallon would be taxed $3,850.

Natural Gas Pricing (PL 95-621). Allowed the price of newly discovered natural gas to rise about 10 percent a year until 1985 when price controls would be lifted altogether.

Oil Tanker Safety (PL 95-474). Authorized the Transportation Department to require a federally licensed pilot on each vessel operating in U.S. waters when state law did not so require; expanded federal authority to investigate accidents at sea and barred any vessel carrying oil or another hazardous material from operating in U.S. waters or from transferring cargo in any U.S. port if the vessel had a history of accidents or failed to comply with U.S. laws and regulations; sought to prevent accidents by mandating better control of ship traffic and by requiring tankers to install electronic navigation and communications equipment.

Pesticides Registration (PL 95-396). Speeded up the process by which the Environmental Protection Agency evaluated the safety of pesticides and thus made it easier for farmers to obtain effective and safe pesticides; extended the Federal Insecticide, Fungicide and Rodenticide Act of 1975 through fiscal 1979; gave the public access to information about the effect of a pesticide on human health and the environment; gave the states new authority to enforce controls on pesticides once they met standards designed to maintain minimum nationwide controls on the substances; retained existing EPA authority to veto a state registration.

Utility Rates (PL 95-617). Required state utility commissions and other regulatory agencies to consider the use of energy-saving methods, such as pricing electricity at lower levels in off-peak hours to avoid heavy loads in peak periods of use and discontinuing discounts for large volume users. The Energy Department was authorized to intervene in the regulatory proceedings to argue for energy-saving measures.

1979

Pipeline Safety (PL 96-129). Provided stronger federal regulation of pipeline transportation and storage of hazardous natural and petroleum gases and liquids; required the Transportation Department to set and enforce safety standards within a year for mandatory participation by pipeline facility operators.

1980

Aircraft Noise Exemptions (PL 96-193). Delayed noise control standards for small two-engine jets until 1988, for larger two-engine jets and aircraft until 1986, and for three-engine aircraft until 1985 if they met certain conditions; authorized funds for planning noise control and land use compatability projects; barred damage suits against airport noise if the persons bringing suit acquired the property after enactment of the legislation and had knowledge of the noise exposure map of the area.

Antitrust Procedures (PL 96-349). Expanded the ability of the Justice Department to analyze complicated business documents and to obtain information from investigative targets; gave the department new authority to investigate possible antitrust violations by unincorporated entities, including partnerships and individuals; enlarged the authority of federal judges to discipline attorneys whose conduct unreasonably delayed antitrust litigation.

Auto Mileage Standards (PL 96-425). Gave auto makers more flexibility in computing average mileage of their fleets; allowed the Transportation Department to adjust mileage requirements for manufacturers of four-wheel-drive vehicles and light trucks if the companies could show that meeting those standards would result in severe economic problems, such as factory closings.

Bank Deregulation (PL 96-221). Permitted financial institutions to diversify the services they offered to attract deposits; set in motion a gradual lifting over six years of the federal interest rate ceilings that prevented financial institutions from paying the going market rate on savings deposits; dismantled federal regulations that had locked banks and thrift institutions into limited loan portfolios and kept them from competing effectively with high-yielding investment opportunities such as money market funds; authorized all federally insured financial institutions — savings and loans as well as banks — to offer interest-paying negotiable order of withdrawal (NOW) accounts; allowed savings and loan associations to offer consumer loans, checking accounts, credit cards and trust services previously reserved for commercial banks.

Deep Seabed Mining Act (PL 96-283). Opened the way for U.S. mining companies to explore the ocean floor for mineral riches while an international seabed mining treaty was being negotiated; required any U.S. miner to obtain from the National Oceanic and Atmospheric Administration a license for exploration of the seabed and a permit for commercial recovery of the minerals.

Federal Trade Commission (FTC) Reauthorization (PL 96-252). Extended the authorization for the FTC through fiscal 1982; permitted for the first time a two-chamber legislative veto by Congress of the agency's regulations without requiring the president's signature; barred the FTC from regulating trade groups that set product and industry standards or from petitioning the patents commissioner to cancel a trademark on the grounds that it had become the common name of a product; permitted the FTC to continue its rulemaking proceeding on television advertising aimed at children and to issue rules governing certain funeral home practices.

Grain Weighing Standards (PL 96-437). Relaxed the federal grain weighing regulations imposed on the export grain industry in 1976; eliminated most of the federal responsibility for checking weights of grain to be exported.

Household Movers Deregulation (PL 96-454). Clarified Interstate Commerce Commission authority to allow truckers to offer customers binding estimates of rates, to charge for the estimate and to offer a variety of services at varying rates; provided consumers with more protections in their dealings with the moving industry and established guidelines to help settle disputes between customers and carriers.

Infant Formula Standards (PL 96-359). Set minimum nutritional requirements for infant formulas; authorized the Department of Health and Human Services (HHS) to enforce standards and periodically revise the list of required nutrients.

International Air Transportation (PL 96-192). Intended to ease the regulation of international air transportation and encourage competition among foreign and domestic airlines; gave the Civil Aeronautics Board new authority to take countermeasures when a foreign government restricted U.S. carriers.

Multi-Employer Pensions (PL 96-364). Tightened the funding requirements of and reduced government liability for multi-employer pension plans covering 8 million workers.

Ocean Dumping (PL 96-572). Reauthorized federal ocean dumping regulations through fiscal 1982; reaffirmed the law's provisions prohibiting dumping of municipal sewage sludge in the ocean.

Paperwork Reduction Act (PL 96-511). Established to reduce the burden of lengthy and redundant federal reporting requirements imposed on individuals and organizations; created within the Office of Management and Budget (OMB) a central Office of Information and Regulatory Affairs with the authority to review all requests for information from the public made by government agencies.

Pesticides Rule Veto (PL 96-539). Provided that any proposed federal pesticide regulation could not take effect if Congress passed a resolution of disapproval within 90 days of the date the regulation was originally proposed.

Rail Safety (PL 96-423). Boosted federal railroad safety programs and strengthened federal powers to deal with hazardous rail conditions; authorized the Department of Transportation to issue orders to abate conditions or practices that were potentially hazardous.

Railroad Deregulation (PL 96-448). Reduced substantially a century of federal regulation of the railroads; gave railroads more price-setting flexibility; promoted competition by removing most antitrust immunity from rates set collectively by railroad carriers.

Regulatory Flexibility Act (PL 96-354). Required any agency proposing a rule to prepare an assessment of its economic and paperwork impact on individuals and small businesses, organizations and governments; set up a procedure for reviewing all major regulations at least once every ten years to see if they could be redrawn to minimize their adverse impact.

Saccharin Ban Moratorium Extension (PL 96-273). Extended the saccharin ban moratorium to June 30, 1981; continued the 1977 moratorium's requirement that saccharin-flavored products bear health warning labels and that stores selling such products post warning notices.

Safe Drinking Water Deadline Extensions (PL 96-502). Gave some cities three additional years to meet federal standards for cleaning up cancer-causing substances in public drinking water supplies.

Superfund Bill (PL 96-510). Established an emergency "superfund," called the Hazardous Substance Response Trust Fund, to clean up toxic contaminants spilled or dumped into the environment; imposed fees on the chemical and oil industries; gave the federal government the authority to act in emergencies to clean up spilled or dumped chemicals threatening public health or the environment; authorized the government to sue the persons or companies responsible for the damage to recoup the cleanup costs.

Swine Feed Regulation (PL 96-468). Regulated the feeding of garbage to swine in an effort to protect the nation's $7 billion-a-year hog industry from potentially devastating effects of African swine fever; required that garbage for swine-feeding be treated at licensed facilities according to methods prescribed by the Agriculture Department.

Trucking Deregulation (PL 96-296). Removed many federal trucking regulations; allowed the individual trucker greater freedom to determine prices; ended antitrust immunity for some collective rate-making; made it easier for newcomers to enter the industry.

Truth in Lending Act Amendments (PL 96-221). Amended the 1968 Act by encouraging the states to set up procedures to help consumers resolve minor complaints without going to court. Required that the consumer's right to rescind within three days an open-end credit loan secured by his residence would exist only at the time of the first transaction.

1981

Consumer Product Safety Commission (CPSC) Reauthorization (PL 97-35). Extended the authorization for the CPSC for another two years, despite the administration's request to abolish it; required a cost-benefit analysis of proposed mandatory standards; allowed one chamber of Congress to veto safety standards and regulations if the other chamber did not object.

Saccharin Ban Delayed (PL 97-42). Extended for two years, through June 30, 1983, the law prohibiting the Food and Drug Administration from banning saccharin, the artificial sweetener that was linked to cancer in laboratory animals.

Steel Industry Air Pollution Deadline Delay (PL 97-23). Gave the steel industry another three years through 1985 to meet air pollution cleanup deadlines; allowed steel companies to negotiate on a case-by-case basis extensions for cleaning up air pollution emissions; required that the money saved by deferring pollution control expenditures must be used to modernize older plants.

Selected Documents

Following are the texts of several laws that regulate the federal regulators. Included are the Administrative Procedure Act, the Freedom of Information Act, the Privacy Act, the Government in the Sunshine Act, the Paperwork Reduction Act, and the Regulatory Flexibility Act.

Also included is the text of Executive Order 12291, issued Feb. 17, 1981, by President Ronald Reagan. That order increased the president's oversight of rules and regulations written by regulatory agencies in the executive branch.

Administrative Procedure Act

Following is the text of the Administrative Procedure Act as it appears in the U.S. Code, Title 5, Chapter 5, Subchapter II, sections 551 and sections 553-559 and Title 5, Chapter 7.

SUBCHAPTER II
ADMINISTRATIVE PROCEDURE

§ 551. Definitions

For the purpose of this subchapter—

(1) "agency" means each authority of the Government of the United States, whether or not it is within or subject to review by another agency, but does not include—

(A) the Congress;

(B) the courts of the United States;

(C) the governments of the territories or possessions of the United States;

(D) the government of the District of Columbia;

or except as to the requirements of section 552 of this title—

(E) agencies composed of representatives of the parties or of representatives of organizations of the parties to the disputes determined by them;

(F) courts martial and military commissions;

(G) military authority exercised in the field in time of war or in occupied territory; or

(H) functions conferred by sections 1738, 1739, 1743, and 1744 of title 12; chapter 2 of title 41; or sections 1622, 1884, 1891-1902, and former section 1641(b)(2), of title 50, appendix;

(2) "person" includes an individual, partnership, corporation, association, or public or private organization other than an agency;

(3) "party" includes a person or agency named or admitted as a party, or properly seeking and entitled as of right to be admitted as a party, in an agency proceeding, and a person or agency admitted by an agency as a party for limited purposes;

(4) "rule" means the whole or a part of an agency statement of general or particular applicability and future effect designed to implement, interpret, or prescribe law or policy or describing the organization, procedure, or practice requirements of an agency and includes the approval or prescription for the future of rates, wages, corporate or financial structures or reorganizations thereof, prices, facilities, appliances, services or allowances therefor or of valuations, costs, or accounting, or practices bearing on any of the foregoing;

(5) "rule making" means agency process for formulating, amending, or repealing a rule;

(6) "order" means the whole or a part of a final disposition, whether affirmative, negative, injunctive, or declaratory in form, of an agency in a matter other than rule making but including licensing;

(7) "adjudication" means agency process for the formulation of an order.

(8) "license" includes the whole or a part of an agency permit, certificate, approval, registration, charter, membership, statutory exemption or other form of permission;

(9) "licensing" includes agency process respecting the grant, renewal, denial, revocation, suspension, annulment, withdrawal, limitation, amendment, modification, or conditioning of a license;

(10) "sanction" includes the whole or a part of an agency—

(A) prohibition, requirement, limitation, or other condition affecting the freedom of a person;

(B) withholding of relief;

(C) imposition of penalty or fine;

(D) destruction, taking, seizure, or withholding of property;

(E) assessment of damages, reimbursement, restitution, compensation, costs, charges, or fees;

(F) requirement, revocation, or suspension of a license; or

(G) taking other compulsory or restrictive action;

(11) "relief" includes the whole or a part of an agency—

(A) grant of money, assistance, license, authority, exemption, exception, privilege, or remedy;

(B) recognition of a claim, right, immunity, privilege, exemption, or exception; or

(C) taking of other action on the application or petition of, and beneficial to, a person;

(12) "agency proceeding" means an agency process as defined by paragraphs (5), (7), and (9) of this section;

(13) "agency action" includes the whole or a part of an agency rule, order, license, sanction, relief, or the equivalent or denial thereof, or failure to act; and

(14) "ex parte communication" means an oral or written communication not on the public record with respect to which reasonable prior notice to all parties is not given, but it shall not include requests for status reports on any matter or proceeding covered by this subchapter.

§ 553. Rule making

(a) This section applies, according to the provisions thereof, except to the extent that there is involved—

(1) a military or foreign affairs function of the United States; or

(2) a matter relating to agency management or personnel or to public property, loans, grants, benefits, or contracts.

(b) General notice of proposed rule making shall be published in the Federal Register, unless persons subject thereto are named and either personally served or otherwise have actual notice thereof in accordance with law. The notice shall include—

(1) a statement of the time, place, and nature of public rule making proceedings;

(2) reference to the legal authority under which the rule is proposed; and

(3) either the terms or substance of the proposed rule or a description of the subjects and issues involved.

Except when notice or hearing is required by statute, this subsection does not apply—

(A) to interpretative rules, general statements of policy, or rules of agency organization, procedure, or practice; or

(B) when the agency for good cause finds (and incorporates the finding and a brief statement of reasons therefor in the rules issued) that notice and public procedure thereon are impracticable, unnecessary, or contrary to the public interest.

(c) After notice required by this section, the agency shall give interested persons an opportunity to participate in the rule making through submission of written data, views, or arguments with or without opportunity for oral presentation. After consideration of the relevant matter presented, the agency shall incorporate in the rules adopted a concise general statement of their basis and purpose. When rules are required by statute to be made on the record after opportunity for an agency hearing, sections 556 and 557 of this title apply instead of this subsection.

(d) The required publication or service of a substantive rule shall be made not less than 30 days before its effective date, except—

(1) a substantive rule which grants or recognizes an exemption or relieves a restriction;

(2) interpretative rules and statements of policy; or

(3) as otherwise provided by the agency for good cause found and published with the rule.

(e) Each agency shall give an interested person the right to petition for the issuance, amendment, or repeal of a rule.

§ 554. Adjudications

(a) This section applies, according to the provisions thereof, in every case of adjudication required by statute to be determined on the record after opportunity for an agency hearing, except to the extent that there is involved—

(1) a matter subject to a consequent trial of the law and the facts de novo in a court;

(2) the selection or tenure of an employee, except a hearing examiner appointed under section 3105 of this title;

(3) proceedings in which decisions rest solely on inspections, tests, or elections;

(4) the conduct of military or foreign affairs functions;

(5) cases in which an agency is acting as an agent for a court; or

(6) the certification of worker representatives.

(b) Persons entitled to notice of an agency hearing shall be timely informed of—

(1) the time, place, and nature of the hearings;

(2) the legal authority and jurisdiction under which the hearing is to be held; and

(3) the matters of fact and law asserted.

When private persons are the moving parties, other parties to the proceeding shall give prompt notice of issues controverted in fact or law; and in other instances agencies may by rule require responsive pleading. In fixing the time and place for hearings, due regard shall be had for the convenience and necessity of the parties or their representatives.

(c) The agency shall give all interested parties opportunity for—

(1) the submission and consideration of facts, arguments, offers of settlement, or proposals of adjustment when time, the nature of the proceeding, and the public interest permit; and

(2) to the extent that the parties are unable so to determine a controversy by consent, hearing and decision on notice and in accordance with sections 556 and 557 of this title.

(d) The employee who presides at the reception of evidence pursuant to section 556 of this title shall make the recommended decision or initial decision required by section 557 of this title, unless he becomes unavailable to the agency. Except to the extent required for the disposition of ex parte matters as authorized by law, such an employee may not—

(1) consult a person or party on a fact in issue, unless on notice and opportunity for all parties to participate; or

(2) be responsible to or subject to the supervision or direction of an employee or agent engaged in the performance of investigative or prosecuting functions for an agency.

An employee or agent engaged in the performance of investigative or prosecuting functions for an agency in a case may not, in that or a factually related case, participate or advise in the decision, recommended decision, or agency review pursuant to section 557 of this title, except as witness or counsel in public proceedings. This subsection does not apply—

(A) in determining applications for initial licenses;

(B) to proceedings involving the validity or application of rates, facilities, or practices of public utilities or carriers; or

(C) to the agency or a member or members of the body comprising the agency.

(e) The agency, with like effect as in the case of other orders, and in its sound discretion, may issue a declaratory order to terminate a controversy or remove uncertainty.

§ 555. Ancillary matters

(a) This section applies, according to the provisions thereof, except as otherwise provided by this subchapter.

(b) A person compelled to appear in person before an agency or representative thereof is entitled to be accompanied, represented, and advised by counsel or, if permitted by the agency, by other qualified representative. A party is entitled to appear in person or by or with counsel or other duly qualified representative in an agency proceeding. So far as the orderly conduct of public business permits, an interested person may appear before an agency or its responsible employees for the presentation, adjustment, or determination of an issue, request, or controversy in a proceeding, whether interlocutory, summary, or otherwise, or in connection with an agency function. With due regard for the convenience and necessity of the parties or their representatives and within a reasonable time, each agency shall proceed to conclude a matter presented to it. This subsection does not grant or deny a person who is not a lawyer the right to appear for or represent others before an agency or in an agency proceeding.

(c) Process, requirement of a report, inspection, or other investigative act or demand may not be issued, made, or enforced except as authorized by law. A person compelled to submit data or evidence is entitled to retain or, on payment of lawfully prescribed costs, procure a copy or transcript thereof, except that in a nonpublic investigatory proceeding the witness may for good cause be limited to inspection of the official transcript of his testimony.

(d) Agency subpenas authorized by law shall be issued to a party on request and, when required by rules of procedure, on a statement or showing of general relevance and reasonable scope of the evidence sought. On contest, the court shall sustain the subpena or similar process or demand to the extent that it is found to be in accordance with law. In a proceeding for enforcement, the court shall issue an order requiring the appearance of the witness or the production of the evidence or data within a reasonable time under penalty of punishment for contempt in case of contumacious failure to comply.

(e) Prompt notice shall be given of the denial in whole or in part of a written application, petition, or other request of an interested person made in connection with any agency proceedings. Except in affirming a prior denial or when the denial is self explanatory, the notice shall be accompanied by a brief statement of the grounds for denial.

§ 556. Hearings; presiding employees; powers and duties; burden of proof; evidence; record as basis of decision

(a) This section applies, according to the provisions thereof, to hearings required by section 553 or 554 of this title to be conducted in accordance with this section.

(b) There shall preside at the taking of evidence—

(1) the agency;

(2) one or more members of the body which comprises the agency; or

(3) one or more hearing examiners appointed under section 3105 of this title.

This subchapter does not supersede the conduct of specified classes of proceedings, in whole or in part, by or before boards or other employees specially provided for by or designated under statute. The functions of presiding employees and of employees participating in decisions in accordance with section 557 of this title shall be conducted in an impartial manner. A presiding or participating employee may at any time disqualify himself. On the filing in good faith of a timely and sufficient affidavit of personal bias or other disqualification of a presiding or participating employee, the agency shall determine the matter as a part of the record and decision in the case.

(c) Subject to published rules of the agency and within its powers, employees presiding at hearings may—

(1) administer oaths and affirmations;

(2) issue subpenas authorized by law;

(3) rule on offers of proof and receive relevant evidence;

(4) take depositions or have depositions taken when the ends of justice would be served;

(5) regulate the course of the hearing;

(6) hold conferences for the settlement or simplification of the issues by consent of the parties;

(7) dispose of procedural requests or similar matters;

(8) make or recommend decisions in accordance with section 557 of this title; and

(9) take other action authorized by agency rule consistent with this subchapter.

(d) Except as otherwise provided by statute, the proponent of a rule or order has the burden of proof. Any oral or documentary evidence may be received, but the agency as a matter of policy shall provide for the exclusion of irrelevant, immaterial, or unduly repetitious evidence. A sanction may not be imposed or rule or order issued except on consideration of the whole record or those parts thereof cited by a party and supported by and in accordance with the reliable, probative, and substantial evidence. The agency may, to the extent consistent with the interests of justice and the policy of the underlying statutes administered by the agency, consider a violation of section 557(d) of this title sufficient grounds for a decision adverse to a party who has knowingly committed such violation or knowingly caused such violation to occur. A party is entitled to present his case or defense by oral or documentary evidence, to submit rebuttal evidence, and to conduct such cross-examination as may be required for a full and true disclosure of the facts. In rule making or determining claims for money or benefits or applications for initial licenses an agency may, when a party will not be prejudiced thereby, adopt procedures for the submission of all or part of the evidence in written form.

(e) The transcript of testimony and exhibits, together with all papers and requests filed in the proceeding, constitutes the exclusive record for decision in accordance with section 557 of this title and, on payment of lawfully prescribed costs, shall be made available to the parties. When an agency decision rests on official notice of a material fact not appearing in the evidence in the record, a party is entitled, on timely request, to an opportunity to show the contrary.

§ 557. Initial decisions; conclusiveness; review by agency; submissions by parties; contents of decisions; record

(a) This section applies, according to the provisions thereof, when a hearing is required to be conducted in accordance with section 556 of this title.

(b) When the agency did not preside at the reception of the evidence, the presiding employee or, in cases not subject to section 554(d) of this title, an employee qualified to preside at hearings pursuant to section 556 of this title, shall initially decide the case unless the agency requires, either in specific cases or by general rule, the entire record to be certified to it for decision. When the presiding employee makes an initial decision, that decision then becomes the decision of the agency without further proceedings unless there is an appeal to, or review on motion of, the agency within time provided by rule. On appeal from or review of the initial decision, the agency has all the powers which it would have in making the initial decision except as it may limit the issues on notice or by rule. When the agency makes the decision without having presided at the reception of the evidence, the presiding employee or an employee qualified to preside at hearings pursuant to section 556 of this title shall first recommend a decision, except that in rule making or determining applications for initial licenses—

(1) instead thereof the agency may issue a tentative decision or one of its responsible employees may recommend a decision; or

(2) this procedure may be omitted in a case in which the agency finds on the record that due and timely execution of its functions imperatively and unavoidably so requires.

(c) Before a recommended, initial, or tentative decision, or a decision on agency review of the decision of subordinate employees, the parties are entitled to a reasonable opportunity to submit for the consideration of the employees participating in the decisions—

(1) proposed findings and conclusions; or

(2) exceptions to the decisions or recommended decisions of subordinate employees or to tentative agency decisions; and

(3) supporting reasons for the exceptions or proposed findings or conclusions.

The record shall show the ruling on each finding, conclusion, or exception presented. All decisions, including initial, recommended, and tentative decisions, are a party of the record and shall include a statement of—

(A) findings and conclusions, and the reasons or basis therefor, on all the material issues of fact, law, or discretion presented on the record; and

(B) the appropriate rule, order, sanction, relief, or denial thereof.

(d)(1) In any agency proceeding which is subject to subsection (a) of this section, except to the extent required for the disposition of ex parte matters as authorized by law—

(A) no interested person outside the agency shall make or knowingly cause to be made to any member of the body comprising the agency, administrative law judge, or other employee who is or may reasonably be expected to be involved in the decisional process of the proceeding, an ex parte communication relevant to the merits of the proceeding;

(B) no member of the body comprising the agency, administrative law judge, or other employee who is or may reasonably be expected to be involved in the decisional process of the proceeding, shall make or knowingly cause to be made to any interested person outside the agency an ex parte communication relevant to the merits of the proceeding;

(C) a member of the body comprising the agency, administrative law judge, or other employee who is or may reasonably be expected to be involved in the decisional process of such proceeding who receives, or who makes or knowingly causes to be made, a communication prohibited by this subsection shall place on the public record of the proceeding:

(i) all such written communications;

(ii) memoranda stating the substance of all such oral communications; and

(iii) all written responses, and memoranda stating the substance of all oral responses, to the materials described in clauses (i) and (ii) of this subparagraph;

(D) upon receipt of a communication knowingly made or knowingly caused to be made by a party in violation of this subsection, the agency, administrative law judge, or other employee presiding at the hearing may, to the extent consistent with the interests of justice and the policy of the underlying statutes, require the party to show cause why his claim or interest in the proceeding should not be dismissed, denied, disregarded, or otherwise adversely affected on account of such violation; and

(E) the prohibitions of this subsection shall apply beginning at such time as the agency may designate, but in no case shall they begin to apply later than the time at which a proceeding is noticed for hearing unless the person responsible for the communication has knowledge that it will be noticed, in which case the prohibitions shall apply beginning at the time of his acquisition of such knowledge.

(2) This subsection does not constitute authority to withhold information from Congress.

§ 558. Imposition of sanctions; determination of applications for licenses; suspension, revocation, and expiration of licenses

(a) This section applies, according to the provisions thereof, to the exercise of a power or authority.

(b) A sanction may not be imposed or a substantive rule or order issued except within jurisdiction delegated to the agency and as authorized by law.

(c) When application is made for a license required by law, the agency, with due regard for the rights and privileges of all the interested parties or adversely affected persons and within a reasonable time, shall set and complete proceedings required to be conducted in accordance with sections 556 and 557 of this title or other proceedings required by law and shall make its decision. Except in cases of willfulness or those in which public health, interest, or safety requires otherwise, the withdrawal, suspension, revocation, or annulment of a license is lawful only if, before the institution of agency proceedings therefor, the licensee has been given—

(1) notice by the agency in writing of the facts or conduct which may warrant the action; and

(2) opportunity to demonstrate or achieve compliance with all lawful requirements.

When the licensee has made timely and sufficient application for a renewal or a new license in accordance with agency rules, a license with reference to an activity of a continuing nature does not expire until the application has been finally determined by the agency.

§ 559. Effect on other laws; effect of subsequent statute

This subchapter, chapter 7, and sections 1305, 3105, 3344, 4301(2)(E), 5362, and 7521 of this title, and the provisions of section 5335(a)(B) of this title that relate to hearing examiners, do not limit or repeal additional requirements imposed by statute or otherwise recognized by law. Except as otherwise required by law, requirements or privileges relating to evidence or procedure apply equally to agencies and persons. Each agency is granted the authority necessary to comply with the requirements of this subchapter through the issuance of rules or otherwise. Subsequent statute may not be held to supersede or modify this subchapter, chapter 7, sections 1305, 3105, 3344, 4301(2)(E), or 7521 of this title, or the provisions of section 5335(a)(B) of this title that relate to hearing examiners, except to the extent that it does so expressly.

CHAPTER 7—JUDICIAL REVIEW

§ 701. Applications; definitions

(a) This chapter applies, according to the provisions thereof, except to the extent that—

(1) statutes preclude judicial review; or

(2) agency action is committed to agency discretion by law.

(b) For the purpose of this chapter—

(1) "agency" means each authority of the Government of the United States, whether or not it is within or subject to review by another agency, but does not include—

(A) the Congress;

(B) the courts of the United States;

(C) the governments of the territories or possessions of the United States;

(D) the government of the District of Columbia;

(E) agencies composed of representatives of the parties or of representatives of organizations of the parties to the disputes determined by them;

(F) courts martial and military commissions;

(G) military authority exercised in the field in time of war or in occupied territory; or

(H) functions conferred by sections 1738, 1739, 1743, and 1744 of title 12; chapter 2 of title 41; or sections 1622, 1884, 1891-1902, and former section 1641(b)(2), of title 50, appendix; and

(2) "person", "rule", "order", "license", "sanction", "relief", and "agency action" have the meanings given them by section 551 of this title.

§ 702. Right of review

A person suffering legal wrong because of agency action, or adversely affected or aggrieved by agency action within the meaning of a relevant statute, is entitled to judicial review thereof. An action in a court of the United States seeking relief other than money damages and stating a claim that an agency or an officer or employee thereof acted or failed to act in an official capacity or under color of legal authority shall not be dismissed nor relief therein be denied on the ground that it is against the United States or that the United States may be named as a defendant in any such action, and a judgment or decree may be entered against the United States: *Provided,* That any mandatory or injunctive decree shall specify the Federal officer or officers (by name or by title), and their successors in office, personally responsible for compliance. Nothing herein (1) affects other limitations on judicial review or the power or duty of the court to dismiss any action or deny relief on any other appropriate legal or equitable ground; of (2) confers authority to grant relief if any other statute that grants consent to suit expressly or impliedly forbids the relief which is sought.

§ 703. Form and venue of proceeding

The form of proceeding for judicial review is the special statutory review proceeding relevant to the subject matter in a court specified by statute or, in the absence or inadequacy thereof, any applicable form of legal action, including actions for declaratory judgments or writs of prohibitory or mandatory injunction or habeas corpus, in a court of competent jurisdiction. If no special statutory review proceeding is applicable, the action for judicial review may be brought against the United States, the agency by its official title, or the appropriate officer. Except to the extent that prior, adequate, and exclusive opportunity for judicial review is provided by law, agency action is subject to judicial review in civil or criminal proceedings for judicial enforcement.

§ 704. Actions reviewable

Agency action made reviewable by statute and final agency action for which there is no other adequate remedy in a court are subject to judicial review. A preliminary, procedural, or intermediate agency action or ruling not directly reviewable is subject to review on the review of the final agency action. Except as otherwise expressly required by statute, agency action otherwise final is final for the purposes of this section whether or not there has been presented or determined an application for a declaratory order, for any form of reconsiderations, or, unless the agency otherwise requires by rule and provides that the action meanwhile is inoperative, for an appeal to superior agency authority.

§ 705. Relief pending review

When an agency finds that justice so requires, it may postpone the effective date of action taken by it, pending judicial review. On such conditions as may be required and to the extent necessary to prevent irreparable injury, the reviewing court, including the court to which a case may be taken on appeal from or on application for certiorari or other writ to a reviewing court, may issue all necessary and appropriate process to postpone the effective date of an agency action or to preserve status or rights pending conclusion of the review proceedings.

§ 706. Scope of review

To the extent necessary to decision and when presented, the reviewing court shall decide all relevant questions of law, interpret constitutional and statutory provisions, and determine the meaning or applicability of the terms of an agency action. The reviewing court shall—

(1) compel agency action unlawfully withheld or unreasonably delayed; and

(2) hold unlawful and set aside agency action, findings, and conclusions found to be—

(A) arbitrary, capricious, an abuse of discretion, or otherwise not in accordance with law;

(B) contrary to constitutional right, power, privilege, or immunity;

(C) in excess of statutory jurisdiction, authority, or limitations, or short of statutory right;

(D) without observance of procedure required by law;

(E) unsupported by substantial evidence in a case subject to sections 556 and 557 of this title or otherwise reviewed on the record of an agency hearing provided by statute; or

(F) unwarranted by the facts to the extent that the facts are subject to trial de novo by the reviewing court.

In making the foregoing determinations, the court shall review the whole record or those parts of it cited by a party, and due account shall be taken of the rule of prejudicial error.

Freedom of Information Act

The following is the text of the Freedom of Information Act as it appears in the U.S. Code, Title 5, Chapter 5, Subchapter II, section 552.

§ 552. Public information; agency rules, opinions, orders, records, and proceedings

(a) Each agency shall make available to the public information as follows:

(1) Each agency shall separately state and currently publish in the Federal Register for the guidance of the public—

(A) descriptions of its central and field organization and the established places at which, the employees (and in the case of a uniformed service, the members) from whom, and the methods whereby, the public may obtain information, make submittals or requests, or obtain decisions;

(B) statements of the general course and method by which its functions are channeled and determined, including the nature and requirements of all formal and informal procedures available;

(C) rules of procedure, descriptions of forms available or the places at which forms may be obtained, and instructions as to the scope and contents of all papers, reports, or examinations;

(D) substantive rules of general applicability adopted as authorized by law, and statements of general policy or interpretations of general applicability formulated and adopted by the agency; and

(E) each amendment, revision, or repeal of the foregoing.

Except to the extent that a person has actual and timely notice of the terms thereof, a person may not in any manner be required to, or be adversely affected by, a matter required to be published in the Federal Register and so published. For the purpose of this paragraph, matter reasonably available to the class of persons affected thereby is deemed published in the Federal Register when incorporated by reference therein with the approval of the Director of the Federal Register.

(2) Each agency, in accordance with published rules, shall make available for public inspection and copying—

(A) final opinions, including concurring and dissenting opinions, as well as orders, made in the adjudication of cases;

(B) those statements of policy and interpretations which have been adopted by the agency and are not published in the Federal Register; and

(C) administrative staff manuals and instructions to staff that affect a member of the public;

unless the materials are promptly published and copies offered for sale. To the extent required to prevent a clearly unwarranted invasion of personal privacy, an agency may delete identifying details when it makes available or publishes an opinion, statement of policy, interpretation, or staff manual or instruction. However, in each case the justification for the deletion shall be explained fully in writing. Each agency shall also maintain and make available for public inspection and copying current indexes providing identifying information for the public as to any matter issued, adopted, or promulgated after July 4, 1967, and required by this paragraph to be made available or published. Each agency shall promptly publish, quarterly or more frequently, and distribute (by sale or otherwise) copies of each index or supplements thereto unless it determines by order published in the Federal Register that the publication would be unnecessary and impracticable, in which case the agency shall nonetheless provide copies of such index on request at a cost not to exceed the direct cost of duplication. A final order, opinion, statement of policy, interpretation, or staff manual or instruction that affects a member of the public may be relied on, used, or cited as precedent by an agency against a party other than an agency only if—

(i) it has been indexed and either made available or published as provided by this paragraph; or

(ii) the party has actual and timely notice of the terms thereof.

(3) Except with respect to the records made available under paragraphs (1) and (2) of this subsection, each agency, upon any request for records which (A) reasonably describes such records and (B) is made in accordance with published rules stating the time, place, fees (if any), and procedures to be followed, shall make the records promptly available to any person.

(4)(A) In order to carry out the provisions of this section, each agency shall promulgate regulations, pursuant to notice and receipt of public comment, specifying a uniform schedule of fees applicable to all constituent units of such agency. Such fees shall be limited to reasonable standard charges for document search and duplication and provide for recovery of only the direct costs of such search and duplication. Documents shall be furnished without charge or at a reduced charge where the agency determines that waiver or reduction of the fee is in the public interest because furnishing the information can be considered as primarily benefiting the general public.

(B) On complaint, the district court of the United States in the district in which the complainant resides, or has his principal place of business, or in which the agency records are situated, or in the District of Columbia, has jurisdiction to enjoin the agency from withholding agency records and to order the production of any agency records improperly withheld from the complainant. In such a case the court shall determine the matter de novo, and may examine the contents of such agency records in camera to determine whether such records or any part thereof shall be withheld under any of the exemptions set forth in subsection (b) of this section, and the burden is on the agency to sustain its action.

(C) Notwithstanding any other provision of law, the defendant shall serve an answer or otherwise plead to any complaint made under this subsection within thirty days after service upon the defendant of the pleading in which such complaint is made, unless the court otherwise directs for good cause shown.

(D) Except as to cases the court considers of greater importance, proceedings before the district court, as authorized by this subsection, and appeals therefrom, take precedence on the docket over all cases and shall be assigned for hearing and trial or for argument at the earliest practicable date and expedited in every way.

(E) The court may assess against the United States reasonable attorney fees and other litigation costs reasonably incurred in any case under this section in which the complainant has substantially prevailed.

(F) Whenever the court orders the production of any agency records improperly withheld from the complainant and assesses against the United States reasonable attorney fees and other litigation costs, and the court additionally issues a written finding that the circumstances surrounding the withholding raise questions whether agency personnel acted arbitrarily or capriciously with respect to the withholding, the Civil Service Commission shall promptly initiate a proceeding to determine whether disciplinary action is warranted against the officer or employee who was primarily responsible for the withholding. The Commission, after investigation and consideration of the evidence submitted, shall submit its findings and recommendations to the administrative authority of the agency concerned and shall send copies of the findings and recommendations to the officer or employee or his representative. The administrative authority shall take the corrective action that the Commission recommends.

(G) In the event of noncompliance with the order of the court, the district court may punish for contempt the responsible employee, and in the case of a uniformed service, the responsible member.

(5) Each agency having more than one member shall maintain and make available for public inspection a record of the final votes of each member in every agency proceeding.

(6)(A) Each agency, upon any request for records made under paragraph (1), (2), or (3) of this subsection, shall—

(i) determine within ten days (excepting Saturdays, Sundays, and legal public holidays) after the receipt of any such request whether to comply with such request and shall immediately notify the person making such request of such determination and the reasons therefor, and of the right of such person to appeal to the head of the agency any adverse determination; and

(ii) make a determination with respect to any appeal within twenty days (excepting Saturdays, Sundays, and legal public holidays) after the receipt of such appeal. If on appeal the denial of the request for records is in whole or in part upheld, the agency shall notify the person making such request of the provisions for judicial review of that determination under paragraph (4) of this subsection.

(B) In unusual circumstances as specified in this subparagraph, the time limits prescribed in either clause (i) or clause (ii) of subparagraph (A) may be extended by written notice to the person making such request setting forth the reasons for such extension and the date on which a determination is expected to be dispatched. No such notice shall specify a date that would result in an extension for more than ten working days. As used in this subparagraph, "unusual circumstances" means, but only to the extent reasonably necessary to the proper processing of the particular request—

(i) the need to search for and collect the requested records from field facilities or other establishments that are separate from the office processing the request;

(ii) the need to search for, collect, and appropriately examine a voluminous amount of separate and distinct records which are demanded in a single request; or

(iii) the need for consultation, which shall be conducted with all practicable speed, with another agency having a substantial interest in the determination of the request or among two or more components of the agency having substantial subject-matter interest therein.

(C) Any person making a request to any agency for records under paragraph (1), (2), or (3) of this subsection shall be deemed to have exhausted his administrative remedies with respect to such request if the agency fails to comply with the applicable time limit provisions of this paragraph. If the Government can show exceptional circumstances exist and that the agency is exercising due diligence in responding to the request, the court may retain jurisdiction and allow the agency additional time to complete its review of the records. Upon any determination by an agency to comply with a request for records, the records shall be made promptly available to such person making such request. Any notification of denial of any request for records under this subsection shall set forth the names and titles or positions of each person responsible for the denial of such request.

(b) This section does not apply to matters that are—

(1)(A) specifically authorized under criteria established by an Executive order to be kept secret in the interest of national defense or foreign policy and (B) are in fact properly classified pursuant to such Executive order;

(2) related solely to the internal personnel rules and practices of an agency;

(3) specifically exempted from disclosure by statute (other than section 552b of this title), provided that such statute (A) requires that the matters be withheld from the public in such a manner as to leave no discretion on the issue, or (B) establishes particular criteria for withholding or refers to particular types of matter to be withheld;

(4) trade secrets and commercial or financial information obtained from a person and privileged or confidential;

(5) inter-agency or intra-agency memorandums or letters which would not be available by law to a party other than an agency in litigation with the agency;

(6) personnel and medical files and similar files the disclosure of which would constitute a clearly unwarranted invasion of personal privacy;

(7) investigatory records compiled for law enforcement purposes, but only to the extent that the production of such records would (A) interfere with enforcement proceedings, (B) deprive a person of a right to a fair trial or an impartial adjudication, (C) constitute an unwarranted invasion of personal privacy, (D) disclose the identity of a confidential source and, in the case of a record compiled by a criminal law enforcement authority in the course of a criminal investigation, or by an agency conducting a lawful national security intelligence investigation, confidential information furnished only by the confidential source, (E) disclose investigative techniques and procedures, or (F) endanger the life or physical safety of law enforcement personnel;

(8) contained in or related to examination, operating, or condition reports prepared by, on behalf of, or for the use of an agency responsible for the regulation or supervision of financial institutions; or

(9) geological and geophysical information and data, including maps, concerning wells.

Any reasonably segregable portion of a record shall be provided to any person requesting such record after deletion of the portions which are exempt under this subsection.

(c) This section does not authorize withholding of information or limit the availability of records to the public, except as specifically stated in this section. This section is not authority to withhold information from Congress.

(d) On or before March 1 of each calendar year, each agency shall submit a report covering the preceding calendar year to the Speaker of the House of Representatives and President of the Senate for referral to the appropriate committees of the Congress.

The report shall include—

(1) the number of determinations made by such agency not to comply with the requests for records made to such agency under subsection (a) and the reasons for each such determination;

(2) the number of appeals made by persons under subsection (a)(6), the result of such appeals, and the reason for the action upon each appeal that results in a denial of information;

(3) the names and titles or positions of each person responsible for the denial of records requested under this section, and the number of instances of participation for each;

(4) the results of each proceeding conducted pursuant to subsection (a)(4)(F), including a report of the disciplinary action taken against the officer or employee who was primarily responsible for improperly withholding records or an explanation of why disciplinary action was not taken;

(5) a copy of every rule made by such agency regarding this section;

(6) a copy of the fee schedule and the total amount of fees collected by the agency for making records available under this section; and

(7) such other information as indicates efforts to administer fully this section.

The Attorney General shall submit an annual report on or before March 1 of each calendar year which shall include for the prior calendar year a listing of the number of cases arising under this section, the exemption involved in each case, the disposition of such case, and the cost, fees, and penalties assessed under subsections (a)(4)(E), (F), and (G). Such report shall also include a description of the efforts undertaken by the Department of Justice to encourage agency compliance with this section.

(e) For purposes of this section, the term "agency" as defined in section 551(1) of this title includes any executive department, military department, Government corporation, Government controlled corporation, or other establishment in the executive branch of the Government (including the Executive Office of the President), or any independent regulatory agency.

Privacy Act

The following is the text of the Privacy Act as it appears in the U.S. Code, Title 5, Chapter 5, Subchapter II, section 552a.

§ 552a. Records maintained on individuals

(a) Definitions

For purposes of this section—

(1) the term "agency" means agency as defined in section 552(e) of this title;

(2) the term "individual" means a citizen of the United States or an alien lawfully admitted for permanent residence;

(3) the term "maintain" includes maintain, collect, use, or disseminate;

(4) the term "record" means any item, collection, or grouping of information about an individual that is maintained by an agency, including, but not limited to, his education, financial transactions, medical history, and criminal or employment history and that contains his name, or the identifying number, symbol, or other identifying particular assigned to the individual, such as a finger or voice print or photograph;

(5) the term "system of records" means a group of any records under the control of any agency from which information is retrieved by the name of the individual or by some identifying number, symbol, or other identifying particular assigned to the individual;

(6) the term "statistical record" means a record in a system of records maintained for statistical research or reporting purposes only and not used in whole or in part in making any determination about an identifiable individual, except as provided by section 8 of title 13; and

(7) the term "routine use" means, with respect to the disclosure of a record, the use of such record for a purpose which is compatible with the purpose for which it was collected.

(b) Conditions of disclosure

No agency shall disclose any record which is contained in a system of records by any means of communication to any person, or to another agency, except pursuant to a written request by, or with the prior written consent of, the individual to whom the record pertains, unless disclosure of the record would be—

(1) to those officers and employees of the agency which maintains the record who have a need for the record in the performance of their duties;

(2) required under section 552 of this title;

(3) for a routine use as defined in subsection (a)(7) of this section and described under subsection (e)(4)(D) of this section;

(4) to the Bureau of the Census for purposes of planning or carrying out a census or survey or related activity pursuant to the provisions of title 13;

(5) to a recipient who has provided the agency with advance adequate written assurance that the record will be used solely as a statistical research or reporting record, and the record is to be transferred in a form that is not individually identifiable;

(6) to the National Archives of the United States as a record which has sufficient historical or other value to warrant its continued preservation by the United States Government, or for evaluation by the Administrator of General Services or his designee to determine whether the record has such value;

(7) to another agency or to an instrumentality of any governmental jurisdiction within or under the control of the United States for a civil or criminal law enforcement activity if the activity is authorized by law, and if the head of the agency or instrumentality has made a written request to the agency which maintains the record specifying the particular portion desired and the law enforcement activity for which the record is sought;

(8) to a person pursuant to a showing of compelling circumstances affecting the health or safety of an individual if upon such disclosure notification is transmitted to the last known address of such individual;

(9) to either House of Congress, or, to the extent of matter within its jurisdiction, any committee or subcommittee thereof, any joint committee of Congress or subcommittee of any such joint committee;

(10) to the Comptroller General, or any of his authorized representatives, in the course of the performance of the duties of the General Accounting Office; or

(11) pursuant to the order of a court of competent jurisdiction.

(c) Accounting of certain disclosures

Each agency, with respect to each system of records under its control shall—

(1) except for disclosures made under subsections (b)(1) or (b)(2) of this section, keep an accurate accounting of—

(A) the date, nature, and purpose of each disclosure of a record to any person or to another agency made under subsection (b) of this section; and

(B) the name and address of the person or agency to whom the disclosure is made;

(2) retain the accounting made under paragraph (1) of this subsection for at least five years or the life of the record, whichever is longer, after the disclosure for which the accounting is made;

(3) except for disclosures made under subsection (b)(7) of this section, make the accounting made under paragraph (1) of this subsection available to the individual named in the record at his request; and

(4) inform any person or other agency about any correction or notation of dispute made by the agency in accordance with subsection (d) of this section of any record that has been disclosed to the person or agency if an accounting of the disclosure was made.

(d) Access to records

Each agency that maintains a system of records shall—

(1) upon request by any individual to gain access to his record or to any information pertaining to him which is contained in the system, permit him and upon his request, a person of his own choosing to accompany him, to review the record and have a copy made of all or any portion thereof in a form comprehensible to him, except that the agency may require the individual to furnish a written statement authorizing discussion of that individual's record in the accompanying person's presence;

(2) permit the individual to request amendment of a record pertaining to him and—

(A) not later than 10 days (excluding Saturdays, Sundays, and legal public holidays) after the date of receipt of such request, acknowledge in writing such receipt; and

(B) promptly, either—

(i) make any correction of any portion thereof which the individual believes is not accurate, relevant, timely, or complete; or

(ii) inform the individual of its refusal to amend the record in accordance with his request, the reason for the refusal, the procedures established by the agency for the individual to request a review of that refusal by the head of the agency or an officer designated by the head of the agency, and the name and business address of that official;

(3) permit the individual who disagrees with the refusal of the agency to amend his record to request a review of such refusal, and not later than 30 days (excluding Saturdays, Sundays, and legal public holidays) from the date on which the individual requests such review, complete such review and make a final determination unless, for good cause shown, the head of the agency extends such 30-day period; and if, after his review, the reviewing official also refuses to amend the record in accordance with the request, permit the individual to file with the agency a concise statement setting forth the reasons for his disagreement with the refusal of the agency, and notify the individual of the provisions for judicial review of the reviewing official's determination under subsection (g)(1)(A) of this section:

(4) in any disclosure, containing information about which the individual has filed a statement of disagreement, occurring after the filing of the statement under paragraph (3) of this subsection, clearly note any portion of the record which is disputed and provide copies of the statement and, if the agency deems it appropriate, copies of a concise statement of the reasons of the agency for not making the amendments requested, to persons or other agencies to whom the disputed record has been disclosed; and

(5) nothing in this section shall allow an individual access to any information compiled in reasonable anticipation of a civil action or proceeding.

(e) Agency requirements

Each agency that maintains a system of records shall—

(1) maintain in its records only such information about an individual as is relevant and necessary to accomplish a purpose of the agency required to be accomplished by statute or by executive order of the President;

(2) collect information to the greatest extent practicable directly from the subject individual when the information may result in adverse determinations about an individual's rights, benefits, and privileges under Federal programs;

(3) inform each individual whom it asks to supply information, on the form which it uses to collect the information or on a separate form that can be retained by the individual—

(A) the authority (whether granted by statute, or by executive order of the President) which authorizes the solicitation of the information and whether disclosure of such information is mandatory or voluntary;

(B) the principal purpose or purposes for which the information is intended to be used;

(C) the routine uses which may be made of the information, as published pursuant to paragraph (4)(D) of this

subsection; and

(D) the effects on him, if any, of not providing all or any part of the requested information;

(4) subject to the provisions of paragraph (11) of this subsection, publish in the Federal Register at least annually a notice of the existence and character of the system of records, which notice shall include—

(A) the name and location of the system;

(B) the categories of individuals on whom records are maintained in the system;

(C) the categories of records maintained in the system;

(D) each routine use of the records contained in the system, including the categories of users and the purpose of such use;

(E) the policies and practices of the agency regarding storage, retrievability, access controls, retention, and disposal of the records;

(F) the title and business address of the agency official who is responsible for the system of records;

(G) the agency procedures whereby an individual can be notified at his request if the system of records contains a record pertaining to him;

(H) the agency procedures whereby an individual can be notified at his request how he can gain access to any record pertaining to him contained in the system of records, and how he can contest its content; and

(I) the categories of sources of records in the system;

(5) maintain all records which are used by the agency in making any determination about any individual with such accuracy, relevance, timeliness, and completeness as is reasonably necessary to assure fairness to the individual in the determination;

(6) prior to disseminating any record about an individual to any person other than an agency, unless the dissemination is made pursuant to subsection (b)(2) of this section, make reasonable efforts to assure that such records are accurate, complete, timely, and relevant for agency purposes;

(7) maintain no record describing how any individual exercises rights guaranteed by the First Amendment unless expressly authorized by statute or by the individual about whom the record is maintained or unless pertinent to and within the scope of an authorized law enforcement activity;

(8) make reasonable efforts to serve notice on an individual when any record on such individual is made available to any person under compulsory legal process when such process becomes a matter of public record;

(9) establish rules of conduct for persons involved in the design, development, operation, or maintenance of any system of records, or in maintaining any record, and instruct each such person with respect to such rules and the requirements of this section, including any other rules and procedures adopted pursuant to this section and the penalties for noncompliance;

(10) establish appropriate administrative, technical, and physical safeguards to insure the security and confidentiality of records and to protect against any anticipated threats or hazards to their security or integrity which could result in substantial harm, embarrassment, inconvenience, or unfairness to any individual on whom information is maintained; and

(11) at least 30 days prior to publication of information under paragraph (4)(D) of this subsection, publish in the Federal Register notice of any new use or intended use of the information in the system, and provide an opportunity for interested persons to submit written data, views, or arguments to the agency.

(f) Agency rules

In order to carry out the provisions of this section, each agency that maintains a system of records shall promulgate rules, in accordance with the requirements (including general notice) of section 553 of this title, which shall—

(1) establish procedures whereby an individual can be notified in response to his request if any system of records named by the individual contains a record pertaining to him;

(2) define reasonable times, places, and requirements for

identifying an individual who requests his record or information pertaining to him before the agency shall make the record or information available to the individual;

(3) establish procedures for the disclosure to an individual upon his request of his record or information pertaining to him, including special procedure, if deemed necessary, for the disclosure to an individual of medical records, including psychological records pertaining to him;

(4) establish procedures for reviewing a request from an individual concerning the amendment of any record or information pertaining to the individual, for making a determination on the request, for an appeal within the agency of an initial adverse agency determination, and for whatever additional means may be necessary for each individual to be able to exercise fully his rights under this section; and

(5) establish fees to be charged, if any, to any individual for making copies of his record, excluding the cost of any search for and review of the record.

The Office of the Federal Register shall annually compile and publish the rules promulgated under this subsection and agency notices published under subsection (e)(4) of this section in a form available to the public at low cost.

(g)(1) Civil remedies

Whenever any agency

(A) makes a determination under subsection (d)(3) of this section not to amend an individual's record in accordance with his request, or fails to make such review in conformity with that subsection;

(B) refuses to comply with an individual request under subsection (d)(1) of this section;

(C) fails to maintain any record concerning any individual with such accuracy, relevance, timeliness, and completeness as is necessary to assure fairness in any determination relating to the qualifications, character, rights, or opportunities of, or benefits to the individual that may be made on the basis of such record, and consequently a determination is made which is adverse to the individual; or

(D) fails to comply with any other provision of this section, or any rule promulgated thereunder, in such a way as to have an adverse effect on an individual,

the individual may bring a civil action against the agency, and the district courts of the United States shall have jurisdiction in the matters under the provisions of this subsection.

(2)(A) In any suit brought under the provisions of subsection (g)(1)(A) of this section, the court may order the agency to amend the individual's record in accordance with his request or in such other way as the court may direct. In such a case the court shall determine the matter de novo.

(B) The court may assess against the United States reasonable attorney fees and other litigation costs reasonably incurred in any case under this paragraph in which the complainant has substantially prevailed.

(3)(A) In any suit brought under the provisions of subsection (g)(1)(B) of this section, the court may enjoin the agency from withholding the records and order the production to the complainant of any agency records improperly withheld from him. In such a case the court shall determine the matter de novo, and may examine the contents of any agency records in camera to determine whether the records or any portion thereof may be withheld under any of the exemptions set forth in subsection (k) of this section, and the burden is on the agency to sustain its action.

(B) The court may assess against the United States reasonable attorney fees and other litigation costs reasonably incurred in any case under this paragraph in which the complainant has substantially prevailed.

(4) In any suit brought under the provisions of subsection (g)(1)(C) or (D) of this section in which the court determines that the agency acted in a manner which was intentional or willful, the United States shall be liable to the individual in an amount equal to the sum of—

(A) actual damages sustained by the individual as a result of the refusal or failure, but in no case shall a person entitled to

recovery receive less than the sum of $1,000; and

(B) the costs of the action together with reasonable attorney fees as determined by the court.

(5) An action to enforce any liability created under this section may be brought in the district court of the United States in the district in which the complainant resides, or has his principal place of business, or in which the agency records are situated, or in the District of Columbia, without regard to the amount in controversy, within two years from the date on which the cause of action arises, except that where an agency has materially and willfully misrepresented any information required under this section to be disclosed to an individual and the information so misrepresented is material to establishment of the liability of the agency to the individual under this section, the action may be brought at any time within two years after discovery by the individual of the misrepresentation. Nothing in this section shall be construed to authorize any civil action by reason of any injury sustained as the result of a disclosure of a record prior to September 27, 1975.

(h) Rights of legal guardians

For the purposes of this section, the parent of any minor, or the legal guardian of any individual who has been declared to be incompetent due to physical or mental incapacity or age by a court of competent jurisdiction, may act on behalf of the individual.

(i)(1) Criminal penalties

Any officer or employee of an agency, who by virtue of his employment or official position, has possession of, or access to, agency records which contain individually identifiable information the disclosure of which is prohibited by this section or by rules or regulations established thereunder, and who knowing that disclosure of the specific material is so prohibited, willfully discloses the material in any manner to any person or agency not entitled to receive it, shall be guilty of a misdemeanor and fined not more than $5,000.

(2) Any officer or employee of any agency who willfully maintains a system of records without meeting the notice requirements of subsection (e)(4) of this section shall be guilty of a misdemeanor and fined not more than $5,000.

(3) Any person who knowingly and willfully requests or obtains any record concerning an individual from an agency under false pretenses shall be guilty of a misdemeanor and fined not more than $5,000.

(j) General exemptions

The head of any agency may promulgate rules, in accordance with the requirements (including general notice) of sections 553(b)(1), (2), and (3), (c), and (e) of this title, to exempt any system of records within the agency from any part of this section except subsections (b), (c)(1) and (2), (e)(4)(A) through (F), (e)(6), (7), (9), (10), and (11), and (i) if the system of records is—

(1) maintained by the Central Intelligence Agency; or

(2) maintained by an agency or component thereof which performs as its principal function any activity pertaining to the enforcement of criminal laws, including police efforts to prevent, control, or reduce crime or to apprehend criminals, and the activities of prosecutors, courts, correctional, probation, pardon, or parole authorities, and which consists of (A) information compiled for the purpose of identifying individual criminal offenders and alleged offenders and consisting only of identifying data and notations of arrests, the nature and disposition of criminal charges, sentencing, confinement, release, and parole and probation status; (B) information compiled for the purpose of a criminal investigation, including reports of informants and investigators, and associated with an identifiable individual; or (C) reports identifiable to an individual compiled at any stage of the process of enforcement of the criminal laws from arrest or indictment through release from supervision.

At the time rules are adopted under this subsection, the agency shall include in the statement required under section 553(c) of this title, the reasons why the system of records is to be exempted from a provision of this section.

(k) Specific exemptions

The head of any agency may promulgate rules, in accordance with the requirement (including general notice) of sections

553(b)(1), (2), and (3), (c), and (e) of this title, to exempt any system of records within the agency from subsections (c)(3), (d), (e)(1), (e)(4)(G), (H), and (I) and (f) of this section if the system of records is—

(1) subject to the provisions of section 552(b)(1) of this title;

(2) investigatory material compiled for law enforcement purposes, other than material within the scope of subsection (j)(2) of this section: *Provided, however,* That if any individual is denied any right, privilege, or benefit that he would otherwise be entitled by Federal law, or for which he would otherwise be eligible, as a result of the maintenance of such material, such material shall be provided to such individual, except to the extent that the disclosure of such material would reveal the identity of a source who furnished information to the Government under an express promise that the identity of the source would be held in confidence, or, prior to the effective date of this section, under an implied promise that the identity of the source would be held in confidence;

(3) maintained in connection with providing protective services to the President of the United States or other individuals pursuant to section 3056 of title 18;

(4) required by statute to be maintained and used solely as statistical records;

(5) investigatory material compiled solely for the purpose of determining suitability, eligibility, or qualifications for Federal civilian employment, military service, Federal contracts, or access to classified information, but only to the extent that the disclosure of such material would reveal the identity of a source who furnished information to the Government under an express promise that the identity of the source would be held in confidence, or, prior to the effective date of this section, under an implied promise that the identity of the source would be held in confidence;

(6) testing or examination material used solely to determine individual qualifications for appointment or promotion in the Federal service the disclosure of which would compromise the objectivity or fairness of the testing or examination process; or

(7) evaluation material used to determine potential for promotion in the armed services, but only to the extent that the disclosure of such material would reveal the identity of a source who furnished information to the Government under an express promise that the identity of the source would be held in confidence, or, prior to the effective date of this section, under an implied promise that the identity of the source would be held in confidence.

At the time rules are adopted under this subsection, the agency shall include in the statement required under section 553(c) of this title, the reasons why the system of records is to be exempted from a provision of this section.

(l)(1) Archival records

Each agency record which is accepted by the Administrator of General Services for storage, processing, and servicing in accordance with section 3103 of title 44 shall, for the purposes of this section, be considered to be maintained by the agency which deposited the record and shall be subject to the provisions of this section. The Administrator of General Services shall not disclose the record except to the agency which maintains the record, or under rules established by that agency which are not inconsistent with the provisions of this section.

(2) Each agency record pertaining to an identifiable individual which was transferred to the National Archives of the United States as a record which has sufficient historical or other value to warrant its continued preservation by the United States Government, prior to the effective date of this section, shall, for the purposes of this section, be considered to be maintained by the National Archives and shall not be subject to the provisions of this section, except that a statement generally describing such records (modeled after the requirements relating to records subject to subsections (e)(4)(A) through (G) of this section) shall be published in the Federal Register.

(3) Each agency record pertaining to an identifiable individual which is transferred to the National Archives of the United States as a record which has sufficient historical or other value to warrant its continued preservation by the United States Government, on or after the effective date of this section, be considered to be maintained by the National Archives and shall be exempt from the requirements of this section except subsections (e)(4)(A) through (G) and (e)(9) of this section.

(m) Government contractors

When an agency provides by a contract for the operation by or on behalf of the agency of a system of records to accomplish an agency function, the agency shall, consistent with its authority, cause the requirements of this section to be applied to such system. For purposes of subsection (i) of this section any such contractor and any employee of such contractor, if such contract is agreed to on or after the effective date of this section, shall be considered to be an employee of an agency.

(n) Mailing lists

An individual's name and address may not be sold or rented by an agency unless such action is specifically authorized by law. This provision shall not be construed to require the withholding of names and addresses otherwise permitted to be made public.

(o) Report on new systems

Each agency shall provide adequate advance notice to Congress and the Office of Management and Budget of any proposal to establish or alter any system of records in order to permit an evaluation of the probable or potential effect of such proposal on the privacy and other personal or property rights of individuals or the disclosure of information relating to such individuals, and its effect on the preservation of the constitutional principles of federalism and separation of powers.

(p) Annual report

The President shall submit to the Speaker of the House and the President of the Senate, by June 30 of each calendar year, a consolidated report, separately listing for each Federal agency the number of records contained in any system of records which were exempted from the application of this section under the provisions of subsections (j) and (k) of this section during the preceding calendar year, and the reasons for the exemptions, and such other information as indicates efforts to administer fully this section.

(q) Effect of other laws

No agency shall rely on any exemption contained in section 552 of this title to withhold from an individual any record which is otherwise accessible to such individual under the provisions of this section.

Government in the Sunshine Act

The following is the text of the Government in the Sunshine Act as it appears in the U.S. Code, Title 5, Chapter 5, Subchapter II, section 552b.

§ 552b. Open meetings

(a) For purposes of this section—

(1) the term "agency" means any agency, as defined in section 552(e) of this title, headed by a collegial body composed of two or more individual members, a majority of whom are appointed to such position by the President with the advice and consent of the Senate, and any subdivision thereof authorized to act on behalf of the agency;

(2) the term "meeting" means the deliberations of at least the number of individual agency members required to take action on behalf of the agency where such deliberations determine or result in the joint conduct or disposition of official agency business, but does not include deliberations required or permitted by subsection (d) or (e); and

(3) the term "member" means an individual who belongs to a collegial body heading an agency.

(b) Members shall not jointly conduct or dispose of agency business other than in accordance with this section. Except as provided in subsection (c), every portion of every meeting of an agency shall be open to public observation.

(c) Except in a case where the agency finds that the public interest requires otherwise, the second sentence of subsection (b) shall not apply to any portion of an agency meeting, and the requirements of subsections (d) and (e) shall not apply to any information pertaining to such meeting otherwise required by this section to be disclosed to the public, where the agency properly determines that such portion or portions of its meeting or the disclosure of such information is likely to—

(1) disclose matters that are (A) specifically authorized under criteria established by an Executive order to be kept secret in the interests of national defense or foreign policy and (B) in fact properly classified pursuant to such Executive order;

(2) relate solely to the internal personnel rules and practices of an agency;

(3) disclose matters specifically exempted from disclosure by statute (other than section 552 of this title), provided that such statute (A) requires that the matters be withheld from the public in such a manner as to leave no discretion on the issue, or (B) establishes particular criteria for withholding or refers to particular types of matters to be withheld;

(4) disclose trade secrets and commercial or financial information obtained from a person and privileged or confidential;

(5) involve accusing any person of a crime, or formally censuring any person;

(6) disclose information of a personal nature where disclosure would constitute a clearly unwarranted invasion of personal privacy;

(7) disclose investigatory records compiled for law enforcement purposes, or information which if written would be contained in such records, but only to the extent that the production of such records or information would (A) interfere with enforcement proceedings, (B) deprive a person of a right to a fair trial or an impartial adjudication, (C) constitute an unwarranted invasion of personal privacy, (D) disclose the identity of a confidential source and, in the case of a record compiled by a criminal law enforcement authority in the course of a criminal investigation, or by an agency conducting a lawful national security intelligence investigation, confidential information furnished only by the confidential source, (E) disclose investigative techniques and procedures, or (F) endanger the life or physical safety of law enforcement personnel;

(8) disclose information contained in or related to examination, operating, or condition reports prepared by, on behalf of, or for the use of an agency responsible for the regulation or supervision of financial institutions;

(9) disclose information the premature disclosure of which would—

(A) in the case of an agency which regulates currencies, securities, commodities, or financial institutions, be likely to (i) lead to significant financial speculation in currencies, securities, or commodities, or (ii) significantly endanger the stability of any financial institution; or

(B) in the case of any agency, be likely to significantly frustrate implementation of a proposed agency action.

except that subparagraph (B) shall not apply in any instance where the agency has already disclosed to the public the content or nature of its proposed action, or where the agency is required by law to make such disclosure on its own initiative prior to taking final agency action on such proposal; or

(10) specifically concern the agency's issuance of a subpena, or the agency's participation in a civil action or proceeding, an action in a foreign court or international tribunal, or an arbitration, or the initiation, conduct, or disposition by the agency of a particular case of formal agency adjudication pursuant to the procedures in section 554 of this title or otherwise involving a determination on the record after opportunity for a hearing.

(d)(1) Action under subsection (c) shall be taken only when a majority of the entire membership of the agency (as defined in subsection (a)(1)) votes to take such action. A separate vote of the agency members shall be taken with respect to each agency meeting a portion or portions of which are proposed to be closed to the public pursuant to subsection (c), or with respect to any information which is proposed to be withheld under subsection (c). A single vote may be taken with respect to a series of meetings, a portion or portions of which are proposed to be closed to the public, or with respect to any information concerning such series of meetings, so long as each meeting in such series involves the same particular matters and is scheduled to be held no more than thirty days after the initial meeting in such series. The vote of each agency member participating in such vote shall be recorded and no proxies shall be allowed.

(2) Whenever any person whose interests may be directly affected by a portion of a meeting requests that the agency close such portion to the public for any of the reasons referred to in paragraph (5), (6), or (7) of subsection (c), the agency, upon request of any one of its members, shall vote by recorded vote whether to close such meeting.

(3) Within one day of any vote taken pursuant to paragraph (1) or (2), the agency shall make publicly available a written copy of such vote reflecting the vote of each member on the question. If a portion of a meeting is to be closed to the public, the agency shall, within one day of the vote taken pursuant to paragraph (1) or (2) of this subsection, make publicly available a full written explanation of its action closing the portion together with a list of all persons expected to attend the meeting and their affiliation.

(4) Any agency, a majority of whose meetings may properly be closed to the public pursuant to paragraph (4), (8), (9)(A), or (10) of subsection (c), or any combination thereof, may provide by regulation for the closing of such meetings or portions thereof in the event that a majority of the members of the agency votes by recorded vote at the beginning of such meeting, or portion thereof, to close the exempt portion or portions of the meeting, and a copy of such vote, reflecting the vote of each member on the question, is made available to the public. The provisions of paragraphs (1), (2), and (3) of this subsection and subsection (e) shall not apply to any portion of a meeting to which such regulations apply: *Provided,* That the agency shall, except to the extent that such information is exempt from disclosure under the provisions of subsection (c), provide the public with public announcement of the time, place, and subject matter of the meeting and of each portion thereof at the earliest practicable time.

(e)(1) In the case of each meeting, the agency shall make public announcement, at least one week before the meeting, of the time, place, and subject matter of the meeting, whether it is to be open or closed to the public, and the name and phone number of the official designated by the agency to respond to requests for information about the meeting. Such announcement shall be made unless a majority of the members of the agency determines by a recorded vote that agency business requires that such meeting be called at an earlier date, in which case the agency shall make public announcement of the time, place, and subject matter of such meeting, and whether open or closed to the public, at the earliest practicable time.

(2) The time or place of a meeting may be changed following the public announcement required by paragraph (1) only if the agency publicly announces such change at the earliest practicable time. The subject matter of a meeting, or the determination of the agency to open or close a meeting, or portion of a meeting, to the public, may be changed following the public announcement required by this subsection only if (A) a majority of the entire membership of the agency determines by a recorded vote that agency business so requires and that no earlier announcement of the change was possible, and (B) the agency publicly announces such change and the vote of each member upon such change at the earliest practicable time.

(3) Immediately following each public announcement required by this subsection, notice of the time, place, and subject matter of a meeting, whether the meeting is open or closed, any change in one of the preceding, and the name and phone number of the official designated by the agency to respond to requests for information about the meeting, shall also be submitted for publication in the Federal Register.

(f)(1) For every meeting closed pursuant to paragraphs (1) through (10) of subsection (c), the General Counsel or chief legal officer of the agency shall publicly certify that, in his or her opinion, the meeting may be closed to the public and shall state each relevant exemptive provision. A copy of such certification, together with a statement from the presiding officer of the meeting setting forth the time and place of the meeting, and the persons present, shall be retained by the agency. The agency shall maintain a complete transcript or electronic recording adequate to record fully the proceedings of each meeting, or portion of a meeting, closed to the public, except that in the case of a meeting, or portion of a meeting, closed to the public pursuant to paragraph (8), (9)(A), or (10) of subsection (c), the agency shall maintain either such a transcript or recording, or a set of minutes. Such minutes shall fully and clearly describe all matters discussed and shall provide a full and accurate summary of any actions taken, and the reasons therefor, including a description of each of the views expressed on any item and the record of any rollcall vote (reflecting the vote of each member on the question). All documents considered in connection with any action shall be identified in such minutes.

(2) The agency shall make promptly available to the public, in a place easily accessible to the public, the transcript, electronic recording, or minutes (as required by paragraph (1) of the discussion of any item on the agenda, or of any item of the testimony of any witness received at the meeting, except for such item or items of such discussion or testimony as the agency determines to contain information which may be withheld under subsection (c). Copies of such transcript, or minutes, or a transcription of such recording disclosing the identity of each speaker, shall be furnished to any person at the actual cost of duplication or transcription. The agency shall maintain a complete verbatim copy of the transcript, a complete copy of the minutes, or a complete electronic recording of each meeting, or portion of a meeting, closed to the public, for a period of at least two years after such meeting, or until one year after the conclusion of any agency proceeding with respect to which the meeting or portion was held, whichever occurs later.

(g) Each agency subject to the requirements of this section shall, within 180 days after the date of enactment of this section, following consultation with the Office of the Chairman of the Administrative Conference of the United States and published notice in the Federal Register of at least thirty days and opportunity for written comment by any person, promulgate regulations to implement the requirements of subsections (b) through (f) of this section. Any person may bring a proceeding in the United States District Court for the District of Columbia to require an agency to promulgate such regulations if such agency has not promulgated such regulations within the time period specified herein. Subject to any limitations of time provided by law, any person may bring a proceeding in the United States Court of Appeals for the District of Columbia to set aside agency regulations issued pursuant to this subsection that are not in accord with the requirements of subsections (b) through (f) of this section and to require the promulgation of regulations that are in accord with such subsections.

(h)(1) The district courts of the United States shall have jurisdiction to enforce the requirements of subsections (b) through (f) of this section by declaratory judgment, injunctive relief, or other relief as may be appropriate. Such actions may be brought by any person against an agency prior to, or within sixty days after, the meeting out of which the violation of this section arises, except that if public announcement of such meeting is not initially provided by the agency in accordance with the requirements of this section, such action may be instituted pursuant to this section at any time prior to sixty days after any public announcement of such meeting. Such actions may be brought in the district court of the United States for the district in which the agency meeting is held or in which the agency in question has its headquarters, or in the District Court for the District of Columbia. In such actions a defendant shall serve his answer within thirty days after the service of the complaint. The burden is on the defendant to sustain his action. In deciding such cases the court may examine in camera any portion of the transcript, electronic recording, or minutes of a meeting closed to the public, and may take such additional evidence as it deems necessary. The court, having due regard for orderly administration and the public interest, as well as the interests of the parties, may grant such equitable relief as it deems appropriate, including granting an injunction against future violations of this section or ordering the agency to make available to the public such portion of the transcript, recording, or minutes of a meeting as is not authorized to be withheld under subsection (c) of this section.

(2) Any Federal court otherwise authorized by law to review agency action may, at the application of any person properly participating in the proceeding pursuant to other applicable law, inquire into violations by the agency of the requirements of this section and afford such relief as it deems appropriate. Nothing in this section authorizes any Federal court having jurisdiction solely on the basis of paragraph (1) to set aside, enjoin, or invalidate any agency action (other than an action to close a meeting or to withhold information under this section) taken or discussed at any agency meeting out of which the violation of this section arose.

(i) The court may assess against any party reasonable attorney fees and other litigation costs reasonably incurred by any other party who substantially prevails in any action brought in accordance with the provisions of subsection (g) or (h) of this section, except that costs may be assessed against the plaintiff only where the court finds that the suit was initiated by the plaintiff primarily for frivolous or dilatory purposes. In the case of assessment of costs against an agency, the costs may be assessed by the court against the United States.

(j) Each agency subject to the requirements of this section shall annually report to Congress regarding its compliance with such requirements, including a tabulation of the total number of agency meetings open to the public, the total number of meetings closed to the public, the reasons for closing such meetings, and a description of any litigation brought against the agency under this section, including any costs assessed against the agency in such litigation (whether or not paid by the agency).

(k) Nothing herein expands or limits the present rights of any person under section 552 of this title, except that the exemptions set forth in subsection (c) of this section shall govern in the case of any request made pursuant to section 552 to copy or inspect the transcripts, recordings, or minutes described in subsection (f) of this section. The requirements of chapter 33 of title 44, United States Code, shall not apply to the transcripts, recordings, and minutes described in subsection (f) of this section.

(l) This section does not constitute authority to withhold any information from Congress, and does not authorize the closing of any agency meeting or portion thereof required by any other provision of law to be open.

(m) Nothing in this section authorizes any agency to withhold from any individual any record, including transcripts, recordings, or minutes required by this section, which is otherwise accessible to such individual under section 552a of this title.

Regulatory Flexibility Act

Following is the text of the Regulatory Flexibility Act as it appears in the U.S. Code, Title 5, Chapter 6.

FINDINGS AND PURPOSES

SEC. 2. (a) The Congress finds and declares that—

(1) when adopting regulations to protect the health, safety and economic welfare of the Nation, Federal agencies should seek to achieve statutory goals as effectively and efficiently as possible without imposing unnecessary burdens on the public;

(2) laws and regulations designed for application to large scale entities have been applied uniformly to small businesses, small

organizations, and small governmental jurisdictions even though the problems that gave rise to government action may not have been caused by those smaller entities;

(3) uniform Federal regulatory and reporting requirements have in numerous instances imposed unnecessary and disproportionately burdensome demands including legal, accounting and consulting costs upon small businesses, small organizations, and small governmental jurisdictions with limited resources;

(4) the failure to recognize differences in the scale and resources of regulated entities has in numerous instances adversely affected competition in the marketplace, discouraged innovation and restricted improvements in productivity;

(5) unnecessary regulations create entry barriers in many industries and discourage potential entrepreneurs from introducing beneficial products and processes;

(6) the practice of treating all regulated businesses, organizations, and governmental jurisdictions as equivalent may lead to inefficient use of regulatory agency resources, enforcement problems, and, in some cases, to actions inconsistent with the legislative intent of health, safety, environmental and economic welfare legislation;

(7) alternative regulatory approaches which do not conflict with the stated objectives of applicable statutes may be available which minimize the significant economic impact of rules on small businesses, small organizations, and small governmental jurisdictions;

(8) the process by which Federal regulations are developed and adopted should be reformed to require agencies to solicit the ideas and comments of small businesses, small organizations, and small governmental jurisdictions to examine the impact of proposed and existing rules on such entities, and to review the continued need for existing rules.

(b) It is the purpose of this Act to establish as a principle of regulatory issuance that agencies shall endeavor, consistent with the objectives of the rule and of applicable statutes, to fit regulatory and informational requirements to the scale of the businesses, organizations, and governmental jurisdictions subject to regulation. To achieve this principle, agencies are required to solicit and consider flexible regulatory proposals and to explain the rationale for their actions to assure that such proposals are given serious consideration.

ANALYSIS OF REGULATORY FUNCTIONS

SEC. 3. (a) Title 5, United States Code, is amended by adding immediately after chapter 5 the following new chapter:

"CHAPTER 6—THE ANALYSIS OF REGULATORY FUNCTIONS

"Sec. 601. Definitions.
"Sec. 602. Regulatory agenda.
"Sec. 603. Initial regulatory flexibility analysis.
"Sec. 604. Final regulatory flexibility analysis.
"Sec. 605. Avoidance of duplicative or unnecessary analyses.
"Sec. 606. Effect on other law.
"Sec. 607. Preparation of analyses.
"Sec. 608. Procedure for waiver or delay of completion.
"Sec. 609. Procedures for gathering comments.
"Sec. 610. Periodic review of rules.
"Sec. 611. Judicial review.
"Sec. 612. Reports and intervention rights.

"§ 601. Definitions

"For purposes of this chapter—

"(1) the term 'agency' means an agency as defined in section 551(1) of this title;

"(2) the term 'rule' means any rule for which the agency publishes a general notice of proposed rulemaking pursuant to section 553(b) of this title, or any other law, including any rule of general applicability governing Federal grants to State and local governments for which the agency provides an opportunity for notice and public comment, except that the term 'rule' does not

include a rule of particular applicability relating to rates, wages, corporate or financial structures or reorganizations thereof, prices, facilities, appliances, services, or allowances therefor or to valuations, costs or accounting, or practices relating to such rates, wages, structures, prices, appliances, services, or allowances;

"(3) the term 'small business' has the same meaning as the term 'small business concern' under section 3 of the Small Business Act, unless an agency, after consultation with the Office of Advocacy of the Small Business Administration and after opportunity for public comment, establishes one or more definitions of such term which are appropriate to the activities of the agency and publishes such definition(s) in the Federal Register;

"(4) the term 'small organization' means any not-for-profit enterprise which is independently owned and operated and is not dominated in its field, unless an agency establishes, after opportunity for public comment, one or more definitions of such term which are appropriate to the activities of the agency and publishes such definition(s) in the Federal Register;

"(5) the term 'small governmental jurisdiction' means governments of cities, counties, towns, townships, villages, school districts, or special districts, with a population of less than fifty thousand, unless an agency establishes, after opportunity for public comment, one or more definitions of such term which are appropriate to the activities of the agency and which are based on such factors as location in rural or sparsely populated areas or limited revenues due to the population of such jurisdiction, and publishes such definition(s) in the Federal Register; and

"(6) the term 'small entity' shall have the same meaning as the terms 'small business', 'small organization' and 'small governmental jurisdiction' defined in paragraphs (3), (4) and (5) of this section.

"§ 602. Regulatory agenda

"(a) During the months of October and April of each year, each agency shall publish in the Federal Register a regulatory flexibility agenda which shall contain—

"(1) a brief description of the subject area of any rule which the agency expects to propose or promulgate which is likely to have a significant economic impact on a substantial number of small entities;

"(2) a summary of the nature of any such rule under consideration for each subject area listed in the agenda pursuant to paragraph (1), the objectives and legal basis for the issuance of the rule, and an approximate schedule for completing action on any rule for which the agency has issued a general notice of proposed rulemaking, and

"(3) the name and telephone number of an agency official knowledgeable concerning the items listed in paragraph (1).

"(b) Each regulatory flexibility agenda shall be transmitted to the Chief Counsel for Advocacy of the Small Business Administration for comment, if any.

"(c) Each agency shall endeavor to provide notice of each regulatory flexibility agenda to small entities or their representatives through direct notification or publication of the agenda in publications likely to be obtained by such small entities and shall invite comments upon each subject area on the agenda.

"(d) Nothing in this section precludes an agency from considering or acting on any matter not included in a regulatory flexibility agenda, or requires an agency to consider or act on any matter listed in such agenda.

"§ 603. Initial regulatory flexibility analysis

"(a) Whenever an agency is required by section 553 of this title, or any other law, to publish general notice of proposed rulemaking for any proposed rule, the agency shall prepare and make available for public comment an initial regulatory flexibility analysis. Such analysis shall describe the impact of the proposed rule on small entities. The initial regulatory flexibility analysis or a summary shall be published in the Federal Register at the time of the publication of general notice of proposed rulemaking for the rule. The agency shall transmit a copy of the initial regulatory flexibility analysis to the Chief Counsel for Advocacy of the Small Business Administration.

"(b) Each initial regulatory flexibility analysis required under this section shall contain—

"(1) a description of the reasons why action by the agency is being considered;

"(2) a succinct statement of the objectives of, and legal basis for, the proposed rule;

"(3) a description of and, where feasible, an estimate of the number of small entities to which the proposed rule will apply;

"(4) a description of the projected reporting, recordkeeping and other compliance requirements of the proposed rule, including an estimate of the classes of small entities which will be subject to the requirement and the type of professional skills necessary for preparation of the report or record;

"(5) an identification, to the extent practicable, of all relevant Federal rules which may duplicate, overlap or conflict with the proposed rule.

"(c) Each initial regulatory flexibility analysis shall also contain a description of any significant alternatives to the proposed rule which accomplish the stated objectives of the applicable statutes and which minimize any significant economic impact of the proposed rule on small entities. Consistent with the stated objectives of applicable statues, the analysis shall discuss significant alternatives such as—

"(1) the establishment of differing compliance or reporting requirements or timetables that take into account the resources available to small entities;

"(2) the clarification, consolidation, or simplification of compliance and reporting requirements under the rule for such small entities;

"(3) the use of performance rather than design standards; and

"(4) an exemption from coverage of the rule, or any part thereof, for such small entities.

"§ 604. Final regulatory flexibility analysis

"(a) When an agency promulgates a final rule under section 553 of this title, after being required by that section or any other law to publish a general notice of proposed rulemaking, the agency shall prepare a final regulatory flexibility analysis. Each final regulatory flexibility analysis shall contain—

"(1) a succinct statement of the need for, and the objectives of, the rule;

"(2) a summary of the issues raised by the public comments in response to the initial regulatory flexibility analysis, a summary of the assessment of the agency of such issues, and a statement of any changes made in the proposed rule as a result of such comments; and

"(3) a description of each of the significant alternatives to the rule consistent with the stated objectives of applicable statutes and designed to minimize any significant economic impact of the rule on small entities which was considered by the agency, and a statement of the reasons why each one of such alternatives was rejected.

"(b) The agency shall make copies of the final regulatory flexibility analysis available to members of the public and shall publish in the Federal Register at the time of publication of the final rule under section 553 of this title a statement describing how the public may obtain such copies.

"§ 605. Avoidance of duplicative or unnecessary analyses

"(a) Any federal agency may perform the analyses required by sections 602, 603, and 604 of this title in conjunction with or as a part of any other agenda or analysis required by any other law if such other analysis satisfies the provisions of such sections.

"(b) Sections 603 and 604 of this title shall not apply to any proposed or final rule if the head of the agency certifies that the rule will not, if promulgated, have a significant economic impact on a substantial number of small entities. If the head of the agency makes a certification under the preceding sentence, the agency shall publish such certification in the Federal Register, at the time

of publication of general notice of proposed rulemaking for the rule or at the time of publication of the final rule, along with a succinct statement explaining the reasons for such certification, and provide such certification and statement to the Chief Counsel for Advocacy of the Small Business Administration.

"(c) In order to avoid duplicative action, an agency may consider a series of closely related rules as one rule for the purposes of sections 602, 603, 604 and 610 of this title.

"§ 606. Effect on other law

"The requirements of sections 603 and 604 of this title do not alter in any manner standards otherwise applicable by law to agency action.

"§ 607. Preparation of analyses

"In complying with the provisions of sections 603 and 604 of this title, an agency may provide either a quantifiable or numerical description of the effects of a proposed rule or alternatives to the proposed rule, or more general descriptive statements if quantification is not practicable or reliable.

"§ 608. Procedure for waiver or delay of completion

"(a) An agency head may waive or delay the completion of some or all of the requirements of section 603 of this title by publishing in the Federal Register, not later than the date of publication of the final rule, a written finding, with reasons therefor, that the final rule is being promulgated in response to an emergency that makes compliance or timely compliance with the provisions of section 603 of this title impracticable.

"(b) Except as provided in section 605(b), an agency head may not waive the requirements of section 604 of this title. An agency head may delay the completion of the requirements of section 604 of this title for a period of not more than one hundred and eighty days after the date of publication in the Federal Register of a final rule by publishing in the Federal Register, not later than such date of publication, a written finding, with reasons therefor, that the final rule is being promulgated in response to an emergency that makes timely compliance with the provisions of section 604 of this title impracticable. If the agency has not prepared a final regulatory analysis pursuant to section 604 of this title within one hundred and eighty days from the date of publication of the final rule, such rule shall lapse and have no effect. Such rule shall not be repromulgated until a final regulatory flexibility analysis has been completed by the agency.

"§ 609. Procedures for gathering comments

"When any rule is promulgated which will have a significant economic impact on a substantial number of small entities, the head of the agency promulgating the rule or the official of the agency with statutory responsibility for the promulgation of the rule shall assure that small entities have been given an opportunity to participate in the rulemaking for the rule through techniques such as—

"(1) the inclusion in an advanced notice of proposed rulemaking, if issued, of a statement that the proposed rule may have a significant economic effect on a substantial number of small entities;

"(2) the publication of general notice of proposed rulemaking in publications likely to be obtained by small entities;

"(3) the direct notification of interested small entities;

"(4) the conduct of open conferences or public hearings concerning the rule for small entities; and

"(5) the adoption or modification of agency procedural rules to reduce the cost or complexity of participation in the rulemaking by small entities.

"§ 610. Periodic review of rules

"(a) Within one hundred and eighty days after the effective date of this chapter, each agency shall publish in the Federal Register a plan for the periodic review of the rules issued by the agency which have or will have a significant economic impact upon a substantial number of small entities. Such plan may be amended by the agency at any time by publishing the revision in the Federal Register. The purpose of the review shall be to determine whether such rules should be continued without change, or should be amended or rescinded, consistent with the stated objectives of applicable statutes, to minimize any significant economic impact of the rules upon a substantial number of such small entities. The plan shall provide for the review of all such agency rules existing on the effective date of this chapter within ten years of that date and for the review of such rules adopted after the effective date of this chapter within ten years of the publication of such rules as the final rule. If the head of the agency determines that completion of the review of existing rules is not feasible by the established date, he shall so certify in a statement published in the Federal Register and may extend the completion date by one year at a time for a total of not more than five years.

"(b) In reviewing rules to minimize any significant economic impact of the rule on a substantial number of small entities in a manner consistent with the stated objectives of applicable statutes, the agency shall consider the following factors—

"(1) the continued need for the rule;

"(2) the nature of complaints or comments received concerning the rule from the public;

"(3) the complexity of the rule;

"(4) the extent to which the rule overlaps, duplicates or conflicts with other Federal rules, and, to the extent feasible, with State and local governmental rules; and

"(5) the length of time since the rule has been evaluated or the degree to which technology, economic conditions, or other factors have changed in the area affected by the rule.

"(c) Each year, each agency shall publish in the Federal Register a list of the rules which have a significant economic impact on a substantial number of small entities, which are to be reviewed pursuant to this section during the succeeding twelve months. The list shall include a brief description of each rule and the need for and legal basis of such rule and shall invite public comment upon the rule.

"§ 611. Judicial review

"(a) Except as otherwise provided in subsection (b), any determination by an agency concerning the applicability of any of the provisions of this chapter to any action of the agency shall not be subject to judicial review.

"(b) Any regulatory flexibility analysis prepared under sections 603 and 604 of this title and the compliance or noncompliance of the agency with the provisions of this chapter shall not be subject to judicial review. When an action for judicial review of a rule is instituted, any regulatory flexibility analysis for such rule shall constitute part of the whole record of agency action in connection with the review.

"(c) Nothing in this section bars judicial review of any other impact statement or similar analysis required by any other law if judicial review of such statement or analysis is otherwise provided by law.

"§ 612. Reports and intervention rights

"(a) The Chief Counsel for Advocacy of the Small Business Administration shall monitor agency compliance with this chapter and shall report at least annually thereon to the President and to the Committees on the Judiciary of the Senate and House of Representatives, the Select Committee on Small business of the Senate, and the Committee on Small business of the House of Representatives.

"(b) The Chief Counsel for Advocacy of the Small Business Administration is authorized to appear as amicus curiae in any action brought in a court of the United States to review a rule. In any such action, the Chief Counsel is authorized to present his views with respect to the effect of the rule on small entities.

"(c) A court of the United States shall grant the application of the Chief Counsel for Advocacy of the Small Business Administration to appear in any such action for the purposes described in subsection (b)."

EFFECTIVE DATE

SEC. 4. The provisions of this Act shall take effect Jan. 1, 1981, except that the requirements of sections 603 and 604 of title 5, United States Code (as added by section 3 of this Act) shall apply only to rules for which a notice of proposed rulemaking is issued on or after January 1, 1981.

Paperwork Reduction Act

Following is the text of the Paperwork Reduction Act as it appears in the U.S. Code, Title 44, Chapter 35, sections 3501-3520.

"§ 3501. Purpose

"The purpose of this chapter is—

"(1) to minimize the Federal paperwork burden for individuals, small businesses, State and local governments, and other persons;

"(2) to minimize the cost to the Federal Government of collecting, maintaining, using, and disseminating information;

"(3) to maximize the usefulness of information collected by the Federal Government;

"(4) to coordinate, integrate and, to the extent practicable and appropriate, make uniform Federal information policies and practices;

"(5) to ensure that automatic data processing and telecommunications technologies are acquired and used by the Federal Government in a manner which improves service delivery and program management, increases productivity, reduces waste and fraud, and, wherever practicable and appropriate, reduces the information processing burden for the Federal Government and for persons who provide information to the Federal Government; and

"(6) to ensure that the collection, maintenance, use and dissemination of information by the Federal Government is consistent with applicable laws relating to confidentiality, including section 552a of title 5, United States Code, known as the Privacy Act.

"§ 3502. Definitions

"As used in this chapter—

"(1) the term 'agency' means any executive department, military department, Government corporation, Government controlled corporation, or other establishment in the executive branch of the Government (including the Executive Office of the President), or any independent regulatory agency, but does not include the General Accounting Office, Federal Election Commission, the governments of the District of Columbia and of the territories and possessions of the United States, and their various subdivisions, or Government-owned contractor-operated facilities including laboratories engaged in national defense research and production activities;

"(2) the terms 'automatic data processing,' 'automatic data processing equipment,' and 'telecommunications system or equipment, the function, operation or use of which—

"(A) involves intelligence activities;

"(B) involves cryptologic activities related to national security;

"(C) involves the direct command and control of military forces;

"(D) involves equipment which is an integral part of a weapon or weapons system; or

"(E) is critical to the direct fulfillment of military or intelligence missions, provided that this exclusion shall not include automatic data processing or telecommunications equipment used for routine administrative and business applications such as payroll, finance, logistics, and personnel management;

"(3) the term 'burden' means the time, effort, or financial resources expended by persons to provide information to a Federal agency;

"(4) the term 'collection of information' means the obtaining or soliciting of facts or opinions by an agency through the use of written report forms, application forms, schedules, questionnaires, reporting or recordkeeping requirements, or other similar methods calling for either—

"(A) answers to identical questions posed to, or identical reporting or recordkeeping requirements imposed on, ten or more persons, other than agencies, instrumentalities, or employees of the United States; or

"(B) answers to questions posed to agencies, instrumentalities, or employees of the United States which are to be used for general statistical purposes;

"(5) the term 'data element' means a distinct piece of information such as a name, term, number, abbreviation, or symbol;

"(6) the term 'data element dictionary' means a system containing standard and uniform definitions and cross references for commonly used data elements;

"(7) the term 'data profile' means a synopsis of the questions contained in an information collection request and the official name of the request, the location of information obtained or to be obtained through the request, a description of any compilations, analyses, or reports derived or to be derived from such information, any record retention requirements associated with the request, the agency responsible for the request, the statute authorizing the request, and any other information necessary to identify, obtained, or use the data contained in such information;

"(8) the term 'Director' means the Director of the Office of Management and Budget;

"(9) the term 'directory of information resources' means a catalog of information collection requests, containing a data profile for each request;

"(10) the term 'independent regulatory agency' means the Board of Governors of the Federal Reserve System, the Civil Aeronautics Board, the Commodity Futures Trading Commission, the Consumer Product Safety Commission, the Federal Communications Commission, the Federal Deposit Insurance Corporation, the Federal Energy Regulatory Commission, the Federal Home Loan Bank Board, the Federal Maritime Commission, the Federal Trade Commission, the Interstate Commerce Commission, the Mine Enforcement Safety and Health Review Commission, the National Labor Relations Board, the Nuclear Regulatory Commission, the Occupational Safety and Health Review Commission, the Postal Rate Commission, the Securities and Exchange Commission, and any other similar agency designated by statute as a Federal independent regulatory agency or commission;

"(11) the term 'information collection request' means a written report form, application form, schedule, questionnaire, reporting or recordkeeping requirement, or other similar method calling for the collection of information;

"(12) the term 'information referral service' means the function that assists officials and persons in obtaining access to the Federal Information Locator System;

"(13) the term 'information systems' means management information systems;

"(14) the term 'person' means an individual, partnership, association, corporation, business trust, or legal representative, an organized group of individuals, a State, territorial, or local government or branch thereof, or a political subdivision of a State, territory, or local government or a branch of a political subdivision;

"(15) the term 'practical utility' means the ability of an agency to use information it collects, particularly the capability to process such information in a timely and useful fashion; and

"(16) the term 'recordkeeping requirement' means a requirement imposed by an agency on persons to maintain specified records.

"§ 3503. Office of Information and Regulatory Affairs

"(a) There is established in the Office of Management and Budget an office to be known as the Office of Information and Regulatory Affairs.

"(b) There shall be at the head of the Office an Administrator who shall be appointed by, and who shall report directly to, the Director. The Director shall delegate to the Administrator the authority to administer all functions under this chapter, except that any such delegation shall not relieve the Director of responsibility for the administration of such functions. The Administrator shall serve as principal adviser to the Director on Federal information policy.

"§ 3504. Authority and Functions of Director

"(a) The Director shall develop and implement Federal information policies, principles, standards, and guidelines and shall provide direction and oversee the review and approval of information collection requests, the reduction of the paperwork burden, Federal statistical activities, records management activities, privacy and records, interagency sharing of information, and acquisition and use of automatic data processing telecommunications, and other technology for managing information resources. The authority under this section shall be exercised consistent with applicable law.

"(b) The general information policy functions of the Director shall include—

"(1) developing and implementing uniform and consistent information resources management policies and overseeing the development of information management principles, standards, and guidelines and promoting their use;

"(2) initiating and reviewing proposals for changes in legislation, regulations, and agency procedures to improve information practices, and informing the President and the Congress on the progress made therein;

"(3) coordinating, through the review of budget proposals and as otherwise provided in this section, agency information practices;

"(4) promoting, through the use of the Federal Information Locator System, the review of budget proposals and other methods, greater sharing of information by agencies;

"(5) evaluating agency information management practices to determine their adequacy and efficiency, and to determine compliance of such practices with the policies, principles, standards, and guidelines promulgated by the Director; and

"(6) overseeing planning for, and conduct of research with respect to, Federal collection, processing, storage, transmission, and use of information.

"(c) The information collection request clearance and other paperwork control functions of the Director shall include—

"(1) reviewing and approval information collection requests proposed by agencies;

"(2) determining whether the collection of information by an agency is necessary for the proper performance of the functions of the agency, including whether the information will have practical utility for the agency;

"(3) ensuring that all information collection requests—

"(A) are inventoried, display a control number and, when appropriate an expiration date;

"(B) indicate the request is in accordance with the clearance requirements of section 3507; and

"(C) contain a statement to inform the person receiving the request why the information is being collected, how it is to be used, and whether responses to the request are voluntary, required to obtain a benefit, or mandatory;

"(4) designating as appropriate, in accordance with section 3509, a collection agency to obtain information for two or more agencies;

"(5) setting goals for reduction of the burdens of Federal information collection requests;

"(6) overseeing action on the recommendations of the Commission on Federal Paperwork; and

"(7) designing and operating, in accordance with section 3511, the Federal Information Locator System.

"(d) The statistical policy and coordination functions of the Director shall include—

"(1) developing long range plans for the improved performance of Federal statistical activities and programs;

"(2) coordinating, through the review of budget proposals and as otherwise provided in this section, the functions of the Federal Government with respect to gathering, interpreting, and disseminating statistics and statistical information;

"(3) developing and implementing Government-wide policies, principles, standards, and guidelines concerning statistical collection procedures and methods, statistical data classifications, and statistical information presentation and dissemination; and

"(4) evaluating statistical program performance and agency compliance with Government-wide policies, principles, standards, and guidelines.

"(e) The records management functions of the Director shall include—

"(1) providing advice and assistance to the Administrator of General Services in order to promote coordination in the administration of chapters 29, 31, and 33 of this title with the information policies, principles, standards, and guidelines established under this chapter;

"(2) reviewing compliance by agencies with the requirements of chapters 29, 31, and 33 of this title and with regulations promulgated by the Administrator of General Services thereunder; and

"(3) coordinating records management policies and programs with related information programs such as information collection, statistics, automatic data processing and telecommunications, and similar activities.

"(f) The privacy functions of the Director shall include—

"(1) developing and implementing policies, principles, standards, and guidelines on information disclosure and confidentiality, and on safeguarding the security of information collected or maintained by or on behalf of agencies;

"(2) providing agencies with advice and guidance about information security, restriction, exchange, and disclosure; and

"(3) monitoring compliance with section 552a of title 5, United States Code, and related information management laws.

"(g) The Federal automatic data processing and telecommunications functions of the Director shall include—

"(1) developing and implementing policies, principles, standards, and guidelines for automatic data processing and telecommunications functions and activities of the Federal Government, and overseeing the establishment of standards under section 111(f) of the Federal Property and Administrative Services Act of 1949;

"(2) monitoring the effectiveness of, and compliance with, directives issued pursuant to sections 110 and 111 of such Act of 1949 and reviewing proposed determinations under section 111(g) of such Act;

"(3) providing advice and guidance on the acquisition and use of automatic data processing and telecommunications equipment, and coordinating, through the review of budget proposals and other methods, agency proposals for acquisition and use of such equipment;

"(4) promoting the use of automatic data processing and telecommunications equipment by the Federal Government to improve the effectiveness of the use and dissemination of data in the operation of Federal programs; and

"(5) initiating and reviewing proposals for changes in legislation, regulations, and agency procedures to improve automatic data processing and telecommunications practices, and informing the President and the Congress of the progress made therein.

"(h)(1) As soon as practicable, but no later than publication of a notice of proposed rulemaking in the Federal Register, each agency shall forward to the Director a copy of any proposed rule which contains a collection of information requirement and upon request, information necessary to make the determination required pursuant to this section.

"(2) Within sixty days after the notice of proposed rulemaking is published in the Federal Register, the Director may file public comments pursuant to the standards set forth in section 3508 on the collection of information requirement contained in the proposed rule.

"(3) When a final rule is published in the Federal Register, the agency shall explain how any collection of information requirement contained in the final rule responds to the comments, if any, filed by the Director or the public, or explain why it rejected those comments.

"(4) The Director has no authority to disapprove any collection of information requirement specifically contained in an agency rule, if he has received notice and failed to comment on the rule within sixty days of the notice of proposed rulemaking.

"(5) Nothing in this section prevents the Director, in his discretion—

"(A) from disapproving any information collection request which was not specifically required by an agency rule;

"(B) from disapproving any collection of information requirement contained in an agency rule, if the agency failed to comply with the requirements of paragraph (1) of this subsection; or

"(C) from disapproving any collection of information requirement contained in a final agency rule, if the Director finds within sixty days of the publication of the final rule that the agency's response to his comments filed pursuant to paragraph (2) of this subsection was unreasonable.

"(D) from disapproving any collection of information requirement where the Director determines that the agency has substantially modified in the final rule the collection of information requirement contained in the proposed rule where the agency has not given the Director the information required in paragraph (1), with respect to the modified collection of information requirement, at least sixty days before the issuance of the final rule.

"(6) The Director shall make publicly available any decision to disapprove a collection of information requirement contained in an agency rule, together with the reasons for such decision.

"(7) The authority of the Director under this subsection is subject to the provisions of section 3507(c).

"(8) This subsection shall apply only when an agency publishes a notice of proposed rulemaking and requests public comments.

"(9) There shall be no judicial review of any kind of the Director's decision to approve or not to act upon a collection of information requirement contained in an agency rule.

"§ 3505. Assignment of tasks and deadlines

"In carrying out the functions under this chapter, the director shall—

"(1) upon enactment of this Act—

"(A) set a goal to reduce the then existing burden of Federal collections of information by 15 per centum by October 1, 1982; and

"(B) for the year following, set a goal to reduce the burden which existed upon enactment by an additional 10 per centum;

"(2) within one year after the effective date of this Act—

"(A) establish standards and requirements for agency audits of all major information systems and assign responsibility for conducting Government-wide or multiagency audits, except the Director shall not assign such responsibility for the audit of major information systems used for the conduct of criminal investigations or intelligence activities as defined in section 4-206 of Executive Order 12036, issued January 24, 1978, or successor orders, or for cryptologic activities that are communications security activities;

"(B) establish the Federal Information Locator System;

"(C) identify areas of duplication in information collection requests and develop a schedule and methods for eliminating duplication;

"(D) develop a proposal to augment the Federal Information Locator System to include data profiles of major information holdings of agencies (used in the conduct of their operations) which are not otherwise required by this chapter to be included in the System; and

"(E) identify initiatives which may achieve a 10 per centum reduction in the burden of Federal collections of information associated with the administration of Federal grant programs; and

"(3) within two years after the effective date of this Act—

"(A) establish a schedule and a management control system to ensure that practices and programs of information handling disciplines, including records management, are appropriately integrated with the information policies mandated by this chapter;

"(B) identify initiatives to improve productivity in Federal operations using information processing technology;

"(C) develop a program to (i) enforce Federal information processing standards, particularly software language standards, at all Federal installations; and (ii) revitalize the standards development program established pursuant to section 759(f)(2) of title 40, United States Code, separating it from peripheral technical assistance functions and directing it to the most productive areas;

"(D) complete action on recommendations of the Commission on Federal Paperwork by implementing, implementing with modification or rejecting such recommendations including where necessary, development of legislation to implement such recommendations;

"(E) develop, in consultation with the Administrator of General Services, a five-year plan for meeting the automatic data processing and telecommunications needs of the Federal Government in accordance with the requirements of section 111 of the Federal Property and Administrative Services Act of 1949 (40 U.S.C. 759) and the purposes of this chapter; and

"(F) submit to the President and the Congress legislative proposals to remove inconsistencies in laws and practices involving privacy, confidentiality, and disclosure of information.

"§ 3506. Federal agency responsibilities

"(a) Each agency shall be responsible for carrying out its information management activities in an efficient, effective, and economical manner, and for complying with the information policies, principles, standards, and guidelines prescribed by the Director.

"(b) The head of each agency shall designate, within three months after the effective date of this Act, a senior official or, in the case of military departments, and the Office of the Secretary of Defense, officials who report directly to such agency head to carry out the responsibilities of the agency under this chapter. If more than one official is appointed for the military departments the respective duties of the officials shall be clearly delineated.

"(c) Each agency shall—

"(1) systematically inventory its major information systems and periodically review its information management activities, including planning, budgeting, organizing, direct-ing, training, promoting, controlling, and other managerial activities involving the collection, use, and dissemination of information;

"(2) ensure its information systems do not overlap each other or duplicate the systems of other agencies;

"(3) develop procedures for assessing the paperwork and reporting burden of proposed legislation affecting such agency;

"(4) assign to the official designated under subsection (b) the responsibility for the conduct of and accountability for any acquisitions made pursuant to a delegation of authority under section 111 of the Federal Property and Administrative Services Act of 1949 (40 U.S.C. 759); and

"(5) ensure that information collection requests required by law or to obtain a benefit, and submitted to nine or fewer persons, contain a statement to inform the person receiving the request that the request is not subject to the requirements of section 3507 of this chapter.

"(d) The head of each agency shall establish such procedures as necessary to ensure the compliance of the agency with the requirements of the Federal Information Locator System, including necessary screening and compliance activities.

"§ 3507. Public information collection activities — submission to Director; approval and delegation

"(a) An agency shall not conduct or sponsor the collection of information unless, in advance of the adoption or revision of the request for collection of such information—

"(1) the agency has taken actions, including consultation with the Director, to—

"(A) eliminate, through the use of the Federal Information Locator System and other means, information collections which seek to obtain information available from another source within the Federal Government;

"(B) reduce to the extent practicable and appropriate the burden on persons who will provide information to the agency; and

"(C) formulate plans for tabulating the information in a manner which will enhance its usefulness to other agencies and to the public;

"(2) the agency (A) has submitted to the Director the proposed information collection request, copies of pertinent regulations and other related materials as the Director may specify, and an explanation of actions taken to carry out paragraph (1) of this subsection, and (B) has prepared a notice to be published in the Federal Register stating that the agency has made such submission; and

"(3) the Director has approved the proposed information collection request, or the period for review of information collection requests by the Director provided under subsection (b) has elapsed.

"(b) The Director shall, within sixty days of receipt of a proposed information collection request, notify the agency involved of the decision to approve or disapprove the request and shall make such decisions publicly available. If the Director determines that a request submitted for review cannot be reviewed within sixty days, the Director may, after notice to the agency involved, extend the review period for an additional thirty days. If the Director does not notify the agency of an extension, denial, or approval within sixty days (or, if the Director has extended the review period for an additional thirty days and does not notify the agency of a denial or approval within the time of the extension), a control number shall be assigned without further delay, the approval may be inferred, and the agency may collect the information for not more than one year.

"(c) Any disapproval by the Director, in whole or in part, of a proposed information collection request of an independent regulatory agency, or an exercise of authority under section 3504(h) or 3509 concerning such an agency, may be voided, if the agency by a majority vote of its members overrides the Director's disapproval or exercise of authority. The agency shall certify each override to the Director, shall explain the reasons for exercising the override authority. Where the override concerns an information collection request, the Director shall without further delay assign a control number to such request, and such override shall be valid for a period of three years.

"(d) The Director may not approve an information collection request for a period in excess of three years.

"(e) If the Director finds that a senior official of an agency designated pursuant to section 3506(b) is sufficiently independent of program responsibility to evaluate fairly whether proposed information collection requests should be approved and has sufficient resources to carry out this responsibility effectively, the Director may, by rule in accordance with the notice and comment provisions of chapter 5 of title 5, United States Code, delegate to such official the authority to approve proposed requests in specific program areas, for specific purposes, or for all agency purposes. A delegation by the Director under this section shall not preclude the Director from reviewing individual information collection requests if the Director determines that circumstances warrant such a review. The Director shall retain authority to revoke such delegations, both in general and with regard to any specific matter. In acting for the Director, any official to whom approval authority has been delegated under this section shall comply fully with the rules and regulations promulgated by the Director.

"(f) An agency shall not engage in a collection of information without obtaining from the Director a control number to be displayed upon the information collection request.

"(g) If an agency head determines a collection of information (1) is needed prior to the expiration of the sixty-day period for the review of information collection requests established pursuant to subsection (b), (2) is essential to the mission of the agency, and (3) the agency cannot reasonably comply with the provisions of this chapter within such sixty-day period because (A) public harm will result if normal clearance procedures are followed, or (B) an unanticipated event has occurred and the use of normal clearance procedures will prevent or disrupt the collection of information related to the event or will cause a statutory deadline to be missed, the agency head may request the Director to authorize such collection of information prior to expiration of such sixty-day period. The Director shall approve or disapprove any such authorization request within the time requested by the agency head and, if approved, shall assign the information collection request a control number. Any collection of information conducted pursuant to this subsection may be conducted without compliance with the provisions of this chapter for a maximum of ninety days after the date on which the Director received the request to authorize such collection.

"§ 3508. Determination of necessity for information; hearing

"Before approving a proposed information collection request, the Director shall determine whether the collection of information by an agency is necessary for the proper performance of the functions of the agency, including whether the information will have practical utility. Before making a determination the Director may give the agency and other interested persons an opportunity to be heard or to submit statements in writing. To the extent, if any, that the Director determines that the collection of information by an agency is unnecessary, for any reason, the agency may not engage in the collection of the information.

"§ 3509. Designation of central collection agency

"The Director may designate a central collection agency to obtain information for two or more agencies if the Director determines that the needs of such agencies for information will be adequately served by a single collection agency, and such sharing of data is not inconsistent with any applicable law. In such cases the Director shall prescribe (with reference to the collection of information) the duties and functions of the collection agency so designated and of the agencies for which it is to act as agent (including reimbursement for costs). While the designation is in effect, an agency covered by it may not obtain for itself information which it is the duty of the collection agency to obtain. The Director may modify the designation from time to time as circum-

stances require. The authority herein is subject to the provisions of section 3507(c) of this chapter.

"§ 3510. Cooperation of agencies in making information available

"(a) The Director may direct an agency to make available to another agency, or an agency may make available to another agency, information obtained pursuant to an information collection request if the disclosure is not inconsistent with any applicable law.

"(b) If information obtained by an agency is released by that agency to another agency, all the provisions of law (including penalties which relate to the unlawful disclosure of information) apply to the officers and employees of the agency to which information is released to the same extent and in the same manner as the provisions apply to the officers and employees of the agency which originally obtained the information. The officers and employees of the agency to which the information is released, in addition, shall be subject to the same provisions of law, including penalties, relating to the unlawful disclosure of information as if the information had been collected directly by that agency.

"§ 3511. Establishment and operation of Federal Information Locator System

"(a) There is established in the Office of Information and Regulatory Affairs a Federal Information Locator System (hereafter in this section referred to as the 'System') which shall be composed of a directory of information resources, a data element dictionary, and an information referral service. The System shall serve as the authoritative register of all information collection requests.

"(b) In designing and operating the System, the Director shall—

"(1) design and operate an indexing system for the System;

"(2) require the head of each agency to prepare in a form specified by the Director, and to submit to the Director for inclusion in the System, a data profile for each information collection request of such agency;

"(3) compare data profiles for proposed information collection requests against existing profiles in the System, and make available the results of such comparison to—

"(A) agency officials who are planning new information collection activities; and

"(B) on request, members of the general public; and

"(4) ensure that no actual data, except descriptive data profiles necessary to identify duplicative data or to locate information, are contained within the System.

"§ 3512. Public protection

"Notwithstanding any other provision of law, no person shall be subject to any penalty for failing to maintain or provide information to any agency if the information collection request involved was made after December 31, 1981, and does not display a current control number assigned by the Director, or fails to state that such request is not subject to this chapter.

"§ 3513. Director review of agency activities; reporting; agency response

"(a) The Director shall, with the advice and assistance of the Administrator of General Services, selectively review, at least once every three years, the information management activities of each agency to ascertain their adequacy and efficiency. In evaluating the adequacy and efficiency of such activities, the Director shall pay particular attention to whether the agency has complied with section 3506.

"(b) The Director shall report the results of the reviews to the appropriate agency head, the House Committee on Government Operations, the Senate Committee on Governmental Affairs, the House and Senate Committees on Appropriations, and the committees of the Congress having jurisdiction over legislation relating to the operations of the agency involved.

"(c) Each agency which receives a report pursuant to

subsection (b) shall, within sixty days after receipt of such report, prepare and transmit to the Director, the House Committee on Government Operations, the Senate Committee on Governmental Affairs, the House and Senate Committees on Appropriations, and the committees of the Congress having jurisdiction over legislation relating to the operations of the agency, a written statement responding to the Director's report, including a description of any measures taken to alleviate or remove any problems or deficiencies identified in such report.

"§ 3514. Responsiveness to Congress

"(a) The Director shall keep the Congress and its committees fully and currently informed of the major activities under this chapter, and shall submit a report thereon to the President of the Senate and the Speaker of the House of Representatives annually and at such other times as the Director determines necessary. The Director shall include in any such report—

"(1) proposals for legislative action needed to improve Federal information management, including, with respect to information collection, recommendations to reduce the burden on individuals, small businesses, State and local governments, and other persons;

"(2) a compilation of legislative impediments to the collection of information which the Director concludes that an agency needs but does not have authority to collect;

"(3) an analysis by agency, and by categories the Director finds useful and practicable, describing the estimated reporting hours required of persons by information collection requests, including to the extent practicable the direct budgetary costs of the agencies and identification of statutes and regulations which impose the greatest number of reporting hours;

"(4) a summary of accomplishments and planned initiatives to reduce burdens of Federal information collection requests;

"(5) a tabulation of areas of duplication in agency information collection requests identified during the preceding year and efforts made to preclude the collection of duplicative information, including designations of central collection agencies;

"(6) a list of each instance in which an agency engaged in the collection of information under the authority of section 3507(g) and an identification of each agency involved;

"(7) a list of all violations of provisions of this chapter and rules, regulations, guidelines, policies, and procedures issued pursuant to this chapter; and

"(8) with respect to recommendations of the Commission on Federal Paperwork—

"(A) a description of the specific actions taken on or planned for each recommendation;

"(B) a target date for implementing each recommendation accepted but not implemented; and

"(C) an explanation of the reasons for any delay in completing action on such recommendations.

"(b) The preparation of any report required by this section shall not increase the collection of information burden on persons outside the Federal Government.

"§ 3515. Administrative powers

"Upon the request of the Director, each agency (other than an independent regulatory agency) shall, to the extent practicable, make its services, personnel, and facilities available to the Director for the performance of functions under this chapter.

"§ 3516. Rules and regulations

"The Director shall promulgate rules, regulations, or procedures necessary to exercise the authority provided by this chapter.

"§ 3517. Consultation with other agencies and the public

"In development of information policies, plans, rules, regulations, procedures, and guidelines and in reviewing information collection requests, the Director shall provide interested agencies and persons early and meaningful opportunity to comment.

"§ 3518. Effect on existing laws and regulations

"(a) Except as otherwise provided in this chapter, the authority of an agency under any other law to prescribe policies, rules, regulations, and procedures for Federal information activities is subject to the authority conferred on the Director by this chapter.

"(b) Nothing in this chapter shall be deemed to affect or reduce the authority of the Secretary of Commerce or the Director of the Office of Management and Budget pursuant to Reorganization Plan No. 1 of 1977 (as amended) and Executive order, relating to telecommunications and information policy, procurement and management of telecommunications and information systems, spectrum use, and related matters.

"(c)(1) Except as provided in paragraph (2), this chapter does not apply to the collection of information—

"(A) during the conduct of a Federal criminal investigation or prosecution, or during the disposition of a particular criminal matter;

"(B) during the conduct of (i) a civil action to which the United States or any official or agency thereof is a party or (ii) an administrative action or investigation involving an agency against specific individuals or entities;

"(C) by compulsory process pursuant to the Antitrust Civil Process Act and section 13 of the Federal Trade Commission Improvements Act of 1980; or

"(D) during the conduct of intelligence activities as defined in section 4-206 of Executive Order 12036, issued January 24, 1978, or successor orders, or during the conduct of cryptologic activities that are communications security activities.

"(2) This chapter applies to the collection of information during the conduct of general investigations (other than information collected in an antitrust investigation to the extent provided in subparagraph (C) of paragraph (1)) undertaken with reference to a category of individuals or entities such as a class of licensees or an entire industry.

"(d) Nothing in this chapter shall be interpreted as increasing or decreasing the authority conferred by Public Law 89-306 on the Administrator of the General Services Administration, the Secretary of Commerce, or the Director of the Office of Management and Budget.

"(e) Nothing in this chapter shall be interpreted as increasing or decreasing the authority of the President, the Office of Management and Budget or the Director thereof, under the laws of the United States, with respect to the substantive policies and programs of departments, agencies and offices, including the substantive authority of any Federal agency to enforce the civil rights laws.

"§ 3519. Access to information

"Under the conditions and procedures prescribed in section 313 of the Budget and Accounting Act of 1921, as amended, the Director and personnel in the Office of Information and Regulatory Affairs shall furnish such information as the Comptroller General may require for the discharge of his responsibilities. For this purpose, the Comptroller General or representatives thereof shall have access to all books, documents, papers and records of the Office.

"§ 3520. Authorization of appropriations

"There are hereby authorized to be appropriated to carry out the provisions of this chapter, and for no other purpose, sums—

"(1) not to exceed $8,000,000 for the fiscal year ending September 30, 1981;

"(2) not to exceed $8,500,000 for the fiscal year ending September 30, 1982; and

"(3) not to exceed $9,000,000 for the fiscal year ending September 30, 1983."

(b) The item relating to chapter 35 in the table of chapters for such title is amended to read as follows:

"35. Coordination of Federal Information Policy.".

(c)(1) Section 2904(10) of such title is amended to read as follows:

"(10) report to the appropriate oversight and appropriations committees of the Congress and to the Director of the Office of Management and Budget annually and at such other times as the Administrator deems desirable (A) on the results of activities conducted pursuant to paragraphs (1) through (9) of this section, (B) on evaluations of responses by Federal agencies to any recommendations resulting from inspections or studies conducted under paragraphs (8) and (9) of this section, and (C) to the extent practicable, estimates of costs to the Federal Government resulting from the failure of agencies to implement such recommendations."

(2) Section 2905 of such title is amended by redesignating the text thereof as subsection (a) and by adding at the end of such section the following new subsection:

"(b) The Administrator of General Services shall assist the Administrator for the Office of Information and Regulatory Affairs in conducting studies and developing standards relating to record retention requirements imposed on the public and on State and local governments by Federal agencies.".

SEC. 3. (a)The President and the Director of the Office of Management and Budget shall delegate to the Administrator for the Office of Information and Regulatory Affairs all functions, authority, and responsibility under section 103 of the Budget and Accounting Procedures Act of 1950 (31 U.S.C. 18b).

(b) The Director of the Office of Management and Budget shall delegate to the Administrator for the Office of Information and Regulatory Affairs all functions, authority, and responsibility of the Director under section 552a of title 5, United States Code, under Executive Order 12046 and Reorganization Plan No. 1 for telecommunications, and under section 111 of the Federal Property and Administrative Services Act of 1949 (40 U.S.C. 759).

SEC. 4. (a) Section 400A of the General Education Provisions Act is amended by (1) striking out "and" after "institutions" in subsection (a)(1)(A) and inserting in lieu thereof "or," and (2) by amending subsection (a)(1)(B) to read as follows:

"(B) No collection of information or data acquisition activity subject to such procedures shall be subject to any other review, coordination, or approval procedure outside of the relevant Federal agency, except as required by this subsection and by the Director of the Office of Management and Budget under the rules and regulations established pursuant to chapter 35 of title 44, United States Code. If a requirement for information is submitted pursuant to this Act for review, the timetable for the Director's approval established in section 3507 of the Paperwork Reduction Act of 1980 shall commence on the date the request is submitted, and no independent submission to the Director shall be required under such Act.".

(b) Section 201(e) of the Surface Mining Control and Reclamation Act of 1977 (30 U.S.C. 1211) is repealed.

(c) Section 708(f) of the Public Health Service Act (42 U.S.C. 292h(f)) is repealed.

(d) Section 5315 of title 5, United States Code, is amended by adding at the end thereof the following:

"Administrator, Office of Information and Regulatory Affairs, Office of Management and Budget.".

SEC. 5. This Act shall take effect on April 1, 1981.

Approved December 11, 1980.

Executive Order 12291

Following is the text of Executive Order 12291 issued by President Ronald Reagan on Feb. 17, 1981.

By the authority vested in me as President by the Constitution and laws of the United States of America, and in order to reduce the burdens of existing and future regulations, increase agency accountability for regulatory actions, provide for presidential oversight of the regulatory process, minimize duplication and conflict of regulations, and insure well-reasoned regulations, it is hereby ordered as follows:

SECTION 1. *Definitions.* For the purposes of this Order:

(a) "Regulation" or "rule" means an agency statement of general applicability and future effect designed to implement, interpret, or prescribe law or policy or describing the procedure or practice requirements of an agency, but does not include:

(1) Administrative actions governed by the provisions of Sections 556 and 557 of Title 5 of the United States Code;

(2) Regulations issued with respect to a military or foreign affairs function of the United States; or

(3) Regulations related to agency organization, management, or personnel.

(b) "Major rule" means any regulation that is likely to result in:

(1) An annual effect on the economy of $100 million or more;

(2) A major increase in costs or prices for consumers, individual industries, Federal, State, or local government agencies, or geographic regions; or

(3) Significant adverse effects on competition, employment, investment, productivity, innovation, or on the ability of United States-based enterprises to compete with foreign-based enterprises in domestic or export markets.

(c) "Director" means the Director of the Office of Management and Budget.

(d) "Agency" means any authority of the United States that is an "agency" under 44 U.S.C. 3502(1), excluding those agencies specified in 44 U.S.C. 3502 (10).

(e) "Task Force" means the Presidential Task Force on Regulatory Relief.

SEC. 2. *General Requirements.* In promulgating new regulations, reviewing existing regulations, and developing legislative proposals concerning regulation, all agencies, to the extent permitted by law, shall adhere to the following requirements:

(a) Administrative decisions shall be based on adequate information concerning the need for and consequences of proposed government action;

(b) Regulatory action shall not be undertaken unless the potential benefits to society from the regulation outweigh the potential costs to society;

(c) Regulatory objectives shall be chosen to maximize the net benefits to society;

(d) Among alternative approaches to any given regulatory objective, the alternative involving the least net cost to society shall be chosen; and

(e) Agencies shall set regulatory priorities with the aim of maximizing the aggregate net benefits to society, taking into account the condition of the particular industries affected by regulations, the condition of the national economy, and other regulatory actions contemplated for the future.

SEC. 3. *Regulatory Impact Analysis and Review.*

(a) In order to implement Section 2 of this Order, each agency shall, in connection with every major rule, prepare, and to the extent permitted by law consider, a Regulatory Impact Analysis. Such Analyses may be combined with any Regulatory Flexibility Analyses performed under 5 U.S.C. 603 and 604.

(b) Each agency shall initially determine whether a rule it intends to propose or to issue is a major rule, *provided that,* the Director, subject to the direction of the Task Force, shall have authority, in accordance with Sections 1(b) and 2 of this Order, to prescribe criteria for making such determinations, to order a rule to be treated as a major rule, and to require any set of related rules to be considered together as a major rule.

(c) Except as provided in Section 8 of this Order, agencies shall prepare Regulatory Impact Analyses of major rules and transmit them, along with all notices of proposed rulemaking and all final rules, to the Director as follows:

(1) If no notice of proposed rulemaking is to be published for a proposed major rule that is not an emergency rule, the agency shall prepare only a final Regulatory Impact Analysis, which shall be transmitted, along with the proposed rule, to the Director at least 60 days prior to the publication of the major rule as a final rule;

(2) With respect to all other major rules, the agency shall prepare a preliminary Regulatory Impact Analysis, which shall be

transmitted, along with a notice of proposed rulemaking, to the Director at least 60 days prior to the publication of a notice of proposed rulemaking, and a final Regulatory Impact Analysis, which shall be transmitted along with the final rule at least 30 days prior to the publication of the major rule as a final rule;

(3) For all rules other than major rules, agencies shall submit to the Director, at least 10 days prior to publication, every notice of proposed rulemaking and final rule.

(d) To permit each proposed major rule to be analyzed in light of the requirements stated in Section 2 of this Order, each preliminary and final Regulatory Impact Analysis shall contain the following information:

(1) A description of the potential benefits of the rule, including any beneficial effects that cannot be quantified in monetary terms, and the identification of those likely to receive the benefits;

(2) A description of the potential costs of the rule, including any adverse effects that cannot be quantified in monetary terms, and the identification of those likely to bear the costs;

(3) A determination of the potential net benefits of the rule, including an evaluation of effects that cannot be quantified in monetary terms;

(4) A description of alternative approaches that could substantially achieve the same regulatory goal at lower cost, together with an analysis of this potential benefit and costs and a brief explanation of the legal reasons why such alternatives, if proposed, could not be adopted; and

(5) Unless covered by the description required under paragraph (4) of this subjection, an explanation of any legal reasons why the rule cannot be based on the requirements set forth in Section 2 of this Order.

(e)(1) The Director, subject to the direction of the Task Force, which shall resolve any issues raised under this Order or ensure that they are presented to the President, is authorized to review any preliminary or final Regulatory Impact Analysis, notice of proposed rulemaking, or final rule based on the requirements of this Order.

(2) The Director shall be deemed to have concluded review unless the Director advises an agency to the contrary under subsection (f) of this Section:

(A) Within 60 days of a submission under subsection (c)(1) or a submission of a preliminary Regulatory Impact Analysis or notice of proposed rulemaking under subsection (c)(2);

(B) Within 30 days of the submission of a final Regulatory Impact Analysis and a final rule under subsection (c)(2); and

(C) Within 10 days of the submission of a notice of proposed rulemaking or final rule under subsection (c)(3).

(f)(1) Upon the request of the Director, an agency shall consult with the Director concerning the review of a preliminary Regulatory Impact Analysis or notice of proposed rulemaking under this Order, and shall, subject to Section 8(a)(2) of this Order, refrain from publishing its preliminary Regulatory Impact Analysis or notice of proposed rulemaking until such review is concluded.

(2) Upon receiving notice that the Director intends to submit views with respect to any final Regulatory Impact Analysis or final rule, the agency shall, subject to Section 8(a)(2) of this Order, refrain from publishing its final Regulatory Impact Analysis or final rule until the agency has responded to the Director's views, and incorporated those views and the agency's response in the rulemaking file.

(3) Nothing in this subsection shall be construed as displacing the agencies' responsibilities delegated by law.

(g) For every rule for which an agency publishes a notice of proposed rulemaking, the agency shall include in its notice:

(1) A brief statement setting for the agency's initial determination whether the proposed rule is a major rule, together with the reasons underlying that determination; and

(2) For each proposed major rule, a brief summary of the agency's preliminary Regulatory Impact Analysis.

(h) Agencies shall make their preliminary and final Regulatory Impact Analyses available to the public.

(i) Agencies shall initiate reviews of currently effective rules in accordance with the purposes of this Order, and perform Regula-

tory Impact Analyses of currently effective major rules. The Director, subject to the direction of the Task Force, may designate currently effective rules for review in accordance with this Order, and establish schedules for reviews and Analyses under this Order.

SEC. 4. *Regulatory Review.* Before approving any final major rule, each agency shall:

(a) Make a determination that the regulation is clearly within the authority delegated by law and consistent with congressional intent, and include in the Federal Register at the time of promulgation a memorandum of law supporting that determination.

(b) Make a determination that the factual conclusions upon which the rule is based have substantial support in the agency record, viewed as a whole, with full attention to public comments in general and the comments of persons directly affected by the rule in particular.

SEC. 5. *Regulatory Agendas.*

(a) Each agency shall publish, in October and April of each year, an agenda of proposed regulations that the agency has issued or expects to issue, and currently effective rules that are under agency review pursuant to this Order. These agendas may be incorporated with the agendas published under 5 U.S.C. 602, and must contain at the minimum:

(1) A summary of the nature of each major rule being considered, the objectives and legal basis for the issuance of the rule, and an approximate schedule for completing action on any major rule for which the agency has issued a notice of proposed rulemaking;

(2) The name and telephone number of a knowledgeable agency official for each item on the agenda; and

(3) A list of existing regulations to be reviewed under the terms of this Order, and a brief discussion of each such regulation.

(b) The Director, subject to the direction of the Task Force, may, to the extent permitted by law:

(1) Require agencies to provide additional information in an agenda; and

(2) Require publication of the agenda in any form.

SEC. 6. *The Task Force and Office of Management and Budget.*

(a) To the extent permitted by law, the Director shall have authority, subject to the direction of the Task Force, to:

(1) Designate any proposed or existing rule as a major rule in accordance with Section 1(b) of this Order;

(2) Prepare and promulgate uniform standards for the identification of major rules and the development of Regulatory Impact Analyses;

(3) Require an agency to obtain and evaluate, in connection with a regulation, any additional relevant data from any appropriate source;

(4) Waive the requirements of Sections 3, 4, or 7 of this Order with respect to any proposed or existing major rule;

(5) Identify duplicative, overlapping and conflicting rules, existing or proposed, and existing or proposed rules that are inconsistent with the policies underlying statutes governing agencies other than the issuing agency or with the purposes of this Order, and, in each such case, require appropriate interagency consultation to minimize or eliminate such duplication, overlap, or conflict;

(6) Develop procedures for estimating the annual benefits and costs of agency regulations, on both an aggregate and economic or industrial sector basis, for purposes of compiling a regulatory budget;

(7) In consultation with interested agencies, prepare for consideration by the President recommendations for changes in the agencies' statutes; and

(8) Monitor agency compliance with the requirements of this Order and advise the President with respect to such compliance.

(b) The Director, subject to the direction of the Task Force, is authorized to establish procedures for the performance of all functions vested in the Director by this Order. The Director shall take appropriate steps to coordinate the implementation of the analysis, transmittal, review, and clearance provisions of this Order with the authorities and requirements provided for or imposed upon the Director and agencies under the Regulatory Flexibility Act, 5 U.S.C. 601 *et seq.,* and the Paperwork Reduction Plan Act of 1980,

44 U.S.C. 3501 *et seq.*

SEC. 7. *Pending Regulations.*

(a) To the extent necessary to permit reconsideration in accordance with this Order, agencies shall, except as provided in Section 8 of this Order, suspend or postpone the effective dates of all major rules that they have promulgated in final form as of the date of this Order, but that have not yet become effective, excluding:

(1) Major rules that cannot legally be postponed or suspended;

(2) Major rules that, for good cause, ought to become effective as final rules without reconsideration. Agencies shall prepare, in accordance with Section 3 of this Order, a final Regulatory Impact Analysis for each major rule that they suspend or postpone.

(b) Agencies shall report to the Director no later than 15 days prior to the effective date of any rule that the agency has promulgated in final form as of the date of this Order, and that has not yet become effective, and that will not be reconsidered under subsection (a) of this Section:

(1) That the rule is excepted from reconsideration under subsection (a), including a brief statement of the legal or other reasons for that determination; or

(2) That the rule is not a major rule.

(c) The Director, subject to the direction of the Task Force, is authorized, to the extent permitted by law, to:

(1) Require reconsideration, in accordance with this Order, of any major rule that an agency has issued in final form as of the date of this Order and that has not become effective; and

(2) Designate a rule that an agency has issued in final form as of the date of this Order and that has not yet become effective as a major rule in accordance with Section 1(b) of this Order.

(d) Agencies may, in accordance with the Administrative Procedure Act and other applicable statutes, permit major rules that they have issued in final form as of the date of this Order, and that have not yet become effective, to take effect as interim rules while they are being reconsidered in accordance with this Order, *Provided that,* agencies shall report to the Director, no later than 15 days before any such rule is proposed to take effect as an interim rule, that the rule should appropriately take effect as an interim rule while the rule is under reconsideration.

(e) Except as provided in Section 8 of this Order, agencies shall, to the extent permitted by law, refrain from promulgating as a final rule any proposed major rule that has been published or issued as of the date of this Order until a final Regulatory Impact Analysis, in accordance with Section 3 of this Order, has been prepared for the proposed major rule.

(f) Agencies shall report to the Director, no later than 30 days prior to promulgating as a final rule any proposed rule that the agency has published or issued as of the date of this Order and that has not been considered under the terms of this Order:

(1) That the rule cannot legally be considered in accordance with this Order, together with a brief explanation of the legal reasons barring such consideration; or

(2) That the rule is not a major rule, in which case the agency shall submit to the Director a copy of the proposed rule.

(g) The Director, subject to the direction of the Task Force, is authorized, to the extent permitted by law, to:

(1) Require consideration, in accordance with this Order, of any proposed major rule that the agency has published or issued as of the date of this Order; and

(2) Designate a proposed rule that an agency has published or issued as of the date of this Order, as a major rule in accordance with Section 1(b) of this Order.

(h) The Director shall be deemed to have determined that an agency's report to the Director under subsections (b), (d), or (f) of this Section is consistent with the purposes of this Order, unless the Director advises the agency to the contrary:

(1) Within 15 days of its report, in the case of any report under subsections (b) or (d); or

(2) Within 30 days of its report, in the case of any report under subsection (f).

(i) This Section does not supersede the President's Memorandum of January 29, 1981, entitled "Postponement of Pending Regulations", which shall remain in effect until March 30, 1981.

(j) In complying with this Section, agencies shall comply with all applicable provisions of the Administrative Procedure Act, and with any other procedural requirements made applicable to the agencies by other statutes.

SEC. 8. *Exemptions.*

(a) The procedures prescribed by this Order shall not apply to:

(1) Any regulation that responds to an emergency situation, *provided that,* any such regulation shall be reported to the Director as soon as is practicable, the agency shall publish in the FEDERAL REGISTER a statement of the reasons why it is impracticable for the agency to follow the procedures of this Order with respect to such a rule, and the agency shall prepare and transmit as soon as is practicable a Regulatory Impact Analysis of any such major rule; and

(2) Any regulation for which consideration or reconsideration under the terms of this Order would conflict with deadlines imposed by statute or by judicial order, *provided that,* any such regulation shall be reported to the Director together with a brief explanation of the conflict, the agency shall publish in the FEDERAL REGISTER a statement of the reasons why it is impracticable for the agency to follow the procedures of this Order with respect to such a rule, and the agency, in consultation with the Director, shall adhere to the requirements of this Order to the extent permitted by statutory or judicial deadlines.

(b) The Director, subject to the direction of the Task Force, may, in accordance with the purposes of this Order, exempt any class or category of regulations from any or all requirements of this Order.

SEC. 9. *Judicial Review.* This Order is intended only to improve the internal management of the Federal government, and is not intended to create any right or benefit, substantive or procedural, enforceable at law by a party against the United States, its agencies, its officers or any person. The determinations made by agencies under Section 4 of this Order, and any Regulatory Impact Analyses for any rule, shall be made part of the whole record of agency action in connection with the rule.

SEC. 10. *Revocations.* Executive Orders No. 12044, as amended, and No. 12174 are revoked.

RONALD REAGAN

The White House,
February 17, 1981.

Selected Bibliography

Books

American Bar Association Commission on Law and the Economy. *Federal Regulation: Roads to Reform.* Washington, D.C.: American Bar Association, 1979.

Anderson, Douglas D. *Regulatory Politics and Electric Utilities: A Case Study in Political Economy.* Boston, Mass.: Auburn House, 1981.

Anderson, Ronald Aberdeen. *Government Regulation of Business.* Cincinnati, Ohio: South-Western Publishing Co., 1950.

Bacow, Lawrence S. *Bargaining for Job Safety and Health.* Cambridge, Mass.: MIT Press, 1982.

Baram, Michael S. *Alternative to Regulation: Managing Risks to Health, Safety and the Environment.* Lexington, Mass.: Lexington Books, 1982.

Bardach, Eugene and Kagan, Robert A. *Going by the Book: The Problem of Regulatory Unreasonableness.* Philadelphia, Pa.: Temple University Press, 1982.

___, eds. *Social Regulation: Strategies for Reform.* San Francisco, Calif.: Institute for Contemporary Studies, 1982.

Benveniste, Guy. *Regulation and Planning: The Case of Environmental Politics.* San Francisco, Calif.: Boyd and Fraser Publishing Co., 1981.

Berenbeim, Ronald. *Regulation: Its Impact on Decision Making.* New York: Conference Board, 1981.

Bernstein, Marver H. *Regulating Business by Independent Commission.* Princeton, New Jersey: Princeton University Press, 1955.

Breed, Alice G. *The Change in Social Welfare From Deregulation: The Case of the Natural Gas Industry.* New York: Arno Press, 1979.

Breyer, Stephen. *Regulation and Its Reform.* Cambridge, Mass.: Harvard University Press, 1982.

Carron, Andrew S. *Transition to a Free Market: Deregulation of the Air Cargo Industry.* Washington, D.C.: Brookings Institution, 1981.

___ and MacAvoy, Paul W. *Decline of Service in the Regulated Industries.* Washington, D.C.: American Enterprise Institute for Public Policy Research, 1981.

Cary, William Lucius. *Politics and the Regulatory Agencies.* New York: McGraw-Hill, 1967.

Cushman, Robert E. *Independent Regulatory Commissions.* New York: Octagon Books, 1972.

Dunlop, John T., ed. *Business and Public Policy.* Cambridge, Mass.: Harvard University Press, 1980.

Ferguson, Allen R., ed. *Attacking Regulatory Problems: An Agenda for Research in the 1980s.* Cambridge, Mass.: Ballinger Publishing Co., 1981.

___ and Leveen, E. Phillip. *The Benefits of Health and Safety Regulation.* Cambridge, Mass.: Ballinger, 1981.

Fritschler, A. Lee and Ross, Bernard H. *Business Regulation and Government Decision-Making.* Cambridge, Mass.: Winthrop Publishers, 1980.

Fromm, Gary, ed. *Conference On Public Regulation: Studies in Public Regulation.* Cambridge, Mass.: MIT Press, 1981.

Gatti, James F., ed. *The Limits of Government Regulation.* New York: Academic Press, 1981.

Goodman, John C. *The Regulation of Medical Care: Is the Price Too High?* San Francisco, Calif.: Cato Institute, 1980.

Government and the Regulation of Corporate and Individual Decisions in the Eighties. Englewood Cliffs, N.J.: Prentice-Hall, 1981.

Government Regulation. Washington, D.C.: American Enterprise Institute for Public Policy Research, 1979.

Gramlich, Edward M. *Benefit-Cost Analysis of Government Programs.* Englewood Cliffs, N.J.: Prentice-Hall, 1981.

Greene, James. *Regulatory Problems and Regulatory Reform: The Perceptions of Business Report #769.* New York: Conference Board Inc., 1980.

Hutzler, Laurie H. *The Regulatory and Paperwork Maze.* New York: Legal Management Services, 1979.

Joskow, Paul J. *Controlling Hospital Costs: The Role of Government Regulation.* Cambridge, Mass.: MIT Press, 1982.

Kahn, Alfred E. *The Economics of Regulation, 2 vols.* New York: John Wiley and Sons, 1971.

Kalt, Joseph P. *The Economics and Politics of Oil Price Regulation: Federal Policy in the Post-Embargo Era.* Cambridge, Mass.: MIT Press, 1981.

Karmel, Roberta. *Regulation by Prosecution: The Securities and Exchange Commission vs. Corporate America.* New York: Simon & Schuster, 1982.

Kaufman, Herbert. *Red Tape.* Washington, D.C.: Brookings Institution, 1977.

Kelman, Steven. *Regulating America, Regulating Sweden: A Comparative Study of Occupational Safety and Health Policy.* Cambridge, Mass.: MIT Press, 1981.

Kohlmeier, Louis. *The Regulators.* New York: Harper & Row, 1969.

Krislov, Samuel. *The Politics of Regulation.* Boston, Mass.: Houghton Mifflin, 1964.

Lave, Lester B. *The Strategy of Social Regulation: Decision Framework for Policy.* Washington, D.C.: Brookings Institution, 1981.

Macaulay, Hugh H. *The Many Costs of Government Regulation.* Greenwich, Conn.: Committee for Monetary Research and Education Inc., 1981.

MacAvoy, Paul W. *The Crisis of the Regulatory Commissions.* New York: W. W. Norton, 1979.

___. *Regulated Industries.* New York: W. W. Norton & Co., 1979.

Mandelker, Daniel R. *Environment and Equity: A Regulatory Challenge.* New York: McGraw-Hill Book Co., 1981.

McCraw, Thomas K., ed. *Regulation in Perspective: Historical Essays.* Cambridge, Mass.: Harvard University Press, 1981.

Mendeloff, John. *Regulating Safety: An Economic and Political Analysis of Occupational Safety and Health Policy.* Cambridge, Mass.: MIT Press, 1979.

Meyer, John R., et al. *Airline Deregulation: The Early Experience.* Boston, Mass.: Auburn House Publishing Co., 1981.

Mitchell, Bridger M. and Kleindorfer, Paul R., eds. *Regulated Industries and Public Enterprise: European and United States Perspectives.* Lexington, Mass.: Lexington Books, 1980.

Mitnick, Barry. *The Political Economy of Regulation.* New York: Columbia University Press, 1980.

Noll, Roger G. *Reforming Regulation: An Evaluation of the Ash Council Proposals.* Washington, D.C.: Brookings Institution, 1971.

Owen, Bruce and Braeutigam, Ronald. *The Regulation Game.* Cambridge, Mass.: Ballinger, 1978.

Peskin, Henry M. et al, eds. *Environmental Regulation and the U.S. Economy.* Baltimore, Md.: Johns Hopkins University Press, 1981.

Phillips, Susan M. and Zecher, Richard J. *The SEC and the Public Interest.* Cambridge, Mass.: MIT Press, 1981.

Pierce, Richard J., Jr., et al. *Economical Regulation: Energy, Transportation and Utilities.* Indianapolis, Ind.: Bobbs Merrill, 1980.

Poole, Robert W., Jr., ed. *Instead of Regulation: Alternatives to Federal Regulatory Agencies.* Lexington, Mass.: Lexington Books, 1982.

Quirk, Paul. *Industry Influence in Federal Regulatory Agencies.* Princeton, N.J.: Princeton University Press, 1981.

Rhine, Shirley Hoffman. *The Impact of Regulations on U.S. Exports.* New York: Conference Board, 1981.

Schwartz, Bernard. *The Economic Regulation of Business and Industry.* New York: Chelsea House Publishers, 1973.

Siegan, Bernard H., ed. *Government Regulation, and the Economy.* Lexington, Mass.: Lexington Books, 1980.

___. *Regulation, Economics and the Law.* Lexington, Mass.: D. C. Heath & Co., 1979.

Stanbury, W. T. *Government Regulation: Scope, Growth, Process.* Brookfield, Vt.: Renouf USA, 1980.

Stone, Alan. *Regulation and Its Alternatives.* Washington, D.C.: Congressional Quarterly Press, 1982.

Strickland, Allyn D. *Government Regulation and Business.* Boston, Mass.: Houghton Mifflin Co., 1980.

Taneja, Nawal K. *Airlines in Transition.* Lexington, Mass.: Lexington Books, 1981.

Weatherly, Charles L., ed. *Mandate for Leadership: Policy Management in a Conservative Administration.* Washington, D.C.: Heritage Foundation, 1981.

Weingast, Barry R. *Bureaucratic Discretion or Congressional Control: Regulatory Policymaking by the Federal Trade Commission.* St. Louis, Mo.: Center for the Study of American Business, Washington University, 1982.

Wellborn, David M. *Governance of Federal Regulatory Agencies.* Knoxville, Tenn.: University Tennessee, 1977.

White, Lawrence J. *Reforming Regulation: Processes and Problems.* Englewood Cliffs, N.J.: Prentice-Hall, 1981.

Wilson, James Q. *The Politics of Regulation.* New York: Basic Books, 1980.

Articles

Bernstein, Marver H. "Independent Regulatory Agencies: A Perspective on Their Reform." *Annals of the American Academy of Political and Social Science,* March 1972, pp. 14-26.

Berry, William D. "Theories of Regulatory Impact: The Roles of the Regulator, the Regulated, and the Public." *Policy Studies Review,* February 1982, pp. 436-441.

Brigman, William E. "The Executive Branch and the Independent Regulatory Agencies." *Presidential Studies Quarterly,* Spring 1981, pp. 244-261.

Calvert, Randall L. "Runaway Bureaucracy and Congressional Oversight: Why Reforms Fail." *Policy Studies Review,* February 1982, pp. 557-564.

Chilton, Kenneth W. and Weidenbaum, Murray L. "Government Regulation: The Small Business Burden." Journal of Small Business Management, January 1982, pp. 4-10.

Christainsen, Gregory B. and Haveman, Robert H. "Government Regulations and Their Impact on the Economy." *Annals of the American Academy of Political and Social Science,* January 1982, pp. 112-122.

Dubnick, Mel and Gitelson, Alan R. "Symposium on Regulatory Policy Analysis." *Policy Studies Review,* February 1982, pp. 423-580.

Eckert, Ross D. "The Life Cycle of Regulatory Commissioners." *Journal of Law and Economics,* April 1981, pp. 113-120.

Fox, J. R. "Breaking the Regulatory Deadlock." *Harvard Business Review,* September/October 1981, pp. 97-105.

Freedman, James O. "Legislative Delegation to Regulatory Agencies." *Proceedings of the Academy of Political Science,* no. 2, 1981, pp. 76-89.

Gordon, Michael R. "Will Reagan Turn Business Loose, If Business Wants to Stay Regulated?" *National Journal,* January 3, 1981, pp. 10-13.

Guzzardi, Walter Jr. "Reagan's Reluctant Deregulators." *Fortune,* March 8, 1982, pp. 34-40.

Hilton, George W. "The Basic Behavior of Regulatory Commissions." *American Economic Review Papers and Proceedings,* May 1972, pp. 47-54.

"Issues in Government Economic Regulation of Transportation in the 1980s." *American Economic Review,* May 1981, pp. 104-121.

Kelman, Steven. "Regulation and Paternalism." *Public Policy,* Spring 1981, pp. 219-254.

McKean, Roland N. "Enforcement Costs in Environmental and Safety Regulation." *Policy Analysis,* Summer 1980, pp. 269-289.

Mescon, Timothy S. and Vozikis, George S. "Federal Regulation: What are the Costs?" *Business,* January/February 1982, pp. 33-39.

Mitnick, Barry M. "The Strategic Uses of Regulation and Deregulation." *Business Horizons,* March-April 1981, pp. 71-83.

Petkas, Peter J. "The U.S. Regulatory System: Partnership or Maze?" *National Civic Review,* June 1981, pp. 297-301.

Prioleau, Gwendolyn D. "Decontrol vs. Deregulation: Heads, They Win; Tails, You Lose." *Howard Law Journal,* no. 1, 1981, pp. 235-243.

"Regulation and Deregulation: Does it Pay and How Much Does it Cost?" *Journal of Contemporary Business,* no. 2, 1980, pp. 1-171.

Schuck, Peter H. "Why Regulation Fails." *Harper's Magazine,* September 1975, pp. 16-30.

Stewart, Milton D. "The New Regulatory Flexibility Act." *American Bar Association Journal,* January 1981, pp. 66-68.

Stewart, Richard B. "Public Programs and Private Rights." *Harvard Law Review,* April 1982, pp. 1193-1322.

Thompson, Fred and Jones, L. R. "Reforming Regulatory Decision-Making in the Regulatory Budget." *Sloan Management Review,* Winter 1981, pp. 53-61.

Thurow, Lester. "Abolish the Antitrust Laws." *Dun's Review,* February 1981, pp. 72-74.

Waters, L. L. "Deregulation for Better, or for Worse?" *Business Horizons,* January/February 1981, pp. 88-91.

Weidenbaum, Murray L. "The High Cost of Government Regulation." *Challenge,* November/December 1979, pp. 32-39.

___. "An Overview of Government Regulations." *Journal of Commercial Bank Lending,* January 1981, pp. 27-36.

___. "Regulation: How Washington Will Switch." *Nation's Business,* February 1981, pp. 26-30.

Wood, Lance D. "Restraining the Regulators: Legal Perspectives on a Regulatory Budget for Federal Agencies." *Harvard Journal on Legislation*, Winter 1981, pp. 1-33.

Government Documents

U.S. Congress. Joint Economic Committee. *Government Regulation: Achieving Social and Economic Balance.* 96th Cong., 2nd sess. Washington, D.C.: Government Printing Office, 1980.

___. *Regulatory Budgeting and the Need for Cost-Effectiveness in the Regulatory Process: Hearing, August 1, 1979.* 96th Cong., 1st sess. Washington, D.C.: Government Printing Office, 1979.

___. Subcommittee on Economic Growth and Stabilization. *Cost of Government Regulation: Hearings, April 11, 13,* Washington, D.C.: Government Printing Office, 1978.

___. House. Committee on Energy and Commerce. Subcommittee on Oversight and Investigations. *Role of OMB in Regulation: Hearing, June 18, 1981.* 97th Cong., 1st sess. Washington, D.C.: Government Printing Office, 1982.

___. Committee on Governmental Affairs. *Regulatory Reform Legislation of 1981: Hearings, May 12, June 23, 1981.* 97th Cong., 1st sess. Washington, D.C.: Government Printing Office, 1982.

___. Committee on Interstate and Foreign Commerce. Subcommittee on Oversight and Investigations. *Cost-Benefit Analysis: The Potential for Conflict of Interest: Hearing, April 17, June 17, August 22, September 24, September 30, 1980.* 96th Cong., 2nd sess. Washington, D.C.: Government Printing Office, 1981.

___. *Regulatory Reform, Volume 1: Quality of Regulators: Hearings.* 94th Cong., 1st sess. Washington, D.C.: Government Printing Office, 1976.

___. *Regulatory Reform, Vol. 2: Federal Power Commission, Food and Drug Administration: Hearings, November 21, 24, 1975; March 15, 19, April 12, 1976.* 94th Cong., 1st sess. and 2nd sess. Washington, D.C.: Government Printing Office, 1976.

___. *Regulatory Reform, Vol. 3: Interstate Commerce Commission: Hearings, Feb. 23, March 5, 1976.* 94th Cong., 2nd sess. Washington, D.C.: Government Printing Office, 1976.

___. Judiciary Committee. *Regulatory Procedure Act of 1982: Report.* 97th Cong., 2nd sess. Washington, D.C.: Government Printing Office, 1982.

___. Subcommittee on Administrative Law and Governmental Relations. *Regulatory Procedures Act of 1981: Hearings, March 24, April 2, 7, 29, 30, May 5, 7, 14, 19, September 10, 1981.* 97th Cong., 1st sess. Washington, D.C.: Government Printing Office, 1982.

___. *Regulation Reform Act of 1979, Part 1: Hearings, November 7, 13, 16, 28, December 3, 5, 1979.* 96th Cong., 1st sess. Washington, D.C.: Government Printing Office, 1981.

___. Committee on Rules. Subcommittee on Rules of the House. *Background Information on Regulatory Reform and Congressional Review of Agency Rules With a Summary of H.R. 1.* 97th Cong., 1st sess. Washington, D.C.: Government Printing Office, 1981.

___. Subcommittee on Legislative Process. *Sunset, Sunrise, and Related Measures: Hearings, April 4, May 10, 23, June 6, 20, July 13, 30, Nov. 12, 1979.* 96th Cong., 1st sess. Washington, D.C.: Government Printing Office, 1980.

___. *Sunset, Sunrise and Related Measures, Part 2: Hearings, November 29, Dec. 5, 1979.* 96th Cong., 1st sess. Washington, D.C.: Government Printing Office, 1980.

___. Committee on Science and Technology. Subcommittee on Science, Research and Technology. *Oversight: The Food and Drug Administration's Process for Approving New Drugs: Hearings, June 19, 21, July 11, 1979.* Washington, D.C.: Government Printing Office, 1980.

___. Senate. Committee on Banking, Housing and Urban Affairs. Subcommittee on Economic Stabilization. *Government Regulation of the Automobile Industry: Hearing, April 26, 1979.* 96th Cong., 1st sess. Washington, D.C.: Government Printing Office, 1979.

___. Committee on Commerce, Science and Transportation. Subcommittee on Aviation. *Impact of Airline Deregulation: Hearings, April 25, 27, 1979.* 96th Cong., 1st sess. Washington, D.C.: Government Printing Office, 1979.

___. Subcommittee on the Consumer. *Cost of Government Regulations to the Consumer: Hearings, November 21, 22, 1978.* 95th Cong., 2nd sess. Washington, D.C.: Government Printing Office, 1979.

___. Subcommittee on Surface Transportation. *Government Regulations Affecting the U.S. Automobile Industry: Hearing, January 28, 1981.* 97th Cong., 1st sess. Washington, D.C.: Government Printing Office, 1981.

___. Committee on Governmental Affairs. *Regulatory Reform Act: Report.* 97th Cong., 1st sess. Washington, D.C.: Government Printing Office, 1981.

___. *Regulatory Reform Legislation of 1981: Hearings, May 12, June 23, 1981.* 97th Cong., 1st sess. Washington, D.C.: Government Printing Office, 1982.

___. *Regulatory Reform Legislation, Part 1 and Part 2: Hearings, March 20, April 16, 24, May 3, 4, 16, 18, 1979, May 23, June 5, 6, 20, 1979.* 96th Cong., 1st sess. Washington, D.C.: Government Printing Office, 1980.

___. Subcommittee on Oversight of Government Management. *Regulatory Negotiation: Hearing, July 29, 30, 1980.* 96th Cong., 2nd sess. Washington, D.C.: Government Printing Office, 1980.

___. *Improving Congressional Oversight of Federal Regulatory Agencies: Hearings, May 18, 20, 24, 25, 1976.* Washington, D.C.: Government Printing Office, 1976.

___. *Study on Federal Regulation, Volumes 1-6.* 95th and 96th Cong., Washington, D.C.: Government Printing Office, 1977-1978.

___. *Study on Federal Regulation: Appendix to Volume 6: Framework for Regulation.* 95th Cong., 2nd sess. Washington, D.C.: Government Printing Office, 1979.

Index